Helping Your Child Choose a Career

by Luther B. Otto, Ph.D.

Helping Your Child Choose a Career
Copyright © 1996 by Luther B. Otto

Published by
JIST Works, Inc.
720 North Park Avenue
Indianapolis, IN 46202-3431
Phone 317-264-3720 Fax 317-264-3709 E-mail JISTWorks@AOL.com

Cover Design: Brad Luther
Interior Design: Debbie Berman

Library of Congress Cataloging-in-Publication Data Applied For

Printed in the United States of America

99 98 97 96 95 1 2 3 4 5 6 7 8 9

We have been careful to provide accurate information throughout this book but it is possible that errors and omissions have been introduced. Please consider this in making any career plans or other important decisions. Trust your own judgment above all else and in all things.

ISBN 1-56370-184-7

To Bob Swofford —
With all best wishes!
~ Otto

To:

William H. Sewell
Archibald O. Haller
David L. Featherman

My mentors

Acknowledgments

Authors are sometimes asked, "How long did it take you to write that book?" Whether the response is several months or a lifetime — either of which may be true — neither is an entirely accurate or satisfactory answer. "Several months" allows no credit to people who form and shape a writer's thinking over the years; and "a lifetime" obscures the same people in lengthy and sometimes prosaic acknowledgments. Perhaps that is why some acknowledgments name typists but not seminal thinkers.

This book has a history, as does every book. It is a product of a long-term and sometimes large-scale research effort: the Career Development Program. The goals of the research are complementary: to generate significant research and to disseminate information effectively. Although the task at hand shifts from time to time — from gathering new data to interpreting results, like this book — the continuing focus is on youth and careers.

This book picks up where *How to Help Your Child Choose a Career* (1984) left off a decade ago. I have developed the themes of that book more comprehensively, with the benefit of an additional 10 years of research and experience in the trenches. The earlier book became the centerpiece of a seminar program for parents, "Today's Youth and Tomorrow's careers," which found its way into high schools in most states. It also became the text for in-service career counselor workshops throughout the country. This book has the same goal, to help parents help their children choose careers. I hope it also will provide a continuing education medium for career counselors.

Over the years, several institutions have given institutional identification for the Career Development Program. The University of Wisconsin-Madison, Washington State University-Pullman, Father Flanagan's Boys' Home — Boys' Town, and North Carolina State University-Raleigh, have each supported the program. Major funding has been received from the National Science Foundation, the National Institute of Mental Health, the National Institute of Education, the U.S. Department of Labor, the W.T. Grant Foundation, the W.K. Kellogg Foundation, Boys' Town, and the College of Agriculture and Life Sciences at North Carolina State University-Raleigh.

I acknowledge my close earlier collaboration with Dr. Vaughn R.A. Call, now at Brigham Young University, and Dr. Kenneth I. Spenner, now at Duke University. More recently, Keith Kimble served as research assistant and helped with data gathering, coding, and analysis. Also, he tracked down much of the detailed information on professional athletes that is the basis for a section in Chapter 5.

Several people readily drew on their experience and expertise to critique parts of the manuscript in draft form, to discuss chapter content, or to provide useful information, notably: William Weston, regarding cooperative education; Sidney Hollway, regarding "what parents can do" sections; Juliette N. Lester, regarding national and state occupational information systems; and the staff at Wake County Schools, regarding vocational preparation programs. Penny Lewter, Michelle Pettiway, and Judy Cline assisted with word processing.

I wrote this book on appointment in the Department of Sociology and Anthropology with the College of Agriculture and Life Sciences at North Carolina State University-Raleigh, without whose support the work could not have been accomplished. I wrote most of the book at home. Thanks especially, therefore, to my wife Nancy, for her patience.

I acknowledge the thousands of participants in the Career Development and Youth and Careers Studies whose real-life experiences illustrate key points throughout the book. I express my indebtedness collectively to the many others, too numerous to mention by name, with whom I discussed one issue or another that appears in the book. So many have contributed to this ongoing effort that the book should bear a group signature.

But when these acknowledgments are made and debts of gratitude paid, I name the three persons who, more than any others, contributed to this book: William H. Sewell, Archibald O. Haller, and David L. Featherman. Truth be known, they gave me more than ideas for a book. They gave shape and substance to my thinking and to my career. As he has done so well for so many, Sewell shared a vision and motivation. Haller gave the theoretical grounding from which I work. And Featherman taught me rigor and discipline. I have freely availed myself of their work, and my real indebtedness is evident on every page. They are my mentors, my friends, and my colleagues.

I did question the appropriateness of dedicating an applied book to three distinguished basic researchers, but the question lingered only a moment; for each recognizes that intervention is the logical extension and scientific complement to description and explanation — they taught me that, too. And I would hope that each will recognize the imprint of his own work on this book.

Luther B. Otto

Foreword

The emerging information-oriented, high-skills occupational society in the United States is rapidly expanding. It now is apparent this type of society will become increasingly needed if the United States is to continue competing with other nations in the international marketplace. The relationship between education and occupational success is becoming closer and closer. This is true both for those who aspire to become four-year college graduates and for those who choose some other form of postsecondary education as preparation for work. Increasingly, a high school education will not be enough to enable most youth to compete successfully for good jobs in the occupational society they will find. In addition, the need to seek educational opportunities essential for changing from one occupation to another is becoming important for more and more adult workers. All of these factors combine to make it increasingly important that parents acquire the basic understanding that will enable them to visit wisely with their children regarding career decisions and their related educational requirements. *Helping Your Child Choose a Career* is a book that can help parents and youth interact as they seek to make career decisions.

I have used the earlier edition of this book for several years. This revised edition will be even more helpful to parents and their children as they deal with career choice problems. I am pleased to recommend it for several reasons.

First, it is written in easy-to-read style while reporting accurate, up-to-date findings on both educational and occupational trends bearing on the kinds of career options available to today's youth. I spent several hours perusing those chapters where research findings are identified, and have found none that appear to be inaccurate or misinterpreted. It is an unusual quality to be able to write in an appealing, popular manner while keeping the content accurate. Dr. Otto has demonstrated this quality in this book.

Second, I like Dr. Otto's chapters in Part I: "The New Realities." The many subtopics in each chapter in this section will be helpful to both parents and students who have questions about the present and projected picture of factors affecting the occupational society. It is easy to identify and find specific short discussions on many of these topics without having to study the entire chapter. The major topics raised in Part I are important and are covered in an accurate fashion. This should be of interest and prove helpful to adults in general — not just to those trying to help their children make career decisions.

Third, the discussion of occupations and jobs appearing in Part II provides a helpful set of ways to consider "work" as part of total lifestyle. Chapter 6, on "Tomorrow's Jobs," is an especially helpful and easy-to-read opportunity to better understand the changing nature of the occupational society and how it affects career choices made by today's youth. It provides parents and children with many opportunities for discussing careers.

Fourth, Part III presents a well-organized set of step-by-step recommendations for high school youth planning to attend a four-year college or university. It is especially good for helping high school students and their parents understand the basic differences among various forms of higher education. There are few questions a high school student could ask about college admission requirements that are not answered in this book.

Fifth, Part IV is a much needed and greatly welcomed addition. Here, Dr. Otto faces head on the fact that almost all high school youth seeking to compete in the emerging information-oriented, high-skills occupational society must seriously consider enrolling in some form of postsecondary education. Dr. Otto speaks directly to the problems, the challenges, and various kinds of postsecondary educational opportunities to be considered by the 70 percent of today's high school youth who will never be four-year college graduates. His approach is rooted in his deep belief that students and their parents should consider all kinds of postsecondary education opportunities together. He has wisely avoided the arbitrary categories some have created by referring to "college-bound" versus "noncollege-bound" youth. Dr. Otto suggests that almost all high school graduates should be thinking about and planning to enroll in some form of postsecondary education.

This is a book that can — and should — be read both by high school students and by their parents. Both will discover many places where natural opportunities for parent/child discussion are appropriate. I hope many will take place. Congratulations, Dr. Otto, on a task well done!

Kenneth B. Hoyt
University Distinguished Professor
of Education
Kansas State University

Contents

ix

PART III CAREER PREPARATION: ADDITIONAL SCHOOLING

PART IV CAREER PREPARATION: EARNING WHILE LEARNING

Today's Youth and Tomorrow's Careers

In the United States today, there are 30 million people between the ages of 14 and 21. More than three-fourths of them graduate from high school (about 2.5 million per year); two-thirds enroll in a college of one kind or another; and one-fourth eventually complete four years of college. Nearly all of them, young women as well as young men, will some-day enter the labor force.

It troubles me, then, both personally and professionally — and I know it concerns counselors, teachers, school administrators, policy analysts, as well as parents — that today's young people say that choosing a career is one of the biggest problems they face.

This is a book for parents. It is about parents, youth, and careers. It explains how parents can help their children choose careers. It is a book for you if you are concerned with your child's future career.

Young people want more help choosing careers, and they've been saying that for 20 years.

I write as a research sociologist. I study how young peoples' careers develop, what makes a differ-ence, and how we can help them. I also write as a parent. I have three sons and have been through the process of trying to help each choose an occupation and a career preparation strategy. Just as each son is a different person, so each has gone about preparing for a career in a differ-ent way. Between the three, they've gone straight out of high school to college, from high school to work, taken some college and then gone to work, attended universities, attended community college, taken industry-sponsored training, dropped out of college, gone back to college, changed college majors, enrolled in cooperative education programs, and learned on their own — so far! I've learned from them.

This book extends parenting into the sometimes troublesome arena of helping young people choose careers. Permit me to explain the rationale for the book by elaborating on seven themes. Then I will explain how the book is organized.

Youth career needs first became apparent in the early 1970s when American College Testing, the same people who provide the ACT tests in high schools, conducted a nation-

1

wide study of the career development needs of 32,000 eighth, ninth, and eleventh graders. Eighty-four percent of the eleventh graders said they could usually or almost always see a guidance counselor whenever they wanted to, yet 78 percent said they wanted more help making career plans.

We could, perhaps, dismiss the ACT study as a musty, dusty, interesting but not very relevant study were it not for the fact that the same theme keeps coming through in more recent studies. Every year since 1975, the Institute for Social Research at the University of Michigan has conducted the Monitoring the Future study that annually surveys about 20,000 high school seniors from across the country. The latest findings are typical. Two-thirds of high school seniors want more counseling on career plans and job choice.

> *Parents, too, are concerned about their daughters' and sons' careers.*

Another example is the High School and Beyond Study, which the National Center for Education Statistics conducted a decade ago. It's a landmark study of 58,000 sophomores and seniors as they made the transition from school to work. Those students were generally positive about their high school experience when it came to academic course work and college counseling, but the seniors were much less satisfied with their school career-related programs. Nearly three-fourths said that schools should place more emphasis on vocational programs, and two-thirds felt that schools did not offer them enough practical experience.

In 1984, American College Testing did another study of the career development needs of the nation's youth to determine what progress had been made since the early 1970s. The second ACT study identifies areas where there has been definite improvement. For example, the proportion of students involved in career planning is higher. Nonetheless, more than 70 percent of the nation's youth continue to say that they want more help making career plans.

My own research, the Career Development Study, followed the progress of 7,000 young men and women from the time they were juniors in high school. When they were 30 years old and established in their early careers, we asked them to look back at the problems they had faced since leaving high school and tell us what might be done to help today's young people prepare for the future. Two-thirds, exactly 66 percent, cited difficulty in establishing careers and lack of career preparation as one of the biggest problems they faced.

As I write, I am analyzing the results of my new study, the Youth and Careers Study, a study of juniors in six North Carolina high schools. At the end of the survey I asked, "As you think ahead to the future, what is your biggest concern?" Seventy-four percent expressed concerns about their careers — figuring out what to do, finding a job, worrying about money for college, being uncertain about the line of work they hope to follow, being uneasy about what to do with their lives.

My first point is straightforward: Two-thirds to three-fourths of today's young people want more help making career plans, and they've been telling us that for twenty years.

In early 1994, the Gallup organization released the findings of a new study of 1,046 adults, the "National Survey of Working America." The general finding from older adults is that high schools aren't doing enough for students, particularly for students who are not headed for college.

> ■ 64 percent say schools should do more to place dropouts and graduates in jobs
>
> ■ 54 percent say schools should do more to help students develop job-seeking skills
>
> ■ 37 percent say their local schools aren't doing enough to prepare students for college

The same poll indicates that young adults, ages 18 to 25, are even more likely to believe that schools focus too heavily on college-bound students.

> ■ 83 percent say they will need more formal training or education to maintain or increase earning power in the next few years
>
> ■ 73 percent say high schools are not doing enough for the noncollege-bound
>
> ■ 58 percent say their high schools are not doing enough to help students choose careers

A tax accountant in our Career Development Study told us his experience:

> *" I am a tax accountant. One reason is my parents are, too, and I was familiar with the job, knew how to get there. I am sure I would work in aviation or carpentry now if I had known more about how to enter those fields when I was younger. It's funny, They are hobbies now and they were then, and my knowledge is greater than that of the average person in those areas, but I could not go to anyone when I was younger and say: 'What the hell do I have to do to get into those areas?'"*

I first began thinking seriously about young people's career problems back in 1978. That year the Ninth Annual Gallup Poll of parents' evaluations of public schools asked parents what areas of parenting concerned them most. Parents of young people ages 13 to 20 said their prime parenting concern was "how to deal with problems of drug and substance abuse." And what was their second biggest concern? "How to help my child choose a career."

The Gallup study pursued the issue further by asking parents how they felt the needs should be met. More than three-fourths said they thought public schools should offer

> *Career decisions involve choosing both an occupation and a career preparation strategy.*

courses for parents in areas that concerned them, and went on to say they would pay increased taxes to support school-sponsored programs for parents. Can you imagine that? In an age of Proposition XIII mentality, fiscal retrenchment policies, school lid bills, and taxpayer revolt, parents said they would pay more school taxes if schools offered programs to help them with their parenting concerns!

My purpose is not to argue that public schools should be more involved in parent education programs. I offer a more modest observation: There is a need out there and that need isn't being met. Parents want to know how to help their children choose careers.

Some of the most depressing research I read reports on young people's knowledge of the world of work — more accurately, I should say their ignorance of the world of work. I'm talking about such basics as what carpenters do on the job, how you get to be a druggist, and what the probabilities are that any little boy or girl will become an Emmit Smith, a Steffi Graf, or a Michael Jordan. Today's young people are misinformed about careers. Sometimes, terribly so.

Of course they're misinformed, because what they learn is a Hollywood version of careers. What do detectives do? They shoot guns. They drive fast cars. And they run around with pretty girls. What do doctors do? Much the same — especially the drive-fast-cars-and-have-fun-with-pretty-girls part. And nurses? Not a hair on their heads out of place. Not a wrinkle on their uniforms. Not a stain on their sleeves.

Young people are equally misinformed about their career preparation options. For example, a recent Gallup Poll reported that young Americans are widely misinformed about the cost of college. Now, a college education is expensive, make no mistake about it. Average annual fixed costs at public four-year colleges are $8,900 per year — plus, it takes an average of 6.2 years after high school to finish, and more than five of those years are spent in college working toward a four-year degree. That means that parents need to budget for at least five years of college, not just four years. No wonder the head nurse in a hospital facing the prospects of educating her son described the costs of a college education as "astronomical." After a while, the costs add up to real money. But the Gallup study indicates that most young people estimate that a college education costs three times more than it actually does. They're mistaken. They're terribly wrong about something that can make an important difference for their futures and for the rest of their lives.

Today's young people have the luxury of choosing not only from an abundance of occupational possibilities, but also from more career preparation options than ever before. In fact, part of the problem young people face is the dilemma of choosing from so many possibilities. Today's career preparation options include nontraditional education programs, industry sponsored training and education, education/industry cooperative programs, occupational training in the military, and on-the-job training programs — to say nothing of additional schooling in comprehensive universities and graduate schools, traditional and specialized colleges, technical colleges, community colleges, business schools, trade schools, proprietary and private and public schools. And the new federal school-to-work and work force preparedness initiatives are opening even more career preparation options.

Choosing a career and a career preparation strategy can be like a grandmother taking her three-year-old granddaughter to the ice cream shop with the promise, "You can have any kind of ice cream you want." But two hours later, the three-year-old still can't decide between chocolate, chocolate fudge, and chocolate goo. The luxury of choice from so many options can be a problem.

Young people don't just need information. They also need guidance. And information and guidance are not the same. Information can be written in books. It can be cataloged. Information can be illustrated, prettied up, captured on video tape, set on tables, stuck on bulletin boards, stacked on shelves, even stuffed into computers. But that isn't guidance. Guidance means showing young people how to find the way and monitoring their progress. Guidance means paying attention to how young people are progressing. Guidance isn't just setting goals, it's also figuring out how to get there. Guidance means helping young people structure their options and being available at those teachable moments when young people want to talk about their futures, not only when we parents want them to talk about their careers, or when the career center happens to be open, or when the counselor is in, or when the computer is turned on. Building career centers and unlocking the doors isn't enough. Young people need to be coached.

Young people want more help choosing careers, and schools, teachers, and career counselors have responded. No institution in society has done more to help young people plan careers than the nation's public schools. Schools have built career centers and stocked them with information on careers and career preparation possibilities. Schools offer courses on career

> *Teachers and counselors have tried to meet young peoples' career needs, but schools don't have the resources to give young people the individualized career guidance they want.*

planning. Schools provide interest inventories, videos and computerized career-exploration and college-choice programs, and the latest information on financial aid. And nowhere is the public school commitment to career guidance more evident than in the number of counselors schools have retained. For nearly two decades enrollments in public schools have declined, but over the same period, the number of guidance counselors has increased.

Just because the nation's public schools are doing what they can to help young people with their careers doesn't mean the students' career planning needs are being met, and it doesn't mean that the career guidance job is getting done — or *can* be done! — in career centers or by career counselors. The Center for Education Statistics reports that there are 527 students for every counselor in U.S. public schools. That means that if all 81,000 guidance counselors came to work every day — eight hours a day, five days a week, four weeks a month, nine months a year — and spent every hour working with students, under those ideal conditions students in our society would have available to them an average of two hours and 44 minutes per student per year for individualized career guidance. That's five minutes a week.

But counselors can't spend every hour counseling — and certainly not individualized career counseling. Counselors have to teach. They are assigned homeroom duty. They take care of problems. A national Educational Testing Services study indicates that counselors spend only 18 percent of their time working on problems brought by students — problems like boy-girl relations, acne, "I think I might be pregnant," or "I need help making career plans." And that suggests that, on average, students in public schools probably get no more than 29 minutes of individualized guidance per year, only part of which is career guidance. That's 54 seconds per week.

These extrapolations are more than an idle exercise in number crunching. I spell out the numbers because they indicate that, even under optimal conditions, young people's career guidance needs are not likely to be met by sending more counselors into the trenches for one-on-one career guidance through the schools. That strategy is fatally flawed, because there are far too many students for far too few counselors. Even if society doubled the number of counselors, hired another 81,000 of them, your daughter or son would still be left with less than two minutes of individualized career counseling per week. And even if you think that a couple of minutes per week ought to be enough, consider that we have no reason to believe that school finances will improve that dramatically in the years ahead. They won't. The number of secondary students peaked at 14,314,000 in 1976, and since then enrollments have dropped 20 percent. In 1991, the students-to-counselor ratio was the lowest ever, but that ratio now appears to be increasing, not decreasing. The nation's social priorities have shifted to crime, health care, and welfare reform. The focus is less on the young and more on the old — and the voting population is growing older. The earlier excellence reports on public education deflected resources back to the basics, away from career preparation. Finally, career guidance is a pupil service, and it is not unusual for 90 percent of school service budgets to be earmarked for personnel, which means that fiscal retrenchment policies and school-budget cuts translate rather directly into personnel reductions. The fact that we don't have enough counselors today, and that the ratio of counselors to students in the years ahead is more likely to erode than improve, suggests that it's time to re-examine how we go about the business of helping our children choose careers.

An Educational Testing Service Study concludes that career centers offer "mountains of information" and "huge collections of facts," but, for the most part, offer young people no way to sort out what information is available to them, how to choose between alternatives, and how to make decisions. I pose two questions: Might we need to reconsider what career information we give young people? And might we also need to give thought to the most effective way to deliver that information?

I think we have to do both.

There is a myth, a widely and uncritically held half-truth, that "parents don't matter," that "my kids don't listen to me." And there are always enough stories circulating about spaced-out teenagers to keep people believing the parents-don't-matter myth.

> *Even if schools had the resources with which to meet young people's career guidance needs, neither teachers nor counselors can replace the critical influence parents have on their sons' and daughters' career plans.*

Now, every parent can think of examples where kids don't listen and parents don't matter. I know I can. When it comes to wearing grubby T-shirts or neatly-pressed Dockers, raggedy Reeboks or the best from Florsheim; when it comes to our sons' and daughters' beliefs about the "latest" and the "biggest" and the "fastest" and the "best," you know they will believe and do what's "in" in the arcades and what's popular in the high school hallways. You can bet on it. But there are other areas where parents have a tremendous influence on their sons and daughters, and one of those areas is in making career plans.

The notion that parents don't matter, along with the idea that there is a generation gap, was popular about the turn of the century. That mode of thinking then reasserted itself in the adolescent-society literature of the 1960s, with its references to a youth "counterculture" or even a "contraculture." But that was 30 years ago. What we have learned since then is that young people are more complex, and that they take a much more differentiated and discriminating view of issues and the opinions of others. We have learned that young people listen to those other people whom they think know something about a particular topic. And so in matters of hairstyle, dress, choice of music — or how loud to play the music — who knows most about these topics? Certainly not parents. And it should come as no surprise that young people listen to their peers on these subjects. But when it comes to issues that are more basic and more important — such as attitudes, beliefs, and values — on these more critical subjects young people listen to their parents.

In his classic book, *Changing Youth in a Changing Society*, Michael Rutter of Harvard University says:

> **"Taken together, the findings from all studies . . . indicate that adolescents still tend to turn to their parents for guidance on principles and on major values but look more to their peers in terms of interests and fashions in clothes, in leisure activities, and other youth-oriented pursuits."**

Rutter later concludes:

> **"Young people tend both to share their parents' values on the major issues of life and also to turn to them for guidance on most major concerns. The concept that parent-child alienation is a usual feature of adolescence is a myth."**

One of the tragedies of our day is that the influence parents have on their children's careers is so greatly underestimated and misunderstood. Our generation of parents has been psyched out. We've been told — and haven't we said it ourselves? — that our kids don't listen to us. And we parents have come to believe it. And so we throw up our hands and do little — not because our kids don't listen to us but because we believe the *myth* that they don't listen to us. And by abandoning serious efforts to communicate with them, we leave them without advice and without guidance in a work world that increasingly requires that they make informed decisions.

To ignore the role of parents in the career development process is to deny what 50 years of studies in child and youth development have taught us. One of the lessons is that even if schools had the resources with which to meet young people's career guidance needs, teachers and counselors cannot replace the primary influence parents have on their children's career plans. My hope is that today's parents will recognize and take seriously the critical influence they have on their sons' and daughters' career decisions, and that they will prepare themselves to use that influence constructively.

Today's parents are poorly informed about the career options available to young people. In addition, many parents are plagued by their own career insecurities. They are trying to sort things out for themselves to say nothing of worrying about the career problems their daughters and sons face.

A different work world exists out there than when we parents made our first career decisions. A generation ago, a father could tell his son: "One thing about being a farmer, Johnny; they can never take the land away from you." But say that to an Iowa farmer today. Fertilizers, pesticides, herbicides, hybrid seeds, mechanization, automation, improved farm management practices, internationalization of markets, and biotechnology have changed all that. A generation ago, a mother could tell her daughter: "One thing about being a stenographer, Honey; those big shots will always need somebody to write their letters." But try to tell that to a Houston executive today. Dictation equipment, word processers, and spell checkers changed all that. A generation ago, the safe advice for parents to give children was, "Go to college so you can get a good job." "Go to college" is still sound advice; but it is not the only way to get a job, and it may not be the best way for your son or daughter to prepare for a career.

Today, most entry level positions are in the fast food industry. Back when Mom and Dad made their first career decisions, McDonald's was probably still working on its first billion hamburgers. Some of us can remember the signs on those golden arches that proudly proclaimed "More than 3 billion sold"; then "More than 4 billion sold"; and then, simply, "Billions sold." Today, McDonald's largest franchise operates five blocks north of Red Square. Today's young people live in a different world.

When the first U.S. census was conducted 200 years ago, the census takers classified workers into three major occupational groups. A person was in agriculture, business, or manufacturing. But how many occupation and industry combinations were used to classify workers in the 1990 census? More than 30,000! Remember that the next time you ask your daughter whether she's figured out what she wants to do with her life. It's no longer a simple matter to choose a career, especially when you're a teenager on the outside of the labor force looking in. Plus, she has to figure out how to prepare for that career.

> *If parents are to be effective career advisers for their children, they must prepare themselves.*

We live in a credentialing society in which the marketability of degrees has decreased but the demand for certificates has increased. That is evident in estimates that there are as many people enrolled in industry-sponsored training programs today as there are people enrolled in all colleges and universities combined — roughly 12.25 million in each. Today, three times as many institutions offer certificates as offer degrees. That makes today's career decisions all the more complex.

Educators have a bias. Understandably, they look at education from an educator's point of view. Educators are concerned about what young people should learn, what they do and do not learn, how subjects can be taught more efficiently, how to motivate students, and the like. These are legitimate concerns about the educational process.

But the world of work — prospective employers, personnel officers, management teams, and project managers — has a different view of what education is all about. From this point of view, the work world needs candidates who meet a certain set of requirements, and employers look to education and training institutions to supply those workers. The work world uses credentials, degrees, and certificates as shorthand codes with which to sort prospective employees. Schools and training institutions "brand" their products, "stamp" them in the same

> *If parents are to advise their children about careers, they need materials and programs with which to work.*

way that the butcher grades and stamps products in the meat counter. Employers who shop for workers look at the labels till they find what they need. Credentials, in the form of degrees and certificates, make the sorting process run smoothly.

Credentials are the keys that open employment doors. Employers sort out prospective workers on paper to come up with a short list they may decide to interview. That makes degrees and certificates critically important as doorways to the labor force. It means that young people must decide not only what line of work they wish to pursue, but also how to qualify, what credentials they will bring to the labor force.

Today's career decisions involve choosing both an occupation and a career preparation strategy; and if parents are to be effective career advisers for their children, they must prepare themselves for both.

For today's young people, knowing what they want to do isn't enough. Their choices have to be based on available options — not on a frontier mentality that everybody can be anything they want to be. Today's young people have to know where the employment opportunities are and how the labor market expands and contracts in response to population and labor force changes.

It isn't enough for today's young people to know about occupations, the lines of work that interest them. They also have to know about industries, the broad fields of activity that engage employers, and whether the fortunes of particular industries are rising or falling.

In our society, it isn't enough for young people to follow employment prospects. Our daughters and sons will live in an increasingly global economy tied together with electronic communications. More information will be needed. More information will be available. Young people need to learn how to access that information and use it to their own career advantage.

It isn't enough for today's young people to decide on an occupational career. They must also decide on a career preparation strategy. On the one hand, a high school diploma may no longer guarantee a good job. On the other hand, college is not the only way to prepare for a career, and it may not be the best way to prepare for a labor market in which one of four workers is already overeducated and underemployed.

Today's young people will be making career decisions every four or five years over their 45-year work histories; and if they are to make intelligent and responsible decisions, someone has to teach them how. That's what this book is all about. My purpose is to help parents help their children choose careers.

My Own Experience

I learned from my own experience as a parent that I had to get my act together if I was to help my children choose careers. I recognized that I needed an organized approach that covered all the important bases. The information had to be accurate and up-to-date. The material had to be practical. It had to be down-to-earth, understandable, and usable.

I became interested in young people's careers for personal reasons, not only for professional ones. When my oldest son turned 16, I, like most parents, wanted to help him think through his career possibilities. I knew the research on young people's career development. I was familiar with the studies that show the importance of parental influence on young people's career decisions. My own research showed the same thing. Yet, like a lot of other parents, I was uncertain about how to use my influence constructively.

I followed my academic instincts and made some trips to the library, went to the book store, even did a computerized literature search. All of those efforts added up to very little because there wasn't much available to help parents help their children choose careers. And there still isn't. "Necessity is the mother of invention," my own father was fond of saying, and my father's advice prescribed the origins of this book. For nearly 20 years, I've developed career materials for parents and counselors, materials that I could use first with my own children. I've hoped that other parents and young people could also benefit, and indications are they have.

The goal of this book is to get parents directly involved in their sons' and daughters' career plans. The book is a tool to help that happen, equipping parents to do that job.

A New Approach

I have an advertisement in my files that someone sent to me. It's for a laser-beam mousetrap — one of those gadgets for the executive who has everything.

The laser-beam mousetrap is a simple contraption — a plain, ordinary mousetrap; a board with a spring on it. But the spring on the laser-beam mousetrap is tied down with a piece of string. Also, the laser-beam mousetrap has an electric eye aimed across the little gadget that holds the cheese. And, of course, the laser-beam mousetrap has a laser beam.

The laser-beam mousetrap works like this: When the bright-eyed, furry little bundle of peace and joy tippy-toes up to the cheese, he interrupts the eye beam; and the eye beam triggers the laser beam. But the laser beam doesn't zap the mouse. Nothing that gross! The laser beam burns the string that holds down the spring, and snap! Wham-O! You got him! Right in the laser-beam mousetrap.

Now, the laser-beam mousetrap is just like the spring-loaded traps you can buy for less than a buck a pair at Kmart. But the laser-beam mousetrap differs from the Kmart trap in three ways. First, the laser-beam trap has an eye beam. Second, the laser-beam trap has a laser-beam. And third, the laser-beam mousetrap has an honest-to-goodness price tag of fifteen-hundred dollars — yes, $1,500! The laser-beam mousetrap is simply the same old Kmart mousetrap with some fancy gadgets attached.

Getting parents directly involved in helping their sons and daughters choose careers is not a laser-beam mousetrap — not the same old stuff rehashed. Focusing on parents is a different approach to the business of helping young people choose careers. It's a strategy that traditional career guidance ignores. It's a strategy that is needed. It's a strategy that works.

Parent Preparation

This book is not an attempt to create another guidance system but, rather, an effort to take the best information available and put it to work more effectively.

Over the years I have attended many national conventions, but I am reminded of the first one I ever attended for career counselors. I walked through the exhibition hall, where booth after booth featured career development materials in all shapes, colors, and descriptions. The exhibits were heavy with promotional gimmicks — helium-filled balloons, colorful plastic carrying bags, free candy and gum. Most of the programs were based on films or videos. Computers weren't around yet. Others were packaged in pink and purple three-ring binders. I thought I had stumbled across a circus.

I listened carefully to the conversations between buyers and sellers. The promoters emphasized how easy the programs were to use, how handy they were, how nice they looked, how little space they took on the shelf, how many young people counselors could process in a single setting, and, of course, special convention rates, quantity discounts, and attractive purchasing plans. The marketing glitz was everywhere, but I heard precious little about how valid and reliable the information was, or any evidence that the programs worked. In too many cases what was pushed, polished, and promoted was another laser-beam mousetrap, the same old stuff with some newfangled gimmicks and a fancy price tag.

The fact is that most career programs are based on information that is readily available at a very modest cost. The information all comes from basically the same sources, and the information is public. I'll put you on to that bargain buy in Chapter 7.

If parents are to take charge, they must prepare themselves. They can't sit back and be spectators or cheerleaders. Parents have to spend at least as much time helping their children choose careers as they spend planning their next two-week vacation. This book gives parents a map of the options young people have for choosing an occupation and choosing a career preparation strategy.

What's Ahead?

Now that you know where I'm coming from, let me explain how this book is organized. The book is divided into four parts. The first half of the book includes "The New Realities" and "The World of Work," which focus on occupational choice. The second half covers career preparation strategies in parts entitled "Additional Schooling" and "Earning While Learning."

Part I, "The New Realities," gives background information to help parents understand the world of work in which today's young people must find their careers. It starts with the big, big picture. In Chapter 1, I overview technology and the global economy — two monumental forces that are reshaping the world of work everywhere and forever. But hang on. The focus of the book narrows, getting more and more specific as the chapters unfold until finally it gives you "to-do" lists to follow. In Chapter 2, I review population and labor force changes that affect career choices in the U.S. — still the big picture, but this chapter reviews national and domestic changes that affect us all. In Chapter 3, I explain how society matches young people with occupations and I explore the critical influence parents have in that process. In Chapter 4, I sketch how society treats women and racial minorities differently in the career development process and provide some suggestions for what parents and young people can do about it. Each topic — technology and the global economy, population and labor force changes, parental influence and equity issues — has an important bearing on young people's career and career preparation choices. I chose Part I with "Next Steps: What Parents Can Do."

Part II, "The Work World," focuses on more considerations that bear on occupational choice. In Chapter 5, I examine how work is central to all of life and introduce important concepts for thinking about and planning careers. Chapter 6 provides employment projections for industries and major occupational groups. Chapter 7 explains where to find and how to use information on occupational careers. I include a section on the probabilities of a young person becoming a professional athlete, which is a career that a lot of young people dream about. I close Part II with "Next Steps: What Parents Can Do."

The second half of the book is about choosing career preparation strategies, which is the second basic career decision every young person must make. Part III, "Additional Schooling," reviews the college possibilities young people have. In Chapter 8, I sketch different kinds of college programs that lead to degrees and certificates. In Chapter 9, I discuss college choice and explain where to get the information parents and young people need to help sort out their college options. Chapter 10 reviews financial aid prospects and procedures. I close Part III with "Next Steps: What Parents Can Do."

Part IV also deals with career preparation strategies but shifts attention to "Earning While Learning" possibilities. I review 15 different ways to put together combinations of education and training programs, none of them requiring a four-year college degree. I cover 12 possibilities in Chapter 11, and then consider apprenticeships, federal civil service, and occupational training in the military in Chapter 12. Chapter 13 summarizes what is known about the benefits, economic and noneconomic, of different kinds of formal education and vocational preparation programs. I end Part IV with "Next Steps: What Parents Can Do," and the book closes with a short Epilogue.

How to Read This Book

There is rhyme and reason to the way the book is organized. The book starts at a general level, exploring the national and international context within which we live and work. Chapters get increasingly specific, finally making recommendations that may apply directly to your circumstances.

But where you and your son or daughter are in the whole business of choosing a career will determine how you choose to read this book. Some young people already know where they intend to go to college, and they're concerned with financial aid. Others want to know what options they have to prepare for a career without going to college. Still others are bogged down with making an occupational choice. You don't have to read this book from the beginning. You can go straight to the part or chapter that interests you, and then return to the earlier materials later if necessary.

The same is true of chapters. You may want to read some of them selectively. For example, Chapter 6 reviews employment projections for both major industry and occupation groups. It's a comprehensive overview, but you may want to read only the sections that interest your son or daughter, and then go on to other chapters. Chapters 11 and 12 also relate to noncollege career preparation possibilities. If your son or daughter is already planning to attend college, you may need only to skim these chapters.

The material in the first part of the book — the way the global economy, technology, population, and labor force changes affect career prospects; and the way society selects, prepares, and sorts young people into occupational positions — is usually ignored by career counselors. Traditional career counseling focuses more narrowly on matching young people's interests with occupational possibilities. It pays little attention to how the labor force is changing, areas of labor force expansion and contraction, industry changes, the emergence of new ways to prepare for careers, and the like. But in periods of employment instability and uncertainty, young people cannot assume that it is sufficient merely to know what they want to do. They also need to take into account the prospects for employment in those occupations and consider how they will prepare themselves for employment in the occupation of their choice. And they are well-advised to learn what drives the labor force. I hope you will pay close attention to these issues in Part I.

Concluding Thoughts

Two themes in the following chapters are critical to the success of involving parents in their daughters' and sons' career plans. The first is a question: Who decides? Who makes a daughter's or son's career choices?

Getting parents more involved in their sons' and daughters' career plans doesn't mean that Mom and Dad should decide for Son or Daughter. The realities are that choosing a career can be frustrating, and sorting out career preparation options includes talking about money (more frustration). It's been said that for every problem there is always somebody with a simple solution, and it's usually wrong! When it comes to choosing a career, there are neither quick and dirty solutions nor magical formulas. There is no "one size fits all" answer. But there are practical approaches and reasonable steps that parents and young people can take together, and this book sketches them for you. The steps are manageable and, when taken together, they teach young people how to make informed and responsible career decisions.

Our sons and daughters must make their own choices, just as we had to make and live with ours. That doesn't mean that we set them adrift. Too much of that has already been done. But it does put parents' advisory role in proper perspective. We should not push, pull, entice, threaten, or cajole our sons and daughters into anything. Career choice is their decision, not ours.

One mother of a high school junior in our Youth and Careers Study, an apple farmer's wife, put it this way:

> *" His career choice is his decision. I want him to think long and hard about that choice. If he changes in mid-stream, I'll support his decision. It's his life, not mine, but I want to be a part of the decision-making process in some way."*

Our job is to give our daughters and sons the best help we can: Help them understand their values and their interests and the labor-market realities; help them sort out their career-preparation options; and, importantly, give them the freedom to make their own decisions. Our daughters and sons need good coaching. We can't play the game for them, but we can show them and teach them and help them. Our job is to explain the play options, help them work out a game plan, show them how to anticipate and evaluate the possible consequences of their decisions, and make sure they understand the rules of the game. It's their ball game, not ours.

Who decides? They do.

The second point is that there may be no quick solution to your son's or daughter's career choice, and there may never be a perfect solution. To think that the question of career choice is settled once and for all is to retreat to the old-fashioned idea that people choose a career for life. That's the way we used to think about it — once a carpenter, always a carpenter — but it's not the way things are today. The average stay on a job in the U.S. labor force is only four and one-half years. That means that today's workers will change jobs seven, eight, or nine times over their work histories, and they may change careers two or three times. Our daughters and sons need to learn how to make informed career decisions, and that means somebody has to teach them. The sooner we teach them, the sooner and longer they will benefit.

We live in a forgiving society. People can change jobs and start over. They need not be stuck. They can always go back to school or get new training. True, the options narrow as we grow older, but we oldsters need to remember that our daughters and sons still have time and they still have options. They have that advantage. They can change their minds, and they will, without jeopardizing their retirement programs. They can make mistakes, and they will. It's one of the benefits of living in a free society. Let them — indeed, help them — play out their options.

The end result may be some temporary peace of mind for parents, but the mind set is not always permanent. The peace of mind comes not from a job that is finished, but from the satisfaction of having done what a parent can do to assist a young person's career decision. The end result for our sons and daughters will be a better understanding of their own interests and abilities, more information about their occupational and career preparation possibilities, and some sense, however tentative, of how and where to begin. That's a start.

The whole approach may come unglued six months later, or just three months later. What do we do then? We pick up the pieces and start over again. Why? Because young people need all the help they can get, and because parents have a critical influence on their son's and daughter's career decisions.

What better reasons are there than that?

Technology and the Global Economy

*"W*hat do you want to do when you grow up?" We ask that question of little boys and girls from the time they are big enough to walk and old enough to talk. It's a tough question. And when we hear their answers — yesterday a space ship commander, tomorrow a motorcycle stunt rider — we realize that our children seem to be living in a different world. They are.

Our sons and daughters will always live in a different world. We hope that by the time they leave high school they will have shed their TV fantasies and have both feet on the ground — be a little more realistic about things. But more realistic about what? About the world we lived in when we were their age — a world of typewriters and 45 rpm records? Or more realistic about the world in which they will live — a world of information highways, DNA testing, and space-age technologies?

Choosing a career involves young people in a decision about how they will fit into a changing world. But what will their work world be like? In this first part of the book, and before getting specific about individual careers, I review new realities that affect us all. This chapter sketches two monumental changes that are reshaping the world of work: the global economy and technology.

THE GLOBAL ECONOMY

There is much discussion about the U.S. economy and its affect on jobs and employment, along with a growing awareness that the U.S. must do something about its economy. The underlying problems may be poorly understood, but the evidence is visible in the unemployment of friends and neighbors, in standards of living that have plateaued if not fallen, in the frantic search for economic development programs at every level — community, state, and federal — and in the growing numbers of homeless and street people.

There is also an increasing sense that the problems have been a long time coming. Perhaps less well-understood is that they may take a while to resolve. The fall of the Iron Curtain and the collapse of the "the evil empire" are but examples of international developments that have cooled the external threat, and, for the first time in a long time, our society has begun to look inward. What we see is not a pretty picture: issues of crime, health care, education, poverty, housing, crumbling bridges and highways and city sewers and airports, unemployment, and fallen wages. The theme that ties them all together is the economy.

We have heard the prophets of profit a bit too often — that the economy is on the "upswing" and the "recovery" is just around the corner — and we're not buying that any longer. We aren't ready to turn to the prophets of doom; but there is a widely shared sense that the old "pump priming" solutions of days gone by aren't working any longer and that we have a serious problem on our hands. The problem is that the pump isn't working. The emerging consensus is that something needs to be done. We need a new pump, a new strategy to compete more effectively in a global economy.

How We Got Where We Are

How did we get into this fix?

We are in a knock-down, drag-out battle over markets — a matter of global economics — and it didn't happen overnight. At the end of World War II, we were in a tremendously advantaged position. We had

- Highly productive industrial capabilities while our competitors' capabilities lay in war-torn ruins
- The largest share of world markets
- The most highly skilled work force
- The best industry and business managers
- Natural resources to draw upon
- Capital for investment purposes
- A sense of moral superiority
- A "can do" attitude

We were #1 on planet Earth, and we knew it. The rest of the world knew it, too. But that has changed. We rebuilt Germany and Japan into political allies, but also into fierce economic competitors. During the '50s and '60s, we enjoyed a standard of living second to none. We welcomed the trickle of imports; we enjoyed the luxuries the good life could afford. We certainly didn't view imports as threats to jobs and the American economy. Other countries specialized in cigars, sugar, coffee, and cameras, but we controlled the high-value, high-wage sectors: computers, advanced materials, machine tools, micro-electronics, biotechnology, and telecommunications — the list goes on. But today and for the foreseeable future, it's open competition with Europe and Asia for the same high-value products. And, truth be known, in many of these areas we are playing catch-up: for example, the auto industry. Another example is education reform. Still another is health care reform.

What Changed?

What changed? A lot changed. No single issue made the difference; rather, a number of things contributed to the change. Here are examples that are often cited:

Competition. Simply stated, the competition has gotten a lot tougher. A generation ago "made in Japan" was a slur, code language for "buyer beware." But not today. Today, "made in Japan" is advertisement promotion, and it sells well: for example, Toyotas and Canon cameras and Sony entertainment centers. Other countries, including Korea, Indonesia, and China, are also weighing in with quality merchandise for the global market.

Process Technologies vs. Product Development. Traditionally, the U.S. dominated because it had natural resources and capital and employed the best technologies. We were leaders in the development of new products, which was the key to competitive advantage under the old system. And we used Henry Ford's assembly line concepts to mass produce the new products in abundance.

But the rules of the new economic game are different. Leadership is now defined not in terms of product development, but in terms of process technologies, which are the strengths of Japan and Germany. Japan, for example — four little islands with a combined land mass no larger than Montana, few natural resources, and with one and one-half times the number of people as live in the entire U.S. — has been amazingly successful at importing raw materials, converting them (adding value) into high-demand products, and exporting them worldwide. Electronic wizardry is but one example. Process technologies rely on work-force productivity, both high-value and high-output, for a competitive edge. And productivity requires workers' education, training, and skill. The demand for highly skilled and highly productive workers comes at a time when our educational system is in crisis. Suddenly, we're unprepared.

Government/Industry Partnerships. Historically, the U.S. has embraced a philosophy of individualistic capitalism — strict separation of government and business. And we have stuck with it in the face of a declining competitive presence in the open market.

Earlier this afternoon, as I write, President Clinton announced a new partnership between the federal government and the big three auto makers to develop the car of the future. By evening, the initiative had been interpreted over national news as having some possible symbolic and political value but little practical significance because government/industry partnerships are not "the American way." Especially in Japan, government, financial institutions, manufacturers, and suppliers are linked — relationships restricted by laws in the U.S. to protect against the anti-trust concerns of an earlier age. Meanwhile, Japan Inc. marches on.

Investment Deficit. The U.S., once a frugal, thrifty, saving and investing society, has become a consuming society. Commerce Department reports that consumer spending continues to rise, for months in succession, in the face of rising unemployment and wage concerns are not uncommon. Indeed, the shift from a saving to a consuming society has progressed over a period of years. Individual consumption behavior is not fueled by a change in public policy, technology, or international affairs, but by changes in peoples' attitudes. Like the change in social values that, in part, prompted women to return to the work force, attitudes about saving and consuming have a direct effect on employment and the national economy.

Competitive countries invest substantially more in their economic futures than does the U.S. In *Job Opportunities Under Clinton/Gore*, Navarro argues that Europeans are investing two times as much as the U.S. per employee on industrial plants and equipment, that Japan is investing three times as much, and that U.S. spending on civilian research and development is 40 to 50 percent less than that of Germany and Japan. Critics argue that the U.S. investment in its future is no longer "world class." At a time when investment capital is needed, consumption has depleted resources.

Worker Skills. High productivity requires more than technology. It also requires highly skilled people to make technology work. Here, too, the critics argue, the U.S. is falling behind, starting with the basics: The U.S. lags in prenatal and infant health care, in the counterproductive and depressing conditions of inner-city neighborhoods, central city decay, mediocre public education, and second-class public health. It ends with deficiencies in worker preparedness, management styles, quality controls, product development, marketing, and profits.

Education and Training. The educational profile of the American worker is mixed and paradoxical. On the one hand, the U.S. college-educated population is among the largest and best educated in the world. That's the top half of the labor force. But competitive countries have learned how to develop a productive bottom half of the work force, persons with a high school education or less.

The bottom half of the labor force is where the problem lies in the U.S., as wage and unemployment figures consistently demonstrate. U.S. high school graduates lag seriously behind their international peers, and high school dropouts are virtually "third world." The U.S. investment in education is comparable to that of industrial competitors, but the U.S. is not getting comparable results from its educational system.

Investments in Workers. How American business views the work force — as another cost factor in production that needs to be reduced to improve profits — is another consideration. Japan and Germany view the skilled, highly productive worker as essential to their competitive positions. They invest heavily in their workers. Their companies concentrate more on the development of general background skills and capabilities, on higher-order thinking and problem-solving skills. They focus less on narrow job skills. By comparison, American companies spend less per worker and concentrate training and investments on the management and professional levels. In competitive countries, training is an investment. In the U.S., it's a perk.

Teamwork. Japan and Germany stress teamwork, cooperation, and collaboration rather than competition in their management styles, in the way they train, compensate people, and organize work. U.S. companies more typically reflect turn-of-the-century hierarchical management styles. That was an era of mass production coupled with management practices that maintained rigid distinctions between owners and workers. The operating concept was that of strong managers who gave orders and compliant workers who did what they were told. Labor unions grew, in part, in response to heavy-handed management and worker abuse.

Hierarchical management has given way to alternative management styles abroad that feature flatter organizational charts, participatory management, psychic investment and psychological ownership, and economic ownership. Flexibility and teamwork characterize the management styles of our economic competitors.

Compensation. Compensation practices also differ between the U.S. and our international competitors. Navarro reports that in 1990 the heads of Japanese companies received about 20 times as much compensation as did the average production worker, whereas chief executive officers in the U.S. made 120 times as much compensation as did the average worker.

Every year *Forbes* magazine publishes "The Forbes Four Hundred," a narrative listing of America's most wealthy. The 1994 listing is headed by 38-year-old William Henry Gates, III, Harvard dropout and head of Microsoft, whose net worth is estimated at $9,350,000,000. "Only in America," some observers would say. "It shouldn't happen in America," some critics would argue.

Technology. Another foreign-domestic comparison is how improvements in technology relate to workers. As automation increased in Germany and Japan, wages also rose. Investments in technology are viewed as ways to increase worker productivity, and profits are returned to labor.

In the U.S., by comparison, management pursues lower wages with religious fervor because lower wages mean short-term higher profits. Improvements in technology are viewed as ways to replace skilled labor with lower-cost, unskilled workers or machines. As sales and profits in the U.S. have risen over the past two decades, firms have reduced wages and shifted more of their activity to contingency employment — lower wage, part-time workers.

Global Unemployment. The magnitude of unemployment around the world is staggering and, in an age of global economics, that has serious consequences for employment in America. The International Labor Organization reports that 47 million additional job seekers enter the already overcrowded labor market every year. Asia suffers chronic unemployment, and Africa and Latin America are in employment crises far worse than anything Americans and Europeans suffered during the Depression.

Several factors contribute to global unemployment, including the press of world population and the return of women to paid employment. The United Nations estimates that 700 million people in impoverished countries are unemployed or underemployed and, that over the next two decades, an additional 750 million will seek to enter the labor force. In countries with the highest population growth rates — such as Mexico, Kenya, and Pakistan — labor supply is growing nearly 3 percent per year, far faster than the demand for workers even in high-growth economies. The birth rate is slightly down in India and China; nonetheless, each birth eventually adds another job seeker to their already staggering combined pool of a billion workers.

Improvements in public health — quality, availability, and practice — contribute further to the problem, however insensitive that may sound. Improved health lowers infant mortality and extends life. Both add numbers to the work force, years to work careers, and further diminish the prospects for hundreds of millions worldwide looking for work at liveable wages.

Large numbers of women have entered paid employment worldwide, including in Asia, Africa, and Latin America. But, in addition to adding to the numbers seeking employment, the worldwide practice of paying women much less than men contributes further to global wage and unemployment problems. In some countries, such as South Korea, women's earnings are no more than 50 percent of men's earnings. The worldwide feminization of the labor force, greater proportions of women working, and women working at lower pay scales exert downward pressures on job prospects and wages globally, which means the least skilled are the most at risk.

Global Competitiveness. Global competitiveness is likely to increase, not decrease, in the foreseeable future. The Japanese economic challenge has been evident and growing for decades. Indeed, one of the main arguments for the North American Free Trade Agreement (NAFTA) was defensive: If we don't capture the south-of-the border market, Japan will. In addition, years of talk and negotiation recently translated into an economically unified Europe and the world's largest market — 380 million people, half again as many as the entire U.S. population. And, if the initial common market consolidation extends throughout Europe as proposed, the world's largest market will more than double to 850 million consumers.

Once upon a time, Europe was the U.S. market!

Where We Are Today

Five factors have brought us to where we are today:

- Continuing wage and unemployment problems
- An increasing awareness that the U.S. standard of living is at stake
- A developing consensus that competing successfully in the global market requires a national initiative
- The election of a new national leadership that, perhaps more than anything else, reflected an acceptance that we need to search for new solutions
- A mid-term repudiation of the new leadership that, perhaps, reflects the national mood of uncertainty and impatience

We are witnesses to history, to a time when people are reluctant, understandably, to let go of a past that has been good to them, but also a time when people, increasingly, have little choice but to embrace change and an uncertain future. Behind the smoke and mirrors of national politics, our leadership is forging, both by design and default, a new economic game plan that will be played on a global field.

It's easy to lose sight of that larger agenda when the issues come at us piecemeal. Nonetheless, the underlying challenge is to craft a viable response to new realities. The components of the blueprint are not yet in place. It may be that all pieces have not yet been identified. NAFTA, the North American Free Trade Agreement, is an example of one component. GATT, the General Agreement Tariffs Trade, is another. Health care is another. New linkages between education and work, a national family policy, insurance and retirement reform, the national investment in high technology, and more reinventing government — the list goes on — are other components that will eventually form sizeable chunks of the total response package. What the specific pieces of the puzzle will be, how carefully they are crafted, the pace and extent to which they are adopted, and how successfully they are implemented will have major impact on today's jobs and tomorrow's careers.

The point is that the U.S. is competing in a global economy with low-wage, low-value-added workers. The emerging U.S. response to the challenge is to produce a high-skill, high-wage, high-productivity labor force. Before turning to what that means, how the U.S. proposes to do this, and how today's youth can prepare themselves for the global economy, I turn to a second major influence on careers: high technology.

HIGH TECHNOLOGY

The depletion of the ozone layer, pollution of the atmosphere, exhaustion of non-renewable resources, the relentless spread of the HIV virus, the world's inability to control its population, each of these together with other issues too numerous to list will affect our daughters' and sons' opportunities and careers. But few forces are as likely to affect their work and the workplace as directly as high technology.

High technology takes many forms, and its applications are as varied as research and treatment in medicine, engineering, and biotechnology. But where high technology touches the lives of citizens and workers on a day-to-day basis is in the vast and emerging arena of electronic communications.

Brief History of the Internet

There was no such thing as an Internet before 1983, and the idea didn't even exist before 1969. In 1969, the Department of Defense set up a research project to solve an increasingly important military problem. Simply stated, if war broke out and one or more critical computer hookups was destroyed, how could the Pentagon route computerized information? The Pentagon had big-time computing horsepower capable of cranking out military solutions, but what good was information if you couldn't get it out? It was an issue of national defense and security.

The Department of Defense set up a project named ARPANET to develop a "war proof" way of connecting computers. The ARPANET project solved the problem by developing packet-switching technology — breaking computer data into packets or chunks, putting proper addressing information on each packet, and then sending the separate packets out into the spider webs of computer networks. The packets don't all have to follow the same route. The technology allows them to seek whatever route is necessary to find their destination. Once the packets of information arrive from hither, thither, and yon, there is technology at the destination to put them back together again.

The notion was simple. Don't restrict the route. And don't send all the packets in one rigid pathway. Don't put all your eggs in one basket. Instead, "Let 'er fly!" Obviously, that can be done only if the information packets can be routed through millions of pathways that include fiber-optic cables, satellite systems, microwaves, and just good old plain copper wiring. The idea was simple, but the solution was complex. The real genius of ARPANET's research, born out of the tensions of the Cold War, is that a way was developed to use those spider webs of connections to assure our military national security.

But Does It Work?

How do we know that it works in wartime? The best evidence is the Persian Gulf War. One of the reasons it was so difficult for the U.S. to knock out Saddam Hussein's command and control headquarters was that Iraqi intelligence used our packet-switching technology against us. Fire the missiles into Baghdad, as we did. Show the pin-point precision targeting on camera, as we did. Even knock out the sights, which we did — but, surprise! The packet-switching technology rerouted the data. It works.

In 1983, the ARPANET research program was split into two projects. Pursuit of military objectives went its separate way under MILNET. A second project was established to develop civilian communications objectives. Thus, 1983 marks the birth of what we know today as Internet. Packet-switching technology, developed for military purposes, entered the public domain.

The National Science Foundation took the lead in developing the civilian communications objectives and initially promoted the Internet concept in the nation's universities. The idea was to connect higher education with the world's supercomputers. Regional computer networks were established to serve universities, and academics became the second wave of Internet users.

Additional years passed — no more than 8 or 10 — before business and individual users perked up. Today, corporations buy high-speed leased-line access and individuals subscribe to dial-up accounts. Anybody with a modem can now connect to the Internet. June 1991 marks another milestone in electronic communications, when more than half of all registered host computers on the Internet were commercial.

Over the short period of 22 years from 1969 to 1991, the Internet idea had matured from a Department of Defense concept, to development of military technology tried under wartime conditions, to regional networks connecting academics in universities, and finally to connections with big business and individual dial-up accounts. Today, nine out of ten new connections are commercial, and the list of Fortune 500 companies that use the Internet is impressive. At this writing, researchers at General Electric send 5,000 messages daily; 20,000 of Schlumberger's 50,000 employees maintain network addresses; and Digital Equipment Corporation links some 31,000 computers to the Internet and sends 1.7 million E-mail (electronic mail) messages every month.

Internet Growth

To say that growth of the Internet has been mind boggling is an understatement. Here is the record:

- In 1969, before ARPANET, there were linkages between only 4 computers.
- By 1985, two years after ARPANET split into Milnet and Internet, some 2,000 computers using some 100 networks talked to each other using packet-switching technology.
- By 1989, 160,000 computers were connected by some 500 networks.
- By 1990, the number of networks expanded beyond 2,000.
- By 1991, the number of networks passed 4,000.
- And by 1994, the communications matrix contained 30,000 networks and more than 2.3 million computers.

In truth, the Internet is a hodgepodge — a strange, unplanned, and anarchic system that has grown like a Frankenstein monster. But it works. The Internet stretches into 137 countries. The number of users worldwide ranges somewhere between 20 and 25 million, with projections of 40 million users by the end of 1995 and 100 million by 1998. The Internet is growing 100 percent a year.

On The Horizon

Of course, the little guy has been left in the dust with these government-supported efforts, but a lot is percolating out there in cyberspace because there are humongous markets for 21st Century electronic pioneers. For example, a consortium of Apple Computer, Sun Microsystems, Bank America, Hewlett-Packard, and Lockheed is building CommerceNet, which promises to be the first large-scale business service on the Internet. It will offer products, visual catalogues, banking, brokerage, and notary services.

Both the Internet concept and its growth are spectacular, but it is likely that we haven't seen anything yet. Media attention to space exploration has focused almost exclusively on the National Air and Space Program to the virtual neglect of private space efforts. That is understandable. Private rockets are low-cost and do not send people into space. The satellites may weigh as little as 50 pounds and cost as little as $1 million — not the kind of drama that ignites network news.

Nonetheless, to date, 10 different private launch vehicles have gone up with small satellites and space sensors, and numerous private satellite-based communications systems are in the works. For example, Orbcomm is developing a communications service that allows customers to use inexpensive hand-held receiver-transmitters to bounce data and messages off a fleet of 26 small, low-Earth-orbit satellites. Orbital's Pegasus Rocket will launch the satellites from a high-flying jet. The first two, scheduled for 1994, were meant to take their positions approximately 500 miles above the Earth. The remaining 24 satellites are scheduled for launch in 1995 and will offer new services. For example, Eyeglass will offer high-resolution satellite imagery for commercial uses, including creating maps and managing natural resources, and Sea Star will use satellites to detect changes in the oceans.

If a private enterprise project built around a fleet of 26 low-Earth-orbit satellites sounds excessive, consider two competing global wireless communications systems. Motorola's Iridium project proposes a fleet of 66 satellites; and the Bill Gates/Craig McCaw Teledesic proposal involves 840 private satellites.

Information Highway

Visualizing a radically different future is difficult because it involves envisioning a world of information highways and superhighways. We don't have a clear understanding of what the commotion is all about. We don't have the necessary new words with which to think about and describe the new concept.

Railroad locomotives were once referred to as "iron horses." The snorting steam engines with their huge pistons and driving wheels may have had some resemblance to an imaginary iron horse, but "iron horse" hardly captures the idea of Japan's 200 mile-per-hour trains or Washington's electric-powered metro system. "Wireless telegraphy" may have borne some resemblance to early radios, but the words don't begin to capture the notions of cellular phones, laser communication links, and satellite communications. And "picture radio" only crudely touched the surface of what television was all about. The words made no allowance for color imagery, cable networks, remote controls, and VCRs. We strain to understand what the future will be like. And the old ideas and words with which we work offer little hint of what life will be like when the innovations take hold.

We have entered an information age in which access to and exchange of information is critical. The current buzz words are "information highway," or sometimes "information superhighway." The concepts conjure up images of black, smoke-belching 18-wheelers hauling gigabyte loads of numbers back and forth, faster than the eye can see, out there in cyberspace (which I can't see and I don't understand, either). The notion of an information highway doesn't take me very far before it runs out of gas.

Perhaps that is just as well, because just as our imagery of new technology is based on dated, even faulty, ideas, the imagery gives us little sense for how the new technology will change the way we live in the 21st Century.

A 17th Century Analogy

Instead of trying to understand the future in terms of our past experiences and limited vocabularies, perhaps we can get a better feel for how things are likely to change by examining a similar shift that occurred earlier. In the 17th Century, as in the 20th Century, the costs of disseminating information suddenly plummeted and, as a result, society changed dramatically and forever.

In 1649, a gentleman named Henry Walker started printing what we might call a shopper's guide or weekly newsletter. Walker ran a registry office in London who's function was to bring buyers and sellers together. He experimented with a hand-printed newsletter to advertise his business to those who

> *" . . . have household stuff to sell, also others that would lay jewels to pawn, gentlemen that want servants and servants that want places. For any business it [costs] but fourpence and doth much good in bringing the buyer and seller together."*

Walker's "classified ad" was a breakthrough in marketing. It made buyers and sellers aware of each other and brought them together. Before the newsletter, buyers and sellers had no easy way to find each other, and the probability of a sale was limited to the chance that a seller happened to bring goods to a village market on the same day that a buyer wanted to purchase those items.

By the early 1800s, 150 years later, Koening cylinder printing and steam presses ran off 1,000 printed sheets per hour, far more than the 150 copies per hour produced by hand presses. Still later, rotary presses turned out 18,000 pages-per-hour. Then the pages, in the form of newspapers, were loaded onto railroads. At this point, the market for buyers and sellers extended well beyond a location in the village square to a news distribution area. The market was no longer a place but, rather, an information system. By the 1920s, information systems became radio networks, then national radio networks, and then national TV networks.

Henry Walker's goal was to promote his registry office. He had no idea that he was putting into motion a concept that would forever change the definition of a market from a place in a village to having access to information. And he had no idea that market information would be distributed by visual, audio, and verbal messages transported by copper wires, fiber-optic cables, and radio and television signals bounced from satellite to satellite around the globe.

So, also, no one knows where the information highway will lead, though it will change our ways of life and living at least as much as was done by the iron horse, wireless telegraphy, and picture radio. There are some clear directions that the technology is headed, and in the next section I sketch what the information highway is, how it works, and what it does — at least at the beginning. Then I discuss some myths about the effect of high technology on the workplace.

The I-Way

Past eras can be characterized in part by what was being moved and how. In the early years, the colonies needed to move people and supplies. Great ships were built, and people and supplies were brought from the old countries to the new. As the population pressed westward, smaller boats carried people and supplies by rivers and lakes, and then wagons carried them by land. The nation became a self-sufficient, agricultural society, and paths were converted to roads for wagons and carts to haul farm produce to and from markets. The Industrial Revolution mass-produced manufactured products, more goods to be moved. And it produced the means to transport them: highways, automobiles, and trucks; railroads and trains; airplanes and airports. Today, information is "the goods" that needs to be transported, and the nation has committed to developing the information superhighway to carry it.

> *" Today more than ever, businesses run on information. A fast, flexible information network is as essential to manufacturing as steel and plastic. If we do not move decisively to insure that America has the information infrastructure we need, every business and consumer in America will suffer."*
>
> **Vice President Gore, The North Carolina Information Highway Project, 1994**

It started with Internet. Now states are expanding on the concept by linking services, and private industry is advancing the technology — building information highways. The federal government is giving financial impetus, coordinating functions, and providing regulatory oversight — nurturing the entire enterprise, building the national information superhighway. Call it what you want: Internet, Information Highway, or Information Superhighway. It's the huge electronic communications network that is leading us into the future. I call it simply the *I-Way*.

What the I-Way Does

The I-Way allows voice and sound, text, data, and video images to be sent and received at the same time at multiple sites around the world. It uses audiovisual equipment — cameras, recorders, monitors, computers, TV sets, video phones, and control equipment in specially equipped rooms; the whole nine yards — to capture information at an origin site, pass it through sophisticated switches and rapid-transmission technology to its destination, then convert the signals back to the original electrical form so they reach the target audience as voice and sound through speakers, as text and data on computer terminals or printers, and as video images on monitors and TV sets.

The I-Way provides a much bigger pipeline for that information, and it flows at far greater speeds than past technology allowed. It is efficient, especially for large-volume data transmissions, including medical video information. For example, an 800-page book transmitted over a current telecommunications system takes about a quarter of an hour and costs $2.00. On the I-Way, the same 800-page book is transmitted in two-tenths of a second at a cost of two-tenths of a cent.

The I-Way enables us to do things we hadn't thought about earlier because the speed, convenience, and flexibility of the technology were not available. For these reasons, the I-Way offers the capability of accomplishing things that are not possible with present technology.

I-Way Benefits

The Internet and beginnings of the I-Way are not science fiction or a pipe dream. They are here today. The advance and acceptance of the new technologies has been spectacular, and one need not be a visionary to imagine what the system will be like. Pilot projects are in service.

The I-Way will offer free-standing information stations that resemble automatic teller machines or phone booths with monitors and speakers situated in public places — shopping centers, public libraries, post offices, and airports. A gentleman uses an information station to check information on property taxes. Another inquires about county population characteristics. A woman calls up school information, then pays some bills and renews her driver's license without standing in line.

The benefits of the information highway fall into four general categories: greater equities, expanded opportunities, increased efficiencies, and more choices. On the surface, these benefits may appear abstract. But when applied to specific areas of society — such as giving a disadvantaged child in a rural area access to special education, or reducing an elderly patient's travel time and costs for medical care — the promise of the new technologies can be grasped more readily. Following are examples of applications in education, crime control, and medical services.

Education. Applications of the I-Way to schools and education are exciting. The I-Way will:

- Allow students at smaller, rural schools to share the resources of larger, urban schools through interactive-video distance learning.
- Make it possible for one remedial education teacher to meet with students from several high schools at one time.
- Bring literacy programs to people in their homes and communities.
- Give teachers and students instant access to university library collections and state government information resources.

Crime Control. The I-Way offers a powerful set of tools for judges, district attorneys, and law enforcement officers to use in solving crimes and arresting suspects. The I-Way will:

- Give law enforcement officers immediate access to information on suspects and crimes from multiple databases.
- Allow interactive video to be used in inmate education and health care evaluations.
- Allow video arraignments, which saves time, eliminates the costs of transporting prisoners, and reduces the chance of prisoner escape.
- Lower the cost of training law enforcement officers, emergency medical personnel, and fire fighters through the use of interactive video.

Health Care. The I-Way will:

- Allow physicians at large hospitals to examine and treat patients at remote locations through "telemedicine." Estimates indicate that one state will save $625 every time medical consultations of inmates can be made via the I-Way instead of transporting the prisoner to a major medical center.
- Store patients' life-time health records and transmit them instantaneously.
- Allow patients to get a rapid second opinion, because images and records can be transmitted quickly from one medical center to another.
- Allow medical personnel at teaching hospitals to train those at remote locations without travel time and expense.
- Provide health information at all times through an interactive health information system.

Medical consultants can clearly distinguish many skin disorders and other external maladies over the I-Way. CAT and EKG scans, electronic stethoscope readings, and videoscopic internal probes can be readily transmitted via electronic communications. New tools are being developed to take advantage of the emerging technology.

Other Benefits of the I-Way

The benefits of the I-Way extend far beyond these examples. The I-Way creates a state-of-the-art telecommunications infrastructure that gives businesses better access to strategic information and market data through worldwide networks. It makes video conferencing and training available to employees, both public and private, which saves travel time and costs. The I-Way also allows emergency management personnel to communicate better, faster, and without travel in times of crisis. Citizens can have direct access to public records.

The backbone of the network, the fiber-optics and special switches, are in place in leading-edge states, and the I-Way opened for business in those areas in the summer of 1994. In North Carolina, for example, 112 initial sites were opened in August, 50 additional sites are scheduled to come online by January of 1995, and more each month and year into the future. North Carolina state government alone has identified 3,400 possible sites.

Home TV

Expanding the band width of computer networks will reach directly into private homes and home TVs. Television will go through another huge change because the broadband will carry 500 channels. Home viewers will no longer have to content themselves with whomever and whatever is playing on the tube. Rather, they will be able to tune in their first choices in entertainment, culture, religion, comedy, sports, news analysis, educational programming, and the like.

Some speculate and hope that a culture of first choices will create a bias toward excellence that will replace lowest common denominator programming with its pandering to the mediocre, convenient, and crude. In a world of band-width scarcity, owners of the conduit control programming. They choose and shape the content. Whether the network is headed by a scheming monster or the world's greatest humanitarian, band-width scarcity requires network managers to determine the video programming. But when there is an abundance of band widths, the viewer will have choices from many options, and the consumer will have much more control over what she or he absorbs.

In sum, electronic communications is real. It is here. It is changing the nature of work (what people do) and the workplace (how they do it). Increasingly, workers are processing information. They are doing it with keyboards, monitors, and other remote devices that physically distance them from the commodities and products they control. The issue young people face is how to prepare themselves for that work and that workplace.

HIGH-TECH MYTHS

When personal computers splashed into the marketplace some 15 years ago, media imaginations ran wild with speculations about how PCs would revolutionize lives and take over the workplace. There was excitement in the air but, truth be known, there was also anxiety. The little beige boxes threatened us and frightened us. They were expensive. They were user unfriendly. And the media hype would have had us believe that, at best, we would all end up sitting at computers or, at worst, we would be replaced by computers. Our only recourse appeared to be to head back to school, master the math we never learned, and learn the high-powered skills it would take to run the whiz-bang boxes.

But little of that ever happened. Nonetheless, today some of the same hysteria resurfaces and fertile imaginations are running wild again. Again, media imaginations are fantasizing about how the I-Way will revolutionize our lives. Again, there is the thinly veiled threat that high tech is taking over the workplace. And, again, there is the worry that we should all be learning sophisticated skills to prepare for jobs that don't yet exist. According to Harper's Index, more than half of the population believes that technology has already gone beyond our capacity to learn it and utilize it effectively.

But we've been down this road before. In this section I, too, examine the impact of electronic high technology on the workplace. But I leave the crystal ball gazing to others — to the visionaries and futurists. Based on what we know rather than what we fantasize or want to believe, I suggest what high tech will *not* do. I seek to dispel five myths.

Myth # 1: "Most Future Jobs Will Be in High Tech"

When discussing future employment, the media tends to focus on the high fliers — biotechnology, microelectronics, laser optics, and anything that smacks of microprocessors and computers. Journalists are quick to conclude that the fastest growing occupations are in high technology (which is right), and they leave the impression that high tech is where most jobs will be (which is wrong).

Often, reporters don't analyze labor force projections carefully. In their quest for developing the big story, they tend to confuse high growth rates with numbers of employment opportunities. They don't follow the projections for, say, retail sales clerks, home health aides, and restaurant cooks. They ignore the ho-hum occupations because their news noses instinctively lead to the razzle-dazzle occupations — and the wrong lists of projections.

In fairness, there are a lot of tables and numbers and lists to sort through when it comes to understanding labor force projections. But to find where most employment opportunities will be, you have to look not at projections for occupations that are growing the fastest and have the highest percentage growth rates, but at projections with the largest job growth and the highest numerical change. There is a difference — a big difference.

Typically, occupations with the most employment opportunities have large numbers of workers compared to what I call the "high fliers" that employ small numbers and, therefore, can post dramatic growth rates. Industries and occupations with the most employees and the most employment opportunities grow slower than the high fliers, and they are not as glitzy. Large numerical growth occupations may even grow slower than the average for the total labor force. And they may have lack-luster titles. Moreover, the high fliers generally require advanced levels of education and high-level expertise. They also offer high pay. But this is not where most employment opportunities lie (more on this in Chapter 6). For the moment, I return to the myth that most future jobs will be in high technology.

There is no single definition of high-technology industries and occupations, though the concept usually refers to some combination of three components: the involvement of scientific and technical workers, a strong commitment to research and development, and the development of relatively sophisticated products. Workers who clearly meet this definition include engineers, life and physical scientists including biotechnologists, mathematical and statistical specialists, engineering and science technicians, and computer, robotics, and microprocessor specialists. High-tech occupations almost always require high school preparation in science and mathematics followed by postsecondary education ranging from an associate degree to a doctorate. They are cutting-edge occupations, using the kind of expertise you can't pick up on a summer job.

In reality, there are few high-tech occupations in the labor force, even when you include associated technical support. High-tech occupations account for small numbers of jobs. In 1982, for example, high-tech workers numbered 3.3 million — little more than 3 percent of the labor force. Since 1982, employment in high tech may have grown as much as 45 or 50 percent, more than double the growth rate of the labor force. But because the size of high-tech occupations is small, the spectacular growth rate generated less than 1.5 million new jobs, which is no more than 6 percent of all new jobs and roughly the same percentage of jobs created by high technology in the 1970s.

Employment in high technology increased faster than the total labor force in the 1970s, the 1980s, and the early 1990s, and it will continue to do so in the years ahead. Nonetheless, because the base number of workers is small, the high-tech contribution to total employment is also relatively small. Even if these estimates are wildly wrong and the proportion of jobs in high technology were, say, to double by the year 2005, no more than 8 percent of all jobs would be in high technology.

When parents and young people hear that so many new jobs will be in high technology, they need to listen carefully to what is being said. Spectacular percentage growth usually means neither many employment opportunities nor a large share of total workers. When projecting employment in high technology, we're not talking about 60 or 80 percent, but about 6 or 8 percent of the labor market. Doubling the share of total workers in high tech, which is very unlikely, isn't a 30, 40, or 50 percentage point increase but a 3, 4, or 5 percentage point increase. Even if 8 percent of all workers were to be employed in high technology in 2005, that leaves 92 percent of the workforce employed elsewhere. Most future jobs will not be in high technology.

Myth # 2: "Everybody Will Have to Learn to Use Computers"

Another myth about the impending high-tech takeover follows these lines: "Bookkeepers' jobs have really changed. They're all using computers now." Or "90 percent of people in New York already work with computers." And "By the year 2000, three-fourths of school kids will carry laptops instead of three-ring binders." Neither the exact year (whether it be 2000, 2005, or even 2225) nor the percentage (whether it be 60, 70, 80, or even 90 percent) is important. The argument, a second high-tech myth, is simply that just about everybody is going to have to learn to use computers in the near future. Again, the magic word "computers" trips fantasy buttons that conjure up Star-Trek imagery about what life will be like: James Bond briefcases, third graders cracking secret Pentagon codes, and death-row inmates controlling the World Bank. Part of the fantasy is the worry that we're going to have to learn all kinds of technical stuff to live that way.

Recently, I interviewed a number of high school students about their career plans — all grades, young men and young women, bright ones, all-American average youngsters, and so-so students. One of the things that concerned me was the number who expressed confusion about how to prepare for careers "that don't exist yet."

The notion that most jobs that young people will take don't even exist today is wrong. All jobs change over time — including motherhood; but the idea that there will be a wholesale replacement of existing jobs with jobs that don't exist yet — and that, therefore, there is no way to prepare for them — is disturbing. Where do these ideas come from? They don't come from what we know about the impact of technology on the workplace. It reminds me of a convention presentation I gave some years ago in Waterloo, Iowa, the home of John Deere. No sooner had I finished than a hand shot up like a spring-loaded trap and a middle-aged woman blurted out: "Do you think I should take a course in computers?"

Part of the high-tech mythology that grips us is a fear of the unknown, a feeling that others may be ready for it but that we ourselves really aren't up to all that high-tech stuff. It threatens us. We worry that we'll be run over and end up as road kill on the I-Way. Media hype nurtures that impression, but we know from past experience and careful studies that most people who end up working with computers need no computer skills whatsoever. Study after study has been done — some by my good friend and associate, Dr. Kenneth Spenner of Duke University — and the general conclusion is that, for all the people who work with computers, only a small number, perhaps 1 percent, will need the sophisticated skills to program computers or take them apart and fix them. For the other 99 percent of us, the computer will simply be something we turn on, use, and turn off again. No big deal.

We already use a wide assortment of computers or microprocessors (small computers that do things for us), and we may not even know it. Examples include the remote control on our televisions, our telephones, our microwaves, and our garage door openers. But does that mean that we know how our microwaves work? Do we fix them when they go on the fritz? Ever have a course in using and fixing your microwave? Or do we just do what the salesperson told us to do, follow the written instructions, and pick up some tips from others along the way? Similarly, we stick our cash cards in the automated teller machine, push some numbers, take our money, and off we go. Did we first enroll in college to learn how to use instant cash machines?

My point is straightforward. We're already using all kinds of high technology. Micro-processors are all over the place. They've been sneaking into our lives. Chalk one up for the computer industry: They've made 'em user friendly — hardly the way the ornery monsters used to be! And the little buggers are extremely contagious. Hard not to want more of them. Or haven't you had a family fight recently about who misplaced the remote control for the TV?

Myth # 3: "Operating High-Tech Equipment Requires Qualitatively Superior Skills"

Do high-tech products and tools require a new work force with advanced skills? Earlier I suggested that 99 percent of us will never access the innards of a computer either by way of keyboard programming or by screwdriver. But do these mostly empty, magical little beige boxes, some of them handbag size, require higher-level skills to operate?

One of the places computers have really taken over is on the desks of secretaries, and there are studies of what happens as secretaries change from typewriters to word processors. It's a change that happens over days, not months or years; and, certainly, it's not a certificate or degree program. It is true that secretaries, like everyone else, don't learn everything at once. And they can constantly improve their computer skills. But they learn by doing — the same way we learn most new things.

But do secretaries need qualitatively superior skills to shift from typewriters to word processors? Does it take a different kind of person with a different set of credentials to operate a computer? Observation, experience, and careful studies suggest that the opposite is true. Secretaries no longer need letter perfect typing skills. It is no longer as important to be able to type/keyboard with blitzkrieg speed, because letters, even whole documents, can be spell-checked and redone easily and quickly. Secretaries need not be able to write a paragraph that the boss forgot in a letter, just find it in some other letter and insert it via cut and paste.

My point is that the role of secretaries has changed, has expanded like most jobs, and that new know-how is needed; but the old tasks of typing have become highly routinized and require few qualitatively superior skills. Indeed, studies suggest that secretaries who only do keyboarding require fewer skills and make fewer judgments. Because a person uses high-tech equipment does not mean that person must have qualitatively sophisticated skills.

Myth # 4: "You've Got to Know a Lot More about a Problem to Run Computers"

Some years ago I totally rebuilt a 1928 Model A Ford. I took apart every piece, every bolt and burr. I laid the whole thing out on the floor of my double garage while my wife's car and my car sat outside through two winters in Madison, Wisconsin. It took me three years to clean everything up, replace bad parts, repaint, reupholster, rechrome, and bring that rusty bucket of bolts back to life in mint condition. You can do that with a Model A Ford. It's been said that all you need is a screwdriver and a pair of pliers.

But that isn't true. You need a lot more than a screwdriver and a pair of pliers to get a Model A running again. At least I did — because it is a lot easier to take the thing apart than to put it back together again. (By the way, if you ever decide to rebuild a Model A, take my advice and join a Model A club so that, when the engine goes *thump, thump, thump* in the middle of the night, you can bring over your cronies the next weekend and, after four beers and a hot afternoon, they'll get you running again.)

There's a parable in this true-life experience. Back in the good 'ole days, the good mechanic was one who could diagnosis problems and fix them. He knew the Model A inside and out. He would figure out what was wrong by sticking his head under the hood, looking around, listening, feeling parts, even smelling them. He would turn off the engine, then start it up again; run the engine fast; run it slowly; let it sit for a while; and then take the car for a test drive. The good mechanic would tune it up until it "sounded right."

My last car was a sports car, low slung with a rotary engine. I seldom opened the hood other than shortly after I bought it when friends would ask to look under the hood, and then ask, "What's that thing?" I seldom knew the answer. So the more I kept the hood closed, the less dumb I looked.

And I never laid a wrench on the engine. Wouldn't have known where to start. That doesn't mean I never had problems. I did. And one of the things I learned is that mechanics no longer stick their heads under the hood to look, listen, touch, and smell. Instead, they plug in diagnostic equipment that runs tests, then prints out a page of numbers that tells them what isn't working. The mechanic doesn't need a lot of hands-on experience with the vehicle — he may never in his life have driven your make and model of automobile — because he doesn't rely on experience to diagnose the problem. The microprocessors do it for him. The mechanic goes through a set of routines and the machines tells him what is wrong and what to do. He puts the red wire on the red thing and the yellow wire on the yellow thing, and then pushes the right buttons and has a cup of coffee while the diagnostic machinery does its thing.

High-tech equipment may be sophisticated, but that doesn't mean that operators have to know a lot about the problem to use it. They don't. Today's high-tech mechanic doesn't have to be as experienced or as knowledgeable as the mechanic who fixed Model A Fords. The new technologies don't require advanced skill, experience, and judgment. New technologies replace the advanced skill, experience, and judgment that mechanics used to need.

Myth # 5: "It Takes a Lot of Smarts to Fix Computers"

Myths 3 and 4 challenge the notion that you have to know a lot more to operate computers, but what about fixing all the computers and high-tech equipment we're putting in place? The fifth myth is that it will take an ever-expanding army of whiz-kid service people to keep a high-tech society going.

Not so. Let me share another personal example. About 10 years ago I had an office in a building that was struck by lightning, and whammo! Everything went bananas, including my computer. Sure, I had a surge suppressor, but it didn't matter. When I turned on my computer, the screen gave me all kinds of mumbo-jumbo.

I had a service contract, so I picked up the phone and the conversation went something like this. The technician said, "Push this button and that button; then tell me what the screen says." The screen gave some numbers. "Okay," he said. "Now do this, that, and that together." I did. The screen gave me more numbers. "I need to ask you to do one more thing," the technician said. "When you push this button and that button together, does the little light in the back blink?" I said, "Yes." "Okay," he said, "you've got a fried mother board. We'll send someone out to fix it."

Within an hour a young person came — I'd guess that he was 19 or 20 years old. He brought with him a thin cardboard box and a screwdriver. He took out four screws and removed the shell from my computer, unplugged a couple of ribbon wires, slid out a piece of gadgetry, took the new piece out of the box and slid that in, put the shell back on, tightened the four screws, and said, "Well, let's see if it works."

It worked. I sat there speechless. So I started asking questions. "What happens when lightning strikes?" "Oh, I don't know," he said. "I guess it just burns something out." "But what does it burn out?" "I don't know," he said. "I just fix these things." "But can it start a fire? Should I unplug it when I go home at night?" I asked. "Oh, I really don't know," he said. "I don't usually work on these. I suppose it wouldn't hurt to unplug it. Let me know if you have any more problems." And, with that he was gone. My computer was back, up and running — thanks to the young Einstein! And I never had any more problems with it.

Who repairs all that fancy stuff? Nineteen-year-old kids with screwdrivers repair that fancy stuff. Most high-tech equipment is modular construction. Other equipment diagnoses the bad module. The technician retrieves the box with the right bar code from the warehouse, replaces the faulty module, tightens the screws on the shell, and flips the switch. The technician doesn't have to know much more than you and I do when we follow the directions to hook up our stereo sets. He just follows directions.

Technology, Work, and the Workplace

The National Academy of Sciences conducted two major studies of jobs that have gone through technological change. The studies inquired into changes in the labor force due to technology, and what changes in the labor force are likely. The answer to both questions? Not much.

The studies conclude that no major changes in education or skill requirements are anticipated. Some jobs are downgraded, and some are upgraded; but most jobs stay basically the same. On balance, it's a wash. And what is required by way of changes in quality of education or changes in level of education? Again, not much. The studies conclude that changes in jobs due to technology will be minor, and that there will be little change in skill and education requirements.

If anything, one might think that small businesses might be affected the most by technological change. Big business has resources with which to hire expertise, but small businesses have fewer options. Two researchers, Levin and Rumberger, followed this logic and did a study of 3,000 firms — a big study. They wanted to understand what happens in the workplace when small to medium-size businesses automate. What happens to personnel? What kind of new personnel are needed? What is the actual human experience of technological change?

This was a study of businesses and workers that actually lived through technological change in the workplace. That's an important consideration because, as I indicated earlier, many who write about high technology are freelance writers. They may not have personal experience with change in the workplace. They may not have hands-on experience with computers and the new technologies. They may not even use computers themselves. Indeed, they may be frightened of computers or, alternatively, impressed by computers. But they are outsiders. They can only imagine what is going on. They guess. And they write on the basis of their imaginations and their guesses. All of this means that what they write may be something quite different from what insiders in business actually experience.

One of the things Levin and Rumberger asked was which characteristics were important for new office employees. Possibilities include previous experience with computers, training with computers, math skills, technical skills, and the like. They studied a whole range of possibilities that are written about in the popular literature. But what did the 3,000 managers say were the most important characteristics needed in new workers? By far, the single most important characteristic managers looked for was interest and enthusiasm for the job. The second most important characteristic was good reading comprehension. And the third was good reasoning ability. Way down on the list were characteristics we so often hear and read about. But few employers, only 4 or 5 percent, said that math skills, experience with computers, and computer training was important.

The characteristics employers look for may be quite different from the popular view. Employers look for high-powered technical skills. How often do popular articles about what's wrong with the labor force — or what's wrong with schools, or what skills young people need in the workplace — conclude that "interest and enthusiasm" is a high priority?

> ## THREE MOST-DESIRED CHARACTERISTICS OF AN OFFICE EMPLOYEE
> *(according to managers surveyed)*
>
> Most important: Job interest and enthusiasm
> Next important: Good reading comprehension
> Next important: Good reasoning ability

A National Commission on Employment study found the same thing. That study expressed surprise that it did not find more need for technical skills in the real world, and that technical skills were not critical needs.

The popular notion that high-tech jobs require new batteries of sophisticated skills isn't supported by the evidence.

Studies of jobs and workplaces that have gone through technological evolutions conclude that skill levels may have to increase in some jobs, but skill levels will decrease in other jobs. In most jobs and most workplaces there isn't much change. People can handle it. On balance, the labor force isn't affected very much by technological change.

This is not to suggest that the current emphases on reinventing the workplace, reinventing education, and reinventing the links between education and work are misplaced. On the contrary, the new initiatives appear to be well-conceived and in step with changing times. But both past experience and the best studies of the impact of technology on work call into question some popular myths. Most of us will increasingly use high technology — as we already do. But the technology itself will remain largely unobtrusive.

Youth and Careers

So what does this all mean for youth and careers? The global economy means that the U.S. must compete, and compete successfully, with more competitors; but it is also competing for larger markets. Competing successfully means producing and marketing more units of better quality at a lower cost. That requires workers who are highly skilled and highly productive.

But the U.S. definition of success means more than being competitive. It also means competing at a world-class profit to maintain if not improve the U.S. standard of living. That means high-wage jobs. High-wage jobs will require even higher levels of skill, greater efficiencies, and more productivity. The challenge to youth is to equip themselves with those capacities.

The U.S. has made a major commitment to develop electronic communication technologies to their full potential as a resource for successful competitiveness. The technologies are manageable and available, and young people are well-advised to master their basic education requirements and to upgrade their technical skills in a timely manner. As I will point out in subsequent chapters, doing that is up to them. They must manage their own careers. The educational infrastructure for doing it is not in place. "Invest in yourself" is the best career development strategy for a global and high-tech economy.

Population and Labor Force Trends

Technology and the global economy are worldwide changes that are giving new form to the nature of work and the workplace. But our society is also in the midst of domestic changes. In this chapter, I narrow the focus to examine two changes — population and labor force changes — that will alter career prospects even further. Both will affect the supply of workers for the labor force and the demands for products that the work force produces. I examine the trends in historical contexts and project them into the 21st Century. The chapter closes with a review of the U.S. response to the new realities.

POPULATION CHANGE

Population changes affect careers in two ways. First, as the population changes, so does the composition of the labor force. More young workers or fewer? More elderly or fewer? More women? Immigrants? Minorities? Who the workers are — their education levels, skill levels, their work ethics — will largely determine whether the U.S. can produce a high-wage and competitive work force. Second, population changes are also engines of demand for new products. Youth require maternity wards, pediatricians, toys, fast food, school supplies, bicycles, and teachers. Ethnic groups create markets for ethnic foods, merchandise, and culture. Older workers require pharmaceuticals, full-service restaurants, home health care, estate planners, and retirement villages. Population changes drive the economy, and the economy creates the jobs.

The U.S. population is changing dramatically. It is growing larger and older. People are living longer and there are more older people. The proportion of non-Hispanic Whites is decreasing noticeably. The population is becoming much more diverse.

Population Growth

When the ball of lights dropped in Times Square and we welcomed 1995 to the refrains of *Auld Lang Syne,* 260 million people were living in the United States. As a nation, we grow about 1.1 percent per year, which is about 3 million people. That's adding more people to the population each year than the number of people who live in each of 21 states. It is like adding another state that size to the union. Most of our growth comes from "natural increase": 4.1 million babies are born and 2.1 million people die, leaving a net increase of 2 million people. In addition, about 750,000 immigrants arrive and about 125,000 U.S. citizens return from foreign lands each year. It all adds up.

Since 1989, the number of births per year has been the highest since the peak years of the baby boom (1954 to 1964). During the baby boom, more than 4 million babies were born each year. The current rate is nearly that high. Birth rates are up not because there are more women of child-bearing age, but because the number of babies women are having has increased. After the baby boom, the U.S. went through a baby bust period, as did many countries. Mothers averaged fewer than two births over their child-bearing years and couples did not reproduce themselves. But in recent years, women's birth rates have been as high as 2.1, which more than reproduces married couples.

The U.S. is now in another growth spurt. Only during the '50s were more people added to the nation's population than will be added during the '90s. If current trends in birth rates, death rates, and immigration rates continue, the U.S. will grow by 20 million persons by the year 2000, which is a 7.8 percent increase. And the U.S. will grow by 50 percent, to 383 million persons, by the year 2050.

Life Expectancy

Births, deaths, and immigration are the prime contributors to population growth, but there is another: life expectancy. Since World War II, the number of deaths annually has been rising, but not as much as one might expect. The number of deaths has kept pace with population growth — between 8.6 and 8.8 persons per 1,000 population die annually. But the proportion of older people in the population has been increasing and one would expect, therefore, that the number of deaths would increase proportionately.

Not so. The death rate has not kept up with the growth rate in the number of elderly in the population because people are living longer. Life expectancy for the total population was 74.2 years in 1981. By 1991, just 10 years later, life expectancy at birth was 75.7 years — a year and one-half longer. The projection for 2050 is that life expectancy will rise to 82.1 years.

The Graying of America

During the '80s, most of the baby boom generation (persons born between 1954 and 1964) entered the 35- to 44-year-old age bracket. They were the fastest growing age group: They increased by 49 percent and accounted for more than half the nation's population growth. The second fastest-growing age group was persons 85 years and older. This group was born during the high birth-rate period at the turn of the century, added enormous numbers of European immigrants to its ranks, and, more recently, enjoyed higher life expectancy. As a result, the 85-years-and-older age bracket increased in size by 35 percent over the '80s. Finally, the third most rapidly growing age group during the '80s was the elderly, including persons 75 to 84 years old. Their numbers increased by 29 percent.

The U.S. population will continue to grow older through 2005. About 30 percent of the population in 1992 was born during the baby boom, and the baby boomers will be ages 36 to 54 at the turn of the century. By 2011, the first members of the baby boom will be 65 years old, and the baby boom will have decreased in size to 25 percent of the population. The last of the baby boom will be 65 years old in 2029, by which time the baby boom will dwindle to 17 percent of the total population and to the status of a footnote in history books.

The median age of the population, the midpoint between the oldest and the youngest, will rise as the population grows older. The median age was 33 years in 1991, but it will increase to 36 years by 2000, rise to nearly 40 years by 2035, and then decrease slightly to 39 years by 2050. That's a 9 percent increase in median age by the end of the century, and a 21 percent increase over the next 40 years.

Diversity

Over the past decade, the U.S. population increased in racial and ethnic diversity, which is another trend that will continue. The non-Hispanic White population grew the least, only 4 percent between 1981 and 1991. The African-American population grew by 15 percent, putting it at 12 percent of the total population.

The Asian and Pacific Islander population grew 90 percent over the decade, the fastest growing of any racial and ethnic group. Its share of the population was 2 percent in 1981 and grew to 3 percent in 1991. The Hispanic-origin population represented 7 percent of the population in 1981, grew 51 percent over the decade, and represented 9 percent of the population in 1991.

The racial and ethnic composition of the population will become even more diverse by the year 2000. The non-White proportion of the population, which now comprises three-fourths of the population, will decrease to 72 percent of the total. African Americans will increase to 13 percent.

By the year 2050, the proportional shares of racial and ethnic groups will shift even further. The non-Hispanic White population will decrease from 72 percent of the total in 2000 to 53 percent in 2050. African Americans will increase from 13 to 16 percent. Persons of Hispanic origin will increase from 11 to 21 percent. And Asian and Pacific Islanders will increase from 5 to 11 percent.

Non-Hispanic Whites are the slowest growing racial and ethnic group, and they will contribute less and less to the future growth of the U.S. population. Although non-Hispanic Whites represent 75 percent of the population today, they will represent only 30 percent of population growth through the year 2000, about 21 percent of growth between the years 2000 and 2010, and 13 percent of growth over the years 2010 to 2030. After 2030, non-Hispanic Whites will contribute very little to population growth in the U.S.

The African-American population will grow 100 percent over the next 60 years. African-Americans will number 35 million by the year 2000, and will increase to 62 million by the year 2050.

The fastest growing racial and ethnic group will continue to be the Asian and Pacific Islanders. Their growth rates may exceed 4 percent annually for the rest of this century and, by the turn of the century, they will number 12 million, will double in size by 2010, and will increase more than five times by the year 2050 (see Figure 2-1).

Composition of the Population, 1990 and 2050

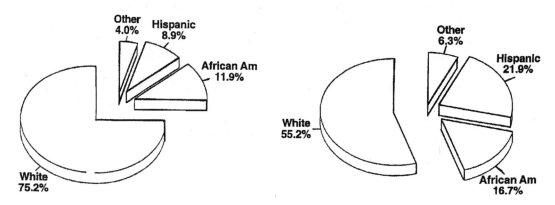

Figure 2-1 *Source: Department of Commerce*

The largest growing group will be persons of Hispanic origin. By the year 2000, the number of persons of Hispanic origin will increase to 31 million, will double by 2020, and will triple by 2050. For the rest of this century and beyond, persons of Hispanic origin will add more people to the U.S. population every year than will the non-Hispanic White population or any other group. The Hispanic-origin population will contribute increasing proportions to the total population growth: 33 percent of the total through the year 2000; 37 percent from 2000 to 2010; 43 percent from 2000 to 2030; and 57 percent of the total from 2030 to 2050.

Population and Change

The population is changing, and it is changing dramatically! Our population is growing larger. Its median age is increasing. And people are living longer. The proportion of non-Hispanic Whites is decreasing. The population is becoming racially and ethnically much more diverse.

How population changes will translate into employment opportunities is the subject of Chapter 6, but consider the effect of earlier population changes on the economy. Think back to the baby boom. The baby boom first flooded maternity rooms — mothers were literally cared for in hospital hallways. Then it spilled out of hospitals into schools and classrooms. School boards were forced to use temporary buildings as school expenditures tripled in the '50s. And then the baby boom hit the labor force, where it seems to be hiding. But it will soon rear its ugly head again as it overwhelms retirement villages and clobbers the Social Security system.

How did the baby boom affect our institutions? Fifteen- to 24-year-olds typically commit about 40 percent of the murders, 50 percent of the rapes, and 65 percent of the burglaries and robberies in society. Obviously, the more people there are of that age, the more crime can be expected. And that's what happened. Seventeen and 18 years after the peak years of the baby boom, murder, rape, robbery, and larceny rates reached all-time highs. The population change had a tremendous effect on social institutions.

And what about retail sales? We gave the baby boomers nicknames along the way, including "hippies," then "yippies," the "now generation," the "Pepsi generation," and finally the "me generation." They bought Davy Crockett T-shirts and coonskin caps. They bought more than $100 million in Barbie dolls (1950s dollars) and related accessories. They gave us rock 'n' roll. They went to Vietnam. They fled to Canada. And they went to Woodstock.

And as the baby boomers grew up, old enough to buy liquor and old enough to vote, society changed with them. Barbie doll's manufacturer, the Mattel Toy Company, moved into the mega-million dollar adult electronic toy industry. Gerber baby food, which once advertised that babies were its only business, expanded into life insurance. The Wrigley Company, makers of chewing gum, introduced Freedent gum for denture wearers. Levi Strauss designed a line of jeans for the guy who needed a little more room in the seat and the thighs. Hospitals closed obstetric and pediatric departments but expanded coronary care. And McDonald's, for years the malt, burger, and fries feedbag for the nation's young, added Egg McMuffin breakfasts for the on-the-way-to-work crowd and Chicken McNuggets for the cholesterol conscious.

The smart money follows population changes!

LABOR FORCE TRENDS

The composition of the labor force has an important effect on the economy. It determines workers' skill levels, education levels, their work ethics, and their interests. And earning wages creates markets, whether for the youth culture, women's accessories, or ethnic tastes. The labor force is changing, and with the changes employment prospects are changing, too.

Trends are understood better when viewed in historical perspective. This section sketches important trends since 1950 that have brought us to where we are today and that shape the labor force we are moving toward.

Labor Force Growth

Over the 30 years between 1950 and '80, the labor force expanded by 44 million workers, which is a 72 percent increase. More than half of that expansion occurred in the '70s, during which time the labor force expanded by more than 24 million workers.

The years between 1950 and 1980, and especially the decade of the '70s, included several notable developments (see Figure 2-2). The most important was the effect of the baby boom generation, persons born between 1946 and 1964, entering the labor force. During the late '70s, the labor force grew by 3 million workers each year, and most of them came from the baby boom. The labor force expanded 29 percent in the 10-year period 1970 to 1980.

The growth rate slowed over the '80s. Nearly all of the baby boom generation that would enter the labor force had already done so, and the labor force expanded by only 17

U.S. Labor Force Growth, 1950–1992

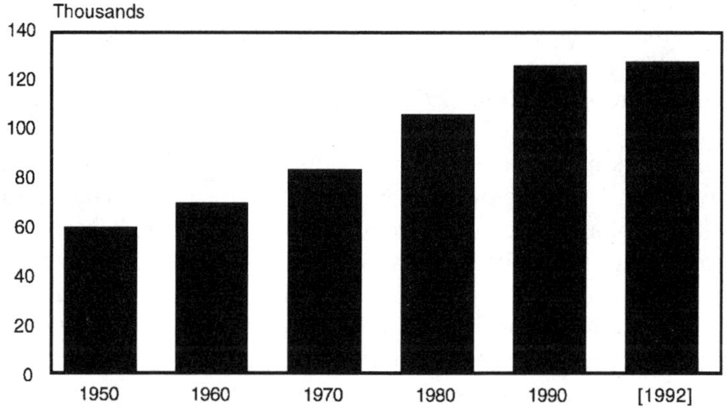

Thousands

140	

Figure 2-2 *Source: Bureau of Labor Statistics*

percent during the decade. The age group born between the end of the baby boom (1965) and before the late 1970s is sometimes called the baby-bust generation, that period of years following the baby boom when the birth rates fell dramatically. Nonetheless, even the slower growth rate added large numbers to the labor force. There were 20 million more workers in 1992 than there were in 1980.

Women Workers

Another contributor to the huge expansion of the labor force over the years 1950 through 1980 was the entrance of women into the paid labor force. In 1950, women comprised less than 30 percent of the labor force; but by 1980, women's share increased to 42 percent — a 40 percent increase. During the three decades, the percentage of working women increased from 34 percent in 1950 to 52 percent in 1980. Growth was even faster for women ages 35 to 44, whose participation rates grew from 41 percent in 1950 to 77 percent by 1990.

The rate of growth in women's participation in the labor force slowed among some age groups by the late 1980s, including participation rates for women in their 20s and 30s. But the rates for women in their 40s and 50s increased, with the result that the total labor force participation rate for women slowed but continued to increase over the '80s.

Another important trend affecting women was that the labor force participation rate of non-Hispanic White women converged with that of African-American women by the early '90s. Earlier, non-Hispanic White women in most age groups had lower labor force participation rates than African-American women. But over the '80s, participation rates for non-Hispanic White women increased faster and, by 1992, the labor force participation rates for many age groups converged between non-Hispanic White and African-American women. Labor force participation rates for Hispanic women remained lower than rates for either non-Hispanic White or African-American women.

Men's Labor Force Participation

Between 1950 and 1980, men's labor force participation followed a gradual but sustained decline from 86 percent in 1950 to 77 percent by 1980. The decline affected most age groups, but it was particularly pronounced among men ages 55 to 64:

Year	Participation Rate
1950	87 percent
1960	87 percent
1970	83 percent
1980	72 percent
1990	68 percent
1992	67 percent (estimated)

The decline in the labor force participation rate of older men accompanied a concurrent trend toward earlier retirement. Some sought earlier retirement. Others, because of industrial restructuring, were unable to find satisfactory employment and chose not to return to the labor force.

Labor force participation rates for African-American men declined more rapidly than rates for non-Hispanic White men. The reasons are complex, but a major contributing factor is the increased education and training requirements for many jobs coupled with differences in levels of education and training among racial and ethnic groups. Another factor is the decline in factory jobs that employed many African-American men. Labor force participation rates declined for older men and for men with lower levels of education and training in both minority and majority cultures.

During the '80s, the labor force trends for men changed from what they were over the years between 1950 and 1980. The change particularly affected men ages 55 and older. This age group experienced steady and sharp declines in labor force participation rates from 1950 to 1980, whereafter the trend leveled off.

Youth Workers

Youth workers, persons ages 16 to 19, experienced considerable year-to-year fluctuation in labor force participation rates over the years 1950 through 1992. This was true of both young men and young women.

The lack of a long-term trend in teenage labor force participation rates reflects the cross pressures of the period. On the one hand, there were pressures for youth to stay in school. On the other hand, there was a growing ideology in support of youth working while in school, at least part-time. An increased number worked out of necessity. Throughout the period, labor force participation rates were substantially lower for minority youth, particularly for African-American males, than for non-Hispanic White youth.

Minority Labor Force Participation

One of the most significant developments over the second half of the 20th Century is the increased share of minority workers in the labor force. In 1980, African Americans, Hispanics, Asians, and other minorities comprised 18 percent of the labor force. Non-Hispanic Whites claimed 82 percent of jobs. By 1992, however, the minority share of the labor force increased to 22 percent.

The numbers are modest, particularly when compared to the 82 and 78 percents for non-Hispanic Whites over the same period; but the 4 percentage point change in minority labor force participation is a 23-percent increase over a period of 12 years, hardly a trivial change! African Americans, whose share of the labor force grew 1 percentage point over the earlier decade, continued at about the same participation rate over the 1980s, but the share of the work force represented by Asians and other races doubled from 1975 to 1992.

The Hispanic share of the labor force also expanded dramatically, from 6 percent in 1980 to 8 percent in 1992. The rapid expansion of Hispanics in the labor force is due to both their high immigration and high birth rates. Both resulted in a younger age distribution for Hispanics with proportionately more people in their child-bearing years compared to the White majority culture.

In summary, not only is the labor force growing, it is growing faster than the population. Not only are there more people, but more of the people are working. There are two major contributors. Decidedly more women are working, while the labor force participation rates for men, particularly for older men, are declining; and there is a significantly larger minority presence in the labor force.

ECONOMIC TRENDS

When considering changes in economic trends, three factors are closely related: growth in domestic productivity, growth in demand for products, and growth in employment.

Productivity

As measured by what economists call the Gross Domestic Product, the U.S. economy increased at an annual rate of 3.3 percent from 1950 to 1980. But analysts mark 1973 as a watershed year when both the rate of growth and the amount of domestic productivity changed. For comparison purposes, the economy grew at an annual rate of 3.7 percent before 1973, and then fell 40 percent to an annual growth rate of 2.2 percent for the years 1973 through 1992. Productivity during the '70s was fueled, in part, by the rapid growth in labor force supply contributed by baby boomers and the increased proportion of women entering the labor force. But by the 1980s, both the number of baby boomers and the proportion of women entering the labor force slowed, with the result that productivity in the 1980s, though somewhat improved over the years 1973 to 1980, was considerably slower than productivity over the years 1950 through 1973.

Demand

The demand for goods and services has increased appreciably since 1950. The increase in personal consumption reflected two trends: growth in personal incomes together with an increase in the proportion of total incomes people spent coupled with a decline in their personal savings. What people bought was more services, particularly higher expenditures for health care.

A second change in the demand for domestic products was in the ratio of exports to imports as the U.S. economy internationalized. Over the years 1980 to 1986, exports grew less than 3 percent, hardly any change at all; and exports actually declined in share of the gross domestic product from 9 percent to 8 percent over the period. Over the same years, imports increased by a staggering 67 percent, which raised imports' share of the gross domestic product from 8 percent in 1980 to 11 percent in 1986. However, from 1986 to 1992, exports expanded at a rapid rate (10 percent per year) while imports slowed from growth of 9 percent to 4 percent per year.

Other major changes in the demand for products over the years 1950 to 1992 include a decline in construction of residential structures, increased business spending for durable equipment (including computers), and a rise in defense spending in the '80s followed by the defense cutback at the end of the Cold War.

Industry Employment

In 1950, 45 million workers were employed in nonfarm wage and salary jobs. Employment doubled over the next 30 years: Workers numbered 90 million in 1980 and 109 million in 1990.

But dramatic growth was only one change that occurred. Major shifts also occurred among industries. The most dramatic was manufacturing's share of employment, which fell from 34 percent of total employment in 1950 to 17 percent in 1992 — a 51 percent decline (see Figure 2-3).

Total industrial employment increased by only 18 percent over the 42-year period spanning 1950 to 1992. Over the same period, employment in service-producing industries increased dramatically. The services industry division, particularly health and business services, added more than 11 million jobs over the years 1980 to 1992 alone, which is a 60 percent increase. Temporary help, one industry within business services, was very small in the 1970s but grew by more than a million workers over the period. By comparison, employment in agriculture, a goods-producing industry, stood at 7 million in 1950 but declined to 3 million in 1992 — a 56 percent loss over 42 years.

Occupational Employment

Several trends in occupational employment mark the second half of the 20th Century, particularly the last two decades. One trend is the steady increase in employment for managers, professionals, and technicians. In 1972, these three occupational groups combined represented 21 percent of total employment, but by 1992 the same three represented 30 percent of total employment — a 43 percent increase.

Industry Employment Change, 1950–1992

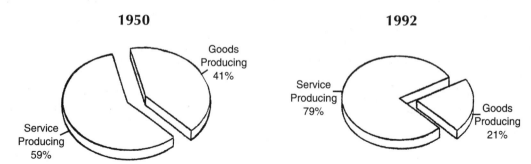

Figure 2-3 *Source: Bureau of Labor Statistics*

Other occupations recorded employment declines. Major declines affected operators and farm occupation categories. The number of clerical workers grew between 1972 and 1980, but grew slower than the total labor force over the past decade as office automation depressed the need for clerical workers.

Parents and young people must not ignore an important characteristic of trends in occupational employment:

- Occupations with increasing shares of total employment almost always require education or training beyond high school.
- Occupations with declining proportions of total employment generally do not require postsecondary education.

The one exception to this trend is service workers, whose share of total employment increased over the past two decades although service occupations usually do not require education and training beyond high school.

Uncertainties

There are always uncertainties about the future; the end of the Cold War, the globalization of the economy, the effect of new technologies, and urgent social and domestic issues raise the level of uncertainty. Following are major unknowns that will also affect careers into the early 21st Century.

Global Uncertainties

The fall of the Berlin Wall and the breakup of the Soviet Union will have far-reaching ramifications. Both will influence military expenditures, Eastern European immigration, and trade. At the same time, Europe is unifying for trade and other common interests and, if successful, trade, immigration, and military expenditures will be affected further by these developments. Concurrently, the U.S. has approved the North American Free Trade Agreement (NAFTA) and the General Agreement Tariffs Trade (GATT), both of which may affect domestic industries, immigration patterns, and the import-export balance.

It has become a truism that we live in a global economy, but what that means remains to be seen. Global factors that add to the uncertainty are the emerging markets in Eastern Europe and the former Soviet Union, the possible emergence of the European common market, prospects for increased trade with China, and our continuing trade relationships, sometimes rocky, with Japan and other Asian countries. Many unknowns remain about how the many factors at work in a global economy will balance themselves out.

Immigration is another wild card. The number of immigrants — whether documented or undocumented — who enter the U.S. over the 1992-to-2005 period will affect growth and the racial and ethnic composition of the labor force. In recent years, Hispanics and Asians dominated the immigration flow, but the annual number of immigrants and their racial and ethnic identities are subject to such vagaries as U.S. policy regarding border enforcement and outbreaks of political repression in other parts of the world.

The Economy and Labor Force

Domestic productivity is a variable, and whether future productivity will be like that of the '60s, the mid- and late '70s, or the '80s is an unknown. The distribution of goods and services is another unknown. For example, the share of domestic productivity devoted to defense has declined since 1987, and continuing declines are anticipated through the year 2000. But beyond the short term, projections for defense spending are subject to two huge unknowns: changes in the international situation, and how the U.S. will deal with obsolescence of its military technology.

Some uncertainties are unique to employment. One is whether the economy will return to longer-term employment growth rates, which is generally taken as an indicator of economic recovery and health, or whether short-term fixes, which can introduce additional ambiguities, will continue. Construction and manufacturing are particularly sensitive to changes in the economy. The overall recovery in employment in these sectors continues to be slow, which has not escaped the critical attention of economists.

Growth in the labor force will also be affected by changes in labor force participation rates. Workers who will join the labor force by the year 2005 are already born — they are 4 or 5 years old — and we know a lot about them. We know their race and ethnicity and the ratio of males to females. We can even count how many will have blue eyes and red hair. But changes in labor force participation rates rest with people's values, and changes in values are difficult to anticipate. For example, over the past quarter-century women's labor force participation rates increased tremendously, but now they appear to have bumped up against an upper limit and are unlikely to continue to increase as in the past.

There are also unknowns about the future labor force participation rates of different age groups among women. For example, the growth in young women's labor force participation rates slowed over the past six years, which raises the question of whether the slowing is permanent or temporary. So also, labor force participation rates of older men declined dramatically, then leveled off over the past six years, raising the same question: Is the trend permanent or temporary?

Another uncertainty is the nature of future jobs. In recent years there has been a major shift to short-term and less-than-full-time work. This is evident in the phenomenal growth of employment in temporary help. As with other uncertainties, questions remain whether this anomaly is a blip on the chart, a short-term cyclical movement, or the beginning of a long-term trend.

Social and Domestic Issues

A major domestic unknown is health care reform. Medical and health care expenditures grew from 5 percent of domestic production in 1960 to 15 percent in 1993 (tripled). Uncertainties include whether increasing costs can be slowed (and, if so, how quickly) and whether costs can be lowered as coverage is broadened. Slowing expenditures for health care at a time when the fastest growing segment of the population is 75 years and older is a nontrivial pursuit. Who will fund the eventual package, whatever its form and coverage, is another major unknown that can affect employment.

Savings in the U.S. have declined to the point that individuals now save less than persons in many other industrialized countries. What this means for the economy is that the U.S., compared with other advanced industrialized countries, is devoting a dwindling share of its receipts to investments. Many economists argue that higher productivity would result if a greater share of national output were reinvested in durable equipment, research, and development. Other questions raised are whether the country has made sufficient reinvestments in its infrastructure — bridges, highways, airports, public buildings, and schools.

Sociopolitical uncertainties also exist. One is occupational segregation, the continuing distribution of jobs by occupation between men and women and among racial and ethnic groups that shows large concentrations of certain groups in particular types of jobs. Women, for example, dominate clerical jobs and men dominate management. Occupational segregation is complicated by differences in educational levels among minority groups that make it difficult for members to compete for jobs. Nonetheless, issues of equity, equal opportunity, and affirmative action remain high on the domestic agenda, and whether they will emerge in corrective legislation and social policy are additional unknowns that may further shape and form tomorrow's work force.

In sum, the world is a very messy place in which to live. Although the emerging direction of labor force growth and composition can be sketched, many uncertainties remain.

THE U.S. RESPONSE TO THE NEW REALITIES

The nation's emerging economic plan covers thousands of pages, crosses federal departments, and goes well beyond the purpose of this book. Even the labor program, which spills into education reforms, exceeds our page limits. Nonetheless, you will find it useful to know the broad outline of emerging federal programs designed to help the nation's youth.

Recognize that these are federal initiatives. As NAFTA and GATT originated during the Republican administration, were then reshaped by the Democratic administration in the '92 national election, and will be massaged into still new forms by Republicans since the '94 mid-term election, so also the problems with education, labor, and the economy are national problems, have been a long time coming, and will occupy Congress and the White House for years to come, whether the leadership is Republican or Democrat. Note that the economy figured prominently in both the defeat of a Republican president in '92 and the repudiation of a Democratic president in '94.

The thrust of the labor initiatives for youth was signalled in the 1994 State of the Union Address when President Clinton stated, "The only way to have real job security in the future, to get a good job with a growing income, is to have real skills and the ability to learn new ones." The administration's plans rest on the assumption that the federal government should actively promote the nation's economy and the public good. A second assumption is that if the nation is to raise productivity, wages, and the standard of living, the government must invest more in people. "Putting people first" was a major theme in the president's campaign rhetoric, and the administration has proposed numerous programs of reform and federal leadership to "invest in people" so that they can deal more effectively with the new realities, including the global economy, and can take advantage of new opportunities, including information technologies.

Federal initiatives are based on the recognition that there continues to be a nagging, collective unease about the nation's economy. The malaise is evident in persisting doubts about whether the country has, in fact, put the recession of the early '90s fully behind it. Unemployment peaked at 9 percent during the recession of 1973 to 1975, and at 10.8 percent in the 1981-to-1982 recession. By comparison, the peak unemployment in the 1990–'91 recession was a modest 7.7 percent. Nonetheless, some reason that the lingering employment situation is worse than that following the past two recessions because it involved more permanent layoffs and increased labor-market problems for white-collar workers.

Permanent Layoffs

A major difference in the last recession was the increase in the proportion of permanent job losses. In past recessions, the proportion of workers who did not expect to be called back to their jobs accounted for less than three-fifths of the job losses attributed to the recession. Since mid-1990, however, the proportion of workers who were laid off with no expectations of ever being recalled has been as high as nine-tenths — a 50 percent increase. This reflects the restructuring pursued by many industries for the purpose of downsizing their operations — that is, bringing about permanent reductions in labor costs. Some of the layoffs were achieved by retirement incentives and buyouts. Others were achieved by pink slips. I recently read of a woman who was informed of her termination by fax.

White-Collar Layoffs

A second difference in the early '90s recession was that a greater loss of white-collar jobs occurred than in past recessions. From the beginning of the recession in mid-1990 through 1991, white-collar employment was stagnant. White-collar workers joined the unemployed at about the same rate as blue-collar workers, which was most unusual. In 1992, white-collar employment increased by 850,000 workers, six times as much as the increase in blue-collar workers; but, concurrently, the unemployment levels for both groups

— and especially for white-collar workers — also rose. Joblessness among white-collar workers rose by 320,000, compared to 90,000 among blue-collar workers.

In sum, the last recession affected the labor market in two new and unanticipated ways. Though the unemployment rate did not rise as high as it has in past recessions, the proportion of permanent job losses was notably higher, as was the proportion of layoffs, both permanent and temporary, that affected white-collar workers.

The administration has argued forcefully that succeeding in a global economy means competing with lower-wage economies. This raises not only the issue of competing for jobs, but also the issue of competing for quality jobs and high-wage jobs. The administration reasons that the solution to both is to equip the American worker to produce high-value products. One way the federal government hopes to accomplish that is to apply U.S. technology to the workplace. A second way is to forge a closer tie between education and work.

But introducing technology is not without costs, as the following section illustrates.

A Modern Parable

In February 1993, Robert Jordan spoke to the Emerging Issues Forum at North Carolina State University on "What it Means to Compete for Business in a Global Economy." Jordan, together with his brother and son, is a partner in the Jordan family lumber company. He told the following story, a compelling story, of how the family company had risen from adversity, changed with the times, and emerged as a stronger, more productive enterprise. The story illustrates the dilemma that faces our nation's business leaders and policy makers.

In September of 1990, the Jordan lumber plant in Mt. Gilead, North Carolina, was destroyed by a devastating fire. The Jordans rebuilt the plant with more modern equipment. They also built another plant, a high-tech lumber plant, near Star, North Carolina. The Star plant had recently completed its first full year of operation.

Jordan stated that over the four years before the fire, the Jordan Lumber Company plant had increased annual productivity by 77 percent. Productivity per employee rose by 104 percent, from $109,000 in annual revenue per employee to $220,000 per employee. But, more, the new Star plant recorded productivity of $1.9 million per employee per year, 18 times as much as employee productivity four years earlier. The Star plant accomplished this with three costs to the company: the initial capital investment, time to retrain workers and involve them more actively in the decision-making process, and an across-the-board 10 percent salary bonus.

Over the same period, however, employment at the rebuilt, modernized plant in Mt. Gilead dropped from 165 to 135 workers, an 18 percent reduction; and it takes only 5 workers to run the entire new high-tech lumber plant in Star, North Carolina. Thus, the dilemma: How does the nation put more people to work in an economic environment in which companies can make themselves stronger with fewer workers?

Labor Secretary Reich on Jobs

Some months ago I attended a conference presentation by Labor Secretary Robert Reich. It isn't enough to get the economy back on track, Reich argued. The track, too, needs to be improved. The real issue is not just the number of jobs, but the quality of those jobs.

It's no great trick to get jobs, Reich reasoned. Just lower wages! You can always improve your competitiveness by getting poorer! For example, some think that the real issue is the balance of trade deficit,

> *". . . a gap has developed between the skill levels of high school graduates entering the labor force and the requirements for employment in the new knowledge-intensive occupations and industries."*

that we have more imports than exports and we simply need to balance the two. We can balance our imports and exports very quickly, Reich continued, by giving everybody in the United States a pay cut. That would make our products less expensive and, comparatively, others' products more expensive. The problem with that solution is that we get more competitive by becoming poorer. The goal must not be competitiveness for the sake of competitiveness, but competitiveness for the sake of a higher standard of living. The problem is to find a solution that not only generates more jobs, but also generates quality jobs, high-wage jobs.

Today, 75 percent of Americans are watching their real incomes and working conditions steadily decline, Reich argued. Three-fourths of Americans are worse off now, in inflation-adjusted terms, than they were in 1980. He cited detailed examples:

- If you did not complete four years of college, you are about 10 percent poorer.
- If you completed high school, you are 17 percent poorer.
- If you dropped out of high school, you are 24 percent poorer.
- Only if you completed college are you better off, on average.

What we are seeing is a gradual divergence in incomes, Reich concluded. Overall, people with college degrees are on an upward income escalator whereas people with less than college degrees are on a downward escalator.

The prevailing diagnosis of the nation's economic ills is that a gap has developed between the skill levels of high school graduates entering the labor force and the requirements for employment in the new knowledge-intensive occupations and industries. Wages for high school graduates and dropouts have fallen compared to wages for workers with additional training or education. That wage differential increased by 40 percent between the mid '70s and the late '80s. Unemployment rates followed the same pattern, with high school dropouts being especially disadvantaged in both wages and employment.

Lester Thurow, dean of the Sloan School of Industrial Management at MIT and a very knowledgeable person on issues of education, work, and the economy, has made the following comparison with Japan. Thurow argues that Japan doesn't have the best upper-half labor force in the world, but Japan does have the best lower-half labor force in the world. By comparison, Thurow argues, the U.S. has the best-trained college graduates in the world. U.S. college graduates take a back seat to no one. For example, U.S. college graduates won the 1994 international Math Olympiad. The problem in the U.S. is not with the top half but with the bottom half of the labor force, where high-school prepared workers try to transition into the labor force. The problem is especially acute for high school dropouts, who are functionally incapacitated in a high-skills society.

Noncollege-Bound Slighted

Most Americans, both youth and adults, agree that high schools aren't doing enough for students who are not headed for college. A 1994 Gallup Poll reports that most Americans say that public schools in their communities should put more emphasis on the needs of students who don't plan to attend college. Here are the findings:

- Three-fourths of young people feel high schools aren't doing enough for those not headed for college.
- Two-thirds of adults feel schools should do more to place dropouts and graduates in jobs.
- Nearly two-thirds of youth say their high schools aren't doing enough to help them choose careers.
- More than half of adults feel schools should do more to help students develop job-seeking skills.

By comparison, only half as many felt that their local schools aren't doing enough to prepare students for college.

As they looked back, the 30-year-old respondents in our Career Development Study echoed the same sentiments. Here is a sampling of some responses:

"I had not received proper counseling. I didn't even know I needed it." — mother of four

"I never felt the need in high school to seek out vocational counseling. . . . Looking back, I wish I knew what training was required for various jobs, and even more basic, what jobs were available." — medical secretary

"Because I was only a C student, I was overlooked in high school. I was not given remedial assistance or any type of college prep. I was not regarded as having any potential . . . there is nothing in the way of programs available to directly motivate or assist the average student. I really see a need in this area." — elementary school teacher

"I was just allowed to 'float along' without any direction, too immature to drift myself toward a goal." — school therapist

> *" If I had known the possible practical applications of the subjects taught in school, I would have been much more interested in those subjects." — radio and television repairman*

Whether or not their criticisms are justified, many young adults look back to the transition from school to work as a time when they were fumbling and had little direction. Some are angry — at high schools, teachers, counselors, and themselves. All would agree that society needs to do a better job of preparing today's young people for careers.

Americans may be changing the way they evaluate schools. They may be requiring more career preparation. The Gallup survey indicates that the public wants schools to pay more attention to helping students make the transition from school to work. Incidentally, the survey also indicates that people who need career guidance the most, the noncollege-bound, use career guidance the least.

The Clinton administration is pursuing school-to-work transition programs to remedy this problem. The programs take three different forms: a national apprenticeship system, a national service program, and an assortment of training and job development programs. Following are the major programs and, where possible, an update on the status of progress toward implementation.

National Apprenticeship System

Both the president and his longtime friend, Labor Secretary Robert Reich, express concerns for the challenges and problems young people face when entering the labor force. Secretary Reich repeatedly points to the decline in wages of high school graduates compared to college graduates, to the lack of work competencies taught in high school curricula, and to the marginal effectiveness of youth training programs. Reich argues that, 10 years ago, college graduates earned 30 percent more than high school graduates, but today the earnings gap has doubled to 60 percent. Thus, the focus of administration policies and programs is on the lower half of the labor market, on high school graduates and dropouts.

Reich, together with Secretary of Education Richard Riley, has sketched a blueprint that introduces major changes in the school-to-work transition that noncollege-bound young people will follow in the future. Essentially, their proposal, modeled largely after Japanese and West German programs, is an apprenticeship program that will combine classroom instruction with on-the-job training and eventually will lengthen the high school educational experience to five years.

One of the criticisms of our current educational system is that we lack linkages between education and work at the high school level. Company recruiters schedule visits to college campuses each spring, but they ignore high schools. The apprenticeship proposal goes beyond getting recruiters into high schools by creating a closer tie between what happens in the classroom and the workplace.

Skills Credential. Another feature of the proposed apprenticeship training program is a certificate of occupational competency for those who complete it successfully. At this writing, seven states have begun programs certifying the job skills and knowledge high school students bring to the workplace, according to a report from the National Center on Education and the Economy (NCEE). Certificates of Initial Mastery guarantee employers that students have learned specific subjects and have acquired certain necessary workplace skills. States are already expected to develop such standards and assessments with funding under the earlier Goals 2000 Reform Law.

The NCEE report documents how the state of Oregon, for example, has begun awarding Certificates of Initial Mastery to 16-year-olds and Certificates of Advanced Mastery to 18-year-olds. After achieving the first certificate, students may choose to learn skills in one of six occupational types identified by a Bush administration panel that recommended that education be reoriented around teaching job skills.

Another state opting for certifying job skills and knowledge is Indiana. Beginning in 1996, high school sophomores will have to pass a statewide achievement test in core subject knowledge. A passing score will earn them a Gateway Certificate. Once the Gateway Certificate is earned, students can go on to earn a high school diploma.

> *"One of the criticisms of our current educational system is that we lack linkages between education and work at the high school level."*

The NCEE report argues that new credentials — job skills and knowledge credentials — are needed because the traditional high school diploma has lapsed into mere certification of student enrollment and/or attendance, not a certification of skill or subject mastery. A school teacher's daughter in our Career Development Study agreed: "After seeing the reading abilities of many graduates, I feel high school diplomas mean little nowadays." The NCEE report argues that diplomas provide employers with no useful information about what young people can do. While the certification efforts in Oregon, Indiana, and other states have not replaced high school diplomas formally, the authors of the NCEE report suggest that diplomas will become irrelevant once employers and higher education institutions begin recognizing the certificates.

Personally, I doubt that the work certificates will ever replace diplomas. Education serves multiple purposes, and only one of the purposes is career preparation — as advocates of the humanities will surely remind society if proposals to replace diplomas with occupational competency certificates ever see the light of day. (More on the multiple purposes of education in Chapter 8.)

In addition to easing young people's transition from school to work, the apprenticeship program has the complementary goal of supplying U.S. industry with the technically trained personnel needed to produce the high-value, high-productivity, high-wage economy the administration envisions. This is a major undertaking during a period of tight budgets, and part of the strategy is to enlist companies that will benefit from trained workers to participate in funding apprenticeship programs. The notion is that with their own resources invested, companies will take an active role in defining the specific skills relevant to their operations and will welcome students who complete the apprenticeship programs to their workplaces.

Beyond improving job opportunities for the noncollege-bound and providing technically trained workers for high-productivity businesses, some see the apprenticeship program as a force that will generate a range of educational reforms at the elementary and secondary levels. The concept is large, but the budget is small — only $32 million in 1994 for pilot programs. The master plan is expansive, however, including a 16-fold budget increase to $500 million per year by 1997. That, of course, could change.

Changing 14,000 public high schools with 12th-grade enrollments of nearly 3 million students is no small undertaking. Someone once said that changing public 3 is like trying to move a national cemetery. The sheer magnitude of the task, to say nothing of the endless complexities, is not for the faint of heart.

National Service

The second component in the administration's plan for preparing the nation's youth for the world of work is the proposed National Service Corps. National service programs have been kicked around in Congress for many years and have been proposed in many forms, but one of the unique features of the current proposal is that it ties national service to financial assistance for college educations.

The National Service Corps was offered, in part, as an alternative to the existing federal student loan program and such widely publicized associated problems as mounting college costs, financial aid, and paying back student loans. The National Service Corps would provide tuition payments in exchange for low-wage public service.

The administration's initial proposal was to shut down the 30-year-old Federal Financial Aid Program that allocates grants, loans, and work-study funds for lower-income students. A National Service Trust Fund would be established that would give all students, regardless of income level, $10,000 a year to attend the college of their choice. After graduating, students could pay off the loans through payroll deductions after they were employed or work off the loans with two years of national service. The service might include work as assistants to teachers, police officers, daycare workers, hospital orderlies, elder-care workers, sensory-impaired workers, parks and recreation leaders, assistants at half-way houses and shelters, and the like.

The administration argued that the National Service Trust Fund could save $2.5 billion that the government currently absorbs in student loan defaults and another $1.5 billion in fees that commercial banks charge to handle student loans. But not everybody is a true believer. Skeptics argue that the federal government is already too far in the red and cannot afford to pay for educations for students who would later work off their grants in national service. Critics argue that it would take years to recoup the expense.

Whether the National Service Trust Fund will materialize will probably depend heavily on whether the administration and Congress can get their separate cost calculations to add up to an acceptable total, and whether tying financial aid to a national service initiative is a help or a hindrance. Whether national service is an idea whose time has come remains to be seen.

Like the apprenticeship proposal, the National Service Corps is a grand design with sweeping reform objectives. Also like the apprenticeship proposal, the National Service Corps proposal has been scaled back already in deference to budget reduction priorities. The program has begun, quite modestly, with a Summer of Service pilot program for 1,000 low-income youth. The next step is to extend the program to 25,000 college-aged youth in a year-round employment program in community support activities such as health care, environmental clean-up projects, public safety, and education. By 1997, the plan is to involve 100,000 participants at an annual budget of $3.4 billion. This, too, could change in the wake of elections.

As with the apprenticeship program, even the 1997 plans for the National Service Corps are modest compared to the lofty goals of reforming barriers to college access and financial aid. About 1.8 million 18-year-olds enroll in colleges and universities each year, which means that, even four years out, the national service program will involve less than 6 percent of the target population. The fact that the administration recently proposed reforms to the federal student loan program that include allowance for loan repayments based on levels of income rather than a fixed schedule suggests that the anticipated pace of change will be slow.

Training and Job Development Programs

The third component of young worker-training opportunities in the administration's labor program is a set of worker-training initiatives. The direction of the administration's labor program came into sharpest focus in the president's 1994 State of the Union Address and subsequent release of the White House proposed budget for '95. The president proposed school-to-work and career center initiatives, and he is clearly focusing both on the noncollege-bound. He stated:

> *" Most of the people we're counting on to build our economic future won't graduate from college, [and] it's time to stop ignoring them and start empowering them. Our school-to-work initiative will, for the first time, link school to the world of work, providing at least one year of apprenticeship beyond high school."*

At this writing, both the House and the Senate have passed versions of the president's school-to-work initiative, leaving House-Senate negotiators to work out a final bill.

One-Stop Career Centers

The administration is especially critical of the nation's fragmented career support services and lack of systematic support for workers making career changes in a period of economic upheaval. At the heart of the administration's proposal is transforming existing employment centers to one-stop career or skill centers. The one-stop centers would offer comprehensive services and program information for dislocated workers and, as the one-stop concept evolves, a wider assortment of services for students and others entering the labor force. The president's Workforce Security Act, currently before Congress, calls for the centers to offer comprehensive career, job training, and course information services. The concept includes providing eligibility information for local, state, and federal education and training programs and unemployment benefits as well as job search services.

The key word in the one-stop concept is "universal" — the system has to be universal, whether it is for a high school student trying to figure out which apprenticeship or school-to-work program to enter or for the dislocated autoworker deciding what to do next with his work career or for a mother returning to the work force. Education and training services would be provided on a referral basis through payments to a vocational or post-secondary school or other area service provider.

The one-stop concept is an effort to consolidate an array of programs operating under such labels as dislocated worker training programs, voc-ed programs, adult ed programs, and job training program. The president argues:

> *" We've got to streamline today's patchwork of training programs and make them a new source of new skills. . . . We've got to have a new system to move people into new and better jobs because most of those old jobs just won't come back."*

One of the president's major themes has been international economic competitiveness. He has repeatedly emphasized that education, training, and national jobs skills standards are the keys to expanding world trade and revitalizing the nation's economy.

The president also ties reforming the nation's welfare system to job training. He argues that job training will be crucial to whether welfare reform works. Indeed, the president redefined the meaning of "support," moving it away from financial assistance to job training:

> *" We will provide the support, the job training . . . but after that, anyone who can work, must. That's the only way we'll ever make welfare what it ought to be: a second chance, not a way of life. "*

The one-stop centers concept, like the National Apprenticeship System and the National Service program, will be phased in over time. Six states received initial "incentive grants" in 1994 to begin setting up career centers, and several waves of competition for implementation grants will follow throughout the decade. The dislocated worker services are scheduled to be in place by July of 1995. More comprehensive services, including education and training programs for youth, are scheduled to follow.

The federal initiatives have far-reaching implications for job training and vocational education programs as we have known them. The administration takes the position that employment instability is not a short-term, but rather a long-term problem, predicting continuing turmoil in the labor force over the years ahead. To quote one policy advisor: "Most of us can expect to hold as many as seven or eight jobs over our work lives, and to change careers once or twice to boot."

Federal Initiatives, Youth, and Careers

Society is changing. Both the population and the labor force are changing in ways that will open employment opportunities and close others. (This is the subject of Chapter 6.)

What the nation's collective response to helping youth choose and prepare for careers will eventually be, what specific programs will emerge, when they will truly become public policy, and how effectively they will be implemented remains to be seen. Thus far, the national temperament has wavered between looking for new solutions and ignoring old problems, between embracing political change and rejecting it, between business as usual and impatience. Adam allegedly said to Eve as they left the proverbial garden, "We are entering an age of great uncertainty!" That is as true today as it was back then.

One of the implications for the short term is that today, more than ever before, young people will need help choosing careers. The world around them is changing, but society does not yet have in place a new set of policies and programs to prepare young people for their futures. Some of the new initiatives are experimental and not yet debugged. Others are in their infancies, fragmented, underfunded, and not yet integrated with established school and labor force policies, programs, and practices. There is no new set of school-to-work or work force preparedness transition programs that are nationally available to parents and their daughters and sons.

The federal initiatives are not band-aid solutions; they are major overhauls of the system to fix the problem. The reforms, whatever their eventual form, will take years to implement. And, of course, they will be reshaped and reformed by the changing political winds and tides. But there are three distinguishing earmarks to the new programs for youth, and I expect that these program characteristics will remain intact:

> - They will focus on the noncollege-bound.
> - They will involve curriculum reform that incorporates workplace knowledge and skills.
> - They will incorporate hands-on work experience in an apprenticeship model.

How these initiatives are taking shape, and where you can get information about programs in your area, is covered in Parts 3 and 4 of this book, particularly in Chapter 11.

Parents:
The Critical Influence

Parents have a critical influence on their sons' and daughters' careers. That's the theme that ties this book together. This chapter examines how society selects, prepares, and places young people in the workforce — starting them out on careers — to do the work that needs to be done to keep the economy going. Parents are central to that process, and in this chapter I examine what their influence is and how it happens. I also illustrate how levels of education and training qualify young people for occupations, and how occupations determine income levels. This chapter also shows beliefs, values, and attitudes young people learn from parents that make a difference in positioning young people in the labor force.

Society is a system that "works." Society is a great big people-processing machine. During the processing, society sorts, prepares, and places young people in different careers, and determines where parents fit into that process.

THE SOCIAL SYSTEM

All societies face a similar problem. Every day of every year workers leave the labor force through choice, retirement, or death, and society must replace them. Some are truck drivers. Some are teachers. Others are nurses, bankers, governors, police officers, cosmetologists, doctors, or sales clerks. Positions open that have to be filled.

Concurrently, every day of every year babies are born. Some are girls and some are boys. Some are African Americans and some are Hispanics. Others are non-Hispanic Whites. The children are reared under vastly different circumstances, and they turn out differently. Eventually they seek employment in the labor force. The problem societies face is how to sort the supply of workers, how to prepare them, and where to place them in the open positions.

Individuals need jobs, and societies must fill their employment openings to maintain their economies. But who gets what jobs? By what rationale are people distributed in the labor force and jobs filled? Who makes the rules and what are the rules that determine the outcomes — the winners and the losers — of competition for the best jobs? How do societies prepare succeeding generations of workers to take the place of the old? These are questions every society faces.

Achievement in the U.S.

In a rigid caste system, such as occurred among the Hindus in India, babies were born into a caste, a strictly enforced social and occupational level. The caste lines were exclusive and restrictive. People weren't allowed to cross them. They couldn't improve their social status but, at the same time, they couldn't lose it either. People were unequal from the day they were born, and they stayed that way for life.

But in our society, "All people are created equal." Or are they? What about women? What about African Americans? What about the physically, mentally, or emotionally challenged?

The notion that our society is made up of equals who all have the same opportunities in life is more of a gradeschooler's view than a mature understanding of the way society works. Equality is an ideal, a very noble ideal, but it's not reality. We do not live in a caste system that rigidly divides society into separate groups; nonetheless, inequalities exist between groups.

Inequalities are of three kinds. First, people differ in terms of their natural endowments — strength, attitudes, dispositions, and intelligence. People are not equipped in the same way. Second, people differ in terms of their opportunities — education, travel, and exposure to fine arts. Everyone does not have access to the same resources. Third, the playing field is smooth and flat for some but bumpy and uphill for others. Some people find themselves in unequal circumstances beginning at birth, and it often lasts a lifetime.

The inequalities also continue from one generation to the next with remarkable regularity. When speaking of the poor, some writers refer to this as the "vicious cycle of poverty." The notion is that the conditions in which people live repeat from one generation to the next. Sociologists have a term for it. They call it *social stratification*. Like layers of rock in a canyon wall, the strata start at one end and, with a few irregularities here and there, the strata continue to the other end of the canyon wall for as far as the eye can see. This is analogous to what happens in society with families over time. Social stratification refers to the fact that sons and daughters regularly end up at about the same social status as their parents. Here's how that happens.

Social Status

People are unequal beginning at birth. They have different heights, weights, gender, race, muscle power, and brain power. And they grow up in different circumstances. Some have many advantages. Some have few. Some are disadvantaged in every way from day one.

One kind of inequality that is particularly important for understanding how careers develop is family socioeconomic status. Socioeconomic status refers to a combination of three things that are closely related in our society: education or training level, occupation level, and income level. Put those three levels of statuses together, and you have a person's socioeconomic status. Sometimes people call it "social class." To keep it simple, I refer to the combination as *social status*.

Occupation Level

Notice that I've referred to occupation, education/training, and income levels. People usually know that levels of education or training mean how many years of schooling or what level of degrees or certificates a person earns. And level of income is easily understood — it means how many dollars. But sometimes level of occupation isn't understood as readily.

Occupation level is shorthand for level of occupational prestige. When people evaluate occupations, they give more prestige to some occupations than to others. For example, doctor and attorney are viewed as high-prestige occupations. Airplane pilot isn't quite so high. Newspaper journalist and law officer are lower yet. And sanitation worker is lower still in terms of prestige. I hasten to add that different levels of occupational prestige do not mean that some occupations are better than others — just like a lot of money isn't necessarily better than a little.

How much prestige an occupation has determines the social status of the person in the occupation. For example, President Reagan had much more social status when he was president than after he left office. Johnny Carson had much more social status when he was host of the "Tonight Show" than after he left the job. Janet Reno has much more social status now as attorney general than before she took the job. In their minds, people assign different levels of prestige to occupations; and people are accorded the prestige of the occupations they have. Occupational prestige is the way people measure social status.

Occupational Prestige Scale

People talk about social status, but social scientists have figured out very refined ways to measure occupational prestige — much the same way that economists use dollars to measure income and educators use degrees and certificates to measure education. Social scientists have developed scales that measure how the public ranks occupations. Some of the most commonly used scales rank occupations from one to 100, much like a thermometer. High-prestige occupations have high numbers, and low-prestige occupations have low numbers. Every occupation can have a prestige score and, therefore, the scales are very long. Following are examples of prestige scores from one widely used scale, called the Socioeconomic Index:

Occupation	Prestige Score
Dentist	96
Airplane pilot	79
Clergy	52
Electrician	44
Piano and organ tuner	38
Gasoline service station attendant	33
Plasterer	25
Shoe repairer	12
Babysitter	7

Since social status is based on occupational prestige, occupational prestige scales provide a convenient way to figure out a person's social status. People rank each other, even when they don't know the other person, by occupation. Some occupations, like doctor and lawyer, have high status. Others have lower status. Unskilled laborer is an example. How society treats a person — that is, what status it accords that person — depends largely on the person's occupation.

How Statuses Fit Together

If you were to ask me what single piece of information I would want to know about a person that would tell me more about that person than anything else, I would say: Tell me that person's occupation. If I knew only the person's occupation and nothing more, I would have a pretty good idea of a lot of other things about that person.

Suppose, for example, that you told me that a person is a dentist. I would assume that the person is well-educated and probably is well-off financially. And, knowing that the person is well-educated, has a high-status occupation, and enjoys a good income, I could then reasonably conclude a number of other things: That the person probably drives a nice car and not a beat-up pickup truck; lives in the suburbs rather than the slums; spends more time on tennis courts than in pool halls; enjoys more fine wines than cold beers; wears more designer jeans than farmer-style overalls; is more likely to be seen at the symphony than the race track; and a lot more. Get the picture? If you know a person's occupation, you can usually figure out a lot about that person — within reason, of course.

Notice, however, that though you may have told me only the person's occupation, I immediately took a couple of other things into account. I assumed, for example, that the dentist is well-educated, because I know that you have to go to school a long time to be a dentist. I also assumed that the dentist has a good income, because I know that people who go to school a long time and become dentists get good paying jobs.

Were those reasonable assumptions for me to make? Of course they were, because we realize that levels of education/training, occupation, and income fit together. To be a dentist, you first have to have the education and training, then you can get the job, and then the income follows. Education/training, occupation, and income are related.

The same is true of other occupations. Suppose you were to tell me that a person is a server at a fast food restaurant. I would conclude that the person is probably a high school graduate, or maybe still in school (education/training level), and that she or he earns modest wages (income). And assuming these are true, I might conclude that the person is not yet financially independent, might still live at home, may not own an automobile, and instead of belonging to a country club probably spends leisure hours playing softball with the gang.

Education/training, occupation, and income levels fit together (see Figure 3-1). This is an important principle for career planners, whether parent or young person, to recognize, because it provides a framework for making career plans.

To review: There are levels of education/training, occupations, and income; and the levels fit together. High levels of education/training prepare people for high-level occupations, and high-level occupations produce high-level incomes. Medium levels of education/training prepare people for medium-level occupations, and medium-level occupations

The Fit between Education, Occupation, and Income Levels

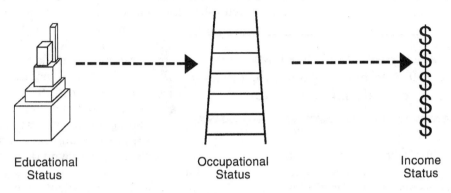

| Educational | Occupational | Income |
| Status | Status | Status |

Figure 3-1

produce medium-level incomes. And low levels of education/training prepare people for low-level occupations, and the low-level occupations produce low incomes. An electrical technician's son, a junior in high school, had it figured out. He told us: "If I have no college education, I think I'll probably flip burgers the rest of my life."

That is the way society works — with occasional exceptions, to be sure. But the way the system works suggests three rules for career planners:

> **Rule # 1:** Level of education/training prepares a person for a level of occupation that produces a level of income, and these three fit together.
>
> **Rule # 2:** Choosing a career involves making decisions about both an occupational career and a career preparation strategy — education/training.
>
> **Rule # 3:** Level of education/training is the key to level of occupation and income.

To get a well-paying job, a person needs a good job. And to get a good job, a person needs a good education or training.

Education and Training

As mentioned earlier, society is a system, and the system works. One of the ways society works is by sorting young people, preparing them for occupations, and placing them in the labor market. It does this through schools and training institutions.

We live in a credentialing society. That means that employers use degrees and certificates to sort out prospective workers. Education and training institutions brand people when they award them degrees and certificates. Institutions stamp them like the butcher stamps meat in the supermarket — pardon the analogy — with labels like "sandwich meat" or "sausage," and with stickers that say "choice" or "prime." To press the analogy, employers are like supermarket customers who shop for a particular kind and quality of product. Not every customer wants hot dogs. Others cannot afford the top-grade steak. So, also, not every employer needs technical-school graduates, and few need the top-of-the-line products supplied by university graduate schools. Thus, schools and institutions "grade" their products (students) with degrees and certificates so the customers (employers) can buy (hire) what they need.

> *To get a well-paying job, a person needs a good job. And to get a good job, a person needs a good education or training.*

Schools and training institutions are society's biggest and most efficient job brokers. They are in the business of preparing workers and sorting them out for the labor market. The degrees and certificates they award become the shorthand labels that employers use to match people with jobs.

Income

So it is that society converts levels of education and training into levels of occupational prestige, but where does income fit into the picture? Clearly, levels of income are tied to levels of occupational prestige. High-prestige occupations, like the professions, pay the most wages, whereas low-prestige occupations, like unskilled laborer, pay the least.

What emerges, then, is a snapshot of the way society works. Levels of education and training determine the levels of occupational prestige for which people qualify, and their levels of occupational prestige largely determine their incomes. People with higher levels of education and training qualify for the better jobs, which also pay better. Or, to think of the process in reverse: How do you get a better paying job? You get a higher income by getting a better job, that is, a more prestigious job. And how do you get a better job? By getting the necessary credentials — that is, the degrees and certificates that come with additional education and training. Indeed, many of the best jobs require that the person be licensed or certified or pass an exam like the bar exam; and, for all practical purposes, the only way a person can do that is through formal education or training.

How the Social System Works

Interestingly, if you compare parents' social status with that of their children, a definite pattern emerges. Children usually end up in occupations that are at about the same level of occupational prestige as their parents. And because childrens' occupational-prestige levels are similar to their parents', parents and their children have comparable social status.

That doesn't mean that children necessarily do the same kind of work as their parents, though they might. Singer Naomi Judd is following her mother's singing career. Michael Andretti is following his father's racing career. Terry Bowden and Dave Shulla are following their father's coaching careers. And George Bush, Jr., Edmund "Jerry" Brown, Jr.,

Richard Daley, Jr., Barry Goldwater, Jr., and Albert Gore, Jr., are but a few examples of sons who are chips off the old political blocks. Following father's footsteps happens, but most often children enter lines of work that are at about the same level of prestige as the work their parents do, not necessarily the exact same occupation.

It isn't that children can't break out of the pattern, but they don't. If children want to change the pattern dramatically — say they come from a family of migrant workers (low occupational prestige) and want to become a Supreme Court justice (high occupational prestige) — they find that to be an extremely difficult change. And it is quite unlikely that, say, a Kennedy or a Rockefeller will aspire to be a common laborer. They are much more likely to stay in public service. The pattern is for levels of family social status to remain remarkably similar from one generation to the next, as Figure 3-2 shows.

Parents' and Children's Socioeconomic Status

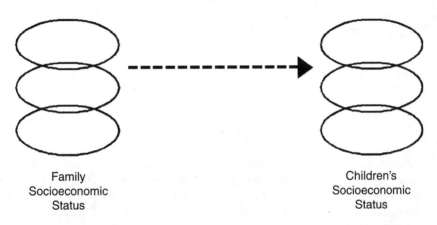

| Family Socioeconomic Status | Children's Socioeconomic Status |

Figure 3-2

But why does the doctor's daughter become a college professor or a lawyer and not a restaurant cook? Why does the truck driver's son become a mechanic but not a pharmacist? It doesn't happen by accident.

There are connections between parents' and children's occupational prestige and, therefore, their social statuses (see Figure 3-3). The most important connection is the education and training that parents provide for their children. By education I mean formal programs of instruction that emphasize the development of knowledge and critical thinking. By training I mean programs of instruction that emphasize skills and vocational preparation. Levels of education are usually identified by degrees. Completion of training programs is usually documented by certificates. Education and training are the main connection to who gets into what occupations.

Levels of family social status remain relatively the same from one generation to the next because parents encourage their children to get about the same or higher levels of education and training as they have. Which parents encourage their children to enroll in professional schools? Typically, it's the professional people. And who can best afford it? Typically, it's the professional people. Parents with less education may also want good educations for their children, but they are less able to afford it. So it is that education and training produce the pattern of comparable levels of social status for parents and children.

Education and Training Connects Family Statuses Across Generations

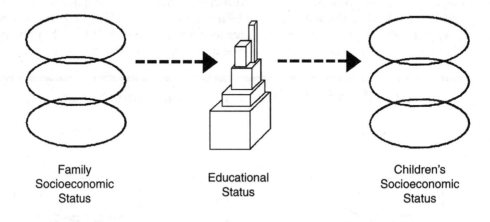

| Family Socioeconomic Status | Educational Status | Children's Socioeconomic Status |

Figure 3-3

This is an important bit of information because it holds the key to how parents can improve the career opportunities of their children, if they are so inclined. The most assured way parents can improve their children's career prospects is to help them gain the necessary credentials that qualify them for higher-prestige occupations. Education and training provide those credentials. That's the way the social system works.

Influence Processes

Parents are central to the career influence process. Young people are like rocks in a rock polisher. Parents are in there with them, grinding away over time. And parents will agree that the younger generation does plenty of grinding back. Parents are the big rocks in the tumbler. They have the big influence.

But parents aren't the only ones involved. There are other rocks in the polisher — some rough, some smooth, some large, and some small. The other rocks are brothers and sisters, friends, neighbors, relatives, and teachers.

The tumbler keeps on turning, year after year. Maybe it doesn't turn very fast. And maybe it doesn't make much noise. But it keeps on grinding, and the job gets done. Young people's attitudes and behaviors are shaped by the people around them. Take the rocks out of the rock polisher and the polishing stops.

What happens in real life as people bump and grind against each other? Three different processes go on. Let's look closely at how parents influence their children.

Rewards and Punishments

When children are very young, parents use rewards and punishments to mold their behavior. Parents reward children for what they do right and punish them for what they do wrong. Many of the rewards and punishments are subtle.

Consider the potty-training stage. After months of changing diapers, Dad and Mom will do anything to get the little heavenly blessing to do the right thing at the right place at the right time. What usually works best is some kind of reward, perhaps M&Ms. In the early years, parents modify children's behavior in much the same way that people train animals.

My wife and I took our three boys to the state fair when they were young, and one of the first things we saw were "smart" chickens. There the first chicken stood, totally bored, in a glass cage. But when I dropped a quarter into the slot, a bell rang, and the chicken perked up and did a lively one-legged dance. After hopping a certain number of times — it probably cost me a penny per hop! — the chicken quit and three or four kernels of corn dropped automatically into its feeder. The dancing chicken was rewarded. The chicken in the next cage had a different specialty, rolling over like a trained dog. The next one "sang." And the last one played tic-tac-toe.

How did these scrubby country chickens make the big-time entertainment world? Simple. A trainer rewarded them when they did the right thing. It's the old M&M trick. After a while a machine gave the rewards. The trainer didn't even have to be there.

Rewards and punishments work with people, too — especially with children. But even adults reward and punish one another. They're just a little more subtle about it. Say things another person likes and they reward with a smile. Say things they don't like and they punish with a frown.

Parents influence their children's ideas about careers at an early age in ways as simple as nods of approval and hints of disapproval. When a six-year-old daughter proudly tells Grandma, "When I get big I'm going to race motorcycles," what does Grandma say? Maybe, "Grandpa would like that!"? Or does Grandma say, "But you'll get grasshoppers stuck in your teeth!"? The first reaction rewards. The second punishes. Parents use rewards and punishments, subtle ones as well as the heavy-duty variety, especially when children are young.

Teaching and Reasoning

As youngsters grow older, parents try to reason with them. Instead of denying them a treat when they don't make their beds (punishment), parents talk to them. Parents try to reason. If the adolescent still wants to race motorcycles for a living, parents ask whether she has ever thought of making films about motorcycle racers. Parents encourage children to think about things that teach their children what, in their judgment, is a good job and what is a bad job.

Parents know most about the kind of work they do themselves, and unconsciously they teach their children most about their own line of work and the lifestyle that goes with it. When my youngest son asked, "Dad, what's in your briefcase?" I could show him. But I couldn't show him what a helicopter pilot carries in his. I could show him my office, the computer, the telephone, the file cabinets, and the books; but I couldn't show him what's inside a shrimp boat. And I really don't know very much about lobster fishing off the Maine coast, either. Children learn most about the work their parents do and about similar kinds of occupations because it comes up in their daily conversations, and youngsters see their parents in particular occupational roles. That's why children often follow the same line of work or work closely related to what their parents do. They know and understand that line of work better than other possibilities.

As children mature, parents increasingly use more words and fewer actions. They give compliments instead of M&Ms. They offer criticism instead of sending children off to bed as punishment. They make suggestions. But both methods get across the message of what parents expect, their ideas about what is good and what is bad, their attitudes and their values. As children mature, parents do more by teaching and reasoning.

Example

Parents also influence by example, and this is the subtlest influence of all. Children copy adults, especially mothers and fathers. Watch children sit in chairs. Often they will cross their legs in the same manner as a parent or stand with the same characteristic posture. Sometimes their imitations are harmless and amusing — little girls in mother's high heels strutting with all the poise of a Kentucky mule. And sometimes the imitations are tragic. More than one little boy has fingered the trigger of a loaded gun or pulled an automatic transmission into gear "just like Dad."

Most learning by example is less spectacular. It involves picking up parents' gestures, using parents' language, observing parental pastimes, and acting like Mom or Dad. Children's work play typically imitates their parents' work. Most parents see a part of themselves in their children, in the way they walk or the way they talk. Sometimes its flattering. Sometimes embarrassing.

I learned the power of parental example when our youngest son, Stephen, was eight years old. Airlines were offering incentives to attract passengers, and we took advantage of a "kids fly free" promotion to take Stephen to New York so he could see what his dad does at work.

Both of us eagerly anticipated the big trip — until the night before the early morning departure. As Stephen headed to bed I casually asked whether he was ready to go to New York, and to my surprise I was answered by a flood of tears and a little boy's sob: "But Dad, I don't have a sport coat or a necktie or a briefcase." I thought I had all the ducks lined up: the airline tickets, hotel reservations, preparation for the meeting, a stroll down Park Avenue, and, of course, the trip to the Empire State Building. Yet I had overlooked the most important things of all: a sport coat, a necktie, and a briefcase for my son.

The story has a happy ending, because his mother was innovative. An older brother's oversized sport coat was retrieved from mothballs. One of Dad's old ties was unceremoniously cut off and shortened. And an old, dusty, square lunch pail appeared from some closet that, with white-lie assurances, miraculously changed into a briefcase — at least in Stephen's mind. Suddenly, we were ready to go. And we had a great trip. Sport coat, tie, and briefcase stayed intact — though my own stayed in the hotel most of the time. That real-life incident is my favorite illustration of how children learn from their parents — what they should wear, how they should dress, and whether or not they need a briefcase. I never sat down and taught this to Stephen. He picked it up by example.

Like rocks in a rock polisher, young people brush and bump against others who smooth their rough edges and polish their surfaces. Young people aren't exactly marshmallows in the whole process. Dads and moms take their own share of bumps and bruises along the way. They're in the mix together with sons and daughters. Consciously or not, parents mold and shape their children from early on. Young people are the result of a lot of tumbles others take with them.

Parents are basic to the influence process. They influence by using rewards and punishments, teaching and reasoning, and by examples. And that influence is critical in shaping their sons' and daughters' career plans.

A carpenter's daughter who graduated from high school, married a truck driver for a logging company, and worked herself up from being a receptionist in a beauty shop to a bank teller in a small town put it this way:

> *" I feel that what I learned from my family and on my own helped me as much as anything I got from high school classes. In fact, it helped me much more."*

BELIEFS, VALUES, AND ATTITUDES MAKE A DIFFERENCE

In the previous section, I explained how the social system works, how education and training prepares people for jobs that, in turn, generate income; and how, through education and training, families perpetuate their social status from one generation to the next. In this section, I examine career development from a different angle by sharpening the focus and zeroing in on what goes on inside young people's heads. This section reviews beliefs, values, and attitudes that young people learn — much of it from their parents — that help or hinder young people's careers.

What's Taught and What's Caught

There are patterns in the levels of family social status from one generation to the next. That happens because parents rear their children to be like they are. Education and training are the main connection between the generations, and other linkages reinforce the patterns. These involve how parents "bring up" their children. A librarian in our Career Development Study told us, "My parents and family have more to do with my ability to deal with the world than school did." Not all child rearing is done consciously. Perhaps more is caught than taught.

Supermarket magazine racks, church pulpits, and PTA programs all voice concern about the influence parents have on their children. There are different opinions about how parents should parent, but on one point there is widespread agreement: How parents raise their children makes a difference in how the children turn out. This section examines where parents get the career values they teach their children.

Occupations Affect Values

Occupations differ in important ways, and some of the major differences depend on whether the occupation is high or low prestige. One of the main differences between high- and low-prestige occupations is how much a person works with people as opposed to things. Another is whether the occupation requires self-direction or conformity. Yet another is whether the occupation requires individual effort or group effort.

Consider the examples in the following sections. Actually, most parents and families are somewhere in between high and low status, so the picture I paint appears in broad-brushed strokes, not fine detail. Figuring out what influences young people is a sticky problem, and I oversimplify in order to focus on important differences in child-rearing practices and how those differences influence a young person's career development.

> *A high-prestige occupation generally requires self-direction and the ability to work with people.*
>
> *A low-prestige occupation generally requires the ability to conform and to work with things.*

The distinction between higher- and lower-status families is a useful way to think about differences in child-rearing strategies. The labels take into account that the values behind child-rearing practices come from parents' work experiences. Work circumstances differ by occupations, and they affect parents' values — what parents feel is important and what they teach their children.

People vs. Things

High-prestige occupations usually involve dealing with people and ideas, whereas low-prestige occupations more often involve dealing with things.

Here's an example. Insurance sales is a higher-than-average-prestige occupation, and people who sell insurance work with ideas like "security," "insurability," "estate planning," and "return on investment." A lower-prestige occupation, by comparison, may involve putting in sidewalks. The worker works with grass and gravel, concrete, hammers, and shovels. Whereas higher-prestige occupations typically involve working with people and abstract concepts, lower-prestige occupations more often involve working with things.

Self-Direction vs. Conformity

Occupations also differ in the amount of self-direction they allow and expect of the worker. Insurance sales people choose their clients and have flexibility about when and how to speak with them. No one is looking constantly over the salesperson's shoulder. It's not a routine job because every client represents a different challenge. The agent figures out ways to get the sales job done, and, to the extent that happens, the salesperson is a good employee.

Lower-prestige occupations usually present a different situation. A boss tells the worker what to do, how to do it, and when to do it. It's routine work. It doesn't take much planning and figuring. And the worker who follows orders is the good employee.

An African-American mother, a registered nurse who wanted her daughter to become a nurse, librarian, or teacher, understood the effects of being taught self-direction vs. conformity. She put it bluntly: "I feel the needs of a child should be met regardless of race or culture. . . . A student should be encouraged to achieve rather than accept."

Individual vs. Group

Higher-prestige occupations usually require much individual effort whereas lower-prestige occupations tend to require that people work together closely. The insurance salesperson figures out a strategy, calls on clients, writes up policy proposals, and reports back to the general agent. The salesperson has little supervision. The construction worker, by comparison, is often part of a crew. The crew travels to work together, puts up scaffolding together, and eats lunch under the same shade tree.

Different work conditions illustrate why higher-prestige occupations require higher levels of education. Education equips people to deal with abstract ideas and complex issues, to work smoothly with others, and to work independently. That's important in the higher-prestige occupations. But in lower-prestige occupations, level of education may have little to do with the job. What may be required is a strong back and a person who will do what he or she is told to do.

Values

Different jobs require different worker values. People in high-prestige occupations learn to value their freedom and pursue opportunities as they see them. By comparison, workers in low-prestige occupations learn to value conforming to the wishes or demands of authorities. After all, isn't the insurance salesperson rewarded for figuring things out and working independently? And isn't the laborer rewarded for doing what he or she is told to do?

Self-direction and conformity are values that are learned in two different workplaces. Both are practical strategies, and they work for the worker. These values become an important part of the work values parents teach their children. Parents in higher-prestige occupations tend to emphasize the importance of self-direction. Parents in lower-prestige occupations tend to stress conformity.

To be sure, life is more complicated than that, and what parents value is a much more complex matter. Parents' values also come from how they were reared when they were children and from their own ideas about young people. But a considerable influence on parent values goes back to the parents' work circumstances. What works in the workplace is different in higher- and lower-prestige occupations.

As children learn their parents' values, they adopt values that fit best with the same kinds of occupations their parents have. Thus, children who learn self-direction at home are better suited for jobs that require freedom and independence, and children who learn conformity are being taught to take orders in the workplace, and they are learning attitudes and behaviors appropriate to lower-prestige jobs.

Life Chances

Higher-status families offer advantages to their children when it comes to career planning and career preparation. They have the resources to provide opportunities for their young people to pursue their ambitions. Thus, approximately half of young people who go to college come from families whose parents earn $35,000 or more per year. In addition, higher-status families are often in a position to provide the psychological support that enables young people to take reasonable risks in starting their careers. Their daughters and sons can afford to start over if they fail.

The lower-status family situation is more tenuous. The resources aren't there to provide economic stability and an emotional safety net. Young people in lower-status families usually can't afford to take career risks. Overdue bills have to be paid. Lower-status families have to be concerned with the here and now. Thinking about the future is a luxury. Young people in lower-status families don't have the same opportunities and life chances as do their age-mates from higher-status families. A registered nurse in our Youth and Careers Study, whose husband is a prison guard, thinks her son would like to be a small business owner, but she was concerned

> *" That he stumbles around and he'll become frustrated and get discouraged, end up with bad choices and it will be very difficult to climb out of the problems and get back on a productive path. We don't have much money to support him as he struggles, and the alternatives he has and may have to choose aren't much, due to not having the opportunity to have a second chance like middle-class white kids do!"*

Parents tend to relate to their children in much the same way that they themselves are treated at work. Workers who deal with people have to be concerned about communication skills and interpersonal relations. Workers who are more accustomed to doing what they are told tend to be more coercive with their children. In both cases, parents teach their children what works for them in the work place, and their children learn to behave in ways appropriate to the same occupational levels their parents have.

Child-Rearing Practices

Differences exist, also, in how parents relate to their children and discipline them. Higher-status parents are more likely than lower-status parents to treat their children as equals. They try to nurture warm and supportive relations with their children. They are interested in why their children behave as they do. They are concerned about how other people interpret their children's behavior, and they try to pass on those sensitivities to their sons and daughters.

Lower-status parents tend to be more concerned with their children's external behavior, with conformity, and they pay less attention to "why" children behave as they do. Lower-status parents are more dominating, more assertive, more demanding of obedience, and less permissive. Sensitivity for interpersonal feelings is not a job requirement in the typical lower-prestige occupation, and parents in those occupations are less likely to pick up interpersonal sensitivities and teach them to their children.

Higher-status parents are usually more verbal. They do more explaining and teaching. Mothers tend to give more exact instructions when dealing with their children. They point out to the child how the child's behavior differs from the directions given. By comparison, lower-status mothers use fewer words, communicate more by gesturing, and give fewer explanations. When they punish, lower-status parents do less by way of explaining why they punish.

How parents relate to their children has consequences for how children develop. Children who learn interpersonal sensitivities are developing skills for working with people, which prepares them to ease into higher-prestige occupations later. Children who learn to do what they are told are molded to fit lower-prestige occupations later.

How People Think the World Works

Is life fair? Is life a game of chance? Or would you say that life is a little of one and a lot of the other?

Some people think that if they plan, use their heads, and work hard, they can pretty much get what they want. Others feel that events are mainly a matter of luck. Studies show that people with higher status are more likely to believe that life is fair and that "they get what they've got coming." People with lower status tend to believe that what happens in life is more "a toss of the dice" — in other words, luck.

The same attitudes and behaviors appear when it comes to planning a career. Higher-status parents and young people do more career planning and more preparing for careers than do lower-status parents and young people. The latter are more likely to believe that life is a matter of chance, so why worry about it? Parents pass their real-life work experiences to their children, and these become a part of what young people believe about themselves and the world around them, whether they think they can take charge of events or believe that circumstances control them.

Self-Concept

Perhaps the most important lesson children learn early in life is what to think about themselves. Some learn to think of themselves as people in control. Others learn to think of themselves more as bystanders or spectators in a chance game of life.

Whether children learn to think of themselves as actors or pawns depends on many of the same parenting practices and family circumstances I described earlier. Parents who hold high expectations for their children, who communicate their expectations clearly, who explain when a young person deviates from those expectations, and who are supportive are encouraging young people to evaluate themselves against set standards. These young people can see what progress they are making. By comparison, parents who are more coercive, who do less explaining, and who are more insistent on obedience and conformity convey a sense of powerlessness and unpredictability to their children.

Young people gain a sense of their "place" in society from interactions with other people. They learn what to think about themselves, their self-concepts, from others. Others teach them. If parents are supportive and nurturant, young people get the impression that others like them. They develop healthy self-concepts and gain self-confidence. These characteristics are less likely to develop under dominating family regimes. What young people think of themselves is important. Their self-concepts and self-confidence are major predictors of their long-term career outcomes.

Expectations

From early on children respond to the expectations others have for them, and they compare themselves and their performance with others. That doesn't mean that others' expectations are necessarily appropriate or even in the child's best interests. They may not be.

Some of the earliest and potentially most damaging inappropriate expectations and faulty comparisons may take place in schools where children are sorted into fast learners, so-so learners, and slow learners. If class files and school records are uncritically passed from one teacher to the next, without teachers making independent and current student evaluations, then teachers' expectations may be passed on, too, from one year to the next. Children change over time and the earlier expectations may be wrong. Expectations, both accurate and faulty expectations, make a difference in how children respond.

Researchers have done experiments in which teachers were given false past grade reports for students. When the bogus grades suggested that a child was a good student, the teacher had higher expectations and the student's classroom performance increased. When the teacher was given false information that the child was a poor student, the teacher had lower expectations and the child's performance dropped off.

High expectations prompt young people to believe that "they can do it," but low expectations dampen their beliefs in themselves and in their own abilities. More is expected of some youngsters than of others, and what is expected of young people often differs by family social status. Others' expectations, not just young people's ability and interest levels, make a difference in their achievements.

Career Expectations

When it comes to planning and preparing for careers, what a young person wants is important; but what young people want reflects the expectations parents and other people have for them. Which young people want to go to college? Most often it's young people from higher-status families. Higher-status families have more resources, fewer children to compete for the resources, offer more parental support, and hold values and expectations that favor education. Their children have an advantage over age-mates from families with fewer resources.

Young people are not just rocks in a rock polisher. They're not just pawns. They also think for themselves. They assess their own ability and their past performances. They measure themselves against their peers. They think about themselves. They draw their own conclusions. These conclusions are formed and shaped by people who are important in their lives — "significant others," social scientists call such important people.

Young people are influenced over the long term by as few as four or five other people who are especially important to them, and as few as two or three others may be particularly influential over their early years when it comes to career plans. Parents figure prominently among those most-influential others. And the way parents influence their daughters' and sons' career outcomes the most is by the level of education and training they expect, encourage, and provide.

What is the single most important way parents can contribute to their daughters' and sons' long-term careers? By providing them with good education and training — because the better their education and training, the better their employment prospects; and the better their jobs, the better their income. That's the way the social system works.

Inequities in the Workplace

Does the social system treat everyone the same, or does the system work better for some than for others? The answers are "no," the social system does not give everyone the same chances, and "yes," the system works better for some than for others. The system treats some groups differently than others, which brings about a fundamental problem in a society that believes that everybody should be treated equally. It's what the civil rights era was all about. It's what much of the women's movement is about.

The social system "works," but it doesn't always work the way it is supposed to. How it *should* work is deeply ingrained in our values and social consciousness:

- People *should* have equal access to education and training.
- People at the same levels of education and training *should* have equal access to occupations.
- People in the same occupations *should* be paid the same.

But the social system doesn't work that way for women, and it doesn't work that way for racial minorities, either.

What's wrong with the system? Where does it break down? The system breaks down at each juncture in the career development process: education, occupation, and income. Society discriminates, first, by denying equal access to education. Consider the civil rights era, Eisenhower and the national guard, George Wallace and the confrontation on the steps of the University of Alabama. The issue, which played itself out in less dramatic scenarios all over the country, was whether African Americans were entitled to equality in college admissions. Until the last decade, when, for the first time, the number of young women exceeded the number of young men on college campuses, society discriminated against women, too — just less visibly. Then, when African Americans and women were admitted, colleges didn't process them as efficiently, with the result that African Americans and women didn't achieve the same levels of education as non-Hispanic White men.

The problem goes beyond discrimination in education. After women and African Americans increased their enrollments and their levels of education, they ran into road-blocks in the labor force. Employers haven't allowed women and African Americans to convert their education and training into the same levels of occupations that are available to White men. Women and African Americans get fewer jobs, and they get poorer jobs. That's why there are equality of opportunity mandates and affirmative action programs.

But, prejudice and discrimination run deeper still. Once women and African Americans get jobs, they get paid less. That's what the "69 cent pay dollar" is all about for women, and the pay dollar is discounted even more for African-American men. Discrimination means that the social system doesn't allow certain groups the full benefit of the way education, occupations, and income are supposed to fit together in our society (see Figure 4-1). Discrimination blocks women, African Americans, and other racial minorities at critical points in their career development. It doesn't necessarily bar them completely, but it slows them down and holds them back.

The Effect of Discrimination in Society

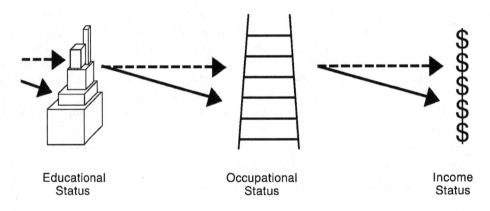

| Educational | Occupational | Income |
| Status | Status | Status |

Figure 4-1

Discrimination is supported by an array of beliefs, values, and attitudes — prejudices — that reinforce the inequities. These are widely shared and may be held by families, friends, teachers, clergy, politicians — the whole society. The cumulative effect is that prejudice and discrimination stop women and racial minorities from achieving what they deserve. It is like paying compound interest on an accumulating debt without being given a chance to pay off the principal. A person pays a little now, a little then, a little here, a little there, but the indebtedness never goes away. Rather, it keeps adding up. A person in that circumstance can never get out from under it, can never break even.

In the following sections I examine the special cases of women's and African Americans' career development in more detail. I present the case for women in narrative style, explaining what happens and why. Then I shift to using numbers to explain the case of African Americans. Here my goal is to show how little differences in career development add up to big differences over a lifetime. I change the style of presenting as a way of explaining the causes and consequences of discrimination more vividly.

WOMEN AND WORK

By the time they start school, two-thirds of little girls have, historically, narrowed their preferences to three occupations: Teacher, nurse, or secretary. And their early aspirations are remarkably similar to the occupations women eventually take. Women take employment in fewer occupations than men, and they tend to end up in the lower-level, poorer-paying jobs — the female ghetto.

Why this happens is a controversial and emotionally charged topic that cannot be resolved here. The main arguments include biological, social structural, and social learning explanations:

> ■ Biological arguments reason that there are gender differences in personality that are fixed at conception, and that sex differences in occupational preferences are an expression of those innate biological determinants.
>
> ■ Social structural explanations focus on discriminatory economic, political, and legal practices that deny equal opportunities to women in the workplace.
>
> ■ Social learning explanations argue that people learn and acquire occupational preferences from others who, knowingly or unknowingly, teach what society defines as "appropriate" roles for men and women to aspire to and achieve.

From a parent's point of view, it is most useful to think of young women's careers from a social learning perspective. This is not to deny that sex differences are apparent already at an early age — that girls, for example, are more verbal and boys more aggressive — and that these differences may have some biological basis. Nor is it to deny that the occupational structure, reinforced by economic, political, and legal practices, disadvantages women in the workplace. But gender is fixed at conception, and the social system and the occupational structure are beyond parents' immediate control. Parents may not be able to do very much about these in time for their daughters to benefit, however important it is to remedy the system. Therefore, I urge parents to focus on the social learning possibilities, because that's where parents can make a difference.

Parents can change some of the beliefs, values, and attitudes that hold young women back. Parents can manage the immediate learning environments in which their daughters grow up, and that gives parents a handle on at least part of the problem. Young women's career opportunities are affected — usually stifled — by the attitudes and behaviors others expect and that women learn and bring to the workplace. Of people with whom young women interact, none is more important than family and school.

Education/training is the main linkage by which young people can improve their occupation and income prospects. But if this doesn't work as well for women as for men — and it doesn't — then we need to ask why women are exceptions to the pattern and what it is about the way families and schools treat women that narrows their options and depresses their achievements. These are strategic points where parents can plug in and make a difference. Unfortunately, traditional ways of rearing little girls often set the stage for the discrimination that occurs later in the workforce and society.

Family Influences

The family has the first, the most sustained, and the most enduring influence on newborn infants. Daughters and sons live with family for nearly a third of their lives, and even after the child leaves home, family influence continues.

A baby's sex is the first characteristic that family, friends, relatives, and community take into account. Before birth there is speculation, "boy or girl?" There is discussion about what the baby "really should be." Birth announcements invariably include the first thing ever said about the baby: "It's a boy!" or "It's a girl!" From day one, gender is central to who the babies are, how others behave toward them, and how they learn to think about themselves.

Parental Expectations and Behaviors

How much expectations are based on gender is evident in the way parents describe day-old infants. Parents describe baby girls as smaller, softer, more finely featured, prettier, and more attentive than they describe baby boys. Similarly, parents overestimate baby boys in terms of strength, features, boldness, and coordination. Traditional gifts for little girls feature delicate fabrics in pastel colors with floral designs. Gifts for little boys come in coarser fabrics and primary colors with bright animals and machines.

Parents behave differently toward little girls and little boys. Mothers look at, stay closer to, and talk more to little girls than to little boys. When playing with them, parents are more likely to throw a ball beyond a child's reach and encourage the child to retrieve it if the child is a boy. This is but one example of ways that higher levels of independence and achievement expectations are placed on little boys, even though parents do it unknowingly. By comparison, little girls are treated more protectively and are kept under tighter restrictions and controls.

Parents, families, and friends treat little boys and girls differently. They expect and reward nurturance and supportiveness in little girls but assertiveness and dominance in little boys.

Children's Behaviors

Not only do others treat little boys and girls differently, but little boys and girls behave differently. Girls are more verbal than boys and boys are more aggressive than girls. Girls talk earlier and speak more frequently. When preschool children are asked to make paper and pencil drawings, over half of the girls but only one of six or seven boys sketch pictures of people. Boys draw cars and trucks. When preschoolers tell stories, more girls than boys tell stories about people. Boys are more likely than girls to tell stories about airplanes and rockets. By age two, boys are more likely to yell, shove, and hit with intention to injure. As boys and girls grow older, the difference in aggressiveness increases.

So, why do little boys and girls behave differently? The biological point of view argues that these are expressions of basic male and female traits — not much help to parents who are trying to help teenage daughters choose careers. More useful to parents is the awareness that children develop along the lines that parents reward and punish them. Child-rearing patterns are important because they may encourage autonomy and independence, on the one hand, or passivity and dependence on the other — attitudes and behaviors that influence occupational choice and achievement later in life and have traditionally differentiated boys and girls already at an early age.

School Effects

Schools, too, are important in career development; and schools, like parents and families, educate young women and men in ways that produce different outcomes.

There are notable parallels between the ways schools and occupations separate girls and boys. One of the most visible ways schools separate students is by classifying them on the basis of gender. At nurseries and kindergartens there may be separate toys, separate chores to do, separate teams on which to play, and occasionally separate assignments for girls and boys. At the elementary level the playground may be organized into boy and girl territories — the boys' turf, of course, includes the athletic field.

But do these divisions make sense in a society that values equality? Or might they suggest to youngsters that gender is an important division and that gender is an acceptable basis for discrimination within society? These are not trivial questions, because opportunity differences translate into differences in what young men and women aspire to, in what areas they develop their abilities, and whether they receive recognition and support for their efforts.

If classifying students by gender were accompanied by separate but equal opportunities and outcomes, the consequences might be less discriminatory, though still unacceptable. But there is evidence that school opportunities and outcomes have been separate and not equal. Athletic programs including coaching staffs, stadiums and courts, uniforms, and community support have long histories and traditions of focusing on male activities. Title IX bars unequal opportunity based on gender, among other things, and litigation before the courts — for example, at Brown University — is likely to highlight and perhaps begin to remedy the inequalities in resources university women allege. If successful, can action against high schools be far behind? Against elementary schools?

Curriculum

Separation of students along male-female lines may be most visible in the extra-curriculum, but the same division affects the curriculum. Traditionally, vocational preparation programs have been male-oriented. They prepare young men for technical jobs and industrial trades that pay better. What has been offered to young women has been preparation for retail trades, health fields, and homemaking, occupations at the lower end of the wage scale.

But the most blatant and damaging discrimination may occur in college preparatory programs, where mathematics and science sequences have been "male subjects." In high school young women who have difficulty drop out of the math and sciences sequences — unfortunately, too often with the consent of teachers, counselors, and parents. This woman spoke for many others. She is a school teacher's daughter, got straight A's in college, and has a master's degree. She felt that high schools must be more demanding:

> *" My standardized test scores in mathematics all through school indicated a real deficiency, but I learned tricks that got me through classes with respectable grades. I wish someone had looked at those test scores and said, 'Now here's a smart girl who ought to be doing better than this. Maybe some remedial work would help.' Instead, I was encouraged to avoid a career that involved math, advice which I was only too happy to follow."*

A part-time waitress in our Career Development Study was angry:

> *" A major problem was the lack of incentive given to female students. . . . I distinctly remember an interview with a high school counselor during which I was encouraged to avoid the trades, instead to look at nursing, teaching, or secretarial work. No mention of management, administrative, or any decision-making jobs!"*

Is it surprising, then, that fewer women than men enter college with strong backgrounds in math and hard sciences?

Most women never catch up, and that effectively disqualifies them from college majors in business, medical, scientific, and technical studies. As a result, twice as many men as women enter business and the physical sciences, and many times more men than women enter engineering. In each of these fields, workers find the higher prestige and better-paying jobs. Women, by comparison, gravitate to education, health fields, and the humanities — lower-prestige and lower-paying occupations in which the majority of coworkers are other women. A bookkeeper in our Career Development study was bitter:

> *" I am really angry that I was encouraged 'not to waste time' with math. . . . I feel my high school teachers didn't want to waste time helping me into a career, or they felt I wouldn't use it because I would get married and be a housewife. The only field they encouraged was typing and secretarial skills and possibly teaching."*

Many 30-year-old women we studied were incensed at the lack of attention high schools gave to their career-planning needs. One put it succinctly: "High schools need to give more encouragement to women, scholastically and personally." A computer equipment operator in government service described herself as a "lost lamb," and then added: "Looking back, I believe I got married my senior year because I didn't know what else to do with myself." And this mother in our Youth and Careers Study undoubtedly spoke for many other mothers: "My child needs someone at high school to encourage her very much."

Until the last decade, fewer women than men enrolled in college, a certain predictor that their occupational achievement levels and earnings would be lower than men. But a change occurred over the 10-year period from 1976 to 1986. In 1976, men and women accounted for 53 and 47 percent, respectively, of enrollments in higher education. But 10 years later, in 1986, the distribution was exactly opposite: 53 percent women and 47 percent men. Over roughly the same period, women's earnings rose 84 percent compared with a 64 percent increase for men. In recent years, women's earnings have fluctuated in a range of 69 to 72 percent of men's earnings, which is less than three-quarters of equality, but progress has been made to raise women's earnings above the 62 percent of men's wages women earned in 1979. Indeed, there are occupations today in which earnings inequities favor women over men. The recent gains in occupations and incomes that women have achieved are closely tied to their increased levels of education and training. They earned it.

Women's Traits and the Workplace

Differences in child-rearing practices affect men's and women's attitudes and behaviors in the family, school, and world of work. As children mature, dependency is allowed if not expected of women, but it is rejected as an inappropriate trait for men. As a result, young women depend on their families for support and affection longer than young men do. Compared with men, women develop a greater need for affiliation with others and for other's approval. Women also develop more fear of rejection.

Young women learn to anticipate and respond to the needs and wishes of others, to be nurturant, caring, and giving. These characteristics suit them well for traditional women's jobs, but the same qualities do not equip them for occupations that require decision making, independent judgment, and leadership, which are qualities needed in the higher-prestige and better-paying jobs. Thus, a business service employee in our Career Development Study suddenly found herself in a whole new ballgame after college:

> *"Although I feel I was a success in school and was able to 'play the game' in an academic environment, I was totally unprepared to be a successful employee. . . . The rules of the 'game' in the working world were very different and were often unrelated to education and background."*

The traditional women's traits — deference, nurturance, and empathy — do not characterize the male-dominated workplace. Thus, it has become commonplace for women to learn "assertiveness training"; but how often are there training programs for men to learn the more characteristically feminine values and skills?

One of our 30-year-old study participants wanted to become a carpenter and attended apprenticeship carpenter courses while she held her job as a typist for the federal government. This is how she described the conflicts she faced:

> *" Adjusting to a 'man's' world has been a terrific problem. When I was in school I was raised to think that a woman's place was in the home or in the office as a secretary. My thinking is now 180 degrees from that. I'm in a blue-collar job traditionally held by men, and it is rough. I wish I had been raised to think that I'm equal to a man and can do a 'man's' job, and that there is nothing wrong with not wanting to get married."*

Nowhere is this twist in society's reaction to traditional feminine values and skills more apparent than in the nation's schools. In grade school, high school, and even in college, young women are the "good students." At every level, young women get better grades than young men. Young women do a better job of adapting to school rules and classroom routines. Particularly at the elementary level, but also beyond, the traditional ladylike traits of neatness, politeness, and silence are welcomed and rewarded. Being feminine and student are highly compatible roles.

Yet the "good student" — passive, anxious to please and win approval — may also be the person who is least willing to take initiative, take risks, and make mistakes. The passive and conforming feminine qualities that so closely parallel the classroom model are not the qualities that give workers an advantage in the labor market.

Expectations and Self-Esteem

Another inconsistency is that, although young women do better than young men in school, their expectations and self-esteem are lower than men's. Compared to young men, young women are less sure of their abilities, underestimate their possibilities, and overestimate their liabilities. In elementary school, young women perform better than young men, yet they are less confident that they will be able to do college work. Young women do better than young men in high school, but they do not translate their school performance into the same levels of occupational aspirations as their male classmates. At the college level, young men with lower grades more often believe they can achieve a doctorate degree than young women with higher grades. And among graduate students with similar grades, young women more often than young men aspire to junior college positions. Young men more often than young women aspire to university appointments.

Where the differences between young men's and young women's patterns of dependence, achievement, aspiration, and self-esteem come from will continue to be a subject of much debate. Some argue that the differences are fixed in natural biological tendencies; and there is little question that the occupational structure, reinforced by economic, political, and legal practice, treats women differently than men. But between birth and employment there is a lengthy learning process that sorts little girls and little boys into "socially appropriate" roles. That sorting teaches what society expects of them and how they should think of themselves and others. It also contributes to the sex-typed educational and occupational aspirations young men and women have and their eventual achievements.

Choice and Conflict

The traditional consensus on appropriate roles for young women is breaking down. How much is evident from the percentage of young women who are high school seniors who want to be full-time housewives at age 30. The decline is especially pronounced among young women who are not college-bound. In 1976, 22 percent choose full-time housewife as their occupation at age 30. Today, 2 or 3 percent want to be full-time housewives by that age.

Further, more young women are going to college, and in college more women are taking math and entering the sciences. More women are working, and more young women are entering "men's jobs." The occupational structure is changing, even if too slowly for some and too fast for others. The change means new opportunities for women, but it also signals new conflicts in how women balance marriage and family roles with their work roles.

The conflicts are apparent in what 30-year-old women told us in the Career Development Study. A four-year-college graduate with a major in home economics works as a statistical clerk in an insurance office. She is confused:

> *" I was raised to believe that I would be a wife and mother as an adult. I have not married, nor do I have children. . . . I'm still not truly positive what my goals are or what is in the future."*

Another took two years of general science in college and now works as a manager for a trade contractor. One of her biggest problems has been "trying to convince parents and close friends that being a young woman didn't mean I had to be married by 19 years of age and begin motherhood." A third respondent took three years of college and now works as a hospital secretary. Her views are much more traditional:

> *" The major problem was the conditioning at that time as to what was appropriate to do because of being man or woman. Girls were not encouraged to seek careers, but to educate themselves enough to support the husband's education and back his career. Things are changing, but I strongly believe that really the only decision in a woman's life is who she marries."*

Young women are resolving the conflicts between family and careers in different ways. Today's young woman has more opportunities than before; but the opportunities require that she make choices. And, in truth, there is little research to inform her decisions. Parents can help their daughters sort out their options. Parents can support and encourage them to follow their career interests, whether traditional or nontraditional. Parents can introduce them rather than shield them from competitive environments. And parents can provide the resources for young women to pursue their careers as, traditionally, parents have done for young men. Absolutely, parents can no longer allow what this participant in our Career Development Study told us — doctor's daughter, college graduate, and mother of three: "I honestly never realized . . . that the primary reason for working is to earn a living."

If I were limited to a single word of advice for young women thinking about a career, it would be this: Remember how the social system works. Education and training are the key to successful employment. The higher the level of education and training, the better are the prospects for employment in higher-status occupations. And the higher the status of the occupation, the higher is the income that is likely to follow.

To be sure, this will not solve all the problems young women face — the put downs, the being passed over for promotions, childcare, sexual harassment — but, in an imperfect world and an unjust society, it is a start. Get the education and training to qualify for the job.

Why the Lady Is a Champ

Several years ago, I came across a review of champion women's tennis players. It described the exceptional talents of the big names, but athletic ability alone did not make them winners. The article described the mental toughness and attitudes of players in the Women's Tennis Association who had won major tournaments.

What set apart the champs? Tracy Austin, a two-time U.S. Open champion by the time she was 20 years old, said it was "the desire to win and knowing you can win." The article described her as hungry for on-court confrontations. "Desire is the key," she said, "because without desire, you're not going to want to kill on each point. . . ."

Traditionally, women more than men have lacked that hunger for hard-nosed competition. Pugnacity, aggressiveness, and the killer instinct have been the antithesis of femininity. Tenacity is unladylike. Most women are taught to be passive, compliant, socially acceptable, and supportive.

By comparison, society expects men to display competitiveness. Witness cocky college jocks! Observe the talking trash in competitive events. Some months ago, Jack Nicklaus was in town inspecting a golf course he had designed. A reporter asked whether people still resented his dethroning the king, Arnold Palmer, during the 1970s. "I'm sure they do," Nicklaus said. "I know they didn't like me beating him. But that's too damn bad. Winning is the name of the game."

Barbara Potter, who in her late teens decided to make a career of tennis, says she had to learn a combative spirit traditionally assumed to be an attribute of achievement-oriented men. "You have to go for it," says Potter. "The chances for success and personal gain are just so much greater if you grasp it by the scruff of the neck."

But no one displays the killer instinct better than Navratilova. Those who follow women's tennis may remember when Martina was a confused and chronic underachiever, though the record books have since enshrined her as a tennis immortal. What made the difference? "Attitude," says Navratilova. She learned to "take the pressure, to be the one to beat."

What distinguishes the winners isn't athletic ability alone but attitude. Each learned winning attitudes about herself and about the game. That's why the lady is a champ.

Competitive and Feminine

Some years ago a national organization for young women asked me to propose program recommendations that would help young women take a more active role in society. One of the recommendations I made was that the organization should teach young women a more competitive attitude, and I suggested that the organization could contribute by emphasizing competitive sports, especially team sports. Soccer is a good example.

Today's young women have a growing number of opportunities in high schools, municipal leagues, youth organizations, and colleges. In my judgment, one of the best ways parents can help their daughters prepare for the real world and the world of work is by taking advantage of these opportunities, encouraging their daughters to participate actively in organized, competitive team sports. Young women need to learn to compete effectively.

In her book *Hardball for Women: Winning at the Game of Business,* author Pat Heim makes the same point but gives the advice a little different spin that I like very much. She urges that it's time to deemphasize the Barbie Doll mystique and sign up our daughters for soccer, and then asks: "But why am I so tempted to say, 'Young lady, play to win, [but] if you get hurt out on that field, I'll be here to dry your tears'?"

Heim makes an important point. Winning isn't everything. I hope we can teach young women the importance of a competitive attitude, but I also hope women will maintain the traditional feminine values. As young women plan how they might storm the workplace bastille and claim their fair share of the workforce, I also hope they will bring the feminine qualities of nurturance and caring with them. We'll all be the richer for it.

RACIAL MINORITIES AND CAREERS

African Americans and other racial minorities also suffer the consequences of prejudice — that is, detrimental beliefs, values, and attitudes — and discrimination. The social system withholds from them the full benefits of living in a just, open, and free society.

In the case of women, I elaborated how family and school contribute to their career disadvantage. My approach was conceptual and qualitative. Similar points could be made about other minorities, but I use a slightly different approach in discussing racial minorities to show how little (and not so little) differences add up to cumulatively big differences in career outcomes. I will be more quantitative (use more numbers) to demonstrate the differences.

I review how minorities are faring on the three basic socioeconomic dimensions — education, occupation, and income — and on associated dimensions of family life and well-being. Then I give some examples of "little differences" in the career development process that add up to big differences in outcomes.

Family Socioeconomic Status

Newton's first law of thermodynamics states that a body in motion stays in motion unless some outside force changes that direction. Social systems operate the same way. They stay in motion. They keep headed the same way unless some outside force changes that direction.

Earlier, I sketched how advantaged and disadvantaged families tend to continue their social status over time, even across generations; and I pointed out how levels of education and training are the critical link in that process. And because education/training, occupation, and income hang together, different levels of education and training prepare young people for different levels of occupations that pay different levels of income.

A key question, then, is who gets access to what levels of education and training? I have noted that parents with higher levels of education and training — for example, the professions — encourage their daughters and sons and commit the resources to prepare their children for the same occupational levels. Disadvantaged families, by comparison, may have lower expectations and certainly have fewer resources with which to support their children. So it is that families tend to perpetuate their social status over time, from one generation to the next. For some, that means advantages. For others, it means disadvantages.

There are exceptions, to be sure. Every youngster who toys with the notion of dropping out of high school can rattle off examples of grade-school dropouts who became millionaires. There are those exceptions. One of the reasons the exceptions are noted, even make the news, is that they are exactly that — exceptions! Exceptions are the rare cases. For that reason, they are interesting — but they are still exceptions. Exceptions are not what usually happens.

One of the limitations of my description of the way the social system works is that I must simplify it. I've left out thousands of details and frills. Because this is a book about career development, I focus only on education, occupation, and income — the big building blocks when it comes to careers. I must ignore the thousands of daily slights and indignities and inequities that are so much a painful part of prejudice and discrimination. I do this because too often we lose sight of the way society works. We prefer to deal only with individuals. We get caught up in little details, perhaps because we would much prefer to deal with little problems and look for little answers that we can deal with while ignoring the big problems.

The biggest exception to the way society processes young people is the way it treats women and racial and ethnic minorities. People have prejudices and society discriminates. This is how prejudices and discrimination affect minority careers.

Minority Statuses

Some children are born and raised in advantaged families, while others are born and raised in disadvantaged families. The advantages and disadvantages include a wide range of economic considerations, including parental occupational, educational, and income statuses, family structure, and related family characteristics that bear on young people's opportunities. The more the advantages — which is to say, the higher the social status of the family — the better the chance that young people can pursue the education and training that prepares them for advantaged occupations and incomes. The lower the family social status — that is, the lower the parents' education, occupation, and income levels — the lower the probabilities the children will have access to resources that assure education and training. In the case of minorities, there is the added consideration that minorities do not get the same return on their education and training investments as do members of the majority culture.

Parental Education

Minority families are disadvantaged on each status dimension: education, occupation, and income. Consider the education levels of African Americans ages 24 to 34, which are the prime child-bearing years. Eighty-two percent of African Americans completed four years of high school in 1992, but the corresponding figure for non-Hispanic Whites is 87 percent, a 5 percentage point difference.

The difference in educational attainment is even more apparent at the college level: The proportion of African Americans with a college education is 12 percent, half as high as the corresponding figure for non-Hispanic Whites, which is 24 percent. That's a 12 percentage point difference.

Parental Occupational Status

Lower levels of parental education suggest that the levels of parent occupational status will be lower, too. And they are lower. Large numbers of African-American men work as operators, fabricators, laborers, janitors, cleaners, or cooks. As a group, African Americans are employed in low-level occupations, and they are located in a narrow range of occupations.

There is also a difference by race in unemployment rates. In 1992, the unemployment rate for African-American males 16 years old and older was 15 percent, more than twice the corresponding unemployment rate for non-Hispanic Whites, which was 7 percent. That's an 8 percentage point difference, but it also means that, proportionately, there are twice as many African-American men unemployed as there are unemployed non-Hispanic White men.

Family Income

Education, occupation, and income hang together, and we would expect lower levels of family income to follow from lower levels of parental education and occupations. In 1991, the median income for African-American families was $21,550, whereas the median family income for non-Hispanic Whites was $37,780. That's a difference of $16,230 per year, $1,352 per month, or $45 per day — every day. The median income of African-American married-couple families was $33,310, for male-headed families it was $24,510; and for families maintained by women with no spouse present, it was $11,410 — which means the family lives on $32 per day!

In 1991, 30 percent of African-American families lived below the poverty line. The corresponding figure for non-Hispanic White families was 9 percent. About 46 percent of African-American children under age 16 lived in poverty, compared with 16 percent of non-Hispanic White children.

Poverty

Another gauge of the economic well-being of families is the poverty rate. In 1991, 12 percent of families lived in poverty. But of families maintained by a woman with no spouse present, 36 percent were poor — three times as many. Among woman-headed families with no spouse present and living in poverty, the proportion of minority families was especially high: 51 percent of African-American and 50 percent of Hispanic families, compared with 28 percent of non-Hispanic White families. Woman-headed families with no spouse present represent 78 percent of all poor African-American families and 46 percent of poor Hispanic families.

In 1991, 41 percent of all poor families were headed by married couples, but 54 percent were headed by women with no spouse present. Only 13 percent of nonpoor families were headed by women with no spouse present. The proportion of woman-headed families among all poor families was 51 percent. Thus, marital status matters: 6 percent of families maintained by a married couple live in poverty, but 36 percent of woman-headed households with no spouse present live in poverty. And race matters. Fourteen percent of all persons live in poverty, but 33 percent of African Americans live in poverty.

Poverty rates also vary dramatically by level of parental education. Twelve percent of all families live in poverty, as do 24 percent of all individuals. But of families where the householder has no high school diploma, 24 percent live in poverty. Compare that, for example, with 2 percent of families living in poverty in which the householder has a college education. In sum, race, family structure, education, and poverty all fit together, and minority families are disadvantaged.

Public Assistance

Fourteen percent of the population participates in some form of major assistance — that is, they live in public housing or are beneficiaries of Aid to Families with Dependent Children, General Assistance, Supplemental Security Income, Medicaid, food stamps, or federal or state rent assistance.

But receipt of public assistance varies by gender: 16 percent of women and 12 percent of men receive assistance. It also varies dramatically by family status: 9 percent of persons in married-couple families receive assistance, but 42 percent of persons who live in woman-headed families with no spouse present depend on assistance. And participation varies by race: 11 percent of non-Hispanic Whites, 27 percent of Hispanics, and 39 percent of African Americans participate in some form of major assistance program.

Disadvantage? Minorities, particularly minorities in woman-headed families.

Health Insurance

Health insurance coverage is yet another indicator of family socioeconomic well-being. In 1990, 87 percent of the population was covered, most people by private insurance. But health coverage is linked to employment. Stable, full-time employment improves one's chances of coverage — only 14 percent of persons who worked full-time experienced lapses in coverage over a 28-month period. In contrast, 43 percent of those unemployed for a month or more experienced a lapse in coverage. Of those who worked part-time, 27 percent had no coverage. Thus, persons with more unstable employment histories — many of them minorities — have lower rates of health insurance coverage.

Health coverage is also linked with education. Taking 26 percent as a point of reference — the percentage of all persons whose health coverage lapsed over a two-year study period — 15 percent of college graduates experienced a lapse, as did 25 percent of high school graduates and 27 percent of high school dropouts. Persons with lower levels of education are more likely to experience lapses in health insurance coverage.

Health care is also linked with income. Falling below the poverty line increases the chances that health coverage lapses. Among those who spent no time over a two-year period living below the poverty line, 15 percent experienced lapses in coverage. But of those who spent as little as one month in poverty, 54 percent have lapses in health coverage.

In sum, health care coverage is linked with race, employment, education, and poverty. Twenty-four percent of non-Hispanic Whites had a lapse in health insurance over a two-year period, but 40 percent of African Americans and 46 percent of Hispanics had insurance lapses.

Disadvantage? Minorities.

Family Discontinuance

Socioeconomic conditions are not just circumstances in which people thrive or survive. Economic stress can be a major factor that dissolves the glue that keeps the family together. And when married-couple families discontinue, reduced income and higher rates of unemployment often follow, which affects the life chances of young people further.

About 1 of every 12 married-couple families that exist at the beginning of a two-year period will discontinue by the end of the second year. This happens, annually, with about 7 percent of non-Hispanic White families but with 12 percent of African-American families.

But several conditions increase the probability that families will discontinue. If the husband is not employed, the likelihood that a family will discontinue nearly doubles, increasing to 14 percent. If the married-couple family lives below the poverty line, the probability that the family will discontinue within two years also nearly doubles, increasing to 13 percent. But if the married couple is African American and lives below the poverty line, the probability of discontinuing over the two-year period rises to 21 percent. If the couple is Hispanic, the probability of discontinuing is 9 percent. And if the Hispanic family is poor, it rises to 11 percent. Clearly, poverty — and, therefore, race — is related to family structure.

Reconstituted Families

Most families reconstruct and merge into new two-parent families. Of every four families headed by a woman with no spouse present, one of the families does not exist two years later. But new family formation varies by race, as evident in that new families form for 27 percent of non-Hispanic White single mothers, but for only 16 percent of Hispanic and 13 percent of African-American single mothers.

New family formations also vary by poverty levels. Of single mothers who are non-Hispanic White and were poor in their previous households, 33 percent are poor in newly formed families one year later, but the percentage for corresponding African-American single mothers who were poor in their previous households and are poor in newly formed families one year later is 46 percent.

Whether considering families from the perspective of basic socioeconomic indicators — levels of parental education, occupation, and income — or such associated conditions as extent of major program assistance and health-insurance coverage, the pattern is clear: Higher-status families are in an advantaged position and, conversely, lower-status families are disadvantaged when it comes to the wherewithal to give their children a leg up on a career advantage. In our society, race is closely linked with socioeconomic status. African-American and, to a slightly lesser extent, Hispanic families are the "have nots." Families are the point of origin for young peoples' careers, and that means that minorities are disadvantaged at the start.

In the next section, I shift attention from parental socioeconomic statuses to young peoples' socioeconomic attainments. I focus on the end of the career development process, how minorities fare in terms of educational, occupational, and income attainments.

Minority Socioeconomic Attainments

With passage of the 1964 Civil Rights Act, the U.S. formally acknowledged the reality of discrimination in our society and introduced a series of equal opportunity and affirmative action programs to assure all people of the benefits of living in a free and open society. The initial programs were targeted at unequal educational opportunities. Subsequently, they were extended to occupations and income. The programs are conscious efforts to break the tendency for family socioeconomic status to continue almost automatically from one generation to the next.

In this section, I review the socioeconomic achievement levels of racial minorities — that is, their educational, occupational, and income levels. I urge the reader to keep in mind that there are two conflicting forces at work in our society:

- ■ The tendency for societies to perpetuate socioeconomic advantages and disadvantages from one generation to the next.
- ■ Legislation and social programming designed to stop that tendency by improving minority socioeconomic statuses.

This review shows evidence of both forces at work. There has been improvement in minority educational, occupational, and income statuses; but there is also evidence of continuing discrimination.

Educational Status

The national level of educational attainment for persons 25 years and older rose dramatically over the past half century. Only 7 percent of African Americans completed high school in 1940, compared with 26 percent of non-Hispanic White men. By 1991, 65 percent of African Americans completed high school, compared with 80 percent of non-Hispanic Whites.

So also, in 1940, 1 of 20 persons who were 25 years old and older completed four years of college, but by 1991 1 of 5 completed college. Although the proportion of African Americans who completed four years of college has increased since 1940, it remains about one-half the proportion of Whites, 11.5 percent compared with 22 percent for non-Hispanic Whites in 1991.

Graduating from high school, completing four years of college, and taking an advanced degree offer different levels of career advantage that have important implications for the prospects of getting a job, the quality of the job, and the income associated with the job. In 1993, 87 percent of all 25- to 29-year-olds were high school graduates, but note how the graduation rate for these young adults continues to vary by race:

Race	Percentage High School Graduates	Percentage 4-Year College Graduates	Percentage Advanced Degrees
Non-Hispanic Whites	91.0	31.0	13.0
African Americans	83.0	16.0	6.5
Hispanics	61.0	9.0	6.5

In sum, racial minorities are making progress in their quest for equal levels of educational attainment. They are nearing the goal in terms of high school graduation rates, but vestiges of prejudice and discrimination remain at all levels of postsecondary education. The fact that a high school diploma today is not an advanced credential but the minimum educational credential for entry into the labor force gives some indication of the distance society has yet to travel in assuring equal educational opportunity at the postsecondary levels.

Occupational Status

African Americans are heavily concentrated in a limited number of jobs. In 1990, 31 percent of African-American men were operators, fabricators, and laborers; and of these, 30 percent were truck drivers, assemblers, stock handlers, and badgers. Within service occupations, 45 percent were janitors, cleaners, or cooks. Another 12 percent were guards and police, except public service. Of African Americans who were managers and professionals, 22 percent were teachers, the majority being elementary teachers. Nearly 30 percent of African-American women who are employed in technical, sales, and administrative support services are cashiers, secretaries, and typists. And half of African-American women who work in service occupations work as nurses' aides, orderlies, attendants, cooks, janitors, and cleaners.

African Americans are disproportionately unemployed, also. An average of 9.4 million persons 16 years old and older were unemployed in 1992, but the unemployment rate for African Americans was 14 percent, double the rate for non-Hispanic Whites and Hispanics, which was 7 percent. For adults, persons 20 years old and older, the pattern was similar. The non-Hispanic White unemployment rate was 6 percent, the African-American rate was 13 percent, and the Hispanic rate was 10 percent. African Americans constituted 11 percent of the civilian labor force, but accounted for 21 percent of the unemployed. Hispanics had an 8 percent share of the civilian labor force, but comprised 12 percent of the unemployed.

In sum, the work force continues to be segregated based on race. Racial minorities are not proportionately distributed across the full range of occupations and industries in the labor force but remain clustered in lower-status jobs. Racial minorities also experience higher rates of unemployment. In some respects, the minority experience reflects their lower educational and training credentials. In other respects, it reflects the continuing presence of prejudice and discrimination in society.

Income

The earnings advantage of a college education increased over the past two decades, and in 1992 the advantage of having a bachelor's degree was more than double the earnings advantage of having attended only some college.

The earnings advantage favors minorities. African Americans who complete their college degrees fare better than non-Hispanic Whites, just as women fare better than men. That is evident in the percentage of earnings advantage of college graduates as compared with high school graduates. Male African-American college graduates earn 183 percent more than African-American young men who are high school graduates. Non-Hispanic White males who are college graduates, by comparison, have an earnings advantage of 155 percent over non-Hispanic White male high school graduates. African-American women's earnings advantage is 213 percent, and the earnings advantage of non-Hispanic White women is 194 percent.

Understand, however, that the favorable percentages for minorities reflects only the advantage of a college education over a high school education. The percentages do not mean an advantage of African-American incomes over comparable White incomes.

Most minorities are not college graduates, however, and a different set of income realities applies to noncollegiates. For example, median incomes for married-couple family households vary, and they vary by race. In March 1992, married-couple family income was $41,584 for Whites, $33,369 for African Americans, and $28,833 for Hispanics. In sum, society discriminates in many ways that disadvantage minorities; but among minorities, it also rewards those who achieve a college education.

Households maintained by women with no husband present represented 12 percent of all households in 1991: 10 percent of non-Hispanic White households, 32 percent of African-American households, and 20 percent of Hispanic households. Because minorities have higher proportions of households headed by women which generate lower incomes, minorities are disadvantaged. The median income for households maintained by women with no husbands present was $17,961 for all households, $21,213 for non-Hispanic White households, $12,196 for African-American households, and $13,323 for Hispanic households.

The same disadvantage occurs with personal income. In 1991, the median earnings of year-round, full-time employed African-American men was 73 percent of the level of earnings of comparable non-Hispanic White men, $22,080 compared with $30,270. That's $8,190 less per year, $682 less per month, and about $4 less per hour. The median earnings for African-American women who worked year-round, full-time were 90 percent of the earnings of comparable non-Hispanic White women, $18,720 and $20,790. In sum, clearly minorities remain disadvantaged in income, which reflects their education, their employment opportunities, and their family composition.

Age and Poverty

Nowhere are the cumulative effects of discrimination more apparent than in the proportions of elderly who live in poverty. Nationwide, 10 percent of the elderly live in poverty. But among African Americans, 65 percent of the elderly live in poverty.

Prejudice and discrimination may no longer mean separate drinking fountains, wash rooms, lunch counters, and schools. More typically, today, it means a few percentage points here and a few more there. But cumulatively and over a lifetime, the results are overwhelming.

Minorities and the Achievement Process

The factors that influence a young person's career development can be reduced to five principles:

Career Development Principles

- Young people are reared in families with different socioeconomic statuses.
- Family socioeconomic advantages and disadvantages are passed on from parents to their children.
- The main connection in the continuation of family socioeconomic statuses from one generation to the next is children's levels of education and training.
- Parents encourage and support their sons and daughters to achieve levels of education and training comparable to their own.
- Young people learn beliefs, values, and attitudes in their homes and schools that fit them for socioeconomic statuses comparable to their parents.

In reviewing how discrimination affects minorities, I noted that minorities typically originate in families that are socioeconomically disadvantaged, and that this disadvantage is passed from parents to their children. Now I turn to the question: How does this happen? What is it about the minority family and educational experience that produces disadvantaged outcomes for children?

This is an important question. If specific points can be located where minority sons and daughters are disadvantaged, then these become places where parents can intervene to overcome career development disadvantages. Obviously, the process is much more complex than I can sketch. I can provide only a few examples, and those are limited to the high school experience. A complete analysis would have to include such experiences as childcare, preschool and elementary school experiences, family and peer relationships.

Parental Involvement

It is important to recognize that differences in student school experiences may occur apart from parental involvement in the education of their children. Thus, African-American parents demonstrate substantial involvements in many forms of school-related activities. Consider, for example, the following comparison of parental involvements by race reported by the U.S. Department of Education in *The Condition of Education, 1994*:

- 93 percent of African-American parents check their daughters' and sons' homework, compared with 90 percent of non-Hispanic White parents.
- 68 percent of African-American parents speak with teachers and counselors about their child's academic progress, compared with 59 percent of non-Hispanic White parents.
- 36 percent of African-American parents visit classes, compared with 26 percent of non-Hispanic White parents.
- 10 percent of African-American students come to school without paper, pen, or pencil, compared with 12 percent of non-Hispanic White students and 14 percent of Hispanic students.
- 16 percent of African-American students come to school without homework completed, compared with 18 percent of non-Hispanic White students and 21 percent of Hispanic students.
- 5 percent of African-American high school students work 20 or more hours per week while attending high school, compared with 13 percent of non-Hispanic White students and 10 percent of Hispanic students.
- 21 percent of African-American students missed no days of school during the first half of the year in 1990, compared with 13 percent of non-Hispanic Whites and Hispanic students; and, of students who missed five days or more, 27 percent were African American, 35 percent were non-Hispanic Whites, and 42 percent were Hispanics.

Each of the above is a parenting behavior that advantages minorities and is a credit to minority parents. Nonetheless, minority children remain disadvantaged on other critical achievement indicators.

Grade Repeats

Studies show that students who repeat a grade are more likely to drop out later. In 1992, for example, the dropout rate for 16- to 24-year-olds who had repeated at least one grade was more than double that of those who had never repeated a grade; and when the highest grade repeated was between grades 7 and 10, the dropout rate was two to three times higher than when grades were repeated at lower levels.

But which students are most likely to repeat grades and, therefore, are predisposed to drop out? It is students from low-income families. And, because minority families are disproportionately overrepresented among lower-income families, more minority children are likely both to repeat a grade and to drop out.

In 1992, one-third of 16- to 24-year-old students from low-income families who earlier had repeated a grade dropped out. Note the pattern of grade repeats and school dropouts across family levels of income and the disadvantage to low-income families.

Family Income	Percentage of Grade Repeats	Percentage of Dropout Rates
Low	17	25
Middle	11	10
High	8	2

Persistent Attendance

Persistent attendance is the proportion of students who enroll in high school over two consecutive years, and it is strongly associated with completing high school. The usual persistence rate is about 96 percent — 96 percent for non-Hispanic Whites, 95 percent for African Americans, and 92 percent for Hispanics.

But the rate for students from high-income families is 10 percent higher than the rate for students from low-income families. For low-income families, the persistence rate is 89 percent, for middle incomes it is 96 percent, and for high family incomes it is 99 percent. Thus, when it comes to staying enrolled over two consecutive years during high school, being both minority and from a low-income family are career disadvantages.

Programs

Academic curriculums prepare students for college, and that means that students who aspire to college need to be enrolled in academic or college prep programs. Following are the percentage of high school sophomores who, in 1991, enrolled in general, college preparatory, and vocational programs by race:

Race	General	College Prep	Vocational
All	51	41	8
Whites	52	42	6
African Americans	43	41	6
Hispanics	55	35	10

High school sophomores who were non-Hispanic White earned an average of 42 college preparatory or academic units. By comparison, African Americans earned 41 and

Hispanics earned 35. Hispanics, in particular, disproportionately enroll in programs that do not prepare them for college, and fewer Hispanics eventually enroll and graduate from college.

So also, more non-Hispanic White students earn the recommended units in core courses — another predictor of college enrollment. Forty-nine percent of non-Hispanic Whites, compared with 44 percent of African Americans and 36 percent of Hispanic students, earned the recommended units.

Of students who earned the recommended units in core courses, 49 percent had parents with a college education, 46 percent had parents with some college, 47 percent had parents with a high school education, and 45 percent had parents who had not completed high school. Both race and parental levels of education advantage or disadvantage students in the academic curriculums in which they enroll.

Dropout Rates

The dropout rate for all tenth, eleventh, and twelfth graders declined over the past decade from 6 percent 10 years ago to 4 percent in 1991. Nonetheless, dropouts remain unevenly distributed across the population: 3.7 percent are non-Hispanic Whites, but nearly double that percentage, 6.2 percent, are African Americans, and 7 percent are Hispanics.

Dropout rates also vary by family income, which further disadvantages minorities. Although 7 percent of high school students from families with incomes below $20,000 drop out of high school, fewer than 1 percent of youngsters from families with incomes of $40,000 or more drop out. Being African American or Hispanic and from a low-income family increases the probability that a student will drop out of high school, a decided career disadvantage.

Proficiency Scores

Average proficiency scores in reading, writing, mathematics, and science also vary by race. For example, in 1992, the comparative scores for 17-year-olds were as follows:

Area	Whites' Score	African Americans' Score	Hispanics' Score
Reading	297	261	271
Writing	294	263	274
Mathematics	312	286	292
Science	304	256	270

On each of the basic skills areas — reading, writing, mathematics, and science — 17-year-old non-Hispanic White students score higher than minority students. The same pattern occurs with proficiency tests at earlier ages. Lower scores disadvantage minorities.

SAT Scores

The Scholastic Aptitude Test (SAT) is the test taken most frequently by college-bound students. The SAT predicts first-year college success and may be used to place students in courses and programs. In 1993, college-bound students scored as follows:

- Non-Hispanic Whites scored 444 on the verbal tests and 494 on the math tests.
- African Americans scored 353 on the verbal tests and 388 on the math tests.
- Hispanics scored 375 on the verbal tests and 428 on the math tests.

As with proficiency tests, minority students score lower on SAT tests, a career disadvantage.

Late Completions and Dropping Out

Dropping out may mean that a student never completes high school, or it may mean that the student completes later. Both have detrimental career consequences though, of course, never graduating has the most severe consequences — the usual meaning of "dropping out."

The dropout rates for the eighth grade class of 1988, as measured by students who had not graduated from high school by 1992, varied by race. Nine percent of non-Hispanic Whites dropped out, but 15 percent of African Americans and 18 percent of Hispanics dropped out.

The same pattern occurs for high school completion rates. Consider, for example, the tenth grade class of 1980. The percentage of students who completed high school on time, 1982, and who completed within 10 years, 1992, are as follows:

Race	Percentage Completed on Time, 1982	Percentage Completed Late, 1992
Non-Hispanic Whites	86	95
African Americans	79	92
Hispanics	73	88

Most students who drop out of high school eventually complete, but note the pattern of completions. The differences are greatest for students who complete on time, which disadvantages minorities. And although African Americans and Hispanics eventually almost equal the completion rates of non-Hispanic Whites, both groups take longer to graduate, and their completion rates never fully equal those of non-Hispanic Whites — a career disadvantage.

Encouragement to Attend College

There are considerable differences by race in percentages of fathers, mothers, guidance counselors, and teachers who, when their daughters and sons are sophomores in high school, encourage them to attend college. Note the differences in 1992:

Race	Percentage of Fathers	Percentage of Mothers	Guidance Counselors	Percentage of Teachers
Non-Hispanic Whites	78	84	65	65
African Americans	69	77	66	70
Hispanics	75	81	65	65

Non-Hispanic White fathers and mothers are more likely than minority parents to encourage their sons and daughters to attend college even though encouragement from guidance counselors and teachers is more evenly distributed.

The percentage of high school sophomores whose fathers, mothers, guidance counselors, and teachers encourage college attendance also varies by socioeconomic status:

Socioeconomic Status	Percentage of Fathers	Percentage of Mothers	Guidance Counselors	Percentage of Teachers
Low	58	67	56	59
Middle	77	84	64	64
High	95	97	78	76

The clear pattern is that the higher the level of socioeconomic status, the more fathers, mothers, guidance counselors, and teachers encourage young people to attend college. Because minority parents, guidance counselors, and teachers are less likely to encourage minority students to attend, and their families have fewer family resources, minority youth are disadvantaged.

Income and Opportunities

How low family incomes, which disproportionately plague minority families, affect opportunities for minority children is vividly illustrated in the example of the relationship of college costs to family income levels.

In 1992, the costs for tuition, room, and board of a college education required an expenditure of 14 percent of median family incomes in the U.S. By definition, therefore, the proportions of family incomes required for sending a child to college varied greatly by the income level of the family. For families in the lowest tenth of incomes, college costs claimed 53 percent of total family incomes, whereas for families in the highest tenth of incomes, college costs claimed only 6 percent of total family incomes (see Figure 4-2).

Proportions of Family Incomes Required for College Costs

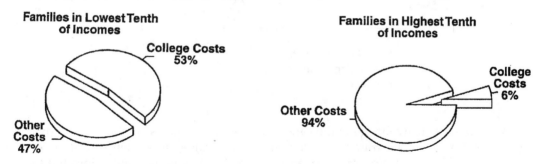

Figure 4-2 *Source: The Condition of Education, 1994*

The example illustrates a more general point: namely, that the disadvantaged not only have fewer resources with which to support their children's careers, but any cost, including the cost of a year of college education, claims a much larger proportion of the scarce resources low-income families have.

Direct College Enrollment

The percentage of high school graduates who enroll in college the following fall is a leading indicator of the total proportion of that year's graduates who will ever enroll in college. It is also a measure of how accessible higher education is to high school graduates.

The proportion of graduates going directly to college has been increasing since 1974. By 1992, it rose 7 percentage points for African Americans, but 15 percentage points for non-Hispanic Whites. In 1992, 62 percent of all high school graduates enrolled in college the following fall. But the proportions vary by race: 64 percent of non-Hispanic Whites and 47 percent of African Americans went directly to college.

Family income status also made a difference. High school graduates from low-income families were twice as likely to go directly to college in 1992 as in 1973, yet only 41 percent from low-income families go directly to college. This compares with 81 percent of graduates from families with high incomes who go directly to college. The combination of race and family income status disadvantages minority youth and predicts the proportion that will eventually graduate.

Program Completion

Completing a postsecondary program, whether that be a vocational certificate or a college degree, is important for maximizing both employment possibilities and income, but the proportions of students who complete programs varies by race. The pattern is largely the same, regardless of the type of certification or degree program. Note, for example, the completion rates for the least demanding program, a vocational certificate, which can be completed on time in as little as nine months (see the following table).

Having begun a program, whether degree or certificate, minorities have higher failure-to-complete rates, which is a career disadvantage.

Race	Percentage Who Ever Complete
All	50
Non-Hispanic Whites	53
African Americans	44
Hispanics	32

In summary, many factors in the career development process combine to disadvantage minorities. I have illustrated but a few that tend to follow in sequence at the secondary level. Most of the differences in performance are small, a few percentage points; but they add up to big differences over the course of a career and lifetime.

Little Differences

Women and racial minorities suffer the consequences of career disadvantages. People hold prejudices, and the social system discriminates against them. But beliefs, values, and attitudes are learned, and parents are critical in controlling what young people learn about themselves and their place in society. And their beliefs, values, and attitudes make a difference in their careers.

We live in a society of small differences and close finishes. That is apparent in one of our most popular forms of entertainment, namely, athletic events. Five-hundred-mile Winston Cup automobile races are won and lost by a front quarter panel — three or four feet. Swimming events and foot races are won and lost by one-hundredths of a second. Golf matches are won and lost by putts made or missed by fractions of an inch. But champions are the competitors who, time after time, win by those same small margins. By analogy, the winners in career development are parents and their daughters and sons who do a little better at each step in the process. The little differences add up to big career differences.

Next Steps: What Parents Can Do

Career choice involves two major decisions: choice of an occupation and choice of a career preparation strategy. All other questions — such as "What kind of teacher or doctor will you be?" or "How will we pay for college?" — follow from the major decisions. Ideally, a young person should choose an occupation first and a career preparation strategy second. But it doesn't always work that way.

There is no single way to make an occupational choice, but this section and "Next Steps: What Parents Can Do" at the end of each part of the book suggest ways parents can assist their daughters and sons with choosing a career.

APTITUDES AND INTERESTS

When young people say that they don't know what interests them, they're probably telling the truth. They may have some vague notions, but they haven't given it much thought, they have little hands-on practical experience, they don't know what the choices are, and they don't know what's involved with getting into some of the occupations they do know about. They just plain don't know. And that's one of the reasons they may go into gridlock — unable "to get their act together" — when it comes to making career choices.

NORMAL "NOS"

Young people often seem to have a better idea of what they don't want to do than what they want to do. They *don't* want to go to college, but they're not sure what they *do* want to do after high school. They *don't* want to be an office worker — or a nurse, plumber, or sales clerk — but they don't know what they *do* want to do. There are three points to keep in mind when working with young adults who know what they don't want to do, but aren't sure what they do want to do.

First, assure them (and yourself) that not knowing what they want to do is common, and there's nothing wrong with that. Young people are often insecure to start with, and they feel it. They don't want to fail. And they're scared. Don't let them use their "undecidedness" as a club with which to beat themselves down further. Rather, build them up.

Developmental psychologists remind us that young people are searching, reaching for that illusive freedom, seeking autonomy. "Is this me?" they like to ask. And they're serious. It takes a while to find "me." In the process they experiment, try things out — hairdos, drugs, clothing, behaviors, lifestyles — and a lot of saying "no" goes on. "I don't like this." "I don't like that." "This isn't me." But occasionally they discover: "This is me." "I like that." The point is that young people experiment for a purpose. They're looking for "me." And that involves saying a lot of "nos." The nos are normal.

Second, saying "no" to career possibilities provides important information parents can sometimes use. What is common in the occupations that the young person doesn't want to pursue? Is it that all require a four-year college education? Are all away from home? Are the "I-don't-like-that-job" possibilities all indoors? Do all involve working in large companies? To the extent that parents can help their sons and daughters see the common themes in what they don't like, that young person is actively sorting out options in much the same way that others follow in the more comfortable route of identifying what they do like.

The important thing in career decision making is that the young person is evaluating and responding, actively involved in sorting out options. One way to do that is by identifying the "nos." Even interest inventories produce little more than a handful of options in which a young person may be interested — which means that inventories allow young people to say a lot more "nos" than "yeses."

Third, parents can use the "I don't like that" response to advantage. All of us use the same sorting process at one time or another when we can't decide. We rule out our dislikes as a way of finding what we do like. Our tastes are not always apparent to us, so we locate them by sorting out what we don't like. It's a process of elimination.

What happens when we evaluate and sort — whether the objects be things we like or don't like — is that we begin to settle on criteria by which we make judgments. Discovering the criteria that are important to us is a big step in determining what we like, and that can often be discovered by figuring out what we don't like, just as it can be discovered by sorting out what we do like. The "nos" are normal.

The idea is to help our daughters and sons build a list of possibilities, then follow the process of elimination in narrowing the choices. Let them eliminate the ones they think are "gross." Keep going till they find the ones that are "awesome!" In the meantime, help them think through what the "no" jobs have in common.

CAREER TALK

Parents have to talk about career options with their sons and daughters if they are to be part of the decision-making process, but how can parents get the discussion started? And, let's face it: You can't talk with them forever about what they *don't* want to do. That gets old after a while. But how do you shift gears? What are some new ways to freshen up the dialogue, get some new possibilities on the table, and keep the dialogue going?

Talk Specifics

Young people often tell me, and I believe them, that they get tired of people (especially Mom and Dad) asking them: "What do you want to do?" They come to detest it. It is painful for them. Mom and Dad want to know. They don't want to push, but they want to know. They, perhaps more than son or daughter, are aware that time is running out. College educations cost a lot of money, and Mom and Dad are antsy about that, too. And son or daughter wants to know, but doesn't know, and doesn't want to make a mistake. These can be uneasy times in households. The subject of careers becomes a touchy topic — a topic that everbody avoids if at all possible.

One of the reasons the subject of career choice becomes painful for some young people is that it is too abstract. It's not concrete. It's hard to handle. In addition, careers sound far away to young people. Son or daughter is at a point in life when long-range planning amounts to figuring out which video he or she is going to watch tonight.

Abstractions are always hard to handle. Suppose Dad and Mom were asked, "What do you want to do with the rest of your life?" If somebody kept after you with that level of abstraction, you might become a bit irritated, too.

Parents need to talk about concrete possibilities with their sons and daughters, and the sooner parents begin to focus on specific possibilities, the more productive the discussions are likely to be. It's a lot easier to consider the pros and cons of being a veterinarian or a journalist than it is to answer: What do you want to do? "Which pie do you want, apple or cherry?" is easier to answer than, "What kind of pie do you want?" — especially when you don't know what kind of pies are available.

One way to start the career dialogue, to freshen it up, or to get some new occupational possibilities on the list is to arrange for your son or daughter to take one or more career exploration programs at school. Aptitude tests show what a young person may be good at. Interest inventories help them focus on occupations that fit their interests.

High schools often provide career exploration exercises as a student service, but the student and parent may have to take the initiative and make the arrangements. Check with your son's or daughter's high school counselors. It may be that they already have a report on file on your daughter or son. Find out.

Usually, there is no cost for interest inventories and aptitude tests administered through high schools, but it is wise to check in advance.

Career Explorations

There are many kinds of career exploration programs. Some are printed in test-type booklets and self-scored, others are scored by machine, and still others are sent away and analyzed by computer. Some are in workbooks and can be scored by the user. Still others are on computers in career centers. Increasingly, career exploration programs are availaable in hardcopy and in personal computer versions. School counselors will tell you what is available through your high school.

If you have a choice, I suggest the Strong-Campbell Interest Inventory for advanced high school students who may be thinking about attending a four-year college. The Kuder General Interest Survey is a good one for young people at the junior high level. The Harrington-O'Shea Career Decision-Making System is useful because it takes into account a young person's interests in school subjects, kinds of postsecondary education, and interests in particular occupations. These are all available in pencil-paper versions. Some may be available to you on computer. Holland's Self-Directed Search is widely used. One reason is that it is very simple. Another is that it was designed for people who do not have access to professional counselors. There are many better career exploration programs available and, fortunately, most parents and young people need not rely on do-it-yourself career counseling.

One of the most comprehensive career exploration programs in book form is the *Guide for Occupational Exploration* (GOE) published by JIST Works. The *GOE* is available through bookstores, and parents may find the volume helpful to use with their sons and daughters at home.

An example of a useful computerized career exploration program is *Choices,* which is produced by Careerware and is increasingly available in high school career centers. One clear advantage of computer systems of career exploration is that a young person can play "what if?" with the automated systems. For example, "what if" I were willing to get a four-year college degree instead of, say, a vocational certificate? How would that change my occupational options? Computer career exploration programs can show such comparisons quickly and efficiently.

All of the systems — whether in test booklet form, workbook or book format, or on computer software — work the same way. The explorations establish an inventory of a young person's interests and aptitudes and then match the young person's traits with occupational characteristics.

Matching individuals' traits with occupational characteristics is a useful exercise, but that exercise alone does not usually take into account employment prospects and projections based on changes in population, labor forces, and national and international policies. How to get information on those considerations is the subject of Part II of this book.

Using Results

Interest inventories don't give answers. Rather, they offer possibilities to think about and discuss. That means that the job isn't finished when the results come back. When the results come back, the job has just begun. And no test booklet or computer program can do that job for you.

Career explorations can give young people some fresh ideas. That's their value. They are not "tests" that give right or wrong answers. There is nothing magical about them. And they won't give a perfect match between a young person's interests and occupations. What the explorations can do is give young people, parents, and career counselors some career possibilities that seem to be in the ball park. But the possibilities need to be thought through.

Because aptitude tests and interest inventories merely offer suggestions, I am not terribly concerned about which tests young people take. It is not as if one kind is a lot better than another. This is not the stuff of "exact science." The explorations are merely tools, nothing more. All of them are good to the extent that they raise possibilities for parents and their children to consider. Use the ones your career center offers.

We're in the age of high tech, and many career centers have computer career exploration programs that are fun to use. Check them out.

Different Results

Don't expect different inventories to give the same results. Chances are, that won't happen. But that isn't bad. In fact, I think it's good.

The idea is neither to narrow everything down as quickly as possible nor to ever narrow everything down to one "right answer." Rather, the idea is to raise as many career possibilities as you can. Think of the process as adding names of occupations to a list on a chalk board. Use every way you can to add new possibilities. Include occupations your son or daughter may have mentioned in the past. Add occupations that grandparents, friends, teachers, or counselors mentioned along the way. Include your own suggestions. Build the list of possibilities.

I encourage parents to arrange for "one or more" aptitude tests and interest inventories. The reason I urge more than one is that your daughter or son is likely to come up with more possibilities doing it that way. The idea is to build the list.

Include Alternatives

Another reason many young people find it difficult to settle on a career is that they're looking for that one "made in heaven match" of an occupation with their interests; and they may unrealistically feel that if they don't find it, they will never be happy. Not so.

Young people — older people, too — should always have alternatives, contingency plans, plan A and plan B, and maybe even plans C and D. Narrowing career choices to a single possibility is both impractical and unwise for three reasons.

> ■ No one's interests are so narrow that there is only one good occupational fit with their interests and aptitudes.
>
> ■ All kinds of circumstances may prohibit a person from following any single choice.
>
> ■ All of us will change jobs — perhaps as often as 8, 10, or 12 times in the years ahead. And we are likely to change careers 2, 3, or 4 times as well. All of us need to think in terms of alternatives.

We need to teach our daughters and sons to keep their options open — indeed, to open up options. Don't focus their interests too narrowly. The goal is to come up with a list of possibilities, not a single occupation.

Two high school juniors in our Youth and Careers Study had the right idea. One, a truck driver's daughter whose mother does not live in the home, told us:

> *" I would love to be a pediatrician, but I don't know if I could handle the economic and academic pressures of medical school. Also, I feel that doctors have tough lives. Being on call all of the time, and they really have no time to spend with family and friends. I know the money is great, but I think I might be just as satisfied helping people being a nurse."*

And a construction worker's daughter whose mother teaches in a community college told us:

> *" I really would like to be an actress, because I am really good. Yet, when I try to be realistic, I realize that it is hard to compete in that field. Therefore, I am going to major in something else I like, biology."*

How to Think about the Work World

The *Dictionary of Occupational Titles* lists more than 30,000 occupations. How can anybody sort through that many possibilities? It's possible, but you have to go about it in an orderly way. We can't assume that young people are prepared to do that, or that they know the basic categories with which to work. A practical nurse in North Carolina told us about her frustration while in high school:

> *" True, I could have asked a counselor, but at 16 or 17 years old, one does not want to appear a fool by asking for basic information. I would have welcomed a rack of brochures in the girls' restroom."*

I begin this chapter with a brief discussion of how work is central to peoples' lives, how work affects everything we do. Then I clarify basic concepts people sometimes confuse. I offer a way to classify occupations that will help parents and young people when they think and talk about career possibilities. The chapter ends with information that is often very much on the minds of young people: The prospect of becoming a professional athlete.

WORK AND LIFESTYLE

For most people, work requires more time and more effort than any other lifetime activity. If you and I live the proverbial three score years and ten, our lives will add up to some 600,000 hours of time. Our work lives are shorter. If we figure they begin at about age 20 and continue to, say, age 65, our work lives will add up to about 400,000 hours. That's two-thirds of our lives.

We spend about a third of our work lives sleeping. That leaves about 260,000 hours, or 16 hours a day for 45 years. Many of us work 8, 10, or 12 hours a day, two-thirds of the remaining time. For many people, work demands more time, provides greater satisfactions and dissatisfactions, and exerts more wear and tear on physical, mental, and emotional well-being than any other single activity. Work is central to life and lifestyle. A lawyer's son with a college degree in political science now works as manager for a business service in Dallas. He said it this way:

> *"Jobs can have a large influence on your life. One must be prepared to actively pursue a career that will fulfill his needs economically, socially, and still allow him to nurture a solid self-image."*

Work is like the hub at the center of a wheel (see Figure 5-1). Other important aspects of life revolve around it. The following sections show how work relates to five important areas of life and well-being.

Earnings and Benefits

We live in a market economy. People use money to buy life's essentials (food, clothing, shelter, medical services) as well as life's luxuries (entertainment, vacations, cosmetics, and club memberships). Money is the way we exchange the sweat of our brow for life's niceties and necessities.

It takes a steady supply of money to keep individuals and families going, money they can exchange to satisfy their needs and wants and maintain their standard of living. How much families need has been steadily increasing, especially during the past two decades. In 1963, it took a minimum of $82 a month to maintain a family of four. In 1973, it took $149 a month. In 1983, it took $296 a month. And by 1993, it took $575 a month. Costs have been doubling every decade.

Most of us earn those resources in wages or salaries. We take a job. Money is the unit of exchange by which we trade our work for food on our tables, roofs over our heads, and the gadgets with which we play.

Fringe Benefits. Part of that exchange takes the form of fringe benefits — retirement programs, medical and dental programs, life insurance, disability insurance, unemployment compensation, sick leave, vacations, and more. Fringe benefits supplement compensation by a fourth to a third of earnings. That means that for every three or four dollars earned, employers set aside another dollar in benefits for the job holder.

Whether people enjoy fringes depends on whether they work. The unemployed are not only without paycheck, they are also without medical and retirement programs. When

The Work Wheel

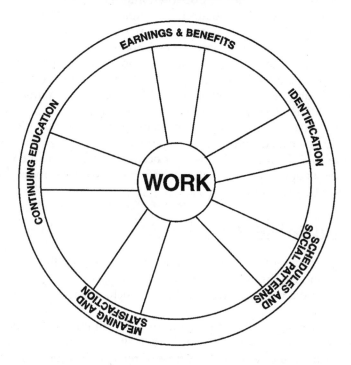

Figure 5-1

catastrophe strikes, the benefits package may be more important to the worker and the worker's family than the earnings. The unemployed are without that safety net.

The amount of fringes workers are entitled to depends on the benefits packages that go with their jobs. How important fringe benefits are is evident from the issues that separate employers and employees in contract negotiations. Listen to the newscasts and follow the newspapers concerning the arguments that forestall contract settlements. Pay hikes and inflationary increments are major considerations, but often the fringe benefits package is the issue. One of the main reasons people work is to acquire the security that comes in the form of earnings and fringe benefits.

Identification

People work to earn a living, but people also work for other reasons. Work tells others who we are. Work identifies us.

Watch and listen as people introduce one another at a party. A host will introduce a couple as "Harry Rouse and his wife, June; Harry is the manager of Piggly Wiggly on East Washington Avenue." A woman introduces herself as "Betty Brandeis; I'm in personnel at

Southern Natural Gas." If a woman does not work, she is likely to say, "I'm Dottie Thomson; my husband is a driver for Middletown International."

Work answers the question, "Who am I?" Occupations tell others that "I am a doctor," "I am a teacher," or "I am a salesperson." If a person has no occupation, that person's status may be ambiguous — which is why Dottie Thomson introduced herself in terms of her husband's occupation. The work a person does and the title associated with the position provide clues. Occupations "place" people in our minds. The labels "doctor" and "judge" give clues about a person's education and income. Occupations and job titles work like signs and signals. They indicate a person's social status.

The point is not that one lifestyle is better than another, but that lifestyles differ. Lifestyles are closely associated with people's occupations, the education levels their occupations require, and the income levels their occupations provide. People identify themselves when they name their occupations, and they give clues about themselves when they name the kind of work they do.

Schedules and Social Patterns

Work dictates how people spend their time and with whom they associate. Work regulates the tempo and rhythm of life. On a day-to-day basis, work schedules dictate when people get up in the morning, when they eat lunch, when they return home, and whether they bring work home in the evening. Work dictates whether they work eight to five, from ten in the evening until six in the morning, or till the job gets done. Work determines whether people are home on weekends, take vacations in the summer or winter, and whether the holiday season is a time of relaxation or busy-busy, push-push activity.

It doesn't stop there. Job requirements spill over into the lives of spouses and families who arrange meals, shopping trips, leisure activities, and holiday weekends around work schedules. More than anything else, work structures people's time. It dictates how people use their time, those 260,000 waking hours of their adult lives.

Associates

Work also determines with whom people associate. People spend more time with others in their own line of work and get to know those people better. What others do on the job affects them, and what they do on the job affects others. Coworkers take each other into account.

Work relationships spill over into friendships and social activities. Coworkers hunt together, bowl together, drink beer and play poker together. Boy meets girl at work. Often work associates live in the same part of town, which means they may attend the same PTA, church, or synagogue. Work associates run into each other at the pet shop. They buy Girl Scout cookies from each other's children. Coworkers meet at the company holiday party, work on committees together, sign the same sympathy cards, pull for the same regional football teams, weep over the same soap operas, and complain about the same ruts in the same city streets.

Work sorts people into groups by regulating their schedules and assigning them common tasks. These associations often extend into off-work hours and shared social activities.

Meaning and Satisfaction

Many people seek purpose and meaning in life from their work. Because work structures the rest of life, it is the main reference point that people take into account when they make other decisions. Can a woman join the Tuesday morning golf club? It depends on her work schedule. Can a man knock off a couple of days and go fishing? It depends on his work load and company policy.

Also, what people think about themselves is tied closely to the work they do. A good job means more than earning good wages. It means doing work that makes a difference, work that is important to the worker and possibly to others.

Studies indicate what people look for in jobs and what gives them satisfaction and dissatisfaction. Particularly among males, jobs are the sources of their greatest likes and dislikes. Studies of marital adjustment indicate that work conditions have a big influence on the husband's marital adjustment. And because the husband's marital adjustment affects the wife's, job satisfaction or dissatisfaction is a big factor in the couple's homelife.

Two sets of job characteristics affect worker satisfaction. Some have to do with working conditions. These include pay, working hours, and supervisory practices. Others have to do with the content of the job: what the person does on the job, responsibilities, and what the end product is. People usually get their satisfactions from what they do on the job, but their dissatisfactions come from working conditions. This means that job dissatisfaction can be reduced by improving such things as pay, work hours, and supervisory practices, but improving working conditions does not necessarily improve worker satisfaction. People get their satisfactions from what they do.

People try to find meaning in their work. What they do and the conditions in which they work affect their attitudes toward other people, their lifestyles, and their quality of life.

Continuing Education

For many people, work is the continuing education department of life. I do not mean on-the-job training programs, but learning experiences that come with the job. These affect workers' mental capacities.

"Substantive complexity" of work refers to the amount of thought and independent judgment work requires. The extent to which work requires workers to think and exercise independent judgment spills over into all areas of life. The more that work requires people to think and make judgments, the more open they are to new experiences, the more independent they become, and the more they think critically in nonwork settings. People who do work that requires thinking and judgment gain confidence in their ability to handle "real world" problems, and they increase their respect for their own capacities. Substantive complexity in work makes people more intellectually flexible.

Even slight differences in the substantive complexity of work early in the career may make large differences in a person's career achievements later in life. Early jobs that require young people to think and make decisions equip them with the intellectual tools and skills to advance to increasingly more complex jobs.

HOW TO THINK ABOUT WORK

Sometimes the words people use are confusing and muddle their own thinking. People may use the same word to mean different things. For example, ask a 17-year-old what a "good" car is, and then brace yourself, because the answer will probably have a lot more to do with twin-turbo engines and mag wheels than monthly car payments, insurance premiums, and gas mileage. "Good" means different things to different people.

The same thing happens when people talk about work. Some use words like "job" and "career" and "work" and "occupation" as though they were the same thing. But a job is not the same as an occupation. A career is not the same as work. Having a job is not the same as having a career.

People think with words and concepts, ideas they share with others. If parents and young people are to think clearly about careers, one place to start is by using key concepts more carefully. This section makes some important distinctions between key words.

Work

What is work? People use the word "work" as if everybody knows what it means and as if everybody means the same thing when they use the word. But consider the following uses:

> *" I have a lot of work to do."*
>
> *" I have to go to work."*
>
> *" My work is interesting."*

"A lot of work to do" refers to the amount of activity and effort that is waiting. "Go to work" implies a place, whether there is a lot of effort waiting to be done there or not. And "interesting work" has to do with what a person does, no matter how much there is to do or where it's done.

Work is a slippery word. It means different things to different people. I use the word "work" to mean expending effort gainfully. I emphasize two points. The first is that work is activity. Work is a verb. Work is doing something. That doesn't mean that people have to get blisters or backaches. Some think that people don't work if they don't flex their biceps, and that people who sit behind a desk "aren't really working." Not so. Work means expending effort. It can be physical, but it can also be mental.

People do many things that involve effort, but that doesn't mean they are working. An infant may wave arms and kick legs excitedly, but that isn't work. Work means expending effort productively. Other people pay for the end product. Work means being gainfully employed. That's the second point.

This definition, that work is expending effort gainfully, helps avoid confusion and arguments. Housewives, for example, expend effort, and they do it productively. But they are not paid. It isn't gainful. Consider also the distinction between work and leisure activity or play. Play is activity engaged in for its own sake. Play is valued for the satisfaction it brings to the person, not for the productivity that others value and are willing to buy.

What is play for one person may be work for another. When my oldest son came home all skinned up, with torn pockets on his blue jeans, he would explain that he was having fun playing tag football. But when Emmitt Smith carries the ball in Texas Stadium on Sunday afternoon, that's work. One does it primarily for personal satisfaction, the other for gain. Work means expending effort gainfully.

Job

When work occurs under a set of arrangements that include payment of wages in exchange for performing regular duties, a person has a job. The notions of work arrangements and regular duties imply a sense of organization and continuity. The arrangements usually include a place where work is done. A person takes a job (work arrangement) in order to work (expend effort gainfully).

Both work and job involve gainful employment. But there is a difference. Work refers to what a person does. Job refers to the set of arrangements or conditions under which wages are paid for productive effort.

Consider an example from my wife's earlier career. Nancy expended effort in three different ways. First, as a mother and housewife she put forth considerable effort around the house. But she wasn't employed to do that and she wasn't paid. It wasn't her job. Second, Nancy was a volunteer library assistant at Columbian Elementary School. She had an assigned set of tasks, and she did them at a particular time and place. But she wasn't employed there. That wasn't her job. Third, Nancy worked in a gift shop called the Candlelighter. She expended effort productively. She followed routines, did her assigned duties, met her responsibilities, and under those arrangements the shop paid her. That was her job.

Having a job means expending effort gainfully under a set of arrangements that pays wages for tasks performed.

Occupations

I work. I seldom sweat from pushing a pencil, dictating a memo, calculating an equation, or writing a chapter. But I expend effort gainfully.

I also have a job. I have students to teach, administrative chores to do, people to supervise, budgets to manage, projects to direct, and manuscripts to write. I do those things in exchange for a salary. I do them in an office. As a matter of fact, I do 95 percent of my work behind the same walnut desk as I sit in the same Herman Miller chair, property code number 766016. That's part of the arrangement. My job is at North Carolina State University.

I also have an occupation. Having an occupation is not the same as doing work or having a job. My occupation is the line of work I do. When my IRS 1040 form asks for my occupation, I write "research sociologist."

Occupations divide the work world into common areas in which people work. Some people, especially young people, don't know how to group occupations. For example, the daughter of a newspaper editor took a bachelor's degree in accounting in Honolulu and now works for a petroleum products wholesaler in Portland. When she thought back to the problems she had had since leaving high school, she said: "I had likes and dislikes, but didn't know how to put them together into available career opportunities."

Occupations group common areas. Teaching is an example. There is a lot of variation within that occupation: Kindergarten teachers and college teachers, music teachers, vocational technical teachers, Sunday-school teachers, teachers who do administration, teachers who do counseling, and the like. All are teachers. Teachers share commonalities in their background and training and in the focus of their activities. And one way or another, they are all involved in the educational enterprise. They are part of the same occupation.

People have occupations, and when they move they take their occupations with them. They apply their line of work in new jobs. My sister in St. Louis is a nurse. She left one hospital and went to work for another. She changed jobs, but she did not change occupations. Jobs stay with employers, but occupations stay with workers.

White-Collar and Blue-Collar Occupations

In the past, people spoke of white-collar and blue-collar occupations. The difference had to do with the extent to which occupations involved working with people and, therefore, with the amount of training or schooling required in the occupation. Because white-collar occupations required better interpersonal skills, white-collar occupations required more education and white-collar workers enjoyed higher social status than blue-collar workers.

But this has changed. As society increasingly moved to a service economy, which requires working with people, and all workers increased their levels of training and education, the former white- and blue-collar distinctions have disappeared. Officially, the Bureau of Labor Statistics no longer makes a distinction between white- and blue-collar, though the concepts still appear occasionally.

When the distinction is made, white-collar traditionally refers to professional and technical workers, managers and administrators, clerical workers, and sales workers. Blue-collar traditionally refers to craft workers, operatives, nonfarm laborers, service workers, and farm workers.

Firms

A firm is the organization for which a person works. Typically, a firm is the place where a person goes to work: Mama's Pizza, Johnny's Cafe, or Southern Gas and Electric. Firms are organizational units. They organize complementary tasks related to production, processing, or marketing and bring people with the necessary skills together to accomplish those tasks. The product may be as intangible as giving psychological advice or as tangible as fabricating steel I-beams. The number of people involved may be as few as one, as is the case with self-employed workers, or as many as hundreds of thousands of workers in multinational corporations. In the latter case, the word "firm" typically refers to the local office of a large corporation. Whatever the size, firms are the organizational structures within which jobs are located. Firms are places of business. They are where people do the work.

Career Lines

People work. They hold jobs that are compatible with their occupations in firms that operate in an industrial sector and division of the economy. People also have careers and follow career lines, two final concepts that are useful to consider.

Career lines are the sequences of jobs people regularly follow. For example, elementary school teachers may change to secondary school teachers and to school administrators over their work histories. That is an example of a string of jobs teachers regularly follow. It's a career line.

There are patterns to people's movements between jobs. They do not change jobs in a helter-skelter way. The changes people make are predictable. There are regularities. Large numbers of people follow the same sequence. It isn't purely a matter of chance. Over time people develop experience, skills, and contacts that open doors to new jobs but close doors on others. Career lines are the job sequences that people typically follow over their work careers.

Career lines are like highway systems that cross the country. Career lines connect jobs like highways connect cities. Some career lines are heavily traveled, like interstate systems. Other career lines have little traffic, like country roads. Some career lines are like roads that go through many intersections where travelers can take different routes — many opportunities to change course. Others go for miles without exits. So, also, with career lines. For example, highly trained neurosurgeons usually don't have many career options. MBAs usually have many.

To press the analogy further, some career lines, like highways, are smooth. Others are bumpy. Some deteriorate over time, get slippery, eventually turn into blind alleys or dead ends (athletes?). Some are more hazardous than others in stormy weather (construction workers and starving artists during recessions?). Just as there are many different kinds of highways people can follow, so there are many different career lines people can follow.

Careers

A *career* is the sequence of jobs that a particular person goes through. A career is the route that one individual follows.

Careers are like motorists who travel the highways. Motorists make choices among routes, and individuals choose among career lines. Motorists can follow different highways to get where they want to go, but their choices are limited to the available road systems. Similarly, consciously or unconsciously, workers choose from career lines that regularly occur in the economy — a fact usually ignored by career counselors, who normally focus on first jobs or next jobs.

This does not mean that all travelers, whether motorists or workers, know where they are going or have maps in front of them. To be sure, many seem to be on a casual Sunday afternoon drive. When the weather looks good — that is, when unemployment is low and earnings are stable — that's an enjoyable way to go. But when travelers' warnings are out, the wind is howling, and a person must travel, that's an especially good time to get started in the right direction, to know where the main roads are, to have a good idea of where you want to go, and to know how you are going to get there. That's true of careers, too.

Industries

The two concepts that are most basic to career planning are occupations and industries. Whereas an occupation is the line of work a person does, an *industry* is the broad field of activity in which the employer is engaged.

Industries indicate what employers do, a second important piece of information about employment possibilities. If a woman says that she works in the petroleum industry, the listener will know the broad area in which her employer operates, namely, the production and distribution of gas and oil. Note, however, that industry does not reveal what the woman does. She may be a chemist, truck driver, office manager, computer programmer, or have any number of other occupations within the petroleum industry. She hasn't identified her occupation. So also, if the woman says that she is an engineer, gives her occupation but not her industry, then the listener knows what she does but is left to wonder in what industry. Is she an engineer in construction? Agriculture? Petroleum?

Knowing both a person's occupation and industry provides maximum information. If the woman says, "I am a chemist for Mobile Oil," the listener would have a pretty good idea what she does. Her occupation, chemist, describes what she does. The industry, oil company, identifies the broad field of activity in which her employer does business.

What would be the next likely question? Probably "Where do you work?" Note that here the question is not about the industry, or about her occupation, but about the firm that employs her. "I work in the western regional office of Sunnyside Oil on Peach Street" gives the firm name and location.

Whereas occupations indicate the line of work a person does, industries indicate the broad field of activity in which the employer is involved. Complete information requires knowing both a person's occupation and industry.

Classification Systems

Young people have problems choosing a career, and helping them sort out the possibilities has been a confusing task in the past. One reason is that the business of classifying occupations and industries has been a terrible mess in our society because the U.S. has not used a uniform occupational classification system. One federal agency would use one system, another would use a different system, researchers would use their systems, and career information books would use still other systems. When parents and young people would go different places to get information — for example, information about occupational descriptions, then employment projections, and finally information on how to prepare for that career — the whole effort would become confusing and frustrating because the systems weren't comparable. Trying to match categories was like trying to fit Ford parts on a Chevy car. Not a good fit.

But take heart. That is changing. In recent years, Congress decided to clean up the mess by developing standard occupational classifications for the entire country. That system is now largely in place and it makes sense for us to use it. The broad occupational groupings I use in this book follow in principle the Standard Occupational Classification (SOC) system that is now used by federal agencies. That means that you should be able to get additional information about occupations if you follow the categories I use in this book. Be forewarned, however, that some commercial publishers of career information are still dragging their feet and reporting information using their old-fashioned categories. If you run into that problem, I suggest you go to a more up-to-date resource.

Occupations and industries are organized into major categories and subcategories, and it is helpful to know what they are. The categories are useful in these ways:

- The categories provide a useful system with which to think about the work world.
- The categories correspond to the way the government and media report on the labor force — for example, unemployment rates.
- Labor force trends and projections are made in terms of the categories.

In the next chapter, I review the employment outlook for the major occupational groups and industry sectors and divisions. We need to learn to think and talk in these categories if we want to use the career information that is available. Once we understand the basic categories, we can limit our information search to the categories that interest us and forget about the rest. It's a time-saver.

Occupational Groups

In our society, there are many, many occupations. For example, the *Dictionary of Occupational Titles*, which is used in the census, organizes more than 30,000 separate occupations into nine primary occupational categories, 82 occupationally specific divisions, and 559 occupational groups. That's a lot of small print to wade through. You need to be able to find the categories that interest you as quickly as possible. The information that follows lists the basic categories for thinking about occupations, the lines of work people do.

Technicians and Related Support Occupations

Workers in this group provide technical assistance to scientists, engineers, and other professionals, and they operate technical equipment. For example, they know how to put information into computers, process the information, get the information out in a usable form, and interpret it. Occupations in this group include computer programmers, health technicians and technologists, paralegals and legal assistants, broadcast technicians, library technicians, science technicians, and others.

Professional Specialty Occupations

People in these occupations perform a wide range of specialized tasks including designing machinery, highways and bridges, shopping centers, calculators, and lawn sprinklers. They do research, figure out how things work, and how to solve problems; they study peoples' attitudes and behaviors; they help people learn, find information, or gain insight about themselves; they prevent, diagnose, and treat illness and disease; they write articles and books, direct films, and entertain. People in professional specialty occupations are engineers, scientists, lawyers, social workers, teachers, doctors, therapists, photographers, announcers, musicians, and many other specialties.

Service Occupations

This group includes a wide range of workers in protective services, food and beverage preparation, health services, and cleaning and personal services. Examples include flight attendants, preschool workers, police officers and firefighters, barbers and cosmetologists, medical and dental assistants, carpet and window cleaners.

Executive, Administrative, and Managerial Occupations

Workers in this group direct the activities of businesses, government agencies, and other organizations. They keep abreast of trends in society that affect their organizations, set directions for their organizations, establish policies, determine staffing requirements, and the like. People in management-support occupations provide technical assistance to managers.

Marketing and Sales Occupations

Workers in this group sell goods and services, purchase commodities and property for resale, and create consumer interest in their products. Occupations include retail sales worker, cashiers, securities and financial service salespeople, real estate agents, and travel agents.

Transportation and Material Moving Occupations

Workers in these occupations operate equipment to move people, material, and other equipment. Examples include bus drivers, aircraft pilots and flight engineers, fork-lift operators, truck drivers, ship pilots, and railroad engineers.

Construction Trades, Extractive Occupations

Workers in these occupations are involved with large projects and structures. They build, maintain, retrofit, remodel, modernize, and otherwise alter buildings, highway systems, dams, and bridges. They operate oil and gas drilling equipment and coal and metal mining equipment. Many operate heavy equipment.

Mechanics, Installers, and Repairers

These workers put in place, set up, and assure that equipment and machinery operates properly. They maintain, adjust, and repair automobiles, home appliances, industrial equipment, computers and other office equipment, tractors, trucks, air conditioners, furnaces, and the like.

Administrative Support Occupations, including Clerical

Workers in these occupations provide the wide variety of administrative tasks necessary to keep organizations functioning smoothly. They prepare memos, letters, and reports; collect accounts; gather and distribute information; operate office equipment including computers, fax and copy machines; do bookkeeping, filing, statistical analysis, and the like. Examples of workers in this group include secretaries, hotel desk clerks, bookkeepers, and word processors.

Handlers, Equipment Cleaners, Helpers, and Laborers

Workers in this group do routine, unskilled tasks that assist skilled workers. For example, they may handle animals, wash semi-trucks, or steam-clean engines. Many work at manual tasks in construction assisting with building and tearing down forms, loading and unloading equipment, gathering and disposing of used material, and doing site cleanup work.

Agriculture, Forestry, and Fishing Occupations

Workers in these occupations cultivate plants, breed and raise animals, harvest forests, and catch fish. They include farm operators and farm workers.

Production Occupations

Workers in these occupations do things that relate to producing goods. They install, adjust, maintain, and operate machinery. They use hand tools and hand-held power tools to make and assemble products. They produce durable goods (for example, furniture and automobiles) and nondurable goods (for example, books, toothpaste, and picnic plates).

These are the major occupational categories used by federal agencies that collect and project occupational employment data. Parents and young people will find it useful to use the same categories to sort out their career interests, seek additional information, and plan ways to prepare for a career.

> **"Occupations are the lines of work people do, and industries are the broad areas of activity in which firms do business."**

Industry Sectors and Divisions

Federal agencies also classify employment in terms of industrial sectors and divisions. Whereas occupations are the lines of work people do, industries are the broad areas of activity in which firms do business. Industry sectors and divisions are the second set of categories that parents and young people can use to think about employment. Industries have been largely ignored by career counselors in the past, though thinking about the industry in which a person wants to work is as important as choosing an occupation.

Why are industries important? And why learn to differentiate among them? The reasons are straightforward:

- Industries provide another increasingly important way to understand today's labor market.
- Some occupations appear in only one or a few industries, whereas other occupations appear in many industries. For example, aircraft mechanics are employed in few industries, but secretaries work in many industries.
- The fortunes of a particular industry are important determinants of the financial stability of firms that employ workers, regardless of their occupations.

Keeping track of every individual industry is impossible — there are thousands of detailed industries — but it is possible to follow the trends that affect major groups of industries. A 30-year-old secretary who has a bachelor's degree in history and works for an engineering and architectural firm in England told me, "If they [young people] want relatively interesting jobs and good salaries, they ought to coolly analyze the job market as you would the stock market before investing." Parents and their sons and daughters need to know how to think and talk about the labor market if they want to make sense out of today's career opportunities. That includes knowing the major industry sectors and divisions.

Industry sectors and divisions, like major occupational groups, provide a convenient shorthand to use in analyzing the job market and in thinking about career possibilities. Industries fall into two major sectors — service-producing and goods-producing industry sectors — and it is useful to keep this basic division in mind because, as the next chapter reveals, employment trends and projections differ greatly for goods-producing and service-producing industries. There are 10 major industry divisions — nine if we combine retail and wholesale trades.

The service-producing and goods-producing industry sectors each consist of several divisions. For example, retail trade is a division within the service-producing sector. Each industry division, in turn, consists of groups of industries. For example, the services division includes: business services; legal services; education services; social services; health services; personal, automotive, and other services. Finally, each group of industries consists of many individual industries. For example, the health services industry includes physicians' offices, dentists' offices, osteopathic physicians' offices, nursing and personal care facilities, hospitals, medical and dental laboratories; and health and allied services that are not classified elsewhere.

For purposes of career planning, we are most interested in the industry sectors and industry divisions. The following descriptions give a more complete picture of the industry divisions.

Service-Producing Industries

There were 127 million people in the U.S. work force in 1992. Three-fourths of those people work in six divisions of the service-producing sector.

Transportation, Communications, and Public Utilities. This is a curious combination of industries that makes sense as a category only if you know a bit of history. These industries are grouped together because, in the past, they provided public services and were owned or regulated by public agencies. The industries provide transportation services: airlines, bus companies, trains, and other forms of public transit; broadcast by radio, television, and satellite; and provide water, electric, sewage, and disposal services.

Transportation companies and warehousing services — such as trucking services, airlines, and railroads — employ more than half the workers in this industry sector. Communications industries employ another fourth, and public utilities employ the remaining fifth of workers. The number of workers totals 5.7 million.

Wholesale Trade. Wholesalers assemble goods in large lots for distribution to retail stores, industrial firms, and institutions such as schools and hospitals. Examples of companies in wholesale trade include petroleum distributors who deliver gasoline to service stations, plumbing suppliers who sell fixtures to home repair stores, and poultry dealers who sell chicken meat to grocery stores. A fourth of all people who work in the trades work in wholesale trades, a total of 6 million people. Most work for distributors.

Retail Trade. Companies in retail trade sell goods in smaller quantities directly to consumers in stores, by mail, and through door-to-door selling. Items sold by wholesale and retail businesses include almost every item produced by manufacturers: automobiles, clothing, food, furniture, toothbrushes, and countless other products. Three-fourths of workers in the trades (19.3 million) work for retail trade businesses. More than two-thirds hold jobs in department stores, food stores, and restaurants.

Finance, Insurance, and Real Estate. Nearly every person and organization uses services provided by this industry division. Financial institutions — banks, savings and loan companies, and consumer-credit organizations — offer services ranging from checking and savings accounts to stock and bond transactions. Insurance companies protect individuals and businesses against loss by fire, accident, sickness, and death. Real estate firms sell and rent buildings and property, and manage large office and apartment buildings. This division employs 6.6 million people. Half work in finance; another third work in insurance; and the remainder hold jobs in real estate.

Services. Services is a subgroup within the service-producing industrial sector. This division is a diverse group of businesses that provide services to people. It includes services in hotels, barber shops, automobile repair shops, business services, laundry and dry cleaning plants, hospitals, computer software firms, and nonprofit organizations. These jobs are located in large corporations and government agencies as well as in one- or two-person firms.

Health services — hospitals, physicians' and dentists' offices, and other medical services such as laboratories and clinics — employ more than a third of the workers in this division. Business services — including advertising and employment agencies, auto repair services, and computer software firms — employ about one out of every six workers.

Government. Government includes such diverse areas as postal services, park and forest services, police and fire protection, social security and public welfare services, and judicial and legislative activities. It does not include public education and health services. Government employees work in large cities, small towns, and in such remote and isolated places as lighthouses and forest ranger stations. A small number of federal employees work overseas. State and local governments — county, city, township, or school districts — employ five out of six government workers. The remainder work for the federal government.

Goods-Producing Industries

Employment in goods-producing industries peaked at 28 million in the late 1970s, then suffered losses of 3 million in the recessions of the 1980s. Today, 24.8 million people, a fourth of all workers, are employed in goods-producing industries.

Agriculture, Forestry, and Fishing. For decades, agriculture meant agricultural production or farming. But today the word encompasses more than farm production. Farms, plant nurseries, cattle feed lots, chicken hatcheries, crop spraying, horticultural services, commercial fishing, and forestry are all examples of agricultural industries. Four of five workers in the agriculture industry work with livestock, livestock products, or agricultural products. Only 1 out of 50 works in commercial fishing and forestry.

Mining. Mining and petroleum industries provide the raw materials and energy sources for industrial and consumer use. Metal mines produce iron, copper, gold, and other ores. Quarrying and nonmetallic mining yields basic materials such as limestone and gravel that are used in school, office, home, and highway construction. Nearly all of the nation's energy for industrial and home use comes from oil, gas, and coal.

Half of all workers in this division work in the exploration, removal, and processing of crude petroleum and natural gas. Coal mining accounts for two-fifths of the industry's workers.

Construction. This division employs 4.5 million workers and divides into three broad categories. General building contractors build houses, apartment buildings, industrial plants, and office buildings. Heavy construction contractors work on large projects such as bridges, dams, missile facilities, radio and television towers, highways, sewers, and swimming pools.

Special trade contractors specialize in one aspect of construction such as excavating, air conditioning, dry walling, roofing, or plumbing and heating. Special trade contractors employ more than half of all workers in construction industries. General building contractors employ over a fourth, and the remaining work for heavy construction contractors.

Manufacturing. Almost everything we use for work, leisure, and even sleep is manufactured. Factories produce goods that range in complexity from simple toys to intricate computers, and in size from miniature electronic components to gigantic aircraft carriers. Manufacturing industries are diverse and employ workers who process foods and chemicals, print books and newspapers, spin and weave textiles, make clothing and shoes, and produce thousands of products needed for our personal and national welfare. Manufacturing employs 18 million workers.

There are two broad categories of manufacturing: durable goods and nondurable goods. Three-fifths of manufacturing employees work in plants that produce durable goods such as steel, machinery, automobiles, and household appliances. The rest produce nondurable goods, including processed food, clothing, and chemicals.

The next chapter projects employment in major occupation groups and industries. A key point we will make is that occupations and industries that grow the fastest seldom offer the most employment opportunities. That is because the number of persons employed is so small.

Nowhere are career prospects more appealing but the probabilities more evasive than a career as a professional athlete. Professional athletics is a stark reminder that it isn't enough for young people to know what they want to do; they are also well-advised to take the opportunity structure into account. Before turning to employment projections for occupations and industries, let's examine the probabilities of a young person becoming a professional athlete, something many young people dream about.

PRO ATHLETES

In a nationally televised "MacNeil/Lehrer News Hour" broadcast, a reporter asked a number of young athletes what they thought their chances were of making it to the pros. Virtually all thought that their chances were pretty good. Even the most modest youngster thought he had at least a 50/50 chance of making it to the National Basketball Association.

But what are the real odds of a youngster making it to the pros? More like 1 in 20,000 — far, far less than 50/50! And the chances of achieving superstar status are about 1 in 500,000.

Probably most young people who have ever thrown, caught, bounced, kicked, or hit a ball have entertained a passing fantasy of doing it for a living. It's an exciting prospect: fan applause, the good life, and, of course, big bucks. Television fuels the fantasy. The grand slams, the slam dunks, the hail Marys, the pressure putts are played and replayed to the adulation of thousands of fans and millions of home viewers. The color and pageantry and action are well-suited to the camera, and visits to the White House have exalted championships to the status of national events. Games blur into real life before our very eyes.

Unfortunately, the cameras in the Goodyear blimp capture only selected parts of the bigger picture. The film isn't rolling during grueling workouts. On game day, the lenses stay focused at a tasteful distance so that not too much blood shows on the tube. Microphones are kept just out of reach of the trash talk. Producers' good taste and sponsors' commercials shield the viewer from seeing real hurt and real pain. Only an occasional spasmodic kick from a pummeled body authenticates the small talk from the booths, that's "its really war down there in the trenches."

When the hype is set aside, the prospects of a career as a professional athlete are illusory — except for the few. The question I pose in this section is: "What do you say to and what do you do about the young person who dreams of becoming a professional athlete?" Before answering, let's look at some realities.

What Are the Odds?

State high school associations together with the National Federation of State High School Associations administer more than 30 competitive sports programs in high schools. Most athletes, of course, are young men; and most of the young men participate in one of three sports: football, basketball, or baseball. In any given year, about

- 1,000,000 young men play high school football
- 500,000 play high school basketball
- 400,000 play high school baseball

Roughly, one of four young men participates in sports in high school — that is, at least gives it a try.

By the time a young person reaches college, the numbers of participants decline dramatically. In any given year, about 110,000 collegiates play football, basketball, and baseball. That means that only 1 of every 80 or 90 young men and 1 of every 17 or 18 high school athletes plays college ball. Only one or two players on a typical high school team ever play college ball.

Only 5 or 6 percent of high school athletes make it to college teams — roughly 1 percent of all young men. Of those who do play college ball, only about 8 percent are drafted by professional teams. Only about 1 percent of young men who play on high school teams are drafted by the pros. What are the chances of a young man in high school ever being drafted? About 1/5th or 1/6th of one percent — something like .002 percent.

But even being drafted is a long way from the popular image of being a pro. Of those who are drafted, only 2 percent ever sign a professional contract. At this point, the odds are down to about 2 of every 10,000 high school athletes ever signing a professional contract. About 1 percent of college football players ever make it to the National Football League.

To put it all in perspective, the chances of a high school student being a professional football, basketball, or baseball player are about 1 in 20,000. The chances of a high school athlete ever becoming a pro are about 1 in 5,000.

One last sobering reflection. The average pro career lasts four years.

Recruitment of New Players: Team Sports

Television displays an endless menu of athletic events. Most of the events, incidentally, are amateur sports. The players don't make a living at it.

In fact, very few athletes ever make a living at such individual sports as track, swimming, gymnastics, bowling, boxing, tennis, rodeo, horse racing, automobile racing, or golf — the individual sports. Most pros make the pros in team sports: football, basketball, baseball, and hockey. A few make it in golf and tennis.

Each sport has its own system for making it to the pros. For those so inclined, these are the systems and the prospects, major sport by major sport.

Baseball

There are 26 professional baseball teams and 725 players on major league rosters. Players enter professional baseball either through the college draft or as free agents in tryouts.

The major league draft takes place in June. To be eligible, a player must be 18 years old or have completed high school. If a person enters a 4-year college, he is eligible for the baseball draft after his junior year or when he is 21 years old.

The number of players drafted each year depends on how many good players are considered prospects by major league teams. Drafting takes place by rounds, and a round consists of each of the 26 major league teams having a chance to choose a player, after which the next round begins. Usually, there are between 25 and 50 rounds. Players drafted in the first 10 rounds have the best chance of making it in pro baseball.

But "making it" means making it to the minor leagues. There are some exceptions, but very rarely does a player bypass the minors and go straight to the majors — not even Michael Jordan. They aren't ready. They haven't learned the necessary skills.

The minors are the proving grounds for aspiring professional baseball players. There are 164 minor-league teams with about 25 players on each team for a total of about 4,000 minor league players. Virtually every player drafted will spend a few years in the minor leagues, and that will be the extent of the professional baseball career for most of them.

Basketball

The National Basketball Association (NBA) has 23 teams, each with a 12-person roster, for a total of 276 professional basketball players. As with baseball, players enter the pro ranks through the college draft or as free agents. Most players eligible for the draft have completed their college eligibility and are seniors, though hardship provisions allow a player to declare his eligibility earlier. Chris Weber of the Michigan Wolverines was a recent example.

Every year teams from the National Basketball Association draft 161 players. About a third — say, 55 players — make the teams. By midseason the number is down to about a fourth, 40 to 45.

Although the National Basketball Association has no formal minor league, the Continental Basketball Association and the European teams function somewhat as minor leagues.

These teams provide playing time and experience for the few who want another chance at the NBA. Most players give themselves two or three years to prove themselves and be picked up by the NBA, whereafter most then call it quits and get on with their lives.

Football

The National Football League (NFL) fields 28 professional teams. Each team has a roster of 45 players for a league total of 1,260. Professional football teams use the draft and tryout camps to recruit players. A draft is held each spring for college players who have completed their collegiate eligibility.

About 15,000 players are eligible for the draft each year. Each of the 28 teams is allowed to choose 12 players for a total of 336 drafted players. About two-thirds of the players come to the pros through the draft. Another third enter through tryout camps. In a typical year, about 1 out of every 100 eligible college players makes it to a professional team's rookie list.

Hockey

There are 21 professional National Hockey League (NHL) teams. Each carries a roster of 24 players for a total of 504. Players enter the league either through the draft or as free agents. The draft is held each June. Eligible players must be 18 years old or have completed high school.

The draft continues for 12 rounds during which the teams choose 252 players. About 85 percent of players enter the league through the draft. Another 15 percent make their way as free agents through tryouts. About half who make the draft come from the Canadian Junior Leagues, about a fourth from U.S. colleges and high schools, and the remainder come from international hockey leagues.

Only about a fourth of those drafted make the National Hockey League roster during their first year. Most play for a few years in the minor leagues, the American Hockey League, or the International Hockey League, to refine their skills. They usually sign three-year contracts with minor league teams during which they hope to make it to the NHL, though the odds are against it.

Recruitment of New Players: Individual Sports

Individual sports such as golf and tennis are usually governed by associations that manage competition and establish rules of eligibility. An athlete's ability is, of course, the key determinant of professional status because individual sports have neither drafts nor tryout camps. Each sport establishes its own rules of eligibility.

Golf

Professional golf is governed by the Professional Golf Association (PGA) and the Ladies' Professional Golf Association (LPGA). Only about 350 men regularly compete on the PGA tour, and about 270 women compete on the LPGA tour.

The PGA and LPGA use basically the same procedures to certify players who are eligible to compete on the tour. There are 9,000 members of the PGA, but a player must have a Tournament Player's Card to compete on the PGA Tour. The Card may be earned in one of two ways. A player can be among the top finishers in the annual PGA Tour Qualifying Tournament, or a player may earn an amount of money from nontour tournaments equal to the amount of money earned by the 150th ranked winner of the previous year.

Players who have earned a Tournament Player's Card must still qualify to compete. Players who have won previous specified tournament victories or are ranked on the tour are exempt from the requirement that they qualify in competition in a qualifying round held the Monday before a tournament. Only a limited number "make the cut" and qualify for a particular tournament.

Tennis

Unlike most sports, there is no minimum age requirement that must be met to be eligible to compete in professional tennis. Ability, not birthday, is the deciding factor, and that explains why there are some very young players in the Association of Tennis Players (ATP) and the Women's Tennis Association (WTA).

Men's tournaments are governed by the ATP, which lists a membership of about 1,100 players from around the world but primarily from the United States. The ATP ranks players. About a third of the ranked players play the circuit full-time. The governing body of women's professional tennis is the WTA. About 400 players regularly play its tour.

A player's ranking is based on the player's earnings and the tournaments in which the player competes. There are about 300 tournaments used in the ATP rankings. To be eligible for associate membership in the WPA, a player must either have earned $500 in one of the past two years or, if the player is an amateur, must have earned $500 in sanctioned tournaments. Full membership requires that a player have earned $15,000 in competitive tennis in one of the last two years or is ranked among the top 100 players by the WTA.

Bowling

Requirements for becoming a professional bowler are established by the Professional Bowlers' Association of America (PBA). To qualify for professional status, a bowler must be 18 years old or be a graduate from high school and must post an average score of 190 for two consecutive years of league play. The PBA has a membership of nearly 3,000 and includes about 150 classified touring pros. Touring pro status makes a bowler eligible for regular competition on the PBA and National Tour.

Boxing

Professional boxing is an international sport and a sanctioned Olympic sport, but it is legal in only 17 states of the United States. Each state establishes its own requirements for becoming a professional boxer.

There is no set career path or rules of eligibility for becoming a professional boxer. Normally, a boxer works his way through the amateur ranks, which probably begins at a local club and progresses to the Golden Gloves competition. A fighter who shows promise may be recruited by a professional boxing trainer or manager who helps him develop his skills to become a pro.

Worldwide, as many as 20,000 boxers fight in any given year. Most fight once and quit. *Ring* magazine is generally recognized as the authoritative magazine for the sport and ranks the top 10 fighters in each of 15 weight classes.

Fewer than half of the ranked fighters in each weight division make a decent living at fighting. Even a good fighter is lucky to make an average workman's wage in a year in the ring. The Mike Tyson and Sugar Ray Leonard multimillion dollar paydays are truly the exception.

Automobile Racing

There are several kinds of automobile races and race cars, and several organizations regulate automobile racing. The International Motor Sports Association (IMSA), for example, sanctions races around the world. It licenses about 2,000 drivers, including most of the top-ranked drivers in the U.S.

Most racing associations require that all drivers attend a professional driving school. Nearly all successful drivers are members of a racing team that has a corporate sponsor. Racing is good advertising for major corporations. It gives them TV time. It takes a major corporation to finance operations for a car on the track. Probably no more than 20 percent of the membership of IMSA make a living from automobile racing.

Racing is one of the most difficult sports to enter. Most drivers of Indy cars, for example, have worked their way up from go-carts through dirt tracks and formula cars. Financial backing is a must, and many racing families have been able to keep the sponsorship in the family or to use their networks to gain it. The Allisons, Andrettis, Unsers, and Yarboroughs are examples.

Horse Racing

People who aspire to be jockeys usually go through various stages, from groom to walker, walker to exercise boy, exercise boy to apprentice jockey, and apprentice jockey to jockey. About 3,000 jockeys ride each year.

Horse racing is probably the most regulated of all sports, and each position, from groom to jockey, requires a license.

There is a practical physical requirement for jockeys. In no other sport is weight so important, and 120 pounds is about the absolute upper limit to what a competitive jockey can weigh. Most jockeys weigh between 110 and 115 pounds.

Rodeo

There are more than 600 rodeos around the country each year that are authorized by the Professional Rodeo Cowboys' Association (PRCA). The PRCA lists more than 5,000 members, but fewer than 200 follow the rodeo circuit full-time. Few if any riders make a living at the sport.

The requirements for being a professional rider are simple: The rider must purchase a permit that allows him to compete, and then the rider must win at least $2,500 in a one-year period.

Money in Sports

Not only are young people prone to grossly overestimating their chances of becoming a professional athlete, they also seriously overestimate the lifestyles that most professional athletes maintain. Of course, this misconception is also part of the media myth. Larry Bird signed a highly publicized contract for $6 million after spending most of the previous year on the Celtics' disabled list. Magic Johnson signed for $14.6 million and didn't play the season. And Glenn Robinson, the current year's top draft pick in the NBA, recently signed for $68 million over ten years as a college junior and before ever playing a professional game. Sounds like easy money. But how many Larry Birds, Magic Johnsons, and Glenn Robinsons are there? Only one of each.

In reality, professional sports is a two- or three-tier system with huge salary gaps between the tiers. No more than 5 percent of the pros are in the top tier, and they are the players who have beaten two sets of odds. They are truly the superstars and, like other superstars, they have survived far longer than the average player. Such athletes are very few and far between.

But it is also true that average pro salaries have increased enormously, particularly since 1980. According to *Forbes* magazine, the average annual salary for Major League Baseball players increased from $144,000 to over $1 million; National Football League salaries climbed from $79,000 to $737,000; and National Basketball Association players' salaries climbed from $180,000 to $1.4 million.

Yet when you combine the two pieces of information — the average length of playing careers and average salaries — an average NFL player, for example, will have earned about $3 million over his gridiron career. Taxes will have reduced the amount by 40 percent to, say, $1.8 million. After living the good life for 4.5 years and paying agents, lawyers, accountants, and advisers, the nest egg may dwindle to $1 million — nice, but not a lifetime of affluence.

All the while, the specter of financial loss looms large. The Bo Jackson story is all too familiar. After just four years, he was badly hurt in football, spent two years recuperating, which included a hip replacement, and then returned to baseball. But the endorsements — which is where the big money is for most athletes — have all but vanished. Forty-three percent of the 40 top-earning athletes on *Forbes'* 1993 list, including 5 of the top 10, were not on the 1994 list. Bad money management is another all-too-common story. Mickey Mantle, Joe Louis, and Kareem Abdul-Jabbar squandered their fortunes.

This is not to deny the huge career success stories. Alan Page, former Hall of Fame defensive lineman for the Minnesota Vikings, earned a law degree in the off season while playing football, became assistant attorney general of Minnesota, and now sits as an associate justice of the Minnesota Supreme Court. Jack Kemp, U.S. Senator and presidential hopeful, was a pro quarterback. And there are the Renaldo Turnbulls, the 28-year-old, 245-pound linebacker who is pursuing his MBA at Tulane and working on his brokerage license while playing for the New Orleans Saints. But these are the exceptions.

Most professional athletes never make it that big to start with. Remember, there are only 1,260 players in the NFL, 725 in major league baseball, and 276 players in the NBA. Most pros are in the minor leagues, and minor league salaries are much, much less than those in the majors. Example: Michael Jordan, the basketball superstar for the Chicago Bulls, earned $1,200 per month playing baseball — less than $10,000 for the entire year — playing for the Birmingham Barons. Minor league football and basketball pay even less — low-grade typists' salaries!

Earnings in individual sports are less. For team athletes, expenses like room, board, and transportation are covered while on the road, but pros in individual sports have to pay as they go. It costs a pro tennis player or golfer at least $2,500 to compete in an event — that's for a week on the road with associated costs. In addition, athletes in individual sports have to cover their own workout costs, equipment costs, insurance premiums, and the like.

Length of a Career

The odds of making it to the pros are pretty slim, as is the pay for most pros. More-over, a pro career is pretty short. The average length of a career ranges from 3.5 years in the National Football League to 5.5 years in the National Hockey League. Even the gifted athlete who makes it to the pros is likely to be out of sports in 4.5 years.

Competition for positions is intense. It never ends. In a television interview at the peak of his career, Mike Tyson observed, "Somewhere out there is a little boy who will someday beat me." There is always a younger athlete out there waiting for the big chance to take the position.

That means that being a professional athlete is a year-round job. It means being in the training room every day, off-season as well as in-season. There is not a lot of time off. It's a full-time job.

Another consideration: The injury rate in the National Football League is 100 percent. Every player receives at least one injury every season, and any one of those injuries can end a career. Troy Aikman, star quarterback for the Dallas Cowboys, recently returned from the injury list and, on "Monday Night Football," was asked how many more years he thought he would play. He answered that he hoped he could play another eight or nine, but then, in a quiet moment of reflection, added that injuries would probably end his career earlier.

Advertising Contracts

There is yet another myth about professional athletes: namely, that pro athletes make a lot of money from advertisements. Some do. But, as with pro salaries, most don't.

The big names earn huge endorsements, but notice how the ratio of money from endorsements to earnings quickly drops even among *Forbes'* 1994 40-top earning athletes.

The 15 top-earning athletes averaged $8.17 million in endorsements, but the last 5 in the 40 top-earning athletes averaged $1.38 million.

Golf Digest featured an article titled "Exclusive: How Much the Pros Really Make" a year or two ago. At that time, the big three in off-course income endorsements and

FORBES' 1994 40-TOP EARNING ATHLETES

Athlete	Sport	Millions Earned		
		Salary/ Winnings	Endorsements	Total
1. Michael Jordan	Minor league baseball	.01	30.0	30.01
2. Shaquille O'Neal	Basketball	4.2	12.5	16.7
3. Jack Nicklaus	Golf	.3	14.5	14.8
4. Arnold Palmer	Golf	.1	13.5	13.6
5. Gerhard Berger	Auto racing	12.0	1.5	13.5
6. Wayne Gretzky	Hickey	9.0	4.5	13.5
7. Michael Moore	Boxing	12.0	.1	12.1
8. Evander Holyfield	Boxing	10.0	2.0	12.0
9. Andre Agassi	Tennis	1.9	9.5	11.4
10. Nigel Mansell	Auto racing	9.3	2.0	11.3
11. Pete Sampras	Tennis	3.6	7.0	10.6
12. Joe Montana	Football	3.3	7.0	10.3
13. Charles Barkley	Basketball	3.3	6.0	9.3
14. Greg Norman	Golf	1.3	7.5	8.8
15. George Foreman	Boxing	3.5	5.0	8.5
36. Parnell Whitaker	Boxing	5.2	0.0	5.2
37. Will Clark	Baseball	4.9	.3	5.2
38. Deion Sanders	Football, baseball	3.3	1.6	4.9
39. Gabriela Sabatini	Tennis	0.9	4.0	4.9
40. Al Unser, Jr.	Auto racing	3.8	1.0	4.8

appearance money were Arnold Palmer, $9 million; Greg Norman, $8 million; and Jack Nicklaus, $7 million. By the time you got to Ben Crenshaw, no slouch on the tour, the endorsement money was down to $600,000. My guess is that it drops even more precipitously thereafter.

"I Want to Be a Pro"

The odds are strongly against anyone making it to the pros. Those who do make it are in the minors, have very short careers, and are not paid well. About 5 percent, one in a half million youngsters, are the fortunate few that make it "big time."

So, what do you say to the youngster with stars in his eyes? I suggest the following. First, there are useful experiences and lessons to be learned from sports, especially team sports. Why throw a wet blanket on youthful dreams and experiences? Second, notice that most young people sort things out for themselves with a little help from teammates, coaches, and opposition teams. Sitting on the bench or being an average player on an average team is a message that they aren't pro material, and nobody has to tell them. Most youngsters weed themselves out. Third, I would not, however, let a young person delude himself or herself with the notion that his or her chances of making it to the pros are something like 50/50. Truth be known, if you calculate the chances for all pros, including pros already on the rosters, of making it the next year, I would guess that not even their average chance is 50/50. Young people, even the most gifted athletes, need to understand that the prospect of making it to the pros is a long shot.

That brings me to the most important point. Although I wouldn't discourage a young person from thinking about a pro career, I would urge budding young athletes to have a contingency plan, something they can fall back on. It is possible to pursue two career-preparation tracks at the same time. The close association between colleges and sports makes that easier. It's also easier to talk young people into having a contingency plan than it is to talk them out of something they want so badly. One possibility is a career in an occupation closely associated with sports that services sports and athletics: from physical education to coaching Babe Ruth League or managing the big leagues, from sports medicine to sports officiating, from being a sports journalist to owning/managing a sporting goods store. These occupations outnumber the opportunities for being a pro athlete many, many times. There are books on these opportunities. Check the careers section in your bookstore.

In sum, don't deprive them of their dreams. But do help them find something they can fall back on. Chances are, they're going to need it.

Tomorrow's Jobs

In 1909, Frank Parsons wrote a book entitled *Choosing A Vocation.* In the book, Parsons advised career counselors to encourage young people to follow three steps when choosing a career:

- First, develop a clear understanding of yourself: your interests, abilities, aptitudes, resources, limitations, and other qualities.
- Second, learn about different lines of work: what is required for success, advantages and disadvantages of each line of work; levels of compensation; opportunities and prospects.
- And, third, follow "true reasoning" to match your individual traits with occupational characteristics.

Parson's three-step approach may have been adequate at the turn of the century — back when nearly everybody worked in agriculture, the Ford Motor Company was not yet a gleam in Henry's eye, and words like "ballpoint pen," "microwave oven," "satellite communication," "computer," and the "information highway" never entered conversations. But it isn't enough for today's young people to merely match their individual traits with occupational characteristics, and young people sense that. A personnel and labor relations worker with a college major in sociology told us: "I guess as far as jobs and careers go, I have a very limited knowledge of the labor market, what jobs are available, types of work, and who employs these people."

Society is changing, and the pace of change is quickening. Young people choosing careers have an advantage if they know where the labor market is headed. That's what this chapter is about.

Knowing a young person's interests and abilities gives parents some cues about what might interest a daughter or son and what they might like to do. But social, political, economic, and technological developments determine where the job opportunities are, and that's important, too. An accountant for an electric utility company put it this way: "Jobs, opportunities, and standards of living are based on the economics of supply and demand, not merely on the years spent in educational institutions."

Change seldom springs upon us unannounced. Rather, the forces that shape the supply and demand for workers develop over a period of years. For example, the decline in employment in agriculture isn't something new. It's been going on for nearly 100 years at a rate of decline of about 1 percent per year. As in the past, employment opportunities in the years ahead will be driven by social, political, population, and labor force changes. These include domestic concerns about crime and health care, the aging of the population coupled with an anticipated spurt in the birth rate, and continuing technological innovation and change. Identifying areas of employment opportunity and decline isn't just a guessing game. The labor force leaves footprints, trends that show us the direction from which things have come. That makes it possible to take labor force trends into account when choosing a career. Knowing the trends improves the probability of making a good fit. A lawyer's daughter who works as a teacher's aid in Oregon told us:

> *"A young person's interests and abilities give you clues as to career possibilities."*

> *" I happened to prepare for a field that had a saturated market by the time I was ready for employment [education], and in retrospect I wish I had understood this and had proper counseling. It might have been avoided."*

Employment projections are available. And they have become increasingly accurate. But parents and young people have to know what the projections are, where to find them, and how to use them. In this chapter, I review the latest employment projections. After a brief section on labor force projections, you will find two major sections — the first on industry employment and the second on occupational employment. You may choose to read these sections selectively. The chapter closes with a section on detailed occupations, which includes listings of the fastest and largest employment growth occupations.

LABOR FORCE PROJECTIONS

The Bureau of Labor Statistics has developed labor force information for nearly 50 years — that's its business — and, in recent years, the Bureau has released revised projections every two years. The projections usually cover a 10- to 15-year period. The most recent projections cover 13 years and extend from 1992 to 2005.

The Bureau uses a series of complex models to develop the projections. The models take into account more than 200 variables and the projections cover about 300 industries and 500 occupations — not a trivial undertaking. The Bureau makes different sets of assumptions about factors that influence the economy and, given different assumptions, the Bureau customarily issues three different sets of employment projections: low-, moderate-, and high-growth scenarios.

These are some of the key assumptions the Bureau made in formulating its most recent projections:

- The federal deficit will be brought under control.
- Foreign trade will be brought into balance.
- The unemployment rate will drop to about 5.5 percent
- Growth in productivity will be higher than over the past decade.
- Growth in health care expenditures will slow, but health care will continue to consume significant resources and account for considerable employment growth.
- The political changes that occurred in Eastern Europe in the late 1980s will lower defense expenditures, and the Armed Forces will shrink to its smallest size since 1945.

As an example of how the different sets of assumptions bear on projections, projected employment in 2005 for the low-growth model is 147 million workers, whereas projected employment for the high-growth model is 156 million — 6 percent higher. But a 6 percent difference in projections over 13 years isn't all that bad. And if you follow the moderate or middle-range projections for career planning purposes, as I do, you won't be off very much even if the labor force grows very fast or very slowly. The moderate-growth projection is that the labor force will grow to 148 million workers by 2005.

Someone once said that hindsight is always 20/20 vision. Unfortunately, foresight can never make that claim. Nobody knows for sure what the employment situation will look like in the future, but the Bureau's projections are respected as a reliable guide by policy makers, industry, educators, and career counselors.

Understanding Projections

Projections are usually more meaningful when compared to the present and the past. For example, to suggest that the labor force will grow by 19 percent and increase by 24 million — which is the moderate-growth projection — may sound "fast" or "much" to some but "slow" or "little" to others. But to point out that the increase is slightly more or that the growth rate is slightly less than the past 13 years puts it in clearer perspective. For that reason, I will compare the Bureau's projections for the years 1992 to 2005 with growth for the previous 13-year period, 1979 to 1992, and, where instructive, with the earlier 13-year period, 1966 to 1979, which differed greatly from 1979 to 1992.

Note: In the pages that follow, I repeatedly say that "the labor force will grow" — or something to that effect. But "will" is a pretty strong word. You know that, and I know that, too. Let's both understand, then, that what I mean is that the labor force "*probably* will grow," or "is *expected* to grow." I use the word "will" as shorthand. I don't want to bore you to tears by constantly saying that "the Bureau of Labor Statistics projects" — even though that's what I mean.

Some projections are virtual certainties. For example, when I say that "the baby-boomers . . . were 46 years old or younger in 1992, but their ages will range from 41 to 59 in 2005," which I do say later on, that's as certain as saying that the sun will rise tomorrow morning and that it will rise in the east. It is always possible, of course, that some wayward black hole out there in the galaxy may decide to gobble up the sun tonight — or gobble up all baby-boomers by daybreak, perish the thought! But, trust me: The chances are very, very good both that the sun will rise in the morning and that the baby-boomers' ages will range from 41 to 59 in 2005 — and that there's no gobbler black hole lurking out there.

Other times the probabilities may be a little more iffy. For example, when I say that women "will constitute 48 percent of the labor force by the year 2005," that's a little less certain — but not much — because that prediction gets into areas of behavior based on beliefs and values. Nonetheless, that prediction, too, is highly probable because the trend is well-established. Understand, then, that in the interest of keeping it simple, I will be guilty of a bit of overstatement in the pages ahead. Occasionally, I will refer to projections — a reminder to us both to keep our feet on the ground.

Employment will increase more during the 1992 to 2005 period than it did during the previous 13 years. Total employment was 121.1 million workers in 1992, and will grow to 147.5 million by 2005, an increase of 26.4 million jobs. These jobs will not be distributed evenly across major industrial sectors and occupational groups. Thus, not only the size but also the occupation and industry composition of the labor force will be different in 2005 than it is today.

I review the projected employment changes in industrial sectors and major occupational groups in the following sections. This is the kind of information that young people want, like this waitress in a hotel who wanted to be an artist or an art teacher; "What I needed and did not get from high school was a clear overview of the employment situation."

Technical note: I follow the conventions of reviewing industries in terms of wage and salary employment, except that agriculture, forestry, and fishing include self-employment and unpaid family workers. I review occupations in terms of total employment — that is, wage and salary, self-employed, and unpaid family workers. Throughout the chapter, "jobs" refers to nonfarm wage and salary jobs.

INDUSTRY EMPLOYMENT

Now 26.4 million jobs added over the next 13 years is a bunch, and it will boost industrial employment by 22 percent. This compares with 19.8 million jobs added over the past 13 years, which raised employment by 19 percent. The average annual growth of employment over the 1979 to 1992 period was 1.4 percent. Employment will grow slightly faster, 1.5 percent per year, through 2005.

Several factors will contribute to industrial employment growth. These include the aging of the population, a tighter labor supply, a continuing decline in defense spending, growth in business investments in equipment, increased personal consumption, lower unemployment, and a gradual decline in the exchange rate for the U.S. dollar accompanying improvements in U.S. exports. All of these will affect industry employment generally, but some factors will affect specific industries, particularly.

The long-term shift from goods-producing to service-producing employment will continue, as Figure 6-1 shows. Almost all new jobs will be in the service-producing sector, 24.5 million of the 26.4 million new jobs. The service-producing industries include transportation, communications, and utilities; retail and wholesale trades; services; government; and finance, insurance, and real estate. These industries alone will account for 93 percent of all employment growth and for 25 percent more new jobs than were created during the past 13 years.

Projected Industrial Growth

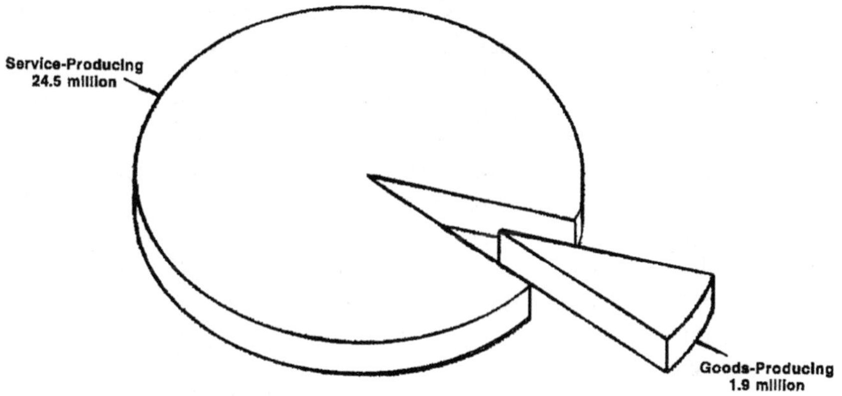

Service-Producing
24.5 million

Goods-Producing
1.9 million

Figure 6-1 *Source: Bureau of Labor Statistics*

Goods-producing industries include manufacturing; construction; agriculture, forestry, and fishing; and mining. There were 26.5 million jobs in goods-producing industries in 1979. Employment dropped to 23 million in 1992, but will increase to 23.7 million by 2005 as the long-term decline in manufacturing jobs slows and employment in construction industries rises.

Service-Producing Industries

Employment will continue to grow in all of the service-producing industry divisions, but two divisions, services and retail trade, will account for four-fifths of the growth.

Services Division

Within the service-producing sector, the services industry is both the largest and the fastest growing division. Of the 25.1 million jobs that will be added to the service sector by the year 2005, more than half, 13.4 million, will be added in the services division.

The services division contains 15 of the 20 fastest growing industries. In 1979, 19 percent of all jobs were in the services division; by 1992, 26 percent were in services; and by 2005, 31 percent will be in the services division. Services accounted for 17 million jobs in 1979, 28 million jobs in 1992, and employment will rise to 42 million by 2005, a 47 percent increase. Services is the only industry division in which employment will grow significantly faster than the average growth of all industries. The services division, alone, will account for half of all new jobs. That's "big time!"

> *"The services division contains 15 of the 20 fastest growing industries."*

Of the many industries in the services division, more than half the increase in employment will occur in health and business service industries. Employment in health services will increase by 4.2 million and account for 17 percent of total job growth. Demand will be prompted by new medical technologies that permit intervention for conditions that previously could not be diagnosed or treated. Demand will also be generated by the aging of the population because requirements for health care increase with age.

Two population changes will put proportionately more of the population in the older age groups. First, the aging of the baby boom will contribute most. As the baby-boomers age, the demands for health care will increase. Individuals who are now ages 32 to 51 will fall in the 45- to 64-year-old group in 2005. In 1990, persons ages 45 to 64 represented 19 percent of the population, but their numbers will increase by a third by the year 2005, when they will account for 25 percent of the population. The second population change is increasing life spans, which further increase the share of the population that is old and very old and in need of increased health care. Note how the number of days of hospitalization per 1,000 population vary by age.

Age	Hospital Days per 1,000 Persons in 1991
15 years old	218
15 to 44 years old	462
45 to 64 years old	859
65 to 74 years old	2131
75 years old and over	4007

Source: U.S. National Center for Health Statistics, Vital Health Statistics, Series 13

Strong growth will also occur in social, legal, engineering, and management services. Employment in social services increased at an annual rate of 4.7 percent during the 1979 to 1992 period, well above average, but employment will increase at an annual rate of 5 percent through 2005, which is even faster. Social services jobs, which numbered 2 million in 1992, will increase by 1.7 million, and almost half of the increase will be in residential care institutions that provide full-time assistance to older persons. Other fast-growing industries within the social services group are individual and miscellaneous social services, which provide elderly daycare, family social services, and child daycare. Residential or home health care services is the fastest growing industry in terms of employment, 7.3 percent annual growth rate, but both child daycare and individual and miscellaneous social services are among the fastest growing industries.

PROJECTED EMPLOYMENT BY MAJOR INDUSTRY DIVISIONS, SERVICE-PRODUCING SECTOR

Service-Producing Industries	1992	2005	Change
	[numbers in thousands]		
Services	28,422	41,788	13,365
Wholesale Trade	6,045	7,191	1,146
Retail Trade	19,346	23,777	4,431
Transportation, Communication, Utilities	5,709	6,497	788
Finance, Insurance, and Real Estate	6,571	7,969	1,398
Government	18,653	22,021	3,368

	% Distribution		Annual % Change
Services	26.3	31.4	+3.0
Wholesale Trade	5.6	5.4	+1.3
Retail Trade	17.9	17.5	+1.6
Transportation, Communication, Utilities	5.3	4.9	+1.0
Finance, Insurance, and Real Estate	6.1	6.0	+1.5
Government	17.3	16.6	+1.3

Source: Bureau of Labor Statistics

Employment in health service industries increased almost three times as fast as total employment increased over the past 13 years. That growth rate will slow somewhat over the next 13 years. Nonetheless, employment in health services will grow almost twice as fast as total employment and will account for 16 percent of all additional jobs from 1992 to 2005.

Business services was the fastest growing industry over the 13 years from 1979 to 1992. Employment increased at an annual rate of 6.3 percent, for an increase of 121 percent over the period. Most of that growth occurred in personnel supply services, which includes temporary help services and computer and data processing services. The past rates of growth for these two industries are not likely to continue, however. Business services will add 3 million jobs through 2005, a 57 percent increase — 14 percent of total job growth. In terms of growth rates, computer and data processing services will be second only to residential care. The industry's rapid growth stems from advances in technology, global trends in automation, and increases in demand from business firms, government agencies, and individuals.

Reduced labor force participation by young women has slowed the rapid expansion of personnel supply firms in recent years, and this industry will grow more slowly through 2005. Nonetheless, personnel supply services will increase from 1.6 to 2.6 million jobs, a 57 percent increase.

Wholesale and Retail Trade

There were more than 25 million jobs in wholesale and retail trade in 1992, of which two-thirds were in retail trade. That number will approach 31 million by 2005, an increase of 5.6 million jobs. The increase will be stimulated by higher levels of personal income.

Wholesale trade will add 1.1 million jobs, increasing the total number of jobs from 6.1 million in 1992 to 7.2 million in 2005, a 19 percent increase. Wholesale trade responds to both foreign and domestic demand for U.S. and imported goods, and the antici-pated growth in foreign trade will contribute to growth in this industry.

> *"Eating and drinking places will add 2.2 million jobs, more jobs than any other retail trade industry."*

Retail trade will gain almost 4.5 million jobs, which will raise employment from 19.3 million to 23.8 million, a 23 percent increase. The fastest projected job growth in retail trade will be in apparel and accessory stores, and in appliance, radio, television, and music stores. Substantial increases in retail employment are also anticipated in large industries including eating and drinking places, food stores, automobile dealers and service stations, and general merchandise stores.

Eating and drinking places will add 2.2 million jobs, more jobs than any other retail trade industry. This will increase employment to 8.8 million workers in 2005. Eating and drinking places are labor-intensive, especially full-service restaurants; and, although there are efforts to increase productivity in the industry by, for example, using automated equipment to dispense drinks, significant labor productivity increases are not expected. Moreover, as the population ages and personal income increases, the demand in eating and drinking places over the next 13 years will shift from fast-food establishments to full-service and casual dining restaurants.

Transportation, Communications, and Utilities

Jobs in the transportation, communications, and utilities division numbered 5.7 million in 1992, and will increase 14 percent, or 788,000, to 6.5 million in 2005. But the fortunes of the two major industries within this division, transportation and communica-tions, will be much different.

The transportation industry will grow by 24 percent, or 824,000 jobs, from 3.5 million to 4.3 million jobs. Half of those jobs will be added by trucking and warehousing, and another fourth will be added by air transportation. As the volume of foreign trade in-creases, so also will the requirements for shipping goods to and from seaports and airports by railroads, trucks, and overseas freight.

Employment in communications peaked at 1.1 million jobs in 1981, but it has been declining steadily. Contributing factors include the divestiture of the American Telephone and Telegraph Company, increased competition for long-distance services, and the continuing pace of technological change accompanied by increases in productivity. In 1992, there were 912,000 jobs in communications, but employment will decline another 12 percent to 724,000 jobs by 2005. Productivity, nonetheless, will continue to grow because of the important role telephone communications will play in providing access to the information highway and computerized data bases.

Employment in radio and television broadcasting will grow by less than 1 percent over the next 13 years, increasing by 37,000 jobs from 355,000 in 1992 to 392,000 jobs in 2005. The dramatic expansion of cable television systems over the past two decades stimulated employment growth from 135,000 jobs in 1970 to the industry's peak of 359,000 jobs in 1990. Less than 10 percent of all households were hooked to cable service in 1970, but almost 60 percent were subscribers in 1990. As a consequence, the cable television market is probably near saturation, which will slow future growth.

Employment in utilities will grow, adding 117,000 new jobs through 2005, prompted by the need for expanded water supply and sanitary services.

Finance, Insurance, and Real Estate

Employment in these industries will increase 21 percent, raising employment from 6.6 million jobs in 1992 to 8 million by 2005. Growth will be prompted by the continuing strong demand for financial services. The fastest growing industries within this sector will be holding and investment offices and mortgage bankers and brokers. The largest numerical increase in jobs, however, will be insurance agents, brokers, and services.

Employment in depository institutions — banks, savings and loans, and credit unions — will increase by 92,000 jobs. Workers numbered 2.1 million in 1992 and will increase 5 percent to 2.2 million by 2005.

Nondepository holding and investment offices, such as finance companies and mortgage brokers, project much faster growth in employment than average. Employment in 1992 was 615,000, but that figure will soar by 334,000 jobs to 949,000 by the year 2005. That is an annual growth rate of 3.4 percent, much faster than the average for all industries; but because the base number of jobs is small, employment opportunities will be limited.

Security and commodity brokers will have higher than average annual employment increases, though the increases will be slower than over the preceding 13 years. The volume of stock transactions increased dramatically in the 1980s due to implementation of computer technologies, offering such additional services as stock market futures, increased corporate merger and leveraged buyout activity, and increased foreign investment. That spurt in industry growth is not expected to continue through 2005, however. There were 439,000 jobs in the security and commodity broker industry in 1992. That total will rise to 570,000 jobs by 2005, an addition of 131,000 workers.

There were 1.5 million insurance carriers in 1992. Another 180,000 will be added by 2005, which will bring the total to 1.7 million. Insurance agents, brokers, and services involve direct contact with customers, and employment is not likely to be affected by automation. The industry expects to add 319,000 jobs over the next 13 years, bringing the total to 971,000 jobs in 2005, up by half from the 1992 level of 652,000 jobs.

Employment in real estate will increase by 300,000 jobs, from 1.3 million in 1992 to 1.6 million in 2005.

Government

Government employment, except for public education and public hospitals, will grow 10 percent over the next 13 years, about half the growth rate for all industries. Employment, not counting public education and public hospitals, will rise by 1 million jobs to 10.5 million in 2005. Growth will occur primarily at the levels of state and local government. Employment in the federal government and U.S. Postal Service will decline by 113,000 and 41,000 jobs, respectively.

When you include public education and public hospitals, however, government will add 3.3 million jobs to the 1992 level of 18.7 million, which will bring total government employment to 22 million. Average growth in state and local government will result in an increase of 3.5 million jobs and will bring the 1992 level of 15.7 million workers to 19.2 million by 2005. Most of the growth, 2.8 of the 3.5 million jobs, will be in state and local education, prompted by growth in the school age population. Over the 15 years from 1990 to 2005, the elementary school population will rise by 3.8 million persons, the secondary school population will rise by 3.7 million, and the postsecondary school population will rise by 1.3 million persons.

| | Population by Age in Millions | | |
Year	5–13	14–17	18–24
1970	36.7	15.9	24.5
1975	33.9	17.1	28.0
1980	31.2	16.2	30.0
1985	30.0	14.9	28.9
1990	32.0	13.3	26.8
2005	35.8	17.0	28.1

Source: Monthly Labor Review, November, 1993

Employment in the federal government will decline slightly as deficit reduction measures go into effect.

Goods-Producing Industries

Employment in the goods-producing sector continues to suffer in the aftermath of the recessions and trade imbalances of the 1980s. Overall employment in goods-producing industries will increase slowly from 1992 to 2005, and growth prospects within the sector will vary considerably. Almost all employment gains will be in construction, with additional small gains in agriculture, forestry, and fishing. Employment in mining and manufacturing will continue to decline.

PROJECTED EMPLOYMENT BY MAJOR INDUSTRY DIVISIONS, GOODS-PRODUCING SECTOR

Goods-Producing Industries	1992	2005	Change
	[numbers in thousands]		
Construction	4,471	5,632	1,161
Mining	631	562	−69
Manufacturing	18,040	17,523	−517
Agriculture, Forestry, and Fishing	1,775	2,000	200

	% Distribution	Annual % Change
Construction	4.1	4.2	1.8
Mining	.6	.4	−.9
Manufacturing	16.7	13.2	−.2
Agriculture, Forestry, and Fishing	*	*	1.4

* Data not available
Source: Bureau of Labor Statistics

Construction

Construction will add 1.2 million jobs between 1992 and 2005, an increase of 26 percent, as it recovers from the residential and commercial building slump of 1990 to 1992, during which time employment fell from 5.1 to 4.5 million. Thus, half of the anticipated gain in employment will merely offset recent losses; but the other half of the gains will be "real" and will lead employment growth in all goods-producing divisions. Employment in construction will be stimulated by spending for domestic infrastructure including roads, bridges, airports, modest growth in residential construction, and educational facilities to accommodate growth in the school-age population.

Mining

Employment in mining declined by 34 percent, or 300,000 jobs, between 1979 and 1992, and that decline will continue through 2005, though at a slower rate. Employment in mining stood at 631,000 in 1992, and will decline by another 11 percent to 562,000, a loss of 69,000 jobs. Crude petroleum and oil and gas field services accounted for half of mining jobs in 1992 and will contribute a loss of 50,000 jobs as imported oil serves domestic consumption. Employment in coal mining will decline by 36,000 jobs as the industry continues to automate. Metal and nonmetallic minerals mining will offset these losses with gains of 17,000 jobs.

Manufacturing

The sustained decline in manufacturing employment will level off. Nonetheless, manufacturing's share of total employment declined from 24 percent in 1979 to 17 percent in 1992, and it will decline to 13 percent in 2005, a loss of an additional 500,000 jobs. By comparison, employment in manufacturing declined by 2.9 million jobs over the past 13 years.

Three demand factors will benefit manufacturing: more favorable foreign trade conditions than those experienced earlier; growth in personal consumption expenditures; and increases in durable production. Conditions that offset these factors are the reduction in national defense expenditures and continuing growth of imports.

Within manufacturing, durable industries — for example, industrial machinery and equipment, electronic and electric equipment, transportation equipment, and instruments — will experience the most growth. Nondurable manufacturing industries that will grow the fastest include paper and pencil allied products, printing and publishing, chemicals, rubber and plastic products.

Agriculture, Forestry, and Fishing

After declines in employment over several decades, overall employment in agriculture, forestry, and fishing will grow from 1.7 million jobs in 1992 to 2 million in 2005. This represents an increase of 13 percent, more than 200,000 jobs, over the next 13 years. Most of the gain will be in agricultural services as more farm owners contract out for services and demand rises for nonfarm horticulture and landscaping services. Employment related to production of crops, livestock, and livestock products will continue to decline.

OCCUPATIONAL EMPLOYMENT

There were 121 million workers in the labor force in 1992, and that number will increase by 22 percent to 148 million in 2005. This projected rate of growth is slightly higher than the increase over the past 13 years, but it is not nearly as fast as growth over the earlier 13 years, 1966 to 1979, when the baby boom entered the labor force and employment increased by 19 percent. Occupations that require a bachelor's degree or other post-secondary education or training will have higher-than-average rates of employment growth, though many occupations requiring less formal education or training will also have above-average growth.

Major Occupational Groups

The rate of total employment growth for major occupational groups will be similar to that of the past 13 years, 1979 to 1992. Among the major occupational groups, employment in three groups — professional specialty occupations, technicians and related support occupations, and service occupations — will increase the fastest. All will grow by a third by 2005. In addition, executive, administrative, and managerial occupations will grow by a fourth, faster than total employment growth; and the number of jobs for marketing and sales workers will increase by 21 percent, about the rate of increase for all occupations, which is 22 percent. Employment in all other major occupational groups will increase, but the increase will be at a rate that is slower than total employment growth.

PROJECTED EMPLOYMENT BY MAJOR OCCUPATIONAL GROUPS, NUMERICAL AND PERCENTAGE CHANGES

	1992 Number*	Percentage	2005 Number*	Percentage	Percentage Change
Total Occupations	121,099	100.0	147,482	100.0	21.8
Executive, Administrative, and Managerial	12,066	10.0	15,195	10.3	25.9
Professional Specialty	16,592	13.7	22,801	15.5	37.4
Technicians and Related Support	4,282	3.5	5,664	3.8	32.2
Marketing and Sales	12,993	10.7	15,664	10.6	20.6
Administrative Support Including Clerical	22,349	18.5	25,406	17.2	13.7
Service	19,358	16.0	25,820	17.5	33.4
Agriculture, Forestry, and Fishing	3,530	2.9	3,650	2.5	3.4
Precision Production, Craft, and Repair	13,580	11.2	15,380	10.4	13.3
Operators, Fabricators, and Laborers	16,349	13.5	17,902	12.1	9.5

* Numbers in thousands
Source: Bureau of Labor Statistics

Growth rates for several major occupational groups will change. For example, the factors that caused sustained employment declines in agriculture, forestry, and fishing, and the factors that prompted declines in employment of fabricators and laborers over the past 13 years have changed. Employment in each of these occupations will increase slowly rather than continue to decline. Employment in manufacturing reached its peak in 1979, but since has declined. That decline will slow through 2005, with the result that employment of operators, fabricators, and laborers, which is concentrated in manufacturing, will not decline as it did over the years 1979 to 1992. Nonetheless, technology and automation will continue to affect employment in these occupations negatively.

Because growth rates will vary across major occupational groups, the distribution of employment across the major occupational groups will change. As a rough guide, consider that a 1 percent change in the employment share of any major occupation group is a notable change. Four groups will change their employment shares by more than 1 percent over the next 13 years:

Professional specialty occupations	+1.8 %
Service occupations	+1.5 %
Administrative support occupations, including clerical	−1.3 %
Operators, fabricators, and laborers	−1.4 %

As a result of these and related changes, service workers will move from second place to first place as the largest single employment group in 2005, and administrative support workers will fall to second place. Professional specialty workers are the most rapidly growing group, and they will rank as they did in 1992, the third largest occupational group.

Executive, Administrative, and Managerial

The number of executive, administrative, and managerial workers will increase 26 percent, or 3.1 million, from 1992 to 2005. This growth will be faster than the total for all occupations, but the rate will be considerably slower than the 50 percent occupational growth rate the group experienced from 1979 to 1992. Managers had the second fastest growth rate over the past 13 years, but they will have only the fourth fastest growth rate by 2005. A contributing reason for the slowdown is the trend toward job restructuring. One way that firms accomplish this is by reducing the employment of middle managers and giving lower-level employees more say in the management process.

The service industry division, which will contribute most new jobs in the economy, will account for nearly half of the total growth in jobs for managers. Particularly large gains will be posted in engineering and management services and business services. Managerial jobs will also open in wholesale and retail trade, finance, insurance, and real estate. In addition, self-employed executive, administrative, and managerial workers will increase by 37 percent and will account for about a sixth, 521,000, of the 3.1 million new jobs in this category.

Professional Specialty

Employment in professional specialty occupations will increase 37 percent, or 6.2 million jobs, the second largest increase following service occupations. In 1992, professional workers claimed 14 percent of all jobs. Their share will rise to 16 percent in 2005. The number of workers in professional specialties grew faster than the average for all employees over the past 13 years. Over the next 13 years, employment of professional employees will rise in all major industrial sectors in the economy — including manufacturing, which will experience a total decline of 518,000 workers but an increase of 230,000 professional workers. Professionals in manufacturing will be mainly computer systems analysts, engineers, and scientists. Nonetheless, most of the increase in professional workers will be in the services industry division, especially in educational services, which will increase by 1.7 million jobs, and health services, which will increase by 1.3 million jobs. Social services, business services, engineering and management services, as well as federal, state, and local governments will contribute further to the growth of professional workers.

Technicians and Related Support

Employment of technicians and related support workers will grow by 32 percent, or 1.4 million workers. Over the previous 13 years, technicians were the fastest growing of any major occupational group. Over the next 13 years, nearly 8 of 10 will take employment in service industries and, within services, almost half of the jobs (651,000) will be in the large and rapidly growing health services industry. Other industries that will employ more technicians through the year 2005 are engineering, management services, and business services.

Marketing and Sales

Employment in marketing and sales occupations will increase 21 percent from 1992 to 2005, about the same as the total economy. This will increase employment by 2.7 million workers. Growth will be slower than it was from 1979 to 1992, when employment in marketing and sales occupations grew faster than the economy. One major reason for the anticipated slowdown is lower growth in employment for wholesale and retail trade, which employs the majority of marketing and sales workers.

The slowing of employment in wholesale trade is based partly on the expectation that manufacturers will take advantage of reductions in the costs of shipping goods and the increased efficiencies in use of computerized inventory and warehouse management systems; and that they will bypass wholesalers and distribute their products directly to retailers. Marketing and sales workers will also find increased employment in the services industry division and in finance, insurance, and real estate.

Administrative Support

The number of workers in administrative support occupations, including clerical workers, will grow by 14 percent, slower than the average for all occupations. However, there were more than 22 million workers in administrative support jobs in 1992 — administrative support was the largest major occupational group — and, because the group is large, even the below-average growth rate will increase employment by 3.1 million workers, the third largest numerical increase following service workers and professionals. However, the below-average growth rate will reduce the share of all jobs claimed by administrative support occupations from 19 percent in 1992 to 17 percent by 2005.

Because administrative support occupations is a large and varied group, there will be a wide range of employment increases and decreases among the detailed occupations in this group, ranging from an increase of 57 percent to a decrease of 60 percent. Employment of telephone operators, typists and word processors, and postal service clerks will be affected negatively by continued technological change and further developments in office automation, but occupations that involve direct contact with people will not be affected significantly and will have average or higher-than-average rates of growth. Examples include hotel desk clerks, receptionists and information clerks, and teacher aides and educational assistants.

The service industry division, which will significantly outperform all other industries over the period of 1992 to 2005, will claim about 80 percent of the job growth in administrative support occupations. Business services will employ another 643,000 workers, health services another 550,000, and educational services another 519,000. Another 401,000 jobs will open in wholesale and retail trade, and another 390,000 jobs in finance, insurance, and real estate. On the down side, a combined 248,000 administrative support jobs will be lost in manufacturing, communications, utilities, and government.

Services

Employment in service occupations will increase by 6.5 million jobs, the largest gain for a major occupational group. Service occupations grew faster than the average for all occupations from 1979 to 1992, but will grow by 33 percent from 1992 to 2005, substantially faster than the past 13 years. Service occupations claimed 16 percent of total employment in 1992, and that share will rise to 18 percent by 2005.

More than half of the jobs in service occupations will open in the rapidly growing services industry division. Health services will add 1.4 million jobs; social services will add 682,000 jobs; and business services will add 658,000 jobs. In addition, retail trade, which employs large numbers of food preparation and service workers, will add 2 million service jobs; and state and local governments, which include large numbers of law enforcement occupations, will add 404,000 service worker jobs.

Agriculture, Forestry, and Fishing

Agriculture, forestry, and fishing will increase by 120,000 jobs from 1992 to 2005, the smallest increase for any major occupational group. However, this 3 percent increase in employment will reverse a sustained decline in employment, a decline of 5 percent between 1979 and 1992 alone, that has gone on for decades. Although the decline will be arrested, if not reversed, the proportion of all workers employed in agriculture, forestry, and fishing will decline from 2.9 percent of total employment in 1992 to 2.5 percent by 2005.

Within agriculture, forestry, and fishing, jobs for farmers will decline by 231,000. This loss will be offset by an increase of 311,000 jobs for gardeners and groundskeepers, who are employed in such rapidly growing agricultural services as gardening and lawn services.

Precision Production, Craft, and Repair

Employment in precision production, craft, and repair occupations will increase by 13 percent, or 1.8 million jobs, from 1992 to 2005. This is an increase over the 4 percent growth rate of the past 13 years. Nonetheless, the share of jobs in precision production, craft, and repair occupations will decline from 11 percent in 1992 to 10 percent by 2005.

Most of the job growth within precision production, craft, and repair occupations will occur among construction trade workers and mechanics, installers, and repairers. In terms of industries, the services division will employ another 666,000 workers; construction will employ 686,000; and wholesale trade will employ 131,000 workers. As noted earlier, some of the increase in employment in construction merely offsets jobs lost during the recent recession. On the down side, employment in precision production, craft, and repair occupations will decline by 156,000 jobs in manufacturing, by 84,000 jobs in communications and utilities, and by 33,000 jobs in mining.

Operators, Fabricators, and Laborers

The number of operators, fabricators, and laborers will increase by 10 percent, or 1.6 million workers, by 2005. This will reverse the trend of the previous 13 years, during which workers declined by 10 percent. Part of the reason for the reversal is that 1979 was a peak year for employment in manufacturing, but in the 1990 to 1991 recession nearly 3 million manufacturing jobs were lost. Employment in manufacturing will decline by 518,000 jobs through 2005, and 454,000 of those lost jobs will be operators, fabricators, and laborers. These losses will be more than offset by new employment opportunities, however: 889,000 jobs in services; 389,000 jobs in transportation; 403,000 jobs in wholesale and retail trade; and 252,000 jobs in construction. Nonetheless, the total share of employment held by operators, fabricators, and laborers will decline from 14 percent in 1992 to 12 percent in 2005.

DETAILED OCCUPATIONS

The Bureau of Labor Statistics has also developed employment projections for more than 500 detailed occupations. These are specific occupations rather than major occupation groups — the level of occupations that most people think and talk about. The rates of change range from an increase of 138 percent for home health aides to a decline of 75 percent for frame wirers.

In this section, I review employment projections for four special categories of detailed occupations: fastest growing occupations; occupations with the most employment growth; occupations that will have the largest decline in employment; and employment projections for self-employment.

Fastest Growing Occupations

The fastest growing occupations have certain things in common. Most are concentrated in one or more of the fastest growing industries. For example, many of the 30 occupations with the fastest growth rates are in the health services industry, which will grow about twice as fast as the rest of the economy. Note, further, that home health aides is the fastest growing occupation and, of course, it is part of the health services industrial

sector. Many human services workers, the
second fastest growing occupation, also work
in the health services industrial sector. More
than a third of the fastest growing occupations have substantial employment in the
health service industry.

> *"Home health aides is the
> fastest growing occupation."*

Another characteristic of many of the 30 fastest growing occupations is that they
serve the elderly, the most rapidly growing segment of the population. The three fastest
growing occupations — home health aides, human services workers, and personal and
home care aides — have substantial employment in the health services industry, which
serves the elderly. Other occupations that will grow rapidly and are part of the health
services industry include physical and corrective therapy assistants and aides, medical
assistants, physical therapists, medical records technicians, occupational therapists,
radiologic technologists and technicians, respiratory therapists, and speech-language
pathologists and audiologists.

Another industry with robust growth that can offer significant employment opportunities is business services, particularly computer and data processing services. Computer
engineers and scientists and systems analysts occupy the fourth and fifth positions in the
listing of fastest growing occupations. These occupations will grow rapidly to satisfy
expanding needs for scientific research and applications of computer technology in business and industry. In addition, increased use of operations research to improve productivity and reduce costs will increase the demands for operations research analysts, the 18th
fastest growing occupation.

Other occupations that will grow rapidly are associated with increases in personal and
business travel. Travel agents are the 14th fastest growing occupation, and flight attendants
are the 26th. Paralegals, the 8th fastest growing occupation, will be in demand in legal and
related fields due to efforts to provide more cost-effective legal services to the public.
Crime has been an issue on the national agenda, and jobs for corrections officers, the 12th
fastest growing occupation, will increase in response to the need to supervise and counsel
the rapidly growing inmate population. An increase in birth rates coupled with the continuing trend for formal institutional childcare and projected increases in preschool and
elementary school levels will stimulate growth in a number of other occupations that
appear in the list of the 30 fastest growing, including special education teachers, childcare
workers, nursery workers, preschool and kindergarten teachers, language pathologists and
audiologists, and psychologists.

In sum, employment opportunities over the next 13 years will be driven by social,
political, population, and labor force changes. These include domestic concerns about
crime, health care, and the aging of the population, coupled with an anticipated spurt in
the birth rate and continuing technological innovation and change.

Occupations with the Most Employment Growth

Several of the occupations with the largest numerical job growth will appear in three
industries that, together, will provide nearly half of the total growth in wage and salary
jobs from 1992 to 2005. These are health services, retail trade, and educational services.

OCCUPATIONS PROJECTED TO HAVE FASTEST EMPLOYMENT GROWTH

Occupation	*Employment		*Numerical Change	Percentage Change
	1992	2005		
Home health aides	347	827	479	138
Human services workers	189	445	256	136
Personal and home care aides	127	293	166	130
Computer engineers and scientists	211	447	236	112
Systems analysts	455	956	501	110
Physical and corrective therapy assistants and aides	61	118	57	93
Physical therapists	90	170	79	88
Paralegals	95	176	81	86
Teachers, special education	358	625	267	74
Medical assistants	181	308	128	71
Detectives, except public	59	100	41	70
Correction officers	282	479	197	70
Childcare workers	684	1,135	450	66
Travel agents	115	191	76	66
Radiologic technologists and technicians	162	264	102	63
Nursery workers	72	116	44	62
Medical records technicians	76	123	47	61
Operations research analysts	45	72	27	61
Occupational therapists	40	64	24	60
Legal secretaries	200	439	160	57
Teachers, preschool and kindergarten	434	669	236	54
Manicurists	35	55	19	54
Producers, directors, actors, and entertainers	129	198	69	54
Speech-language pathologists and audiologists	73	110	37	51
Flight attendants	93	140	47	51
Guards	803	1,211	408	51
Insurance adjusters, examiners, and investigators	147	220	72	49
Respiratory therapists	74	109	36	48
Psychologists	143	212	69	48
Paving, surfacing, and tamping equipment operators	72	107	35	48

* Numbers in the thousands

Source: Bureau of Labor Statistics

The health services industry will not only grow rapidly, it will also offer substantial employment opportunities based on numerical job growth. The second largest numerical increase, 765,000 jobs, will open to registered nurses. Nursing aides, orderlies, and attendants or other health-related occupations will expand by 594,000 jobs — 7th on the list of occupations with the largest job growth. Home health aides, 11th on the list, will increase by 479,000 jobs; and licensed practical nurses, 26th on the list, will increase by 261,000 jobs.

OCCUPATIONS PROJECTED TO HAVE THE LARGEST EMPLOYMENT GROWTH

Occupation	*Employment 1992	*Employment 2005	*Numerical Change	Percentage Change
Salespersons, retail	3,660	4,446	786	21
Registered nurses	1,835	2,601	765	42
Cashiers	2,747	3,417	670	24
General office clerks	2,688	3,342	654	24
Truck drivers, light and heavy	2,391	3,039	648	27
Waiters and waitresses	1,756	2,394	637	36
Nursing aides, orderlies, and attendants	1,308	1,903	594	45
Janitors and cleaners, including maids and housekeeping cleaners	2,862	3,410	548	19
Food preparation workers	1,223	1,748	524	43
Systems analysts	455	956	501	110
Home health aides	347	827	479	138
Teachers, secondary school	1,263	1,724	462	37
Childcare workers	684	1,135	450	66
Guards	803	1,211	408	51
Marketing and sales worker supervisors	2,036	2,443	407	20
Teacher aides and educational assistants	885	1,266	381	43
General managers and top executives	2,871	3,251	380	13
Maintenance repairers, general utility	1,145	1,464	319	28
Gardeners and groundskeepers, except farm	884	1,195	311	35
Teachers, elementary	1,456	1,767	311	21
Food counter, fountain, and related workers	1,564	1,872	308	20
Receptionists and information clerks	904	1,210	305	34
Accountants and auditors	939	1,243	304	32
Clerical supervisors and managers	1,267	1,568	301	24
Cooks, restaurant	602	879	276	46
Teachers, special education	358	625	267	74
Licensed practical nurses	659	920	261	40
Cooks, short-order and fast-food	714	971	257	36
Human services workers	189	445	256	126
Computer engineers and scientists	211	447	236	112

* Numbers in the thousands

Source: Bureau of Labor Statistics

Note that home health aides is first on the list of fastest growing occupations and 10th on the list of largest growing occupations.

Eating and drinking places within retail trade is a large and continually growing industry and will provide numerous additional jobs: 637,000 jobs for waitpersons; 524,000 jobs for food preparation workers; 308,000 jobs for food counter, fountain, and related workers; 276,000 jobs for restaurant cooks; and another 257,000 jobs for short-order and fast-food cooks. Other occupations in retail trade on the list of largest job growth are cashiers, retail salespersons, and marketing and sales worker supervisors.

School enrollments will increase by 14 percent from 1992 to 2005, and this will open employment for another 311,000 elementary school teachers and 462,000 secondary school teachers. The trend toward more use of teacher aides and educational assistants will create another 381,000 jobs in elementary and secondary schools.

The remaining occupations on the list with the largest job growth appear across a variety of industries, and their growth depends on assorted factors. As noted earlier, employment for systems analysts will grow with the spread of computer technology. Jobs for receptionists and information clerks will grow because these workers deal directly with people and their duties are difficult to automate. General office clerks will continue to replace administrative support workers, including clerical workers, in response to automation and improved technologies. Other slower growing occupations that will provide numerous additional jobs due to their size are general managers and top executives, truck drivers, janitors and cleaners, marketing and sales workers supervisors, and guards.

It is interesting to compare the total increase in employment that can be credited to occupations that will grow the fastest with the increase that will be due to occupations with the largest numerical increase. The fastest growing occupations will contribute 17 percent of growth in employment through 2005, but the occupations with the largest numerical growth will account for almost 50 percent of employment growth (see Figure 6-4). Several occupations appear in both groups. The comparison illustrates why career planners, when they are assessing employment prospects, need to take into account numerical change and not be swayed too much by growth rates.

Projected Sources of Occupational Growth

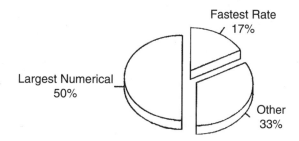

Figure 6-2 *Source: Bureau of Labor Statistics*

Occupations with Declining Employment

Some industries are declining, and changes are afoot regarding management staffing — for example, middle management positions are being phased out. Both industry declines and management changes will be major contributors to employment declines in some occupations over the next 13 years.

Of the two contributors, change in industrial employment is the major cause for declines in employment for farmers, textile draw-out and winding machine operators and tenders, precision electrical and electronic equipment assemblers, and two occupations in the private household industry, cleaners and servants and childcare workers. The declining

OCCUPATIONS PROJECTED TO HAVE LARGEST EMPLOYMENT DECLINES

Occupation	*Employment 1992	2005	*Numerical Change	Percentage Change
Farmers	1,088	857	−231	−21
Sewing machine operators, garment	556	393	−162	−29
Cleaners and servants, private household	483	326	−157	−32
Farmworkers	849	716	−133	−16
Typists and word processors	789	664	−125	−16
Computer operators, except peripheral equipment	266	161	−104	−39
Packaging and filling machine operators and tenders	319	248	−71	−22
Inspectors, testers, and graders, precision	625	559	−65	−10
Switchboard operators	239	188	−51	−21
Telephone and cable TV line installers and repairers	165	125	−40	−24
Textile draw-out and winding machine operators and tenders	192	157	+35	−18
Machine forming operators and tenders, metal and plastic	155	123	−32	−21
Bartenders	382	350	−32	−8
Butchers and meatcutters	222	191	−31	−14
Billing, posting, and calculating machine operators	93	66	−28	−29
Central office and PBX installers and repairers	70	45	−25	−36
Central office operators	48	24	−24	−50
Bank tellers	525	502	−24	−4
Electrical and electronic assemblers	210	187	−23	−11
Cutting and slicing machine setters, operators, and tenders	94	73	−21	−23
Electrical and electronic equipment assemblers, precision	150	129	−21	−14
Station installers and repairers, telephone	40	20	−20	−50
Machine tool cutting operators and tenders, metal and plastic	114	95	−19	−17
Peripheral EDP equipment operators	30	12	−18	−60
Welding machine setters, operators, and tenders	97	80	−17	−17
Crushing and mixing machine operators and tenders	133	117	−16	−12
Industrial machinery mechanics	477	462	−15	−3
Directory assistance operators	27	13	−14	51
Head sawyers and sawing machine operators and tenders, setters and set-up operators	59	46	−13	22

* Numbers in the thousands

Source: Bureau of Labor Statistics

occupations that will be affected the most by changes in industry employment and by changes in the occupational structure are farm workers, central office and PBX installers and repairers, central office operators, station installers and repairers, and directory assistance operators.

Most of the other declining occupations will be affected more by changes in the occupational structure than by changes in industry employment. For example, the anticipated decline in employment for bartenders in eating and drinking places is due to local law enforcement practices that reduce the consumption of alcoholic beverages outside the home. Employment of bartenders will decline by 32,000 jobs. Advances in office automation and user-friendly software coupled with increased use of word-processing equipment by professional and managerial employees will substantially reduce dependency on typists and word processors, whose employment will decline by 125,000 from 1992 to 2005. So also, the demand for computer operators will fall due to increased use of personal computers and decreased use of mainframe computers. Employment for bank tellers will decline due to increased use of automated teller machines, terminals, and other electronic equipment for customer funds transactions.

Several detailed occupations in the manufacturing industry will decline because of advances in technology, changes in industry organization, and other factors that affect how workers are used. For example, industry installation of computer controls that link machines and monitor production will reduce the demand for several occupations, including machine-forming operators and tenders, and metal and plastic machine tool cutting operators and tenders. Welding machine setters, operators, and tenders will be affected by the increased diffusion of robotics technology in industry.

Employment of Self-Employed Workers

In 1992, 10 million workers were self-employed. That number will rise by 15 percent or 1.5 million jobs by 2005, which means that growth in self-employment will be slower than the average for total employment, which is 23 percent (see Figure 6-6). Among the detailed occupations in which 50,000 or more self-employed people work, however, there is much variation in the rates of growth that will occur, and in some occupations the growth rates will exceed the average growth of the labor force.

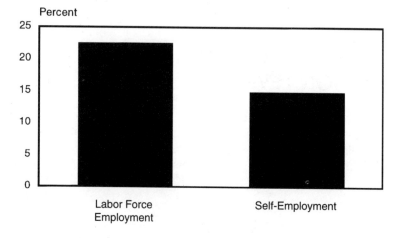

Figure 6-3 *Source: Bureau of Labor Statistics*

Over the next 13 years (1992 to 2005) executive, administrative, and managerial occupations will account for more than one-third of the increase in self-employed workers, 521,000 of the 1.5 million new jobs. As over the past 13 years, employment growth of self-employed managers will be faster than the growth for wage and salary managers. Many individuals, many of them past wage and salary managers, will start their own businesses. At the same time, employment of wage and salary managers will decline because of the squeeze on middle management.

Another 466,000 self-employed workers will identify with service occupations. And 238,000 self-employed childcare workers will be added as more families turn away from at-home to institutional childcare. Janitors and cleaners, including maids and housekeeping cleaners, will add 80,000 positions. And hair dressers, hair stylists, and cosmetologists will contribute another 90,000 jobs.

Professional specialty occupations will open 271,000 self-employment opportunities, and precision production, craft, and repair occupations will add 233,000. Both of these occupational groups have a large number of detailed occupations with a high proportion of self-employed workers.

Marketing and sales fields had the most self-employed workers in 1992, with 1.8 million. This group will increase by 100,000, or 6 percent, over the next 13 years — slower than their wage and salary counterparts. Nonetheless, in such sales occupations as real estate and insurance, the self-employed will continue to account for sizeable amounts of total employment growth. The number of self-employed technicians and related support workers will grow rapidly, at a 34 percent increase. Nonetheless, only 98,000 people worked in these self-employment jobs in 1992, which means that the increase will be only 33,000 additional jobs by 2005. Administrative support occupations and operators, fabricators and laborers are two other major occupational groups that will have little increase in self-employment through 2005.

Within the major occupational groups, self-employment in agriculture, forestry, and fishing will continue to decline, falling by another 230,000 jobs due to the continuing reduction in the number of small farms. One dramatic exception to the decline in employment in this major occupation group is the number of new self-employed workers in gardening and groundskeeping. Their numbers will increase by 76,000 from 1992 to 2005.

FASTEST GROWING OCCUPATIONS FOR EDUCATION LEVELS

This chapter closes with three tables. Each is a listing of projected 20 fastest growing occupations for the years 1992 to 2005. The first is a listing of fastest growing occupations that require a bachelor's degree. The second is a listing of fastest growing occupations that require some vocational education or extensive employer training. And the third is a listing of fastest growing occupations that require about a high school education.

FASTEST GROWING OCCUPATIONS THAT REQUIRE A BACHELOR'S DEGREE

Occupation	Percentage Growth
Computer engineers and scientists	112
Systems analysts	110
Physical therapists	88
Teachers, special education	74
Operations research analysts	61
Occupational therapists	60
Teachers, preschool and kindergarten	54
Speech-language pathologists and audiologists	48
Psychologists	48
Construction managers	47
Management analysts	43
Recreational therapists	40
Social workers	40
Recreation workers	38
Podiatrists	37
Teachers, secondary school	37
Teachers and instructors, vocational education and training	36
Instructors and coaches, sports and physical training	36
Personnel training and labor relations specialists	36
Marketing, advertising, and public relations managers	36

Source: Occupational Outlook Quarterly, Fall 1993.

Note that of the 20 fastest growing occupations that require a bachelor's degree, more than half are in health and education services industries. Other occupations relate to computers and the growing complexity of business in our society.

FASTEST GROWING OCCUPATIONS THAT REQUIRE SOME VOCATIONAL EDUCATION OR EXTENSIVE EMPLOYER TRAINING

Occupation	Percentage Growth
Physical and corrective therapy assistants and aides	93
Paralegals	86
Occupational therapy assistants and aides	78
Medical assistants	71
Radiologic technologists and technicians	63
Medical records technicians	61
Legal secretaries	57
EEG technologists	54
Producers, directors, actors, and entertainers	54
Nuclear medicine technologists	50
Insurance adjusters, examiners, and investigators	49
Respiratory therapists	48
Cooks, restaurant	46
Data processing equipment repairers	45
Medical secretaries	45
Food service and lodging managers	44
Dental hygienists	43
Surgical technologists	42
Pharmacy assistants	42
Licensed practical nurses	40

Source: Occupational Outlook Quarterly, Fall 1993.

Note that of the 20 occupations that require some postsecondary training or extensive employer training, 13 are health-related occupations. Within the list of 20, there is considerable variety with regard to skill levels required, number of employment openings, and earnings.

FASTEST GROWING OCCUPATIONS
THAT REQUIRE A HIGH SCHOOL
EDUCATION OR LESS

Occupation	Percentage Growth
Home health aides	138
Human services workers	136
Personal and home health care aides	130
Electronic pagination systems workers	78
Detectives, except public	70
Corrections officers	70
Childcare workers	66
Travel agents	66
Nursery workers	62
Subway and streetcar operators	57
Manicurists	54
Flight attendants	51
Guards	51
Paving, surfacing, and tamping equipment operators	48
Bakers, bread and pastry	47
Laundry and dry-cleaning machine operators and tenders, except pressing	46
Amusement and recreation attendants	46
Baggage porters and bellhops	46
Nursing aides, orderlies, and attendants	45
Bicycle repairers	45

Source: Occupational Outlook Quarterly, Fall 1993.

Note that of the 20 fastest growing occupations that require a high school education or less, 7 are involved with providing personal services. Many of these occupations require some on-the-job training. Some offer very low pay, but others pay at or above average earnings.

Where to Find Occupational Information

Choosing a career can be a lot like shopping for a necktie for good ol' Granddad. The tie shop offers hundreds of possibilities, and at first glance the whole process of finding the right one may be confusing. The sooner you can categorize them — sort them into silks and woolens, paisleys and stripes and plains, too expensive and too cheap, too wide and too narrow, too gaudy and too funky — the sooner you can eliminate most of them and concentrate on the real possibilities.

Whether you are sorting neckties or career options, it helps to have a system, a set of categories by which you can evaluate possibilities. We've been outlining such a system in the last two chapters. First you learned the basic categories: industrial sectors, divisions, and major occupational groups. Then you reviewed the employment projections for each category. This chapter develops the system further by pointing you to resources that compare specific career possibilities on a number of important points.

> *"Sorting career options is like sorting neckties — rule out the ones that definitely won't work and choose the ones that might be possibilities."*

Sorting career possibilities is much more complicated than buying a necktie for Granddad, but the sorting process is much the same. A good way to begin is to rule out the ones that would never work and pick the ones that, at first glance, might be possibilities — knowing that you will eventually discard all but one or two. Similarly, when it comes to choosing a career, the first task is to identify the realistic possibilities from which to choose. Build a list. Rule out the groupings of industries and occupations that just don't fit. Don't let the misfits clutter up your daughter's or son's thinking.

But whether buying neckties or choosing a career, the time comes when a person has to narrow the options. A person must look more carefully at how the colors and patterns and material will blend with Granddad's favorite shirts and 20-year-old suitcoats. At that stage, it is no longer enough to sort into browns and blues — or industrial sectors and divisions. It helps to have more refined categories for sorting possibilities, and it helps to have more detailed information than national employment projections. It's time to check such details as entry requirements, pay, working conditions, and how employment projections vary by regions of the country and from one state to another.

One of the recurring themes I hear from young people is their complaint of lack of information. A health technologist for the state board of health in Mississippi told us, "Let them know early what types of jobs are available, their requirements and future demand, and projected level of earnings, be they college education type or simply technical." Fortunately, that information is available. And the access to and quality of the information is getting better every year.

This chapter begins with six keys to understanding employment projections. Then I explain where to get and how to use information to sort out career options — and maybe add some new career possibilities. I describe an excellent source of national information on occupations and tell how to use it. I explain where to go for more detailed state information. I list sources of information for people with special needs — the disabled, blind, minorities, and women. I close the chapter with suggestions for what parents can do in this part of the process.

KEYS TO UNDERSTANDING EMPLOYMENT PROJECTIONS

Webster defines a "key" as something that locks or unlocks, holds parts together, reveals or conceals, gives access, or explains or solves something else.

Labor force information can be mysterious, confusing, even overwhelming. The information certainly involves a lot of numbers. But there are keys to keep in mind that will help you sort it all out. Here are six keys that reduce confusion. Keep these in mind when you review employment information and projections.

Key #1: Growth rate and numerical growth are different concepts.

One important consideration in career planning is identifying occupations and industries that have favorable job prospects. Several factors need to be considered, but two of the most important are the employment growth rate and the numerical growth of jobs in an occupation or industry.

The first key to understanding employment projections is to remember that rate of growth and number of employment opportunities are two different concepts, and the two must not be confused. High growth does not necessarily mean many employment opportunities. And when considering employment opportunities, numerical opportunities are almost always more important than rate of growth.

Unfortunately, the media tends to confuse growth rate with numerical employment opportunities, and it does us a disfavor by confusing the two. In its passion for reporting the big story and "making" news, the media is quick to seize on what, in Chapter 5, I referred to as the "high fliers" — laser optics, microchip technologies, wonder drugs, and anything that smacks of the words "high technology" or "computers." But more often than not, the high fliers are small, just-getting-started enterprises, and they employ few people.

Consider an example. Gertrude's Pork & Beans Factory employs 2,000 people, and the Chamber of Commerce predicts that employment at GP&BF will grow 10 percent over the next 13 years. On the other side of town, Johnny's new Microchip Mouse Trap Company has 6 people on the payroll, and Johnny expects that JMMTC will grow by 50 percent over the next 13 years. Gertrude's projects 10 percent employment growth, and Johnny's projects 50 percent growth. But which offers the most employment opportunities? Obviously, Gertrude's. Gertrude's 10 percent growth rate will create 200 jobs, while Johnny's 50 percent growth rate will produce only 3. Don't confuse growth rate with employment opportunities.

There is another consideration. Not only may the number of jobs available in high-growth industries be small, but the qualifications required for getting those jobs may be steep. For these reasons, the anticipated numerical growth in employment is almost always more important than the employment growth rate, which is usually discussed as percentage of growth rate. Slow or moderate growth rates of a large occupation normally provide more employment opportunities than do small, fast-growing occupations.

Key #2: Increased productivity does not necessarily mean more employment opportunities.

The second key to understanding employment projections is to remember that high productivity does not necessarily mean that there will be employment opportunities. High output does not mean that more people are working. In fact, fewer people may be working. Increased productivity may be due to technological innovation or automation.

The agricultural industry is a prime example. Year after year, American farm productivity has been going up. First it was due to industrial improvements. Then productivity was boosted further by the green revolution — fertilizers. Technology added hybrid seed, herbicides, and pesticides. Then came a restructuring of agriculture that introduced large-farm economies and improved management practices. Transportation and geopolitical changes opened new markets. And we're just beginning to see the fruits of biotechnology. But over the same 100 years that productivity was soaring, the number of people directly engaged in farming was declining at a rate of about 1 percent per year, to the point that, today, only about 2 percent of the population are farmers. Increased productivity does not necessarily mean more employment opportunities.

Another example: Employment growth in banks, savings and loans, and credit unions is projected to be only three-tenths of one percent per year over the next 13 years; but productivity will increase nearly tenfold. The high rate of productivity will occur, in part, due to increased use of automated tellers and other computer equipment that provides customer services without adding employees. Increased productivity does not necessarily mean more employment opportunities.

Key #3: Take both occupation and industry projections into account.

The third key to understanding employment projections is to take into account both occupation and industry projections. In Chapter 5, I pointed out the difference between occupations and industries. An occupation is the line of work in which an individual is engaged — for example, nursing; an industry is the major field of activity in which a firm is active — for example, oil. In that discussion, I made the point that knowing only a person's occupation or knowing only a person's industry leaves a lot of questions.

A person may be a secretary, but that doesn't tell you whether she types for a priest or the CIA. Or a person may work for General Motors, but what does that mean? Does he paint cars? Count spark plugs? Spy on Ford? To know what a person does, you have to know both what his or her line of work is and the major field of activity in which the employer is involved.

The same is true of making career plans. Choosing a career involves choosing both an occupation and an industry. Thus, the employment prospects for being a bookkeeper are much better in, for example, health services than in mining; and the prospects for climbing the ladder or making a lateral job transfer are much better in a large industry than in a small one. Industries experience growth and decline just as occupations do, and the intelligent career planner takes both occupations and industries into account. Even a growing occupation in a declining industry is likely to be a career dead end.

Unfortunately, career counselors continue to give little attention to industries — a blind spot that is probably due to their being trained in psychology and education. They usually are not conversant with the literature and resources in such other disciplines as demography, economics, and sociology. Nonetheless, the Bureau of Labor Statistics projects employment for industries using the same methods and following the same schedule and distributes the projections in the same materials as it does for employment in occupations. The informed parent and young person will study employment projections for industries with the same vigor as they explore projections for occupations.

People take employment in both an occupation and an industry, and choosing a career involves choosing both an occupation and an industry.

Key # 4: Most employment openings occur because workers need to be replaced, not because there is employment growth.

The fourth key to understanding employment projections is to recognize that most employment openings occur, not because of labor force growth, but because workers need to be replaced. More than 90 percent of employment opportunities occur because workers retire, change jobs, become disabled, go on leave, die, or need to be replaced. This, again, means that an occupation or industry's growth rate is not likely to be the most important consideration. Replacement needs vary by occupations and industries but, generally speaking, more replacement workers are needed in large than in small work forces. The size of the work force is an important consideration.

In most occupations, openings occur because workers need to be replaced, not because there is employment growth. For that reason, there are employment opportunities even in declining occupations, though it is true that employment prospects are usually not as favorable in declining as in growing occupations.

Key #5: Labor force projections are perishable.

The fifth key to understanding labor force projections is to remember that employment projections are perishable. Data get old, and projections become dated. And when they do, projections can be misleading.

Obsolete information is a particular problem in periods of rapid change. World events, changing technology, federal legislation regarding crime or welfare or health care, or a presidential election can dramatically change the underlying assumptions on which employment projections rest. For example, a renewed military buildup would have tremendous implications for employment in manufacturing. The quality of labor force information, including how old the projections are, is always an important consideration for parents and young people making career plans. Related considerations include whether the information is national, regional, state, or local; whether the information is gathered objectively or is provided as a marketing tool for a training program; and whether the coverage is comprehensive or provides selected information. The quality of the information is critical.

Key #6: Examine both national and state employment projections.

The sixth key to understanding labor force projections is to pay close attention to the area of the country to which employment projections apply. National information gives a broad-brush sketch of employment opportunities over space and time, but regions and states differ widely in their labor force composition. For example, about 41 percent of jobs in the District of Columbia are in government, but government claims only 14 percent of jobs in Indiana. And 18 percent of workers in North Dakota are in farming, but 0 percent of workers in Alaska, Connecticut, Massachusetts, and the District of Columbia are involved in farming.

The same can be said of differences between counties within many states. There is much more variation in industries and occupations by counties in such diverse states as California and Washington than there is in Iowa or Kansas. And though the nation may be short of, say, computer systems analysts, employment opportunities for systems analysts will be much more abundant in Silicon Valley than, for example, in the iron range region of northern Minnesota.

The point is that there is employment information available for the nation, states, and many areas within states. A key to using labor force information intelligently is to examine both the national and local employment projections. I explain the services of the National Occupational Information Coordinating Committee and parallel State Occupational Information Coordinating Committees in sections that follow.

NATIONAL OCCUPATIONAL INFORMATION

The Occupational Outlook Handbook (OOH) is the bible of occupational information. It is the best — the most comprehensive, the most accurate, and the most up-to-date — single source of information on occupations and career possibilities in the nation. In addition to being the most authoritative, the *OOH* has these features to recommend it:

■   It is the most common single career information resource. More than 90 percent of high schools nationwide have one or more copies.

■   It is the single most frequently chosen resource by students.

■   It, together with computerized systems, is identified by students as the most valuable resource overall.

■   Parents and young people who are serious about making informed career choices will want to be familiar with the *OOH*. It's a superb reference. It may not be as eye-appealing as some of the more popular resources, but the information is all there. It's the best place to start.

The Department of Labor publishes a new edition of the *OOH* every two years. It is about the size that Sears Roebuck catalogs used to be, 400 to 500 pages long; and you use it like a mail-order catalog. Start with the table of contents in the front or the index in the back, or just thumb through it.

The *OOH* is a reference volume, not the kind of book you will curl up with by the fireplace and read from cover to cover, but it is an excellent answer to the problem many young adults mentioned in our Career Development Study — like this Air Force officer's son who works as a computer systems analyst: "The expectations I had upon graduation were smashed by the realities of a job market for which I was totally unprepared." A young woman, a junior in a rural high school in our Youth and Careers Study, voiced a similar concern:

" My biggest concern for the future is the types of jobs that will be available to me when I've completed my education, I don't want to get my degree in law only to discover that the field is flooded. I don't want to have to go to work in some factory or fast food place after spending most of my life in preparation for the job of my choice, then find out that I can't pursue my dreams in life."

Use of the *Occupational Outlook Handbook*

The current edition of the *Occupational Outlook Handbook* (1994–95) provides detailed information on about 250 occupations. These occupations cover about 104 million jobs, or 85 percent of all jobs in the nation. In addition, the *OOH* provides summary information on 77 more occupations in a separate chapter, which accounts for another 6 percent of all jobs and brings the total coverage of the book to 91 percent of all jobs in the economy. The remaining 9 percent of jobs are varied and difficult to nail down. Also, the *OOH* has a short section on job opportunities in the armed forces. The occupations in the *OOH* are grouped into occupational categories that largely follow the Standard Occupational Classification system (SOC), to which you were introduced in Chapter 5.

There are two ways for you and your daughter or son to use the *OOH*. If you have some idea of his or her interests, you can begin with the table of contents, which lists about a dozen large groups of related occupations plus job opportunities in the armed forces. The large groups of related occupations subdivide into categories, then into smaller groupings, and, finally, into specific occupations. For example, one cluster of related occupations is "Professional Specialty Occupations." Within that cluster there is a separate grouping for "Engineers"; and within "Engineers" there are ten different kinds of engineers. If your son or daughter is interested in something having to do with engineering, the table of contents offers several engineering specialties that you can review.

A second way to use the *OOH* is to start with the alphabetical index to occupations at the back of the book. Here the approach is to seek out specific occupational titles and pursue those of interest. There are several routes to follow. Turn directly to the information on a general heading — for example, again, engineers. Under "Engineers" the index lists several subcategories under "see also," and then it lists alphabetically the same ten specific kinds of engineers as appeared in the table of contents. No matter how or where a person starts, the *OOH* provides information on occupations and refers the reader to related occupational titles.

Occupational Information

Whether you get into the *Occupational Outlook Handbook* through the table of contents at the front of the book or the index at the back, the *OOH* provides a wealth of information on occupations — and the quality of the information can't be beaten. The *OOH* tells what each occupation is like; education and training requirements; advancement possibilities, earnings, and employment outlook; related occupations to explore; and where to get more information. The *OOH* is a treasure chest.

Each section of the *OOH* follows a pattern that makes it easy to compare one occupation with another. The information for each occupation is summarized in about two pages. It's quick reading and follows this format:

Nature of the Work. This section describes the main duties for people employed in an occupation. For example, the OOH notes that electricians' work is sometimes strenuous. Electricians may stand for long periods of time. They frequently work on ladders and scaffolds, as well as in awkward or cramped positions. Electricians risk injury from electrical shocks, falls, and cuts. They must follow strict safety procedures to avoid injuries.

Work settings vary. Neither we nor our daughters and sons will know in advance the exact working conditions in which they might find themselves, but knowing the normal working conditions is an important consideration in choosing a career. These may be different than they've seen on TV.

Employment. This section reports the number of workers in the occupation and tells whether they are located primarily in certain industries or geographical areas of the country. For example, in 1992 about 266,000 people worked as computer operators, and most were employed by wholesale trade establishments, manufacturing companies, data processing service firms, banks, government agencies, and accounting, auditing, and bookkeeping service firms. The *OOH* indicates what proportion of workers in an occupation work part-time — 1 of

10 in the case of computer operators — and the proportion who are self-employed. If region of the country and size of residential areas are considerations, the *OOH* discusses these.

The size of an occupational group and the number of people in an occupation who work in particular settings are important considerations to people looking for employment, because large occupations, even if growing slowly, offer many openings when workers retire or die. Information on full- and part-time employment may be an important consideration for students, homemakers, or retired persons who want to work part-time.

Training, Other Qualifications, and Advancement. An insurance underwriter with a master's degree in economics said, "It would have been helpful to have had more awareness as a high school student as to what was available as a career and how to best prepare for it." Career preparation considerations are an increasingly important part of the career choice process as levels of education and training in the general population continue to rise, workplace routines become more automated and computerized, and employers' requirements become more specialized.

Not all occupations are open to everyone. Some require that applicants have certificates, licenses, advanced degrees, or pass examinations to enter a field. Other occupations list preferences for candidates with high school or college course work in particular areas.

There are various ways to prepare for employment:

- College study leading to a certificate or degree
- Programs offered by public or private postsecondary vocational schools
- Home study courses
- Government training programs
- Experience or training obtained in the armed forces
- Apprenticeship and other formal training offered by employers
- High school courses and tech prep

The *OOH* indicates the preferred preparation for each occupation. If employers accept alternative programs, it lists these, too. The book also indicates whether continuing education is required to maintain the position. The level of qualifications workers possess often determines the level at which they enter an occupation and how quickly they may advance. This kind of information would have been useful to a nurse in the Career Development Study, who told us:

> *" I chose a three-year nursing program instead of a four-year bachelor's degree program, not knowing until after I got into nursing school that the three-year programs were soon to be phased out. I wasn't made to realize that four-year nurses were the only ones who could do public health, supervise, etc."*

This section specifies common forms of certification and licensure required to enter an occupation. However, states vary regarding certification and licensure requirements for certain occupations, and parents and young people should always supplement *OOH* data with information from the appropriate state agency. The *OOH* also lists other qualifications, including personal characteristics, that are generally needed or desired of workers in the occupation.

The *OOH* indicates that some occupations are natural stepping stones to others. If a pattern of movement from one occupation to another exists, the *OOH* discusses it. For example, experienced dietitians may advance to assistant or associate director, or to director of a dietetic department, or they may become self-employed. They may leave the occupation and become sales representatives for equipment or food manufacturers.

Information on career possibilities is useful. Skills gained working at one job may enhance a person's "working capital," making him or her employable for another position, perhaps a more desirable job. Sometimes moving from one occupation to another requires more than the training or experience acquired on the job. The *OOH* outlines the possibilities for advancement with additional training and indicates in-service programs available by which employees may enhance their skills.

Job Outlook. A person's interests, abilities, and career goals are important considerations in selecting a career, but whether the job market is favorable is also an important consideration for young people in determining whether to pursue a specific career. What can be done to help young people prepare for careers? A flight attendant with a college major in fine arts said, "Being realistic with individuals, letting kids know what areas of the market are glutted." A teacher spoke from his personal experience:

> *" I now feel that if I'd known the facts about the saturated market and had been encouraged to pursue other career goals, I might have entered an entirely different field and found satisfying employment sooner."*

The job outlook section outlines the employment prospects for each occupation. The information includes a statement of the expected change in employment in the occupation and whether the job opportunities are likely to be favorable or unfavorable. In some cases, the *OOH* provides information on the supply of workers. It also indicates how soon employment prospects are likely to develop. In other cases, the *OOH* comments on the effect fluctuations in economic activity are likely to have on employment in the occupation.

The *OOH* uses standard rhetoric for describing projected changes in employment. Following are key phrases and their meaning for employment projections:

Statement	Projection
"Much faster than average"	41% or more increase
"Faster than average"	27% to 40% increase
"About as fast as average"	14% to 26% increase
"Little change or grow more slowly"	0% to 13% increase
"Decline"	1% or more decrease

So, also, the *OOH* has a standard way of describing job opportunities and employment competition:

Statement	Comparison of Job Openings to Job Seekers
"Excellent opportunities"	Much more numerous
"Very good opportunities"	More numerous
"Good or favorable opportunities"	About the same
"May face competition"	Fewer
"May face keen competition"	Much fewer

Information on expected changes in employment is useful, but it should be used carefully. No one can predict labor market conditions perfectly, the number of job openings and job seekers changes constantly, and employment prospects in a particular state or locality may differ from the national outlook described in the *OOH*. Later in this chapter, I explain where to get information on state and local employment conditions.

Areas of slow growth, strong competition for available positions, and few openings should cause young people to pause, but this information alone should not prevent them from pursuing careers that really interest them. Even occupations that are small or overcrowded offer jobs that are vacated when people retire or die, and there is always a need to replace those who leave the occupation. If the occupation is large, the number of job openings that occur from replacement needs is generally much larger than the number that occurs in small occupations, even those with high growth rates. But replacements are needed even in small occupations. Parents and young people should not rule out a potentially rewarding career simply because the employment outlook for that occupation is not favorable.

Earnings. The earnings level for a prospective occupation is another important career consideration.

People tend to think of earnings in terms of money — a check deposited in the bank or cash in the pocket at the end of the month. But money is not the only financial reward for work. Earnings and pay plans take many different forms.

Workers may be paid a straight annual salary, an hourly wage, commissions based on a percentage of what they sell, a contracted price, a piece rate for items they produce, or tips for service to customers. Combination payment plans are common, in which workers are paid salary plus commissions, or salary or hourly wage plus tips, piece rate, or bonuses.

Benefits are a major consideration and include Social Security contributions; workers' compensation; vacation, holiday and sick leave; life, health, dental, and accident insurance; retirement plans; and supplemental employment benefits. Employees may receive stock options, profit sharing plans, savings plans, tuition assistance, tuition for dependents, expense accounts, bonuses, professional development reimbursement, parental leave, childcare, and employee assistance programs.

Other forms of salary supplementation may occur from working overtime, night shifts, or irregular hours. Workers may receive part of their earnings in the form of goods and services. Sales workers in department stores may receive employee discounts on purchases. Private household workers may receive free meals or free housing. Academics may receive sabbatical leaves. Plumbers and electricians may be allowed to supplement their wage or salary income with jobs on the side. Workers in other jobs may receive uniforms, business expense accounts, use of company cars, or free transportation on company-owned planes.

In 1991, benefits totalled 28 percent of total compensation — hardly just "fringes." All are provided in total or substantial part by employers and are a major consideration for people making career decisions.

It is not easy to determine which occupations provide the highest earnings because good information is available only for wages and salaries. In some cases, not even that is available. In addition, pay levels may depend on the worker's experience, seniority, or qualifications. Pay levels differ between occupations and within occupations. Earnings may vary by geographic location, by industry, or by the specialty or type of work performed within occupations.

The earnings reported by the *OOH* generally are the figures for workers in private industry who are not in supervisory positions or engaged in farming, and the earnings information is normally two to three years old. For all of these reasons, it is always wise to check with local employers about earnings for a particular occupation, and parents and young people must exercise caution when interpreting earnings information.

Related Occupations. This short section lists occupations that require similar worker aptitudes, interests, education, and training. These occupations may be viable alternatives to a young person's primary interests, and it is useful to read about them to get the bigger picture. One of the young women in our Career Development Study criticized high schools and colleges, saying: "The practical, realistic approach to life was sadly missing." What did she say could be done to help young people prepare for the future?

> *" Better programs exploring a much wider range of career opportunities. Many people fall between auto mechanics and attorneys. A much wider approach is vital."*

The related occupations section in the *OOH* gives that wider approach.

Sources of Additional Information. This section appears at the end of every occupational description in the *OOH*. It identifies government agencies, professional societies, trade associations, unions, corporations, and educational institutions that provide additional information about specific occupations. Much of the information is free and may be available in career centers, guidance offices, or libraries.

The *Occupational Outlook Handbook* is the single best source of occupational information for the entire country. It is an ideal resource for persons like this participant in our Career Development Study, now a receptionist in a doctor's office:

> *" High school prepared me to do well in college, but neither prepared me or showed me the opportunities for work . . . no one ever showed me the options."*

The *OOH* is a valuable resource, and I explain where you can get and use copies in "Next Steps: What Parents Can Do" at the close of this chapter. But parents and young people should supplement that national information with information on their state and region. Fortunately, state and regional information has improved greatly and has become much more accessible in recent years.

STATE INFORMATION

A college graduate who now works as a sales manager for a department store on the West Coast speaks for many young people when he answered our questions about the major problems he had encountered since leaving high school. "The major problem was I had no clear idea of what I wanted to do and what most occupations involve," he said. Fortunately, there is good information available on what occupations involve, and it is becoming more and more accessible through Occupational Information Systems (OIS) and Career Information Delivery Systems (CIDS).

National Occupational Information Coordinating Committee

In 1976, the U.S. Congress established the National Occupational Information Coordinating Committee (NOICC) to promote the development and use of labor market information. NOICC (pronounced "no-ik") gives common direction and integration to the activities of 10 federal agencies that focus on different aspects of the U.S. economy, including the Departments of Labor, Education, Commerce, Defense, and Agriculture. Since its inception 18 years ago, NOICC has developed a remarkable system through which the career development needs of the nation's youth and adults are being addressed with increasing efficiency and effectiveness. The system gets better every year. What is available to young people (and adults) today was unheard of 10 years ago — even 5 years ago. Every parent needs to know about the NOICC system, and every young person needs to use it.

NOICC's activities focus on creating labor market and occupational databases for public use, linking education and work through career education and career development programs, and providing training and technical assistance to users of labor market and occupational information and career development programs.

Good occupational and labor market information is critical if individuals are to make responsible and informed career decisions and if society is to deal with work force issues effectively; but the information must be organized so that it is understandable and useful to individuals making decisions about education, work, and careers, to educators and trainers engaged in the development of work force preparedness programs, and to decision makers who establish work force policy. NOICC is charged with generating and disseminating valid and reliable information that addresses work force and workplace needs, current and future. NOICC's operations are funded by the U.S. Departments of Labor and Education.

State Occupational Information Coordinating Committees

Under NOICC's direction, state occupational information coordinating committees (SOICCs) are established to coordinate activities at the state level. SOICCs (pronounced "so-iks") work with state producers and users of occupational, educational/training, and labor market information. Together, NOICC and the SOICCs have developed a network that generates, integrates, and delivers career and labor market information that federal and state agencies collect. NOICC is the super committee that works at the federal level and comes up with the grand design. SOICCs are the worker bees at the local level. Together the NOICC/SOICC network makes available national and state occupational, educational, and labor market information that is designed to serve the career development needs of individuals.

If I sound like a cheerleader for the NOICC/SOICC network, I am. I have watched the development of the network since its inception in the mid-'70s, and I am truly impressed with the progress these agencies have made in developing and disseminating occupational, educational, and labor force information, together with a variety of supporting programs, to serve the career development needs of youth and adults. Reviewing the many programs and products generated by NOICC/SOICC goes beyond the purposes of this chapter, but every parent and young person needs to know about and can benefit immensely from the career information that is available through the NOICC/SOICC system.

The Occupational Information System

Since 1977, NOICC has worked with the SOICCs in each state to develop state-level occupational information systems (OISs). In its most advanced form, an OIS is a computerized database that combines multiple-source occupational and educational data for use by state and local program planners. In their earlier and more primitive form, the databases were not computerized but took the form of information files, printed materials, visual presentations, and the like. Today, the state of the art is computerized database systems, though SOICCs also continue to use other methods to distribute information. For example, many SOICCs annually publish a career information tabloid. The newspaper contains information about state-specific career planning, education and training opportunities, promising occupations, and sources of career planning and assistance. The information is updated every year and is widely distributed through schools. Typically, the little newspaper is the finest review of career planning resources available in a particular state.

Each SOICC develops and implements its own occupational information system (OIS) program with financial and technical assistance from NOICC. This gives state OISs the capability of combining data from many sources. Thus, an OIS database may contain extensive state and local labor market information, such as current and projected demand for workers by occupation as well as information on the supply of graduates of related training programs. Some OIS systems also contain information on working conditions, educational requirements, and wages in specific occupations, as well as information about training programs, educational institutions, industries, and employers in the state. This capacity and flexibility enables state OIS systems to meet multiple needs and serve various users. These include the information needs of vocational education, economic development, and employment and training program planners and managers. It allows users to link projected occupational needs with existing training programs and to plan future program offerings — all of this in addition to serving the career development needs of individuals.

Currently, the OIS is undergoing a major redesign in order to provide a more comprehensive database and user-friendly features. The redesign will include development of a microcomputer-based Occupational Information System that will increase the use of occupational information to support programs in the vocational/technical and employment and training areas. NOICC will customize the new system for each state. A core set of databases will be available to each state OIS, and these will be supplemented by state and local-level occupation and labor market information databases. The new system will allow states to upgrade their systems as they improve their computing capabilities and data sources.

Following are examples of questions the new OIS systems will answer for residents of each state:

- What are the fastest growing industries in my state?
- What are the fastest growing occupations?
- What occupations will have the most job openings?
- What occupations require licensing?
- What industries are declining in employment?
- What occupations are declining in employment?

The new OIS systems was delivered to all SOICCs in 1994. States are now incorporating their state-specific data and testing the system for wide-scale distribution and use. The system should be available in your state as you read this chapter.

Career Information Delivery Systems

Career Information Delivery Systems (CIDS) are computer-based systems that provide information about occupations and education/training programs within a state. CIDS are important resources in career and employment counseling, job placement, educational planning, and vocational and career education programs. They are critical tools for career counselors. They are a welcomed resource and may be used directly by individuals at selected sites for exploring options and opportunities.

CIDS contain information about hundreds of occupations and related education and job training programs. Each occupation is described in terms of duties, employment outlook, earnings levels, working conditions, and licensing and educational requirements. Education and training information in the systems includes descriptions of postsecondary and job training programs, as well as the admissions policies, services, financial aid, and other programs at specific institutions. Most CIDS also include information on military occupations and training opportunities.

CIDS are a tremendous resource for young people making career plans. They use computers to relate personal characteristics — such as interests, aptitudes, and educational goals — to occupations and career possibilities. Using a computer, young people (and adults, too!) can request information about particular occupations or ask the computer to match their personal characteristics with possible occupations. The responses are displayed on a computer screen and may be printed for later review.

State CIDS are located at about 20,000 sites across the nation. The systems are used widely, especially in public schools. About two-thirds of all CIDS are located in high schools, junior high schools, and elementary schools. Together, the CIDS serve an estimated 10 million people every year.

CIDS programs are also increasingly available where career development services are provided for adults. These include job service offices, continuing education centers, social service agencies, rehabilitation agencies, military bases, state correctional institutions, librar-ies, and private industries. CIDS are located in state employment and training agencies, community colleges, and four-year colleges and universities. In the future, assuming the one-stop career centers concept develops, they will certainly be available in the centers.

The NOICC/SOICC network is continually developing new features to address the needs of the citizens of each state. These include graduate school files, financial aid and scholarship files, employer files, entrepreneurial files, and job bank files for the impaired. Some CIDS have information files about the world of work, writing resumes, and interview techniques. Other systems include current job listings from the state's job service agency.

In summary, the *Occupational Outlook Handbook* provides the best occupational information available on a nationwide basis, and the SOICCs provide the best informa-tion available on occupations for each state. The name of the particular career information delivery system may differ from one state to another, but keep three points in mind:

> ■ State occupational information is available through your State Occupa-tional Information Coordinating Committee (SOICC).
>
> ■ States have Career Information Delivery Systems (CIDS) that are designed to serve the information needs of state residents.
>
> ■ The SOICCs and CIDS provide the best occupation, education, and labor market information available for your state and, possibly, for your locality within your state.

You pay for these programs with your tax dollars. Use the services. The next section tells you how.

Finding Your SOICC

"SOICC" may not be listed in your telephone directory for two reasons. First, most states incorporate the name of the state in the name of the committee. For example, the state of Michigan doesn't have a SOICC, but it has a MOICC — that is, the Michigan Occupational Information Coordinating Committee. And there are COICCs (Colorado), GOICCs (Georgia), KOICCs (Kentucky), LOICCs (Louisiana), TOICCs (Tennessee), UOICCs (Utah), VOICCs (Virginia), and (WOICCs) Wisconsin — to name just a few. Check an abbreviation that incorporates the name of your state. Usually the name of the state comes first.

But your SOICC may not be listed for a second reason. States, like the federal government, have a habit of reorganizing themselves every now and then — about every time there is an election. When reorganization fever sets in, people change, agency names change, and organizational charts change. This means that the occupational information coordinating committee in your state may have its own identity or, alternatively, may be hidden in the state Department of Labor, the Department of Employment and Training, the Division of Employment Security, or wherever.

But it exists! The trick is to track it down. How can parents and young adults find their State Occupational Information Coordinating Committee and find out where they can use their state Career Information Delivery System? Here are two foolproof ways to track down the systems — and you may have to use them:

> ■ Call your State Department of Labor and ask where you can get information from your State Occupational Information Coordinating Committee.
>
> ■ Write or call the director of your state system directly. The most recent title, address, and telephone number of your state employment security agency director of research and SOICC directors are listed in an appendix at the back of the *Occupational Outlook Handbook* (pages 465–467 in the '94–'95 edition). You can locate a copy of the *OOH* in a school career center or public library.

Additional Labor Force Information

As I have emphasized, labor force information is perishable; it gets old. Parents and young people should always use the most recent information. That applies to the information in this book, too. By January 1996, the Bureau of Labor Statistics will begin publishing new projections; and by mid-1996, the new projections will be available, if you know where to find them. It may take another year or two before the projections are widely available from commercial publishers. Let me tell you where to find the information earlier.

The Bureau of Labor Statistics projections and related publications appear in several forms and in various formats. Nonetheless, there is a pattern to the release of the projections. Following is the sequence in which the projections normally occur and a brief description of the publications.

New projections usually are first distributed in the *Monthly Labor Review (MLR)*, and the November *MLR* in odd-numbered years is usually the lead issue. For example, the November 1993 issue, which released the most recent projections, contained five articles on projections. Four focused on major components of the projections — labor force, economic growth, industry employment, and occupational employment — and the fifth summarized the projections and discussed major related issues. The *MLR* tends to get a little bit technical, however, leaning toward overkill for many readers, and it is not always easy reading.

But the information is all there, and it is important because it is the first public release of new projections. Most libraries carry the *MLR*.

The most popular, concise, and illustrated discussion of major work force projections appears slightly later, in the Fall issue of the *Occupational Outlook Quarterly (OOQ)*. The Fall 1993 issue, for example, sketched the major projections in terms of labor force growth and employment in industries and occupations. The *OOQ* is highly illustrated and easy reading. It, too, is available in libraries.

The *MLR* articles are republished or reworked and appear in other forms. For example, the Bureau's *The American Work Force: 1992–2005*, which was published in early 1994, contains the five *MLR* articles, articles on the documentation of methods used to develop the projections, plus some additional tabulations that were not published as part of the original five articles. Much of this is technical reading.

The popular *Occupational Outlook Handbook (OOH)*, which I discussed earlier in this chapter, is also published every two years. It abstracts and popularizes the same information that appears in the *MLR* and the *OOQ*. The next edition of the *OOH*, the 1996–97 edition, should appear in the Spring of 1996, following late Fall release of the new projections. At about the same time, the Bureau also publishes 20 reprints from the *OOH*, each focusing on a set of related occupations that appear in the *OOH*.

Also published in Spring following the Fall release of new information is the *Occupational Projections and Training Data (OPTD)*, which is a statistical supplement to the *OOH* used by educational planners and career guidance specialists. The *OPTD* contains comprehensive information about the age, sex, and race of workers in more than 600 detailed occupations; provides tabular summaries on growth rates and replacement rates for detailed occupations; and reports data on completions of education and training programs by field of training. It also ranks occupations by growth rate, earnings, unemployment rate, and a number of other considerations that are important in evaluating employment prospects in various occupations. This tends to be technical data that is usually not of interest to parents.

"The Job Outlook in Brief" is an article that appears in the Spring issue of the *OOQ*, following release of new labor force projections. It reports the latest employment levels, usually two years after the data are gathered, and it projects employment 12 or 13 years for the same occupations that appear in the *OOH*. The article also gives a short explanation of the expected trends.

"The Outlook for College Graduates" is normally the last article on projections to appear, focusing on the supply-demand situation for college graduates. The *Outlook* is published in the Summer issue of the *Occupational Outlook Quarterly*.

In 1992, the Bureau produced a new product, *The Career Guide to Industries*, a companion volume to the *OOH*, which focuses on occupations. The *Guide* outlines the nature of the work, working conditions, occupations, and earnings in industries that make up the economy, ranging from the oldest (agriculture) to the newest (computers and television). A regular printing schedule for the *Guide* has not yet been established.

Three of the above publications are particularly noteworthy for parents with children choosing careers: The *Monthly Labor Review (MLR)*, because it is the first source of new labor force projections; the *Occupational Outlook Quarterly (OOQ)*, because it presents the new projections in condensed, graphical, and highly readable form; and the *Occupational Outlook*

Handbook, which, earlier in the chapter, I described as the bible of occupational information. Each of these is available in most public libraries and all may be purchased from the Government Printing Office (see "Next Steps: What Parents Can Do" at the end of this chapter).

Other Sources of Information

Parents and young people have access to other sources of career information. Libraries, career centers, and guidance offices in schools are the most common resource centers. Typically, they have copies of the *Occupational Outlook Handbook* as well as other reference books, brochures, magazines, and audiovisual materials on occupations, careers, self-assessment, and job hunting. Collections of occupational materials are also available in public libraries, college libraries, learning resource centers, women's centers, and career counseling centers. Check with your librarian and also with the telephone operator. They can help you get information.

Counselors play an important role in making career information available. You should use their knowledge and expertise. Counseling and vocational testing are available in a number of places:

- Guidance offices in high schools
- Placement offices in vocational schools
- Career planning and placement offices in colleges
- Job service offices affiliated with the U.S. employment service
- Vocational rehabilitation agencies
- Counseling services offered by community organizations
- Commercial firms and professional consultants

Most career guidance offices offer a variety of services, materials, and activities. Materials include films, filmstrips, cassettes, tapes, kits, interest and aptitude inventories, and occupational information systems. Many of these career exploration activities are now on computer — fun and easy to use. Activities include individual advising, group discussions, guest speakers, field trips, and career days. It is useful to have some general career areas in mind when you and your son or daughter visit these centers, although counselors are able to help people in the early stages of career choice, too.

The important thing is to start the career search process using whatever resources are available. It's like climbing a ladder or stairway. Every step you take gives a clearer picture of what lies ahead. That's what you want.

If I had no idea where to start, I would do two things:

- I would begin by paging through the *Occupational Outlook Handbook.* It's available in high school career centers and libraries.
- Next, I would work through the information from my State Occupational Information Coordinating Committee.

And don't overlook the staff at resource centers. They are there to help you, too, and most are eager to do so.

A young man who studied psychology in college and now works for his family's construction firm told us that "educated adults are the kids' best bet." One of the ways parents and other adults can help young people is by knowing where to go and where to start when searching for good career information.

Information for Special Groups

One of the benefits of living in the U.S. is that ours is a society that believes and acts to level the playing field, to provide equal opportunity and take affirmative actions to correct inequities. Certain groups — including youth, the disabled, the impaired, women, and racial minorities — face special challenges in securing viable careers and employment. Our sociopolitical system may be less than perfect, but there are agencies, public and private, that are dedicated to creating opportunities for people with special needs. The following organizations provide career information for people with special needs.

Disabled

The President's Committee on Employment of People with Disabilities, 1331 F Street, NW, 3rd Floor, Washington DC 20004; Phone: (202)376-6200.

The Sight Impaired

The Federation of the Blind provides a free national reference and referral service for the sight-impaired. Information may be obtained by contacting Job Opportunities for the Blind, National Federation of the Blind, 1800 Johnson St., Baltimore, MD 21230; Phone: (800)638-7518.

Women

U.S. Department of Labor, Women's Bureau, 200 Constitution Avenue, NW, Washington DC 20210; Phone: (202)219-6652.

Catalyst, 250 Park Avenue South, 5th Floor, New York, NY 10003; Phone: (212)777-8900.

Wider Opportunities for Women, 1325 G Street, NW, Lower Level, Washington DC 20005; Phone: (202)638-3143.

Minorities

Inquire with the National Association for the Advancement of Colored People (NAACP), 4805 Mt. Hope Dr., Baltimore, MD 21215; Phone: (410)358-8900.

The National Urban League is a nonprofit, community-based social service and civil rights organization that assists African Americans in the achievement of social and economic equality. The League has 113 local affiliates around the country that provide services related to employment and job training, education, and career development. Check your telephone directory for the National Urban League affiliate in your locality.

Next Steps: What Parents Can Do

A major Educational Testing Service (ETS) study of career information systems is critical of students and career counselors. The criticism of students is that they don't take advantage of the career information resources high schools make available. The criticism of counselors is that many could not identify a single resource for up-to-date information on local wages and salaries, job security and tenure, jobs that involve helping others, or occupations that are accessible to the handicapped. It is not my purpose to throw stones at either students or counselors, but I emphasize two themes that appear throughout this book: Young people need help choosing careers, and parents can help them.

In Part II, I focused on the world of work, how it is changing, where it is going, and the importance of knowing the key resources parents and young people can use in choosing a career:

> - If you, a parent, have never been to your son's or daughter's high school career center, I urge you to go. You will be impressed by the amount and variety of career information materials that decorate the shelves and fill the filing cabinets.
>
> - If you haven't seen the career explorations programs on computer in your high school career center, ask the people in the career center to show you how they work. You will be wowed!
>
> - If you have never met your daughter's or son's career counselor or don't know who the counselor is, call your high school. Find out. Make an appointment. Meet your son's or daughter's career counselor.
>
> - If your daughter or son has never taken an interest inventory or aptitude test, find out what is available in your career center and make arrangements for one.

Unfortunately, too many students don't use the career centers; and too many parents aren't aware of what resources they've paid for with their tax dollars that are available to them through the schools.

Let me share some important information with you. For more than a decade public high schools in more than 40 states have used a program I wrote that is designed to help parents help their sons and daughters choose careers — the same purpose as this book. An important part of that program is getting parents into the high school career centers with their daughters and sons to use the materials together. And here is the point: Never — not once in more than 10 years and in more than 40 states! — have I ever gotten a complaint from a high school career counselor, principal, or superintendent that they didn't want parents in the career center. Never have I received that complaint. Always, the opposite is true. Schools have welcomed parents.

> ■ Go to the career center with your daughter or son.
> ■ Afraid they don't want to be seen with you? Ask them to show you how the computerized career explorations programs work.

Parents can help their sons and daughters choose careers, and one of the best places to start is the *Occupational Outlook Handbook* (OOH).

> ■ Consider buying a copy of the *OOH*, available in paperback and hard-cover editions (the cost of the 1994–'95 hardcover edition is $23), and keep it at home on the coffee table.

The *OOH* is the best information on occupations you can buy. Send for it from the Government Printing Office, Superintendent of Documents, Washington, DC 20402. You will have to pay in advance, so check the current cost before ordering. Phone: (202) 783-3238, for price and ordering information.

Let me suggest two other widely used references for occupational information. One is *The Encyclopedia of Careers and Vocational Guidance*, which is a commercial product. The *Encyclopedia* is well-written and illustrated and is also fairly widely available. Many students and counselors find it helpful and easier reading than the *Occupational Outlook Handbook*. Many career centers and libraries have the *Encyclopedia*. It's there for your use.

Exploring Careers is a good resource for middle school/junior high school students. It promotes career awareness through stories about people at work, photographs, evaluative questions, suggested activities, and career games. *Exploring Careers* is available from the Government Printing Office. The information for ordering is the same as for the *OOH*.

Information about the employment outlook for regions of the country comes out irregularly in the media. Be aware, however, that each year, about mid-October, the *New York Times* publishes a special Sunday supplement on careers that projects the effects of social, political, and economic changes on the labor market. Often the *Times* supplement focuses on the impact of these changes for regions of the country. Watch for it. The *Christian Science Monitor* occasionally, but irregularly, also publishes articles on careers. And, of course, the popular news magazines — *Time*, *Newsweek*, and *U.S. News and World Report* — sometimes feature the employment outlook and give attention to regions of the country.

> **Find out what career information is available for your state by calling your State Occupational Information Coordinating Committee (SOICC). The phone number for your SOICC is listed on pages 465–467 of the Occupational Outlook Handbook.**

But take advantage of national, state, and local information available through your State Occupational Information Coordinating Committee and Career Information Delivery Systems.

Decision-Making Steps

The problems young people have with choosing careers can be broken down into smaller components. Learning more about occupations, industries, and career preparation options are examples. But there is another problem that a lot of young people have. They don't know how to make decisions — about anything!

I urge parents to teach their children a simple four-step decision-making strategy. These are the four steps:

Step #1:   Identify interest

Step #2:   Get Information

Step #3:   Evaluate information

Step #4:   Narrow choices

Following these four steps can help youngsters make decisions in a lot of different areas, including about occupational careers and career preparation possibilities.

Example: Suppose a young person wants to buy a car. Step 1 is to identify interests, and those might be something like this: "Need a four-wheel drive vehicle with lots of power and big wheels; must be rugged and 'open'; can't cost more than $5,000; must be able to pull a boat; must be able to do routine maintenance myself."

Step 2 is to get information. Who makes such a vehicle? Certainly not Cadillac, but Jeep does. Additional information will reveal that Toyota, Suzuki, and some other manufacturers also produce such a vehicle. And the less-than-$5,000 price limit suggests that going to new car dealers will be a waste of time, so it probably makes sense to check the advertisements in the paper and to visit used car lots. This will probably produce six or eight vehicles to check out.

Step 3 is to evaluate the information. That includes checking how many miles are on each vehicle; checking the tires and battery and condition of the body; possibly reading *Consumer Reports* about the repair records of each vehicle; road testing the vehicles to see whether each one holds the road, needs brakes, leaks oil, and whether the clutch slips; and determining whether the vehicle with 105,000 miles is worth $2,900.

Step 4 is to narrow the choices. That means rejecting the one with 105,000 miles (too many miles). It means ruling out the one that is really neat but sells for $7,400 (can't afford it). It means ignoring the one with spongy brakes that also leaks transmission fluid (don't need those expenses). It means selecting two or three from which a final decision will be made, and eventually choosing from them.

Parents can use the same four steps to choose new carpeting for the den, buy a fishing boat, or make vacation plans. More important, young people can use the four-step procedure to sort out their occupational career and career preparation options.

To-Do Check List

❏   Visit the high school career center.

❏   Observe how computer career explorations programs work in the high school career center.

❏   Meet your son's or daughter's high school career counselor.

❏   Arrange for your daughter or son to take an interest inventory and aptitude test.

❏   Buy a copy of the *Occupational Outlook Handbook* for home use.

❏   Call your State Occupational Information Coordinating Committee and ask for career planning information on your state.

❏   Teach your daughter or son a simple decision-making model.

❏   Visit your local library to find out what materials are available for career planning.

❏   If your daughter or son has special needs, contact the information sources for special groups listed in this chapter.

College Degrees and Certificates

CHAPTER EIGHT

C hoosing a career involves two decisions, not just one. The first decision is choosing an occupation. That's what the first half of the book is about. The second decision, choosing a career preparation strategy, is every bit as important. That's what the second half of the book is about. Just as there are more occupational possibilities to consider than ever before, so also there are more ways to prepare for a career than ever before. And the luxury of choosing from so many options — both occupational possibilities and career preparation possibilities — can be a big part of the problem young people face. My purpose in Parts III and IV is to provide a road map for parents and young people to follow as they sort through their career preparation options.

Basically, there are three things young people can do after they graduate from high school:

> ■ They can go straight into the work force (get a job).
> ■ They can get additional schooling (go to college).
> ■ They can earn-while-they-learn (follow a vocational preparation program).

Most young people will end up following some combination of the three: work and college together; vocational preparation and then college; some college and then vocational preparation; some college, then work — there are all kinds of possibilities. But the three components, no matter how young people put them together, will be work, schooling, and vocational preparation. I don't say very much about going straight to work — in my judgment, there isn't much to be said for that! But I do outline the additional schooling possibilities in Part III, and earning while learning, the vocational preparation possibilities, in Part IV.

If I had my choice, I would reverse the order of presenting the options. I would outline the vocational preparation possibilities first, and then discuss the college possibilities. I tried to write the book that way for three reasons. First, most young people will never get a four-year college degree. Of those who enroll in college, only half will get a bachelor's degree. Most young people follow a vocational preparation strategy, not a college education strategy; and it would make sense to write this book in ways that would help most young people. Second, most employment openings in today's labor force do not require a college degree. As we move toward the year 2005, jobs that require education beyond high school will grow the fastest and pay the best, but the largest number of job openings will require only a high school education. Most job prospects do not require a college education.

Education Requirements for Fastest Growing Jobs, 1992–2005

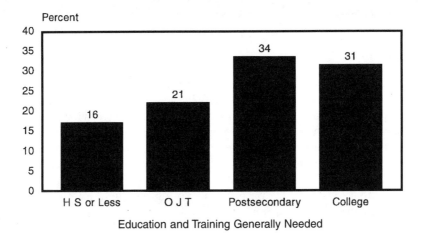

Figure 8-1 *Source: Occupational Outlook Quarterly, Spring 1994*

And, finally, not only is the greatest need in the area of understanding vocational preparation possibilities, that's also where most of the action is. Government initiatives and education and work force reforms all stress vocational preparation. Vocational education programs are every bit as important as college — and they affect more than three times as many people. I discuss the additional schooling possibilities first, not because they are better or more important, but because most vocational preparation programs include a schooling component. So, it is easier to review today's career preparation possibilities by starting with additional schooling.

Work, additional schooling, and vocational preparation are the three tracks a young person can follow after leaving high school. Actually, the vocational preparation options I outline include some possibilities that begin while the student is still in high school, but let's keep it simple. Both career preparation tracks — additional schooling and vocational preparation — offer a range of possibilities and, therefore, decisions that a young person must make. When you map out the possibilities, they take the form of the chart shown in figure 8-2. I call it my Career Preparation Chart, or the CPC.

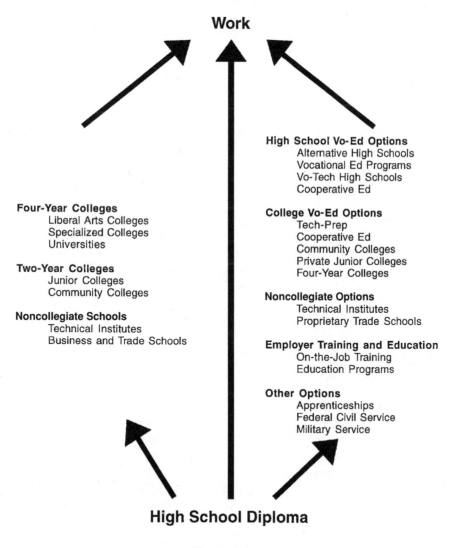

The Career Preparation Chart (CPC)

Work

High School Vo-Ed Options
Alternative High Schools
Vocational Ed Programs
Vo-Tech High Schools
Cooperative Ed

Four-Year Colleges
Liberal Arts Colleges
Specialized Colleges
Universities

College Vo-Ed Options
Tech-Prep
Cooperative Ed
Community Colleges
Private Junior Colleges
Four-Year Colleges

Two-Year Colleges
Junior Colleges
Community Colleges

Noncollegiate Schools
Technical Institutes
Business and Trade Schools

Noncollegiate Options
Technical Institutes
Proprietary Trade Schools

Employer Training and Education
On-the-Job Training
Education Programs

Other Options
Apprenticeships
Federal Civil Service
Military Service

High School Diploma

Figure 8-2

Let me walk you through the CPC. Start at the bottom of the page with a high school diploma. There are three basic paths to the top, to a career. The middle path goes straight to work. Take a full-time job. It's the most direct, right up the middle of the page. I needn't tell you that I don't recommend that path. I do agree, however, that the path is there.

The path to the left offers options, and it certainly enhances career prospects. It's the additional schooling path. If a young person decides on additional schooling as a career preparation strategy, there are follow-up decisions to make: What kind of schooling? The choices are between four-year colleges and universities, two-year colleges, and noncollegiate schools (technical institutes, business, and trade schools). Each additional schooling possibility has its advantages and disadvantages.

The path to the right is vocational preparation, and it offers the most possibilities of all. I've packaged the possibilities in terms of high school options, college options, noncollegiate options, and "other" options — apprenticeships, federal civil service, and occupational training in the military. All together, I review 15 vocational preparation possibilities that young people can follow.

Deciding on a career preparation strategy is what Parts III and IV are all about.

THE PURPOSES OF EDUCATION

"You have to go to college to get a good job." Most people believed that in the past, and many still do. Education has been as much a part of the American value system as hot dogs, Chevrolet, and apple pie.

But as a parent, what do you want your son or daughter to learn? And why? Most likely, you will be paying much of the cost. What do you want to buy? These are old, old questions, and people have answered them in different ways over the centuries:

- The purpose of education is to teach what is true and good and beautiful, to pass the classics to the next generation, whether that be Latin or Shakespearean prose. That's the answer 17th-Century Erasmus and the 20th-Century Dewey gave.

- Forget about the classics, the world is a Tower of Babel — everybody babbling unintelligible sounds. The purpose of education is to train the mind, to teach how to think — logic, rationality — and how to organize knowledge, regardless of what people talk about. That was the Greek philosopher Aristotle's answer in the 3rd Century B.C.E.; and it enjoys much company with those concerned about the information explosion today.

- Get an education to get a job. The goal is vocational training, whether that be agriculture in the 1860s, engineering in the 1900s, or business and computer science in the l990s. That purpose of education is equally at home with Plato in the 3rd Century B.C.E., the career education movement of the 1970s, and college freshmen in an age of high technology and global economics.

> ■ The purpose of education is neither to recite the classics nor to learn to think like Aristotle nor to get a good job. The purpose of education is personal liberation and the development of the individual's potentialities. Education as a personal quest was the rhetoric of the 1960s, but it has its advocates on today's campuses too — though you have to look harder for them.
>
> ■ The goal of education is informed decision making that takes into account a moral and ethical component to life. This position extends beyond the historic claims of religious colleges to include former Harvard University president Derek Bok's emphasis on applied ethics: "A university that refuses to take ethical dilemmas seriously violates its basic obligations to society."

To be sure, the purposes of education blend and blur. No college would say it serves but one purpose. All, particularly as we near the 21st Century, would claim to serve each purpose. Yet the particular mix of purposes varies from one college to the next and, in the case of large and comprehensive colleges, the emphasis will also vary within colleges. I concentrate on career preparation possibilities in this book, but I urge parents and their sons and daughters to recognize that the purposes of a college education are broader than career preparation. To get a job is not the only reason to go to college, and it may not be the best reason.

No other country in the world has as many colleges from which to choose — 3,638 two- and four-year institutions (public and private) at last count that grant degrees, and another 6,961 vocational institutions that award certificates. That's one of the luxuries of living in a free society. But the many possibilities can confuse and further complicate the career choice process. Parents and young people need to decide what they want out of college, and they have to know what colleges have to offer.

An elementary school teacher who recently returned from teaching in Indonesia echoes this point and feels that high schools need to do more to explain schooling options to young people. She told us:

> *"It would be helpful if they [high schools] could tell them [young people] about the different types of schools, colleges, technical training schools, apprenticeship-type programs, and the like. Also, it would be good if they would help the student make the initial contact with these schools or programs."*

Colleges are society's largest talent sorting, career equipping, and job placement institutions. But colleges come in many shapes, sizes, and kinds, and parents and young people need a way to sort through the possibilities. In this chapter, I help you work through the additional schooling options. I discuss the difference between degrees and certificates, consider how colleges have changed since parents may have attended them some years ago, and outline the kinds of colleges from which today's young people can choose.

DEGREES AND CERTIFICATES

The word "college" has become a catch-all category that loosely applies to a variety of education and training programs, whether these offer degrees or certificates, and whether the programs are for four years, more than four years, two years, or less than two years. What the additional schooling and training experiences have in common is that they occur after high school. They are postsecondary programs, and they are offered by three kinds of postsecondary institutions: four-year colleges, two-year colleges, and noncollegiate schools (technical institutes, business schools, and trade schools). Postsecondary institutions offer education and training for students who have completed high school graduation requirements.

There are many kinds of college programs. I sort them into two major groups — degree programs and certification programs — for purposes of thinking through the possibilities. As the labels suggest, degree programs lead to a degree, and certification programs lead to a certificate. Degree programs are broad programs of study that teach knowledge that is generalizable to a variety of work settings. Certification programs emphasize learning and skill training for near-term employment in specific vocational areas.

Differences and Similarities of Degrees and Certificates

Consider the basic difference. A degree program in physics offers the student a broad understanding of physical properties and processes, mechanics, and principles of energy transfer. The degree program includes the theory of physics so that the learner can use that general knowledge across a broad field of applications. By comparison, a certificate program in, say, transmission repair also deals with energy transfer, but it prepares a trainee for a specific line of work: namely, fixing automobile transmissions. The certificate program emphasizes specialized knowledge, skill, and ability in a narrowly defined area. The focus is on how transmission parts work together rather than on the theory of energy transfer.

> *"The goal of certification programs is to prepare people for narrow specialties, and there are many areas in which a person can prepare for certification."*

Degree programs are standardized across institutions so that students may transfer credits from one institution to many others. Also, degree programs are cumulative. Lower-level degrees are the basis for continuing study toward advanced degrees. By comparison, certificate programs are shorter term and closed-ended. They are not designed to provide the groundwork for advanced study, and a program at one institution is not necessarily compatible with programs offered elsewhere. It is not likely that a trainee can transfer any "credit" from one institution to another. A certificate program may be offered at only a single institution. Once certification is achieved, the program is over. The goal of certification programs is to prepare people for narrow specialties, and there are many areas in which a person can prepare for certification.

In some cases, a degree and certificate may mean much the same. For example, an associate degree may indicate that a person completed a two-year vocational program that is skill-oriented. The program includes related general courses and therefore qualifies the student for an associate degree, which is an academic credential. Alternatively, a certificate might be awarded after two years. It indicates that the person is trained in a specific area and that the program of study has been completed. In either case, the student has completed a terminal vocational preparation program, and the holder of the degree or certificate is ready to go to work.

Levels of Degrees

There are four levels of degrees. In ascending order of accomplishment they are: associate degree, bachelor's degree, master's degree, doctorate or other professional degree.

The most general four-year degree is the B.A. (Bachelor of Arts). The B.A. is required or accepted as general preparation for professional programs that lead to master's and doctoral degrees. Other kinds of bachelor's degrees indicate more specialized academic preparation. The B.S. (Bachelor of Science) degree indicates completion of a four-year academic program that is more focused and specialized than a B.A. program. It is of longer duration and less specific than a certificate program. B.S. degrees are awarded for preparation for a career in such areas as science, business, engineering, agriculture, and education. The B.D. (Bachelor of Divinity) degree is another example. It indicates preprofessional preparation in theology.

A basic question young people have to answer if they want to go to college is whether they are interested in a degree or a certificate program. Both offer career-oriented programs, and the quality of one may not be better than the other. Yet there are differences, and the differences are important. Though both degree and certificate programs may claim to prepare a person for an occupation, the actual entry requirements to an occupation may specify one or the other, often a degree. For example, a person can take computer programming in many kinds of colleges, and the course of study may lead to a certificate after as few as six weeks or to a degree in computer science after four years. But many employers require a degree for entry-level computer programmer positions. Alternatively, even if both degrees and certificates are accepted, employers may look more favorably on degrees than on certificates. This may be true for both initial employment and later advancement or promotion. A purchasing agent in our Career Development Study admitted: "It took a long time for me to realize that I made working hard for myself by trying to bypass college." Similarly, an automobile mechanic concluded: "If I would have studied harder and went to college, I would not have to work with my hands all my life." This mother of two didn't attend college, but she is convinced of the merits of a college education:

> *" I tell my kids they should get a four-year degree. Then their choice of careers is much broader. If they still want to drive a truck, they can still do that and so many other things."*

The same mother offered advice to parents, teachers, and counselors who try to help young people prepare for the future:

> **" Encourage college to all students who are capable. Make sure they know all the ways financially they can be helped — i.e., grants, loans, scholarships."**

The number of degree and certificate programs and the necessity to choose between them is one of the big differences between colleges today and colleges back when you and I may have attended college. "Don't go to college without some clear idea of an occupation or occupational area you want to practice. Otherwise, it is not worth the money." That's what a variety-store department head in Oregon told us, a young man with a bachelor's degree in math. Before considering the kinds of colleges from which today's young people may choose, I review other ways colleges have changed over the years. They've changed with the times.

COLLEGE THEN AND NOW

"Things have changed." That's true of colleges, too. At the turn of the century, only 6 percent of the population graduated from high school, and only 4 percent enrolled in college. By 1940, more than half the population completed no more than an eighth grade education and, of all persons 25 years and older, a quarter completed high school and no more than 5 percent completed college. By 1960, 42 percent of men 25 years and older completed no more than the eighth grade, but 40 percent completed high school and 10 percent completed four years of college. During the 1960s, enrollments rose by 120 percent and educational levels followed suit. Then, from the mid-1970s to 1991, educational levels remained very stable, though the average educational level of the population rose as the more highly educated younger cohorts increasingly replaced older Americans who had lower education levels. By 1991, 78 percent of all persons 25 years old and older completed four years of high school and 21 percent completed four years of college. Of the 25- to 29-year-old age group, 85 percent graduated from high school and 24 percent graduated from college.

Growth

Since World War II, the percentage of people who complete four years of college has moved upward steadily. Rates of college-age enrollments doubled or tripled since 1950, with much of the increase occurring in the 1980s. In 1950, for example, only 30 percent of 18- and 19-year-olds enrolled in school, compared to 60 percent in 1991. Enrollments for 20- to 24-year-olds rose from 9 percent in 1950 to 30 percent in 1990. During the 1960s alone, society dedicated over 700 new collegiate institutions — that's one new college every five days for a decade! Undergraduate enrollments doubled. Between 1980 and 1992, enrollment increased about 20 percent. In 1992, 14.6 million Americans enrolled in colleges at some level.

Why the tremendous growth? You guessed it: The baby boom grew up and that was a big part of it. Also, the economy of the 1960s generated a strong demand for college graduates in managerial and professional jobs. That made a difference, too.

But since 1970, the demand for college graduates and professionals slackened, revenues softened, and enrollments slowed down. That doesn't mean that college enrollments have declined. They haven't. At last count, total undergraduate enrollment was 12,539,820, up 16.6 percent over the past decade. And more than two-thirds of administrators at public universities anticipate further growth in enrollments of 1 to 5 percent for the next five years.

Government Involvement

Two-year colleges gained the lion's share of expanding enrollments. In the early 1960s, only 14 percent of college enrollments were in community colleges. In 1985, 37 percent, more than a third of all college students, attended community colleges. In 1992, 48 percent of students enrolled in public colleges enrolled in two-year colleges; and more than half who enter college enroll in a two-year college.

A long-term trend toward more public funding for higher education accompanied growth in the number of colleges. Over the past 45 years, the amount of public funds going to public colleges rose from less than half to three-fourths of total college revenues, not counting increases in student aid. Student aid programs grew even more dramatically. Federal spending for student aid was $40.3 million in 1958, when the first major federal program of general aid for college students was enacted. Today, annual federal spending for generally available student aid is more than $23.5 billion, and 56 percent of all undergraduates receive some kind of financial aid.

Strings are attached to increased government support. State and federal agencies that administer government funds have taken an increasingly strong hand in college administration and have steadily eroded the policy-making role of trustees, faculties, and administrators. For example, the most recent Almanac Issue of *The Chronicle of Higher Education,* which provides a detailed annual review of the state of higher education across the nation, begins its review of my state as follows: "Politicians in North Carolina have never been reticent about getting involved in higher education, and 1994 was no exception." Today more than ever before, higher education is big business, and it is a regulated industry.

Government involvement has had three effects on the nation's colleges:

- ■ More growth in public than private schools
- ■ More public support for higher education and training
- ■ More government regulation and scrutiny of postsecondary education and training, including institutional reviews, demands for accountability, and restructuring.

The number of colleges has grown. The number of enrollments has grown. The size of institutions of higher education has also grown. In 1955, 8 percent of all students were enrolled on campuses with fewer than 500 students, and only one out of four were enrolled on a campus with a student body numbering over 10,000. Today, 95 percent of all public universities enroll more than 10,000 students; and the third largest campus in the country is a community college — Miami-Dade Community College. It enrolls 51,768 students.

With their higher tuition and more limited curriculum and social life, small private colleges have been losing ground steadily to large public colleges and universities.

Student Body Composition

The makeup of college student bodies has also changed. During the 1960s, the civil rights and feminist movements stirred the nation's conscience on whether college education should remain the restricted privilege of young white males from well-to-do families. Large numbers of previously excluded groups enrolled, particularly minorities and women.

Minorities and Women. Minority students increased from 15 percent of all students in 1976 to nearly 23 percent in 1992. During the 1970s alone, the number of African-American students in higher education more than doubled to nearly 1.25 million. By 1992, 10 percent of all college enrollments were African Americans. Hispanics also enrolled in greater numbers. Hispanics contribute over 7 percent and Asian Americans contribute about 5 percent of total college enrollment. American Indians contribute 1 percent.

During the 1970s, the number of women enrolled in higher education rose from three million to nearly five million. In Fall of 1992, 55 percent of college enrollees were women. Over one five-year period, 1974 to 1979, enrollments of women over age 35 increased by 67 percent.

The turning point occurred in 1979 when, for the first time, more women than men enrolled in U.S. colleges. In 1972, the college enrollment ratio of women and men was 74 women to 100 men, but by 1992 it was 89 men to 100 women. Between 1980 and 1992, the number of men enrolled on college campuses increased 13 percent, but the number of women increased 27 percent. Today, women in the 30-and-older age group outnumber men of the same age by almost two to one on college campuses.

Fifty-six percent of full-time undergraduates are women, 54 percent of graduate students are women, 62 percent of part-time undergraduates are women, and 61 percent of part-time graduate students are women. Also, more than half of students enrolled in noncollegiate institutions are women. Finally, the percentage of degrees awarded to women increased from 24 percent in 1950 to 55 percent in 1992.

Age and Part-Time Students. The age of students also changed during the 1970s, particularly for women. In one four-year period, 1972 to 1976, the proportion of college students over age 25 increased from one out of four to one out of three. By 1981, most college students were over 21 years old, and by 1992 nearly two out of five, 39 percent, were 25 years and older. Between 1980 and 1990, enrollments of students under 25 years old increased 3 percent, but enrollments of persons 25 years and older increased by 34 percent.

Today's colleges accommodate the part-time student, especially the older part-time student. From 1970 to 1992, the proportion of full-time students declined from 68 to 56 percent. In 1992, 22 percent of students under age 25 were part-time students, as were 72 percent of students 25 years and older. Colleges offer them flexible and split schedules, off-campus learning sites, and evening classes. A generation ago, dropping out to work or travel was highly discouraged. Courses followed in rigid sequence and students who dropped out got out of sync with their programs. Today's patterns of college attendance are much more flexible, and "stopping out" is common practice. Academic programs accommodate schooling interruptions.

Student Interests. Student bodies changed in other ways over the past quarter century. Average academic ability, as measured by math SAT scores, was 24 points lower in 1993 than it was in 1967, and verbal SAT scores dropped 32 points over the same period. Over the past decade, math scores increased 10 points, from 468 to 478, but verbal scores declined another point, 425 to 424. Colleges responded by offering remedial courses. In one five-year period, 1975–1980, the number of remedial mathematics courses offered by public four-year colleges increased by 72 percent. By 1992, 95 percent of public four-year colleges and universities and 96 percent of public two-year colleges and universities offered remedial education programs.

The career education movement of the 1970s introduced a significant change in college life. Career education placed strong emphasis on marketable skills, and many liberal arts colleges responded by changing into comprehensive institutions offering business, engineering, computing, nursing, health-related programs, and the like. Student interests changed from political activism to more traditional concerns for jobs and careers, as reflected in these comments from an ex-marine who works for a telephone company in Seattle. He encouraged us to:

> *" . . . emphasize vocational skill training needed for living in the real world. If a student does happen to be of a scholarly frame of mind, that's fine. That's why we have colleges and universities. But the notion that everyone, regardless of personal inclination, should go on to a formal four-year institution is ridiculous."*

Many of our other study respondents reacted in the same way. A stock clerk in the navy said: "Having a blue-collar job and working with your hands does not necessarily mean a lack of intelligence." And a crane operator for the railroad in the state of Washington said that today's young people "should be taught that it is not a sin to work with their hands." Many people agree with the civil engineer who told us that "college and the degree have been oversold to high school kids."

One of the big changes in student interests and program offerings has been a steep increase in the number of certification programs. The proportion of college students majoring in the humanities, social sciences, and physical sciences has declined, while the number of majors in professional and vocational programs has increased.

Lifestyles

Campus lifestyles have changed. Government financial aid programs reduced students' monetary dependence on their families, with the result that many are less dependent on their parents' preferences. Few colleges today take seriously the old *in loco parentis* function, namely, that school administrators take the place of parents in supervising students' personal lives. Many colleges continue to have strict rules on the books about alcohol, drug consumption, and residence hall visiting hours for the opposite sex, but in reality these are often enforced weakly, if at all.

The proportion of students living in college housing dropped from a third in the mid-1960s to a fifth by the 1980s, which is where it remains today, as living arrangements have shifted to private apartments. Today, only a few liberal arts colleges remain largely residential campuses.

Changing Institutional Emphases

Colleges have been responding to change since the beginnings of higher education in America. The first colleges, including Harvard and Yale, were established to maintain society's religious consciousness. The educational programs were primarily theological.

As society became increasingly diversified and secular, course offerings included professional training in law and medicine. After the Civil War, the modern university emerged with emphases on agriculture, industrial production, engineering, science, and business administration. Since World War II, higher education diversified and developed programs for such varied occupations as police officers, fire fighters, nurses, and skilled trades workers. Today's colleges and universities offer career preparation for many students who would not have considered going to college a generation ago.

Colleges approach the year 2000 following a quarter century of difficulties. The boom times of the 1950s and 1960s were followed by the belt tightening of the 1970s, 1980s, and 1990s, when growth rates tapered off and educational costs skyrocketed. Fear for survival replaced the optimism and expansiveness of earlier eras. Some traditional departments in prestigious universities have shut down. And some colleges, particularly private colleges, have closed their doors.

Recruitment

Today's colleges are faced with a very practical problem: how to keep classrooms full. Colleges concentrate on meeting the budget. The strategies include attracting more students, lowering admission requirements, actively recruiting students ignored a few years earlier (minorities, women, older students, foreign students, part-time students, married students), inflating grades so that fewer students flunk out, emphasizing career preparation programs, making arrangements with companies to provide job-relevant continuing education programs for workers, increasing athletic revenues, emphasizing grants and contracts, advertising popular courses, reducing faculty size, replacing senior-level retiring faculty with entry-level faculty, and delaying capital expenditures for equipment and facilities. All of this has required a new breed of university administrators: people skilled in financial management and marketing rather than in educational philosophy and policy.

The financial health of today's colleges overwhelmingly depends on public support and high enrollments, and higher education responds to the demands of the marketplace. Colleges use marketing consultants and market research techniques, the kind used by soap and cigarette companies. Colleges advertise on roadside billboards, make their pitch on radio and in newspapers, purchase mailing lists and mail unsolicited recruitment letters with glossy, four-color brochures to high school seniors — marketing techniques that were unheard of when we parents went to college. Truth in advertising suits against a few schools are pending. Higher education is part of today's consumer society. It caters to what the consumer wants and will buy.

There is a note of caution here: *Caveat emptor,* let the buyer beware. The emphasis has shifted to attracting more new students because that's the source of substantial revenues. Colleges' primary concern may not always be to place products in the labor force.

Today's college graduate glut — a worsening situation — is ample evidence of higher education's ability to recruit, even recruit into areas where the labor market is saturated! But that doesn't mean that a job or career is waiting after college. Many a family has been lulled into believing that, because a son or daughter was accepted for enrollment, somehow that young person was on the way to a first job and a promising career. That isn't necessarily so.

A doctor's daughter who started out in education told us: "I pursued study in the field of elementary education for two years before I found out that there were very few jobs available for graduates once finished, so I decided to drop out of college." She now works as a therapist in elementary and secondary schools in California. Historically, colleges and parents have focused on entry-level requirements. The time has come to give equal attention to exit-level requirements.

Enrollment Outlook

The number of college age young people continues at a low ebb as we approach the 21st Century as a result of the depressed birth rates that followed the baby boom. The depressed supply will continue for several more years before the recent revival in birth rates translates into more applicants. That means that colleges may have to expand their recruitment efforts even further if they are to survive. And some will have to cut back. In Fall 1982, for example, the University of Washington eliminated 24 degree programs and reduced its enrollment by nearly 5,000 over a three-year period. The changes were described by university president Gerberding as permanent reductions in size and scope. Many colleges and universities have followed suit, particularly since 1985. Since 1969, 319 colleges, including branch campuses, have closed their doors — 119 since 1985. Of the 319, 285 — or 89 percent — were private colleges.

So far public colleges have done pretty well. The earlier prophets of doom with their forecasts of huge enrollment declines have been wrong. The recruitment efforts directed at new customers ("customers" rather than students is the new buzzword on campuses these days) have paid off. After peaking in 1981 and stabilizing in 1982 and 1983, higher education enrollment declined only slightly, and then picked up again. The National Center for Education Statistics projects a continuation of current trends, a 14 percent increase in enrollments of persons 25 years and older and a 6 percent increase in the number of students 25 years and younger. What happens will depend heavily on the federal government's education program, which tends to change with national elections.

During the decade ahead, colleges and universities will have little choice other than to compete more effectively for student enrollments. While they go after an even more diverse lot of education buyers at increased costs to the consumer, there will be more critics and skeptics who will argue that a college education isn't worth the cost. Whether a college education is likely to pay in the years ahead is the subject of Chapter 13. I also look at the investment prospectus for returns on a vocational education. To portend the answers: Yes, education and training will pay — big time! — in the years ahead. But that's getting ahead of ourselves. Let's explore the kinds of colleges from which young people can choose.

KINDS OF COLLEGES

The changes that have occurred in higher education over the past three decades, including the development of vocational preparation programs, have changed the forms that today's colleges take.

Earlier, I suggested that a basic decision young people headed for college must make is whether to enroll in a degree or certificate program. In today's colleges, both degree and certificate programs are likely to appear in the same institutions. It is no longer the case that you go to college if you want a degree, and you go to a vocational-technical or trade school if you want a certificate. Both degrees and certificates may be pursued in many colleges, and vocational preparation studies may occur in either degree or certificate programs.

In the following sections, I identify the main kinds of colleges that exist on the current educational scene. I distinguish between three kinds: four-year colleges, two-year colleges, and noncollegiate schools. I discuss three kinds of four-year colleges — liberal arts colleges, specialized colleges, and comprehensive universities — and I refer briefly to doctoral and professional degree-granting institutions. I then discuss two kinds of two-year colleges: junior colleges and community colleges. I also discuss four- and two-year colleges in the next chapter but shift attention to vocational preparation programs in those contexts. Finally, I consider noncollegiate institutions (technical institutes, business schools, and trade schools). My purpose is to explain the unique features of each kind of college, to examine how these institutions are similar and different, and to point out the programs identified with each.

Four-Year Colleges

When people use the word *college,* they often have in mind one of the more than 2,000 four-year colleges that offer programs of study leading to a bachelor's degree. I usually use the word that way, too; but here I use the word more broadly to apply to all institutions that offer training and education beyond high school. So it is important to differentiate kinds of colleges.

Colleges offer specialized groups of courses, and the nature of the programs distinguishes three kinds of four-year colleges: liberal arts colleges, specialized colleges, and comprehensive universities. College and university enrollments grew rapidly in the 1960s and 1970s, then slowed beginning with the late 1970s. Today, college and university undergraduate enrollments are nearly 13 million and will probably remain within 1 percent of that figure over the next five years. Growth in four-year colleges has not kept pace with growth in two-year colleges, however. According to the National Center for Education Statistics, the proportion of students in public four-year colleges declined from 48 percent to 41 percent between 1972 and 1992, and the proportion of full-time students declined from 68 percent to 56 percent.

Four-Year Liberal Arts Colleges

Four-year liberal arts colleges offer general programs of study in the arts, humanities, social sciences, and sciences. The arts include courses of study in people's conscious use of skill, taste, and creative imagination to produce objects that are aesthetically pleasing. Music and drama are examples of arts.

Humanities refers to branches of learning that are primarily cultural and have to do with the development of intellectual and moral faculties. Courses in cultural anthropology, English, literature, and comparative religion are examples of humanities.

Social sciences study how people relate to each other, especially as groups. Sociology and political science are examples.

The sciences, as defined in liberal arts colleges, refer to systematized knowledge governing general truths or the operation of general laws. The natural sciences — physics, chemistry, and biology — are examples of courses in the sciences offered by four-year liberal arts colleges.

Within the general programs of study, liberal arts colleges offer majors in specific areas such as mathematics, literature, political science, psychology, or biology. A *college major* is the particular field of study in which a student chooses to concentrate.

Four-year liberal arts colleges award a Bachelor of Arts degree (B.A.). Liberal arts colleges may also be distinguished by their sponsorship and size. Most are private or denominational colleges, and most have fewer than 5,000 students.

Four-Year Specialized Colleges

Specialized colleges put more emphasis on career preparation in a specific area such as business, engineering, education, agriculture, music, art, or home economics; and they put less emphasis on liberal arts. Specialized colleges offer four-year programs that culminate in a bachelor' s degree, usually the Bachelor of Science (B.S.).

Although there are still a few four-year colleges that offer only a Bachelor of Arts or a Bachelor of Science degree, today's four-year colleges usually offer a variety of degrees and, sometimes, certificates. The trend is away from single-focus institutions to institutions with expanded course offerings.

Universities

Universities are the best examples of four-year institutions with expanded course offerings. Colleges offer specialized groups of courses, and when several colleges are brought together under one administrative unit, it is called a university. The prefix "uni-" emphasizes the presumed oneness or unity in the course offerings, though "multiversity," which emphasizes the plurality of colleges and the diversity of course offerings, probably would be a more appropriate label for today's universities.

The distinguishing feature of four-year colleges is that they offer four-year programs of study and award bachelor's degrees. They may be differentiated by the number of specialized groups of courses they offer, those ranging from simply a Bachelor of Arts program to the multiple specialized programs offered by universities. To be sure, there are four-year colleges that offer several programs of study and there are universities that offer few. At those points, the differences between colleges and universities blur.

The distinction between colleges and universities goes beyond the number of under-graduate degree programs offered, however, and extends to graduate programs of study — that is, to programs of study and degrees beyond the bachelor's level. In addition to undergraduate programs, universities may offer graduate programs leading to the master's degree. The Master of Arts (M.A.) and Master of Science (M.S.) degrees are the most common, though other examples include the Master of Business Administration (M.B.A.) and Master of Social Work (M.S.W.). Some university graduate schools also offer the most advanced degrees, the Doctor of Philosophy degree (Ph.D.) or other professional degrees such as law (J.D.) or medicine (M.D.).

Vocational Preparation in Four-Year Colleges

The career education movement of the 1970s encouraged institutions to expand course offerings to include areas of vocational preparation. The movement had these important effects on the nation's four-year colleges:

- Many liberal arts colleges added programs in business, engineering, health-related areas, and the like, that went beyond traditional liberal arts offerings.
- Large numbers of students enrolled in career preparation programs rather than in liberal arts programs.
- The distinctions between liberal arts and career preparation programs became blurred.
- There was increased pressure on colleges to offer higher level degrees, especially master's degrees, for short-term specialized courses.

Computer sciences and health profession programs grew the most, while mathematics, library science, letters, foreign languages, and social sciences experienced the greatest decrease during the 1970s. Over the past decade, a fourth of college-bound seniors chose business and management courses, the most popular choice of major fields. Other fields of study, including the social sciences and liberal arts, have regained their original vigor.

Today's four-year colleges have broadened their programs of study in two ways: They offer multiple bachelor's degree programs and often include career preparation programs. Four-year colleges continue to be oriented to bachelor's degree programs, but about 600 four-year colleges offer undergraduate programs that lead to a two-year associate degree or certificate and attract 5 percent of all students enrolled in vocational preparation programs.

Two-Year Colleges

There are 10,599 institutions that offer some type of postsecondary education. Of that number, 1,469 are two-year colleges — 1,024 public and 445 private — that enrolled 5,723,244 students in 1991.

The label *two-year colleges* refers to the time required for a full-time student to complete requirements for an associate degree. The two major types of two-year colleges are junior colleges and community colleges. Both offer associate degree programs and often some assortment of certificate programs.

Junior Colleges

Junior colleges and community colleges have different origins. Junior colleges are older. They were originally established to offer courses that parallel freshmen and sophomore programs at four-year colleges and universities. Junior colleges were established as "transfer institutions" that high school graduates could attend for two years and then transfer to a four-year college or university. Often the junior college was located close to home and had comparatively modest costs.

Many junior colleges maintain strong liberal arts programs, although since World War II, almost all have expanded their programs to appeal to the same diverse populations as community colleges. Today's junior college is hardly distinguishable as a transfer school.

Community Colleges

The Vocational Education Act of 1963 stimulated the development of community colleges, which emerged with a character of their own. Unlike junior colleges that began with an emphasis on liberal arts programs, community colleges developed in response to industry demands for employees at the skilled, technical, and paraprofessional levels.

Community colleges have diffuse goals and programs. Open-admission policies invite all adults, whether or not they are high school graduates. Community colleges offer a wide variety of programs and appeal to diverse interests and needs. Local services vary but generally include instruction in convenient locations and flexible times.

Community college open-admission policies are an outgrowth of the Great Society programs of the early 1970s and Lyndon Johnson's goal to provide educational opportunities to the extent of every person's interest and ability. Open admission means that almost anyone can enroll, without regard for high school grades or performance requirements on entrance examinations. Generally, community colleges require a high school diploma or equivalency credit, but some will admit anyone over 18 years old. Convenient locations, flexible hours, and low tuition bring programs within reach of large segments of the population that otherwise were denied further education and training. Almost every sizable city has at least one community college, and most colleges extend classes to off-campus sites.

Community colleges are often part of a statewide college system designed to meet the varying needs of diverse populations. The number of community colleges has increased dramatically over the past two decades, and community college enrollments have been increasing faster than any other kind of college. Part of that is due to a relatively recent phenomenon on the U.S. education scene, "reverse transfers," students who enroll in community colleges to improve their employment prospects after attending or graduating from four-year institutions.

Vocational Preparation in Two-Year Colleges

Today's junior colleges and community colleges offer a blend of vocational preparation and other types of programs:

- Associate degree and transfer programs that may be accepted for credit at four-year colleges
- Vocational-preparation programs that may grant an associate degree or certificate to students seeking employment soon after finishing high school
- Noncredit life enrichment courses that are offered apart from a more comprehensive academic program or a vocational preparation program

The distinction between degree and certificate programs may be fuzzy at the two-year college level. The two coexist, as the listing of programs indicates, but how they coexist varies from one two-year college to another. Some offer programs of study that integrate degree and certificate studies. Sometimes the only difference is that the degree program adds general courses in the humanities, social sciences, and natural sciences. Under other circumstances, the programs are under the same roof but operate quite independently.

Over half of today's students who enroll as college freshmen attend two-year colleges. That is one of the big changes in college enrollments over the past decades. Another significant change has been the dramatic increase in vocational preparation programs available to today's young people. When it comes to preparing for today's careers, taking a college degree program is one way to go. Taking a vocational preparation program leading to a certificate is another way to go.

Noncollegiate Schools

The 1994 Almanac Issue of *The Chronicle of Higher Education* indicates that there are 6,961 vocational institutions in the United States. These are technical institutes and trade schools that award certificates but generally do not award degrees. In that sense, they are noncollegiate, even though some include the word "college" in their name. Although I include them in my broad definition of colleges, I prefer to think of them as "schools," as a reminder that they are noncollegiate institutions.

Noncollegiate schools may be either public or private. About .75 million students annually enroll in public noncollegiate schools, and about 1.25 million enroll in private schools. These are rough estimates. There is no way to gather exact data.

Private noncollegiate schools are of two types: proprietary and nonprofit. Proprietary means they are owned and operated for profit — they are businesses — whereas nonprofit means they are operated in the public interest and not for profit. Proprietary schools operate on business principles. Nonprofit school operate on conventional academic principles. Nearly two-thirds are proprietary, and the following discussion pertains primarily to that group.

Most proprietary noncollegiate schools are small businesses, though some are operated by large corporations including International Telephone and Telegraph, Control Data, and Bell and Howell. Most train students in only one or two areas, though some offer extended courses. Enrollment may vary from fewer than 10 (usually hospital schools) to more than 1,000 students (usually institutes). Trade schools are small. Institutes may be large. Only about half of proprietary schools are accredited.

Technical Institutes

Technical institutes developed along several lines. Some were offshoots of engineering colleges. Others rose in response to an imbalance in regional and local labor-market supply and demand. Still others grew out of the needs of industry to update and upgrade workers' skills and proficiencies in a systematic way and to introduce new technologies.

Technical institutes are similar to two-year colleges in that both offer vocational preparation programs. They differ from two-year colleges in that technical institutes are concerned almost exclusively with preparation for immediate employment. They offer closely focused and detailed training of shorter duration than that offered in two-year colleges, although some technical institute programs are general and may extend beyond two years. Technical institutes also differ from two-year colleges in that they are not likely to include general subject matter in their vocational preparation programs. They do not offer credit transfer programs that are aligned with four-year college programs. They are not feeder schools.

These may be advantages or disadvantages, depending on the point of view that parents and young people have. In contrast to the open-admission policies of community colleges, technical institutes may be very selective, and the competition for admission to highly specialized programs may be fairly intense. Training is strictly technical and geared to specific occupations. By comparison, community colleges balance specialization with breadth by including some general course offerings in their vocational preparation programs.

Many technical institutes have full-time placement staff and virtually all present their programs in terms of job-placement prospects. Most institutes will not guarantee placement, however, although their reputations depend heavily on their ability to help their students find jobs upon graduation. A few offer college equivalency courses and grant specialized associate degrees.

Trade Schools

Trade schools offer more flexibility than any other kind of school. Courses may begin as often as 12 times a year, and some schools enroll new students weekly. Morning, afternoon, and evening classes are usually available. The class schedule is intensive and may last five to six hours daily. The average student has fewer hours of assigned homework than students at two- and four-year colleges. Nearly all trade school students work part-time.

Trade schools emphasize practical, hands-on experience. Normally, instruction is modular and competency-based, meaning that each study unit can be repeated until the student meets the required skill level.

Most trade schools are too small to have full-time placement staffs, though virtually all present their programs in terms of job-placement prospects. Most trade schools will not guarantee placement, although their sole purpose for existence is to quickly prepare people for the labor force. Some trades, such as barber and cosmetology, presume that the person will set up her or his own shop. Other trades, for example art, design, and allied health, may have position openings to fill.

Many trade schools are not accredited or, alternatively, the accreditation is meaningless. This means that there are few standards and regulations that govern trade schools and, unfortunately, trade schools have been known to fold up over night. Many are small and unstable.

Variety of Schooling Options

Today's young people can pursue their degree or certificate interests in a variety of institutional settings. Four-year colleges continue to be the primary route to a bachelor's degree and provide the basis for advanced degrees. Two-year colleges provide a mix of associate degree and certification programs that vary with the particular junior or community college. Noncollegiate schools offer certificates in areas of local industry and consumer interest and demand.

These distinctions are an oversimplification, to be sure. Certificates are also awarded by four-year colleges, and some technical schools award associate degrees. Yet the distinction between degree and certificate programs represents a fundamental difference in how people view the preferred outcomes of education and training programs. Whether parents and their sons and daughters seek a broad and generalizable education, specific vocational preparation, or some combination of the two will largely determine what kind of college or school best suits their career interests and needs.

Choosing a College

C hoosing a college can be frustrating for both parent and child. The decision often produces anxiety because college choice comes early in a young person's career, awakens parents to financial realities, and alerts both parties to the fact that the time for leaving the nest is fast approaching.

Choosing a college involves three steps: deciding what a young person wants from the college experience, deciding which colleges and programs offer what the young person is looking for, and then getting into that college — which includes financial aid. In this chapter, I discuss sorting out a young person's goals and interests and point to sources of information about colleges. Additionally, I review what college admissions tests are all about.

Personal Goals and Interests

Young people may enroll in a particular college for different reasons:

- Because Mom or Dad went there
- Because it's close to home
- Because it's far from home
- Because a best friend goes there
- Because a counselor went there
- Because she or he didn't know where else to go

Under appropriate circumstances, each of these reasons may be compelling; but ordinarily, there are better reasons for choosing a college.

The most important reasons to choose a particular college have to do with a young person's goals. As young people think about what they want from college, they should consider the way they are today and the way they would like to be in the future — say, 5 and 10 years from now. Young people have considerable choice about what they will become. That's what the business of choosing a college is all about.

College should help a young person reach one or more personal development or career preparation goals. Most positions available today require some kind of preparatory education or training beyond high school. College — whether in a four-year, two-year, or noncollegiate school — is one way to get that preparation. If parents and young people conclude that going to college is the best way to achieve a young person's goals, then they have taken the important second step in choosing a career.

Whether to attend college is one question. But what to study and where are important questions, too. Lynne Cheney, past chairperson of the National Endowment for the Humanities, recently stated: "Colleges cost so much — it's sort of like buying a car without looking under the hood to pick a college without looking at the curriculum."

Programs of Study

> *" Maybe this is passing the buck, but I think my parents left my future (college-wise) pretty much up to me. A little more guidance or direction would've helped me to define a better future for myself — that is, in selecting a major."*

This secretary, the daughter of a chemical engineer, felt let down by her parents when it came to planning for college. A dental assistant feels the same way. What can be done to help young people prepare for the future? Get "parents more involved in career exploration and college searching," she told us.

A program of studies or college major is an important consideration, and parents can help young people think it through. If a young person has a tentative idea or general occupational area in which she or he may want a career, then the information on education and training requirements in the *Occupational Outlook Handbook* will suggest appropriate programs of study. Start with the *OOH*. That's the way to avoid the kind of frustration experienced by this young man who majored in theology and now works as a routeman for a newspaper: "Whenever I became interested in a possible career, I couldn't find out how to start," he told us.

It is possible, of course, that your son or daughter has not settled on a specific career objective and that you are not able to work backward from an occupational objective to a program of study and preparation. In that case, it makes sense to try to choose from general areas of study and possible college majors. In other words, work the other way around. The strategy is to try to find a career by sorting through courses of study. (See "Bill's Story" in Chapter 13.) Consider also the following listing of college programs with examples of accompanying college majors that may suggest some career preparation possibilities.

Fortunately, colleges do not require students to "declare a major" until the third year. That means students don't really have to know what they want to study when they start. It gives young people two years to try out and think about areas of study before they have to commit themselves. That's an excellent time for young people who don't know what they want to do to explore possibilities.

COLLEGE PROGRAMS WITH ASSOCIATED MAJORS

Program Area	Majors
Agriculture	Agronomy, Animal Husbandry, Fish, Wildlife Management, Forestry, Food, Science and Technology, Farm Management, Natural Resources Management
Business	Accounting, Business Management and Administration, Banking and Finance, Marketing and Purchasing, Insurance, Real Estate, Transportation and Public Utilities, Secretarial Studies
Communications	Journalism, Radio and Television Broadcasting, Advertising, Communications Media
Education	Elementary Education, Secondary Education, Special Education, Adult Education, Art Education, Industrial Arts, Library Science
Engineering	Chemical, Civil, Electrical, Mechanical, Industrial, Aeronautical, Petroleum
Fine/Applied Arts	Architecture, Art, Dance, Dramatic Arts, Music, Applied Design
Foreign Language	French, German, Spanish, Russian, Latin, Greek
Health Professions	Predentistry, Dental Hygiene, Premedicine, Medical Technology, Nursing, Occupational Therapy, Physical Therapy, Radiology, Pharmacy
Home Economics	Clothing and Textiles, Family Relations, Child Development, Foods and Nutrition, Consumer Economics, Interior Design
Humanities	Creative Writing, History, Literature, Philosophy, Religion, Speech
Mathematics and Sciences	Mathematics, Statistics, Computer Sciences, Physical Biology, Chemistry, Physics, Earth Sciences, Astronomy
Social Sciences	Law Enforcement, Corrections, Social Work, Geography, Prelaw, Psychology, Sociology, Anthropology, Archeology, Political Science

Deciding whether to go to college and what to study go hand in hand. Those are the two big questions a young person has to answer. One way to answer the questions is to think in terms of an occupational career objective and how a program of study contributes to that goal. A second way is to think of more immediate courses of study that interest the young person and to use the college experience to explore and narrow career interests. The son of a labor relations officer in a nuclear power plant offered this advice:

" I would encourage those who intend to attend college not to be too sure initially about what course of study they wish to pursue. I found many courses in college to be extremely interesting where I had found them unchallenging or even boring in high school. A good general studies curriculum for the first two years would allow the majority of students to make a more enlightened decision on their eventual major."

Social Climate

Extracurricular activities and the social climate of the school are other factors to think about. A few colleges are single sex, for men or women only. These may not be good selections for the person who wants an active social life, though they may be an excellent choice for a person with other goals. Similarly, a young person with strong interests in hobbies, leisure-time activities, and avocations might reasonably inquire whether these can be pursued at a particular college.

The mix of the student body — whether predominantly in-state, regional, or of national and foreign composition — also bears on the social climate and lifestyles at the school. That's another factor to consider. A young lady who studied humanities for three years in college, then dropped out, and now lives in Alaska, said her biggest problem since leaving high school was attending college. Why?

> *" I was not prepared for the experience or able to cope adequately. Alternate lifestyles should have been presented with equal emphasis. I didn't know I had a choice."*

Student services are another consideration. Is counseling available? Is there an employment service to help undergraduates find part-time jobs? Is there a job-placement service for graduates? Are there facilities and services for those with disabilities? Does your son or daughter need remedial instruction in some area, and does the college offer it? Are there fraternities and sororities? Does that matter? These are questions to ask and answer.

College Size

Colleges vary in size from fewer than 100 to more than 55,000 students on a single campus. But college size means more than the number of people enrolled. Large enrollments often indicate:

- Large undergraduate classes
- More areas of specialized study
- More course offerings in program areas
- Larger and more specialized libraries and laboratories
- Greater demands for student self-direction and self-sufficiency
- Presence of graduate departments and advanced degree programs
- A more research-oriented faculty

Similarly, small enrollments on college campuses may mean:

- Less privacy and anonymity
- More student-faculty interaction
- Faculty who are more teaching-oriented
- Better opportunities to participate in extracurricular activities
- Smaller classes and more classroom discussion
- A more personal atmosphere

Not all of these characteristics are always true, of course, but they do tend to be associated with college size.

Distance and Location

Distance from home is a consideration. Number of miles raises different questions: How long will it take to get home? How much will the trip cost? How often is it feasible to return home? How much advanced planning will be necessary? And what form of transportation is available? Physical distance is one thing, but what that distance means to a young person is another matter. How far is 600 miles — psychologically? A long way? Or not so far — something they can live with? For one young lady, now a statistical clerk for a newspaper, going to college was quite an adjustment. We asked her about her biggest problems since leaving high school. She answered:

> *"Moving from home to school. Also, adjusting to life in a fairly large city compared to a small community and farm life."*

A secretary for an investment firm said much the same. Her biggest problem was to "adjust to college life away from home."

Parents share those concerns. A high school English teacher who participated in our Youth and Careers Study told us:

> *"My daughter wants to be a nurse. . . . I'm concerned that she might get 'lost' in a bigger school and not get the attention, guidance, and encouragement she'll need."*

Another teacher expressed a similar concern for her son:

> *"I fear that he may have some difficulty adjusting to a large school. . . . I would like for him to go to a smaller college for a year or two and then transfer, if necessary, for his major."*

And a third mother, a receptionist for a chamber of commerce, was worried about her son's lack of maturity: "I feel my child is still fairly immature and this worries me as to letting him go on to a higher educational institution that is very far from home."

Distance raises other questions. Is the college in another state? If so, is out-of-state tuition required? Out-of-state tuition and fees for students attending public four-year colleges can easily add $1,500 to $2,000 per year in costs. Does your state have a reciprocity agreement with that other state that exempts your son or daughter from out-of-state tuition? You can find out by asking the college admissions officer.

Distance may not affect tuition costs if the college is private. Private colleges usually charge a set tuition and may not distinguish between in-state and out-of-state tuition.

Distance may mean a difference in climate and scenery. A distant campus may be snuggled in a mountain valley, conveniently located next to the beach, crammed downtown in the inner city, or spread out on a Midwestern plain. Weather and climate may differ. Ann Arbor gets cold and Miami gets hot. Seattle is wet and Phoenix is dry. Are these important considerations for your son or daughter?

Admissions and the Intellectual Environment

College admission policies translate into two practical considerations: whether a young person will be admitted and, if admitted, whether the level of classroom competition will be comfortable.

It is wise to check college entrance standards to get some idea of the academic demands a young person can expect. Straight A's in high school means acceptance at colleges that enroll the top 10 percent of high school graduating classes, whereas grades of B's and C's are less likely to qualify for top-tier colleges. However, even straight A's do not assure admission to colleges with limited enrollments that may also consider personal recommendations and achievements in extracurricular activities.

But college admission is only the first step. The intellectual environment of the college is the second. How does your son or daughter perform under pressure? Does she or he like intellectual challenges? How about competition? Too much pressure can be overwhelming, and too little may encourage coasting. Parents and young people will want to decide on the best fit between student and college characteristics.

Students should consider their Scholastic Aptitude Test (SAT) scores when deciding whether to apply to college and, if so, to which college. It's a good indicator of how well they will fit with others on a particular campus. Later in this chapter, I explain where to find the test scores of other students who enroll in the same colleges your daughter or son may be considering, so you can make such comparisons.

Accreditation

Colleges indicate their accreditation status in their printed materials. If they don't, it is wise to inquire further. Whether a college is accredited may make a difference later, when it comes to landing a job or transferring credits to another institution.

Accreditation is a seal of approval. Accreditation is to a college what an audit is to a business or what a credit rating is to an individual. It means that the college has met certain standards for its faculty, program of studies, and facilities. The standards are set by associations of schools and colleges in order to establish quality controls in education.

Six regional associations are the main accrediting agencies that give institutional accreditation to schools and colleges: Middle States Association; New England Association; North Central Association; Northwest Association; Southern Association; and Western Association. There are also national accrediting associations that accredit specific kinds of schools. Examples include the Association of Independent Colleges and Schools, the National Association of Trade and Technical Schools, and the American Association of Bible Colleges. There are others, but the regional accrediting associations are recognized most widely.

In the case of noncollegiate schools, it is wise to check whether the state's department of education approves the school. Be cautious if it does not. There are "fly by night" operators in education just as there are in any other business. *The College Blue Book* gives good advice when it says: "We urge our readers for their own peace of mind to check out institutions thoroughly through correspondence, phone calls, state bureaus, accrediting agencies, or on-site inspections."

Colleges jealously guard their accreditation. One way is by accepting grades, credits, and degrees earned only at other accredited colleges, and not accepting transfers at all or at full value from nonaccredited schools. If you are considering a college that does not list its accreditation status, check with the college admissions office. Know what you are buying and what you are getting for your money. A degree or certificate from a nonaccredited school is normally not worth as much as a degree or certificate from an accredited school.

Specialized Accreditation

Institutional accreditation applies to the total college. That does not mean that all departments in a college are of equal quality. On the contrary, colleges may contain a mixture of strong, average, and weak programs.

Some forms of specialized accreditation are awarded to individual programs in colleges. Specialized accreditation assures that particular programs meet professional standards. Specialized accreditation is most common in health-related programs, though it also appears in other areas. Parents and young people considering studies in a particular area might consult the *Occupational Outlook Handbook* to determine whether graduation from an accredited program is a requirement for employment, and then determine whether the college department they are considering has that specialized accreditation.

College Affiliation

Colleges may be public or private. If private, they may be private-independent or private church-related. These designations say nothing about the quality of education in the institution, but private church-related institutions may have requirements that affect the campus environment and religious life of students on campus. These may take the form of compulsory attendance at worship services, requirements for religious courses, participation in service programs, and the like.

There is considerable variation in the campus life of private church-related schools. The denominational influence may be strong or weak. Parents and young people will want to consider the match between their lifestyle preferences and the environment offered at both public and private colleges.

INFORMATION ON COLLEGES

There are nearly 3,200 accredited four-year and two-year colleges in the United States. Fortunately, many good reference books are published each year that provide thorough descriptions of what each college has to offer. Some of the better known ones are *The College Handbook, Peterson's Annual Guide To Undergraduate Study, Barron's Profiles of American Colleges, Chronicle Four-Year College Data Book, College Planning/Search Book,* and *Lovejoy's College Guide.*

My personal preference is *The College Handbook* published by the College Board. It is updated each year. The College Board is a nonprofit organization that provides tests and educational services for students and membership colleges, and the descriptions in the *Handbook* are based on detailed information provided by colleges. The *Handbook* covers more colleges than most — twice as many as some references. It is to the point and easy to use. I've used the *Handbook* in my research and writing for years, so allow me to use it here as an example of the kind of information on colleges that is available — as close as your high school career center, your local library, or bookstore.

I have a bias. It is that information is better than ignorance, and that good information is better than bad information. If parents are to advise their children intelligently, responsibly, and effectively, they need good information. *The College Handbook* provides good information about colleges.

Organization of the *Handbook*

The *Handbook* (1995 Edition) is a big, bulky volume, nearly 1,700 pages of small print. But whatever it lacks in appearance, it more than compensates for in information breadth and depth. The *Handbook* is an encyclopedia of factual information on the nation's accredited colleges. It is the best answer I can give for young people who have complaints, like this practical nurse in Baltimore:

> *" I was told by my parents and counselors I 'should go to college' because I was 'smart.' But no further aid or guidance was given. I did not know where to send for college catalogs, how to apply for financial aid, or when and where to apply for acceptance as a college student. . . . I didn't ask because I felt it was expected of me to already know how to apply."*

The *Handbook* begins with special topics related to choosing a college that is useful to parents, including how to pay for college, the new SAT, and listings of major fields of study in academic disciplines. For example, one special topic is an extensive list of words and abbreviations that college administrators often use like Advanced Placement Program (APP), College-Level Examination Program (CLEP), and Federal Supplemental Educational Opportunity Grant (FSEOG). Another special topic covers the most common tests and programs.

The remaining pages are filled with important information about colleges. First the *Handbook* presents about 40 indexes of types of colleges — business colleges, predominantly African-American institutions, women's colleges, colleges with NCAA sports programs, small colleges, religious colleges, colleges with ROTC programs, and the like. Want to narrow down the kind of college you're looking for? Just check the index. Colleges are listed alphabetically by state in each index.

Then comes the bulk of the material, about 1,500 pages of college descriptions. Each description is about a half-page long — small print. Large schools get more coverage than small schools because their programs are more extensive. The college descriptions are also listed alphabetically by states. In the case of complex systems, such as state systems with branch campuses or satellite campuses, the college your son or daughter is interested in may be listed as part of the general information following the system name. For example, the listing for Pennsylvania State University includes three-quarters of a page describing the main campus at University Park. The general information section notes that most associate degree programs are offered at two-year campuses and Erie Behrend College. Erie Behrend does not have a separate listing.

The College Handbook is a reference volume — not exactly bedtime reading. It presents information in short descriptors rather than in elaborate narration. But the information is comprehensive and useful.

Handbook Use

You can use *The College Handbook* in three ways. If you know the kind of academic program you're looking for, check the college index. For example, are you interested in Hispanic-serving institutions? There's an index that lists 105 colleges located in 10 states and provinces. Or if you know the state in which a college that interests you is located, use the college descriptions section, the largest section in the *Handbook*. Turn to the state and the college will be listed alphabetically. Finally, if you know the name of the college but don't know the state in which it is located, start with the alphabetical listing of colleges in the back of the book.

The descriptions of colleges follow a standard outline that makes it easy to locate information and to compare one college with another. Of course, there is some variation across college descriptions, and I can review only the main parts of the information. Let me walk you through the general outline.

The descriptions begin with brief information that tells what happens to students who apply for enrollment at the college. *Admissions* is the percentage of persons who apply that are accepted as freshmen. This will give you some sense of what the probabilities are that you'll be admitted. *Basis for selection* explains what the college takes into account in selecting applicants — for example, high school records, test scores, application essay, and maybe an interview. This is more information to help you calculate your chances of getting in. *Completion* is the percentage of freshmen who complete the freshmen year in good academic standing — some idea of the chances of making it through the first year, which can be the toughest one, if you are admitted. Finally, the percentage who graduate and the percentage who enter graduate study are typically given. This gives some indication of what your chances might be for settling in for the long haul.

General information is given on the major characteristics of the college: the number of years of undergraduate education it offers; the type of institution — whether, for example, community college, arts and sciences, upper-division college, or university; whether the college is public, private, or proprietary; whether the college enrolls only men, only women, or both; whether the college has a religious affiliation; and when the college was founded. Interested in an all-boy or all-girl college? Here's the place to look.

Accreditation indicates what national accrediting association and/or specialized bodies accredit the college. The *Handbook* lists only accredited institutions, so you needn't worry too much about shoddy operators. *Undergraduates and Graduates* indicates the number of men and women, full- and part-time enrollments. *Faculty* indicates the total number of faculty, full- and part-time, and the number who hold doctorates. These give you an idea of the size of school. *Location* gives an indication of the campus environment and size of the city in which the campus is located. *Calendar* indicates whether the college follows semesters, quarters, trimesters, and the like. *Microcomputers* tells whether microcomputers are available to students, how many, where they are located, and whether there is a campus-wide communications network. *Special facilities* designates such things as observatories and nuclear reactors on the campus. *Additional facts* includes such things as multicampus locations and extensive evening courses.

Degrees Offered

This paragraph lists the kinds of degrees the college awards, how many were awarded in the last reporting years, and what percentage were awarded in major program areas. It tells you whether the college offers the undergraduate degree program that interests your son or daughter — pretty important information. This paragraph also gives you a sense of the college's graduate programs and, therefore, gives a feeling for the campus environment. Thus, DVM means the college has a veterinary college and JD means it has a law school (see abbreviations in the *Handbook* glossary). A college with a veterinary school will have a different campus environment than a college with a law school.

Undergraduate Majors

In 1990, the U.S. Department of Education produced a standard list of majors, and the *Handbook* lists alphabetically which majors the college offers. Majors are broad categories. For example, psychology is a major, but within that major there are more specific areas. Thus, in the index of major fields of study the *Handbook* lists 11 specific areas — such as clinical psychology and social psychology. This is more information with which to assess the fit between a particular college and your son's or daughter's interests.

Academic Programs

Colleges may offer special programs that allow accelerated study, study abroad, cooperative education, honors programs, independent study, weekend college, semester at sea, United Nations semester, transfer programs, and the like. The Glossary in the *Handbook* describes many of these programs. *Remedial services* indicates what kind of special counselors, learning centers, preadmission summer programs, tutoring, remedial instruction, and reduced course loads are available to help students improve their basic academic skills or provide instruction. Check out the possibilities. Find the best fit for what you want and need — and will be paying for. If a college provides Air Force, Army, or Navy officer training, these are designated under ROTC. Colleges list the tests they use for *Placement/ credit examinations.* Colleges indicate their policies on the use of selected national and local programs or tests to determine a student's placement in courses, use in counseling students on academic programs, or for granting college credit for experience or informal learning. Take advantage of these provisions. They may save you money and save your son or daughter time in earning a college degree.

Academic Requirements

This section indicates the requirements freshmen must meet to remain in good academic standing. An example is minimum grade point average (GPA). The percentage of freshmen who return for their sophomore year may be given. Colleges may indicate at what point students must declare their major. *Graduation requirements* specify the number of credit hours required for associate and bachelor's degrees and the number required to complete a major field of study. If the college has general education requirements that students must meet, these are listed. It's a good idea to know exactly what is expected because it certainly doesn't make sense to have to hang around for an extra semester just to pick up a couple of credits that could have been taken earlier. *Postgraduate studies* indicates the percentage of students who go on to graduate school within one year of taking their undergraduate degree.

Freshmen Admissions

This paragraph reports the college's admissions criteria, sometimes by order of importance. Colleges may report minimum qualifications required, such as minimum grade point average or rank in the applicant's high school class. Indication is given if special consideration goes to particular groups of applicants, such as children of alumni, foreign students, out-of-state applicants, minorities, and others. Private schools sometimes include experiential criteria. For example, Trinity Bible College includes "evidence of Christian testimony and lifestyle very important" as a basis for selection. Colleges indicate what they require by way of *high school preparation.* Many colleges have specific educational background requirements and specify the minimal, and sometimes the recommended, number of course units applicants should have and in what fields of study. *Test requirements* indicates whether the college requires national, standardized admissions tests, such as ACT or SAT, the name of the test, and the date by which scores must be reported. The college may also indicate how the test scores are used, whether for admissions or for counseling and placement only.

Freshman Class Profile

The current freshman class is described in terms of the number of men and women who applied, the number who were accepted, and the number who enrolled. This gives another rough indicator of an applicant's chances of being accepted. Additional information about an applicant's chances of being accepted is given in *Academic background*. Colleges indicate the percentages of freshmen with grade-point averages above 3.0 and between 2.0 and 2.99, the percentage of freshmen who were in the top tenth or top quarter of their high school graduating class, the SAT I (verbal) and ACT score ranges of the middle 50 percent of enrolled freshmen together with the percentage of freshmen who submitted SAT I and ACT scores. Information provided under *Characteristics* includes the percentages of freshmen who are in-state residents, who live in college housing, who commute, who are minority students, who are foreign students, and who join fraternities/sororities. Finally, the college gives the average age of entering freshmen.

The freshman class profile is some of the best information a young person can use to sense how she or he might fit with a particular college campus. It tells a lot about who one's classmates will be.

Fall-Term Applications

This section includes deadlines and special admission procedures such as Early Decision Plans (EDP) or Candidate Reply Date Agreements (CRDA). These procedures are defined in the *Handbook* glossary. The college indicates when applicants are informed of their admission decisions and may provide information about interviews, portfolios, auditions, essays, and the like. A word to the wise: The deadlines are firm.

Student Life

This section describes important information regarding student housing and activities. *Housing* lists the kinds of residential accommodations available, including whether dormitories are coed, whether married student and cooperative housing is available, whether the campus offers fraternity and sorority housing, and whether the college guarantees housing for freshmen.

Colleges list student *Activities* available, such as student government, band, orchestra, religious organizations, and yearbook. This listing may be long, especially for large colleges. *Additional information* may comment on student life. For example, Iowa State University notes that "quality of student life rated very high in Eli Lilly Foundation study."

Athletics

This section indicates the college's membership in an athletic association — such as the NCAA — and lists the range of athletics available by *intercollegiate* and *intramural* levels. For example, the University of Wisconsin-Madison lists 13 intercollegiate and 25 intramural programs. Some colleges also list *clubs.* Sports offered for men only are designated "M" and for women only, "W." The College Indexes section of the *Handbook* shows the division level of play a college offers in a sport-by-sport index.

Student Services

This paragraph provides information on personal and career counseling, health services, employment service for undergraduates, placement service for graduates, facilities and services for the handicapped, veterans, and others. If your daughter or son has special needs, this is the place to check out the special services.

Annual Expenses

This is a brief statement of the average costs of full-time freshmen for the current academic year. *Tuition and fees* may be listed separately or combined with *Room and board* and quoted as a comprehensive fee. Colleges may offer a variety of living arrangements and meal plans that provide a range of room-and-board plans. If out-of-state fees are assessed to nonresidents, the added amount is indicated. The costs for *Books and supplies* and other expenses are reported separately. *Other expenses* refers to estimated normal costs for clothing, laundry, entertainment, medical insurance, and furnishings, but does not include transportation costs. You can get additional information from the college, but this information will give you an accurate first approximation.

Financial Aid

This section gives practical information, appropriate procedures for making application, and details about how the college awards financial aid. It lists the percentage of freshmen and continuing students who receive some form of aid. It reports the percentages of need-based financial aid distributed to students in the form of grants, loans, and jobs. Colleges are asked to report how many enrolled freshmen were judged to have need and how many were offered aid. Colleges also indicate whether scholarships are available based on criteria other than need — such as academics, music/drama, art, athletic abilities, minority status, and the like. *Application procedures* lists important dates for applications and the dates the college will notify applicants of application decisions. *Additional information* may indicate related services the college provides — for example, a short-term loan program or financial counseling clinics. If you have questions, call and get the answers.

Address/Telephone

Each description ends with a name and title, mailing address, telephone and possibly a fax number that parents and applicants may use to get further information.

INFORMATION ON NONCOLLEGIATE SCHOOLS

Career preparation programs are growing and changing rapidly. Indeed, there are twice as many noncollegiate schools — including business, trade, and technical schools that award certificates but do not award degrees — as there are all two- and four-year colleges and universities, public and private. Noncollegiate schools are popular and in demand. Increasing numbers of high school graduates feel like this young lady, who received a certificate in visual arts from a technical school in Minneapolis: "Although a college degree is important to some careers, it is not mandatory for success." A young man making a career of the Navy agrees:

> *" I believe technical skills should be given more emphasis as a satisfying way of life. Today it's the blue-collar workers who are making the most money and I think, on the whole, they are more satisfied with their jobs."*

Noncollegiate Schools

Noncollegiate schools — including business, trade, and technical schools that give certificates but do not award degrees — are the only place a person can learn some skills. There are few other places to learn to fly airplanes, repair shoes, practice cosmetology, or drive diesel trucks. Noncollegiate schools do not offer academic programs but, rather, training in narrowly focused fields. Their purpose is straightforward: to prepare a person for a specific job, many of which involve self-employment.

Noncollegiate schools vary considerably from one school to the next. There is little that holds them together, little regulation and, therefore, there may be little comparability from one to the next. This includes the credentials of teachers, whose levels of training and experience may vary from that of a grand master to a novice. Likewise, their programs may be different, as well as the quality of school recordkeeping — whether they keep the kind of information prospective students need.

Essentially, noncollegiate schools are small businesses. Their primary method of attracting students is advertisement. Most are private and proprietary. And the laws of the marketplace prevail: What you see is what you get. They may be established features of a community or here today and gone tomorrow.

Noncollegiate schools are a loose assortment and, unlike professions and collegiate institutions, generally do not police themselves through associations and ethics committees. They are not backed by infrastructures that collect detailed information under rigorous conditions, as the College Board does for collegiate institutions. They do not use standardized testing, as Educational Testing Services and American College Testing provides for colleges and universities. Noncollegiate schools operate under few, if any, shared education regulations. Their accountability is more likely to be to the Chamber of Commerce than to a county or state department of education and professional associations.

Noncollegiate Programs

Noncollegiate programs, like noncollegiate schools, are not well-organized into recognized fields of study and course offerings. They don't offer degrees of learning subject matter but, rather, certification that skills and techniques have been adequately mastered. Moreover, there are few reference books and handbooks with customary documentation to assist comparisons and evaluations of programs. This makes it difficult to describe the programs of the nearly 7,000 schools that fly noncollegiate banners, and it makes it even more difficult to evaluate specific programs. It puts customers largely "on their own" and at some risk when evaluating training possibilities.

The best advice is to exercise due diligence in evaluating a particular school and program. There are precautions you can take:

- Visit the school. Establish that the school is accredited by the National Association of Trade and Technical Schools. Accreditation will be noted in the school's descriptive literature. If not, be especially wary.
- Talk with others who have attended the school. Better yet, consult with people who have been through the specific program that interests you.
- Inquire about the reputation of the proprietary trade school from your state department of education and your local chamber of commerce.
- Ask questions. Speak with high school principals and people in business. Find out who owns the school, how long they have been in business, and about the reputations of the school and the owner.
- There are no regional accrediting associations for noncollegiate schools that correspond to the six regional college associations, but there are several accrediting associations for noncollegiate programs. Make sure you understand the nature of the program accreditation.

Important Note

State Occupational Information Coordinating Committees and Career Information Delivery Systems (see Chapter 7) provide both state-specific occupational information and career preparation possibilities. This is usually your best source of state information. Call your State Occupational Information Committee and ask questions. If you have difficulty locating the phone number, ask for the number through your state department of labor or check the number directly in pages 465–467 of the '94–'95 *Occupational Outlook Handbook.*

The SOICC/CID information services are excellent resources for people like a young lady in Idaho who held seven different jobs in twelve years and feels herself "drifting":

> *" Had I been directed toward vocational school, my life may be different today. I wouldn't be drifting jobwise."*

Finally, in the past Macmillan has published a guide, *The College Blue Book: Occupational Education*, that has been a useful general reference on noncollegiate schools. There are three problems with *The Blue Book:* It has been published irregularly, every few years, and the information is quickly dated; the data are not gathered rigorously and the quality of the information is uneven and suspect; and *The Blue Book* is expensive and not widely available. These limitations aside, I recommend it. First of all, in my opinion *The Blue Book* is the best approximation to comprehensive and useful reference material on noncollegiate schools and programs. And second, it includes a handy reverse index for many specialized training programs. If, for example, you want to take training in underwater salvage, *The Blue Book* is the best resource that I know of where you can check an index for training in underwater salvage and find a listing of schools that offer this training. Even though the information is dated and may be suspect, it is a place to start. It may be the best resource for people like this physics major now working as a product researcher for a manufacturing company, who wants to "be exposed to the great diversity of jobs, trades, and opportunities in the real world such as house builder, entrepreneur, and business executive."

SAT/ACT-COLLEGE ADMISSIONS TESTS

The two most frequently used, nationwide college-admissions tests in the United States are the Scholastic Aptitude Test (SAT) and the American College Testing Program's Assessment (ACT). The SAT or ACT is normally required by two- and four-year colleges but seldom by noncollegiate institutions — business, trade, and technical schools. Few colleges base their admissions decisions solely on SAT or ACT scores. Most also consider such other information as high school grade point average, extracurricular activities, and special talents. Many colleges use admissions test scores to identify students for advanced placement or remedial courses.

College reference books including *The College Handbook* indicate the basis on which each college makes its admissions decisions; therefore, it is wise to check the admissions section in the description for colleges you are considering. One of the things prospective applicants are sure to find is whether they must take the SAT or the ACT.

About a million high school seniors take each test each year. Colleges in the Midwest, South, and some in the West generally require the ACT — probably because the American College Testing Program is located in Iowa City, Iowa. Colleges on the East Coast and some on the West Coast require the SAT — probably because the SAT is administered by the College Board in Princeton, New Jersey. Some colleges will accept either the SAT or the ACT.

At the end of Part III in "Next Steps: What Parents Can Do," I provide a timetable for parents and young people to follow that alerts them to when they should be concerned about taking college admissions tests, applying to colleges, applying for financial aid, and the like.

The SAT

The College Board makes available booklets that describe the SAT test, give specific instructions for completing the necessary forms, and provide testing tips and sample test questions. The booklets are generally available in high school counseling centers.

The SAT test score report is mailed to the student's home about six weeks after the test. The report lists separate scores for the verbal and math sections of the SAT.

Scores for the SAT sections range from 200 to 800. Two-thirds of college-bound students score between 320 and 525 on the verbal section, and between 355 and 585 on the math section. The SAT score report enables parents and their son or daughter to compare their scores with college-bound seniors in the current high school graduating class across the nation and recently enrolled freshmen in colleges that the student named to receive the scores. This information gives the prospective applicant an indication of the general academic level of entering freshmen classes at these colleges.

The report makes comparisons by using percentile ranks that indicate the percentage of people who earned scores lower than the student. The College Board provides information with the SAT test report that helps parents and students interpret the scores.

SAT Achievement Tests

A college may also require one or more SAT Achievement Tests for admission or placement purposes. Achievement tests are one-hour, multiple-choice, and measure a student's knowledge of a particular subject. SAT offers achievement tests in 14 areas. College reference books may indicate if particular achievement tests are required by specific colleges; but it is wise to discuss details and arrangements directly with high school counselors or, if necessary, with the college admissions office. Registration for the SAT or ACT must be completed about a month in advance, so note the registration dates.

Test registration packets are available in high school counseling centers, and many high schools notify parents and students when the packets are available. The packets provide specific information about testing dates, registration deadlines, and testing fees for the SAT and ACT. The SAT and ACT may be given more than once between September and June, usually on a Saturday morning. The deadlines for submitting registration forms and test fees are rigid and, therefore, must be observed.

The ACT

The American College Testing Program provides booklets that describe the ACT test, give examples of test questions and answers, and provide helpful suggestions about taking the ACT. This information is generally available in high school counseling centers.

The ACT test score report is mailed to the student's high school about four weeks after the test. The ACT report lists five scores: English, math, social studies, natural sciences, and a composite, which is the average of the four other scores. Two-thirds of all college-bound students earn composite scores between 12 and 24 on a scale that ranges from 1 to 36. The report enables parents and students to compare their scores with college-bound students who took the ACT in their high school, college-bound students in their state, college-bound students from across the nation, and recently enrolled freshmen in one or more colleges that the student named to receive the scores. This information gives the prospective applicant an indication of the general academic level of entering freshmen classes at these colleges.

The ACT score report makes comparisons using percentile ranks that indicate the percentage of people who earned scores lower than the student. The report also includes summary biographical and educational information about the student and interest inventory information that enables students to compare their interests with the interests of people in various college majors or employed in different occupational groups. The American College Testing Program provides information that helps parents and students interpret the results of the test. This information is included with the ACT score report that is sent to the student's high school.

Special Preparation and Retaking the Tests

Both the SAT and the ACT measure abilities and knowledge that students acquire over a period of years. Short-term drills and intense cramming sessions are not likely to increase scores, though practice on sample test questions may familiarize students with the form of the tests and the different types of questions. This may help reduce test anxiety, especially for young people who tend to get "uptight" about taking tests.

The results of longer term preparation courses vary from program to program and from student to student. Some studies of special preparation programs in high schools indicate that the courses tend to raise scores 10 to 15 points on the SAT. In most cases, an increase this small is not likely to make a difference in admission to a particular college.

What about retaking the test? Studies show that young people who retake the test only because they scored low on an earlier test are not likely to greatly increase their scores by retaking the test. About two-thirds raise their scores a few points, and about one-third lower their scores. However, occasionally something happens while a student takes a test that may negatively affect the score. Good reasons for retaking a test include illness, high anxiety levels, or misunderstanding instructions.

When considering either special preparation courses or retaking the test, weigh the time and money required against the likelihood that it will favorably affect a college admissions decision.

Changes in the SAT

The SAT introduced changes recently. The first changes occurred in October 1993. A second set of changes occurred in March and May of 1994. And a third set of changes occurred in April 1995. You need to understand the changes to avoid confusion with earlier scores and earlier versions of the SAT. These are the changes.

PSAT/NMSQT and SAT Program

PSAT/NMSQT is an abbreviation for Preliminary SAT/National Merit Scholarship Qualifying Test. This is a shorter version of the SAT I, which is the verbal and mathematical reasoning test, and it is administered in high schools each year in October. This preliminary test helps high schools in the early stages of advising students who plan to attend college and serves as the qualifying test for the prestigious National Merit Scholarships awarded by the National Merit Scholarship Corporation. It also serves as the qualifying test for the National Hispanic Scholar Awards Program. Students are encouraged to take the PSAT/NMSQT whether or not they believe themselves to be in contention for the National Merit or Hispanic Awards scholarships because it provides excellent practice for the SAT.

After taking the PSAT/NMSQT, students get back their test books together with a report showing how they did on each question so they can apply the experience of taking the PSAT in their junior year when they take the SAT I: Reasoning Test in the Fall of their senior year.

Because the PSAT/NMSQT is a shorter version of the SAT I, which has been changed (see below), the PSAT/NMSQT reflects the changes. There is more emphasis on critical reading in the verbal section. In the math section, there are questions that require students to work out answers, and use of a calculator is recommended.

SAT I and SAT II

SAT I: Reasoning Test and SAT II: Subjects Tests replaced the earlier SAT and Achievement Tests, respectively, beginning in the Spring of 1994.

SAT I is a revised and expanded version of the traditional SAT verbal and mathematical tests. Differences include longer reading passages with questions that measure critical reading skills and vocabulary and math questions that require students to work out answers. Use of calculators is allowed. Like the traditional SAT, SAT I takes three hours to complete.

The Subject Tests are revisions of the traditional Achievement Tests (additional subject matter that is tested) and include a major new test in writing. Students need not wait until their senior year to take subject tests, but may take them as soon as they finish high school courses on the subjects. Subject-specific exams take one hour to complete.

New SAT Scoring System

Beginning in 1995, SAT scores are reported on a different scale and one-to-one comparisons cannot be made with earlier scores, including those listed in the college reference books for previous years. The average SAT verbal score is now 424, and the average math score is 478. The new scale will put the average score for both the verbal and math sections back to 500, which will make it easier for students to interpret their scores.

"Recentering" the scores has the effect of raising most scores of students who took the tests after April 1995. An equivalency table will be used to compare the old scores with new scores.

The new scores will not affect admissions to college because the equivalency tables will assure that the value of new scores will remain the same as old scores.

College Costs and Financial Aid

My father attended college in the late 1920s. He was fond of relating how he worked for a county road maintenance department in rural Iowa and finished one summer with savings of $104. His room, board, and tuition costs for the following year were $102.

Things changed by the time I went to college in the mid-'50s. Unlike my father, I never earned more money from summer employment than the costs for my tuition, room, and board for the following year. I made up the difference with scholarships and by working during the school year. Working always involved a tradeoff because scholarships were based primarily on achievement and merit. I didn't want my grades to slip because of work, yet the scholarship situation was always "iffy," and that left me little choice but to work. It was an uneasy compromise.

Today, most awards are based not on merit but on need. Few students earn enough during the summer months to cover their costs for an academic year. Most students apply for financial aid, and, in one form or another, 44 percent receive it. The average amount of aid received by full-time, full-year undergraduates in 1990 was $4,732. Nonetheless, the financial aid process is cloaked in mystery and shrouded in bureaucracy for parents, students, and even for funding agencies. A 1994 report from the Institute for Higher Education Policy reports that the Education Department unnecessarily burdens post-secondary institutions with more that 7,000 federal aid regulations. The report concludes that although "few individual regulations can be described as onerous, their collective weight is immense."

Financial aid doesn't just concern parents. It concerns their daughters and sons as well. An electrician's daughter whose mother is a childcare worker told us her biggest concern in our Youth and Careers Study: "My biggest concern is how my family and I will be able to afford college." Another young woman whose father, a part-time farm worker, supports her mother, three daughters, and three other relatives told us:

> *"My biggest concern as I look ahead to the future is that my parents nor I won't have money to send me to college. It is very hard for us to save money because we have a lot of bills to pay."*

In this chapter, I overview what parents should know about college costs and financial aid. I review ways to increase resources and reduce costs. I suggest references to consult for additional financial aid possibilities, and I suggest questions to ask and answer about some college financing plans. I close with "Next Steps: What Parents Can Do," which has a timetable for parents and young people to follow for making college plans and suggestions to follow when making college plans.

ESTIMATING COSTS AND RESOURCES

Paying for a college education is a bad news and good news topic. There is also ambiguous news. In this section, I identify the bad, the good, and the ambiguous as they relate to meeting college costs.

College Costs

The bad news is that college costs have increased steadily in recent years, faster than the cost of inflation. Since 1980, tuition, room, and board has increased 58 percent at private colleges and 34 percent at public colleges. Over the same period, the median family income for all families with children 6 to 17 years old fell 3 percent. The income for families at the 25th percentile — a fourth the way up the nation's income ladder — dropped 10 percent. Family incomes at the 75th percentile rose 2 percent. At public institutions, the costs for tuition, room, and board rose from 10 percent of the family income for families with children 6 to 17 years old in 1980 to 14 percent in 1990. Costs in tuition and fees rose 6 percent from 1993–1994 to 1994–1995. For the 12 months ending in August, the Consumer Price Index, a common measure of the rate of inflation, rose 2.9 percent. Many young people feel like the young lady who dropped out of college after one year and told us that young people's biggest need is "advice on financial assistance for those who wish to attend college but feel financially unable to do so."

The table on page 229 lists the average costs for resident students at four kinds of colleges in the 1994–1995 academic year. Of course, some colleges have lower and others have higher costs.

The nation's most expensive institution continues to be Landmark College, which specializes in teaching students with learning disabilities. Its tuition (alone) for the '94–'95 school year is $23,700.

Over the next few years college costs are likely to continue to rise by 7 to 9 percent per year while the Consumer Price Index may increase only 3 or 4 percent. The increases occur, in part, because of past efforts to keep costs down during the double-digit inflation days of the late 1970s and early 1990s. Eventually the piper had to be paid in the form of overdue capital expenditures, building maintenance, library books, laboratory equipment, and faculty and staff salaries. The result is that today's college costs outstrip inflation, and that's a concern for anyone who has to pay the bill.

Here's the good news. The amount of money available for student aid has increased substantially — indeed, monumentally! In 1958, 35 years ago, the federal government initiated student aid with a $40.3 million program. Over the years, federal student aid increased 620-fold to nearly $25 billion per year, and student aid from all sources increased

AVERAGE COSTS FOR RESIDENT STUDENTS, 1994–1995

Item	2-Year Public	2-Year Private	4-Year Public	4-Year Private
Tuition and fees	$1,298	$6,511	$2,686	$11,709
Books and supplies	566	522	578	585
Room and board	*	4,040	3,826	4,976
Transportation	*	569	592	523
Other costs	*	975	1,308	991
Total	$1,864	$12,647	$8,990	$18,784

* Insufficient data
Source: The Chronicle of Higher Education, October 3, 1994

AVERAGE ANNUAL INCREASE IN TUITION AND FEES, 1991–1995

Item	2-Year Public	2-Year Private	4-Year Public	4-Year Private
1990–'91	5%	7%	8%	8%
1991–'92	13	12	6	7
1992–'93	10	10	6	7
1993–'94	10	8	7	6
1994–'95	4	6	5	6

Source: The Chronicle of Higher Education, October 3, 1994

868-fold to about $35 billion per year. That amount has held relatively constant in recent years, which means that it has had to stretch further because college costs continue to rise while inflation erodes the buying power of the dollar, which leaves more young people competing for the same amount of financial aid.

So much for the bad news and the good news. The ambiguous news is that federal aid programs change from time to time, even from year to year, in ways that are not altogether predictable. Parents need to follow the developments on the financial aid scene as these occur. It also is useful to keep in mind the history of financial aid when contemplating where the program is likely to go in the future.

A Brief History of Financial Aid

Beginning with the G.I. Bill after World War II and the post-sputnik National Defense Education Act signed by Eisenhower in 1958, programs of financial aid for students in postsecondary education enjoyed more than two decades of remarkable growth, and there was an era of unprecedented access to higher education. Congress expanded financial aid programs with passage of the Higher Education Act in 1965. As part of Kennedy's New Frontier legacy and Johnson's Great Society program, the Higher Education Act emphasized several forms of aid for low-income students: Educational Opportunity Grants; federally insured student loans; work-study programs; and Social Security funds underwriting the cost of a college education for children of deceased, disabled, or retired workers.

In 1972, Congress added a matching-funds program to induce states to establish their own financial aid programs. In 1978, the Middle-Income Student Assistance Act permitted more families to receive some forms of aid.

But the 1980s ushered in a period of uncertainty regarding the future of federal financial aid programs. Several factors contributed to the change. The prolonged economic recession early in the decade left students caught between rising educational costs and a tightening supply of money available for financial aid programs. In the face of difficult budgetary decisions, the consensus regarding the principle underlying financial aid programs began to weaken. A new ideology broadened the question from "Can we maintain these programs?" to "Should we maintain them?" In this climate, it was probably inevitable that financial aid would, for the first time, become a highly politicized issue. What for a quarter of a century was a virtually protected area suddenly became the topic of heated debate and political tradeoffs, often with little regard for academic calendars and individuals' attempts to make rational academic plans. In 1992, Congress reauthorized the Higher Education Act and put in place an unsubsidized student loan program that makes everyone eligible for aid, albeit not without cost.

That's where the matter of federal financial aid continues to linger. It is politicized. It is under debate. The future of financial aid programs is uncertain, and it is likely to remain that way, perhaps changing year by year with the possible exception of election years, when it may be convenient to rest the issue. Meanwhile, a foreman for an auto repair service in Tacoma, Washington, spoke for a lot of young people when he said, "The biggest problem I've encountered is. . . . no money to be able to go to college."

The issue facing parents is how to meet college costs under uncertain conditions. Four of five people who participated in a national public opinion poll said that college costs are rising so fast that they will be out of reach in the near future. Seven out of ten said that right now they would not be able to pay for college without a grant or loan. Not only parents are concerned. About half of today's college students report that lack of money is a problem.

Principles of Financial Aid

The financial aid picture is unsettled and unsettling, but there are some guidelines for parents to follow. Close observers suggest that there will be less public money for financing education in the future, and the money will be more difficult to obtain. Eligibility rules for grants and loans are likely to tighten up, and the government has cracked down on former students whose loan payments are in arrears. I expect that future programs will favor the self-help concept, such as college work-study, and there may be a tax incentive for families to contribute to savings accounts for their children's college education, perhaps modeled after IRA accounts.

Both the self-help and savings emphases are consistent with current administration philosophy, which suggests that an affordable education will require that parents and their young people do more careful planning and perhaps make some difficult choices.

But it is highly unlikely that all federal financial aid will suddenly disappear. History suggests that when it acts, the federal government adjusts, refines, realigns, relabels, and changes priorities. It would be out of character for the federal government to chop an entire program with one fell swoop. Rather, new programs are likely to follow the current emphases on school-to-work transitions and tying work force preparedness to secondary education. For example, AmeriCorps, the first phase of a national service program, ties community service to payments for college tuition and repayment of college loans. A wide range of postsecondary financial aid options will probably continue to be available for qualified and motivated students.

Family Responsibility

In whatever manner specific programs may be adjusted, it seems clear that certain basic principles of financial aid will continue. First among these is the principle that the family, together with the student, bears primary responsibility for meeting postsecondary education costs. This is not a change of philosophy or policy. Rather, this has been the basic principle undergirding the federal financial aid program from the beginning. Although the principle might have suffered some erosion in earlier years, it remains a workable way to provide the greatest benefit to the largest number of people, a goal that is at the heart of our democratic process.

A family's ability to pay is determined by a fair, reasonable, and uniform analysis of means. That is the reasoning behind family need analysis statements, which produce estimates of need based on carefully defined rules for estimating resources and costs.

Estimated Need

The second principle is that financial aid is intended to meet estimated need. Estimated need is the difference between what the formulas indicate the family and student can pay and the actual costs of attending a particular institution. This principle, too, has suffered some erosion in recent years as some colleges have introduced "no-need" scholarships as a way of attracting students. However, no-need scholarships are few in number and usually small in size — often less than $500 — relative to total college costs. "Full scholarships" independent of need are about as common as a "free lunch." They seldom exist.

The Package Concept

The third continuing principle in financial aid is the package concept. The total aid given any student consists of a combination of "gift aid" (scholarships and grants that need not be repaid) and "self-help aid" (loans or work that involve obligations on the part of the student). The principle is that of fairness to students, so that some don't receive all gift while others are burdened with intolerable loans, coupled with the effort to distribute available funds to achieve the most widespread benefit.

Amounts, regulations, forms, and deadlines may shift from year to year, but I suggest that the basic financial aid system is here to stay. Given this background, there are some practical steps parents and young people can take to meet college costs.

Practical Steps to Take

In his book, *Cost of Children,* Lawrence Olson estimates that families earning $42,000 a year at the time a child is born will spend $323,000 to raise a son to age 22, and $21,000 more if the child is a daughter. Olson's figures include tuition at private colleges, which may put his estimate on the high side. Nonetheless, the costs of raising children are substantial. One way to partially reduce that expense is to qualify for financial aid. But you have to meet certain policies and practices to qualify.

Apply

Young people can't get financial aid if they don't apply for it. This may seem obvious, but every year many families automatically rule themselves out without good reason. Some think that applying for enrollment and applying for financial aid are one and the same, but not so. There are two separate procedures involved including different forms and different deadlines. Other parents and students hear the rumors that financial aid funds have been radically reduced, assume that no aid is available, and, therefore, don't even make an effort. Such reports may or may not be true.

Still others think that there is no reason to apply for financial aid because they won't get anything anyway. The fact is that some families with incomes of $60,000 qualify for need-based aid because of their particular circumstances. It is also true, however, that families with annual incomes exceeding $50,000 normally find it difficult to qualify. Nonetheless, about 5 million students receive about $25 billion each year in federal aid and another $10 billion from other sources. The table on page 233 shows the percentage of students who receive financial aid from various sources and the percentage who receive $1,500 or more from the sources.

Meet Deadlines

To be successful, it is absolutely necessary that applicants meet all financial aid deadlines and apply as early as possible within the time limits. Processing the nation's financial aid applications is a huge undertaking, and the deadlines are real. Although funds are limited, colleges try to distribute all the money they have. It is to their advantage to do so. The first piece of the pie is likely to be more generous than the last, and tardy applicants may not find anything remaining but crumbs.

Investigate

Parents and young people should also check the possibilities of scholarships offered by private groups, businesses, unions, clubs, and civic organizations. Investigate the "no-need" scholarships offered by colleges for academic, athletic, or extracurricular achievement.

But don't count on unrealistic hopes. No-need scholarships are rare, if available at all: Consider them to be the frosting on the cake. Seventy-four percent of all college aid comes from the federal government, and 90 percent of financial aid money is distributed through

PERCENTAGES OF STUDENTS RECEIVING AID

Source	% Receiving Aid	% Receiving $1,500 + Aid
Parents' assistance	78	49
Savings from summer work	51	6
Other savings	30	6
Part-time employment	26	2
College scholarship or grant	24	11
Federal Stafford Loan	23	11
Federal Pell Grants	23	6
Part-time job on campus	20	2
State Scholarship or grant	14	3
Federal Work-Study Program	12	1
Other scholarship or grant	10	3
Federal Perkins Loan	8	2
College loan	6	3
Other loan	6	3
Federal Supplemental Educational Opportunity Grant	6	1
Full-time employment	3	1
Other aid	3	1
Other government aid	2	2
Student's spouse	2	*

* Indicates less than 1 percent
Source: The American Freshman: National Norms for Fall, 1992

colleges. Therefore, be skeptical of claims that hundreds of millions of dollars in financial aid goes unused every year. Often these can be traced to advertisements for fee-based computerized scholarship services. Moreover, generally the claims have not been supported. Following a year-long study of 45 computerized scholarship services, the California Student Aid Commission concluded as follows:

- ■ The claim that large amounts of financial aid go unused "could not be documented."
- ■ Though some college officials see the computer services as potentially helpful in saving students time, others point out that the same information is available without cost from reference books and campus financial aid advisers.
- ■ There is some unclaimed student assistance, but the amount of financial aid that is not used is "infinitesimally small."
- ■ Computerized services appear to do very little by way of matching student characteristics with financial aid program requirements.

The notion that there are large amounts of unclaimed financial aid lying around is largely myth. There is a small grain of truth to it — occasionally there are no takers for the money; but the notion that this happens often and that large amounts of money are available is misleading and doesn't square with the realities and opportunities most people face.

Stay in Touch

Parents and young people should stay in touch with high school counselors and college financial aid officers. They are the people in the best position to have information. College financial aid officers live with the complexities of financing a college education, and they must stay current. In addition, they may have some flexibility determining and packaging financial aid awards if parents can present a reasonable case. Remember, the financial aid officer's job is to do everything possible to help the student enroll in that institution. Financial aid officers are reasonable people.

College education is a big investment, and it deserves careful thought and planning. As complicated as it may seem, financial aid is one way to cut the costs of a college education for families and young people.

Financial Aid Application

Financial aid application and award procedures are highly standardized across colleges. All applicants for federal aid must submit a need analysis form called the Free Application for Federal Student Aid (FAFSA). In addition, many colleges and most private scholarship programs require one of these:

- The American College Testing Program's Family Financial Statement (FFS)
- The College Scholarship Service's Financial Aid Form (FAF)

The FFS and FAF are general-purpose application forms. In addition, some states have their own forms. For example, there are Pennsylvania Higher Education Assistance Agency forms and Student Aid Application for California forms. Reference books on colleges including *The College Handbook* indicate what form a particular college requires, but it is wise to verify this information directly with the college's office of financial aid.

Financial aid forms are useful tools for estimating need. However, before considering how to meet estimated need, let's look at how college financial aid offices determine need.

The basic formula is simple:

Estimated costs – Estimated resources = Estimated need

In the following sections, I review how each component in the formula — estimated costs, estimated resources, and estimated need — is calculated. I use Jim's costs as a hypothetical example.

Estimated Costs

Costs vary from one school to another, and so does the amount of financial aid available. It is important, therefore, to have a particular school in mind when estimating costs and needs.

The annual cost of a college education has two components: direct and indirect costs. *Direct costs* include tuition and fees, books and supplies. *Indirect costs* include housing and meals, transportation, and personal expenses — clothing, local travel, laundry and dry cleaning, and entertainment. Add these together and you have estimated costs.

Parents can make preliminary estimates of direct costs from information in reference books such as *The College Handbook.* However, parents and young people should not assume that the direct cost figures listed in printed materials are

JIM'S ESTIMATED COSTS	
Direct Costs	
Tuition and fees	$2,350
Books and supplies	520
Indirect Costs	
Housing	2,420
Meals	1,080
Transportation	550
Personal expenses	1,180
Estimated costs	$8,100

up-to-date. Typically, published material is at least a year old and sometimes two years old. That means that the actual costs could be 12 to 18 percent higher than the published costs. Direct costs change annually, and reported figures should be used only as first approximations. Colleges will gladly respond to inquiries about current direct costs. Write or telephone the financial aid office listed in college reference books.

College catalogs and college financial aid and admissions offices may also be helpful in providing estimates for indirect costs — housing, meals, and personal expenses. College reference books may provide estimates, but these should be verified against current costs. The one item of indirect expense for which neither college catalogs, admissions directors, nor college reference books can provide a reasonable estimate is the cost of transportation. Families can make a better estimate of transportation costs than anyone else. They need to take three things into account: distance, mode of transportation, and number of trips.

In making estimates, it is wise to err on the safe side — that is, err too high rather than too low. Generally speaking, undergraduates spend at least $525 a year on books and supplies and, say, $1,000 per year on personal expenses. Transportation costs? Your best estimate. The point is: Keep the total formula in mind. What a college education actually costs you and your daughter or son depends on several different cost considerations. Take them all into account.

Estimated Resources

Today's colleges expect that both the student and family will contribute to meeting the costs of a college education. The need analysis forms request detailed information on family size, income, assets, and expenses, which are used to establish the parents' and student's expected contributions. Let's go back to Jim's example. The major components to the expected student and family contribution are these:

JIM'S ESTIMATED RESOURCES

Student's Resources
A set percentage of savings and other assets	$ 0
Portion of summer earnings*	1,400
Earnings during school year*	850
Other benefits	0

Part of Family Contribution
Formula based on income	975
Formula based on savings	650
Formula based on other assets	800
Estimated resources	$4,675

* Based on prior year earnings

Several considerations bear on estimating the family contribution. These change from year to year.

Estimated Need

Estimated need is the difference between estimated costs and estimated resources. In Jim's case, his anticipated costs exceed his estimated resources, and he will probably be eligible for financial aid. Whether he is eligible will be determined officially by processing the Free Application for Federal Student Aid form.

JIM'S ESTIMATED NEED

Estimated costs	$ 8,100
Estimated resources	4,675
Estimated need	$ 3,425

Processing Services

The Free Application for Federal Aid form is processed by an independent corporation, either the College Scholarship Service or the American College Testing Program's Student Need Analysis Service. The service forwards the results to the colleges to which a young person applies. The goal of the standardized procedures is to equalize costs to students and families as much as possible.

There is another advantage to mailing the form to a financial aid processing service. The information isn't released to local school and community authorities. A young woman living in North Carolina told us: "My mother refused to complete a form for a scholarship that somebody gave me because she said the 'confidential financial info' in a small town was not so confidential." That might have been true when that young woman's mother was in high school and information was processed locally. But today, family financial information never comes back to the community and school. It is confidential. The system works remarkably well in protecting family information. Indeed, I have never heard of an instance where information about family finances was leaked or disclosed by the financial aid processing services. And the local school and community authorities never see the applications.

The estimate of resources available from parents and students will remain the same whether the college costs are high or low, so the estimates of a student's need will vary by college costs. Therefore, parents and their young people should not rule out colleges with higher costs, because students may be eligible for higher levels of financial aid at more expensive colleges. Financial aid is based on total expenses, not just tuition and fees.

Financial Aid Programs

Colleges receive reports from the financial aid service based on the need analysis forms, and the college decides on the level of resources it will commit to a particular student. Colleges administer financial aid in three basic forms, and financial aid packages consist of some combination of these sources:

> ■ Grants or scholarships: aid that does not have to be repaid
> ■ Loans: low-interest-bearing notes that must be repaid
> ■ Work study: jobs for students who need financial aid

Financial aid resources come from the federal government, state governments, colleges, and private organizations and scholarship programs. Colleges usually put their own money into the ablest students. By comparison, when colleges administer federal programs, the funds tend to go to the neediest students. The way financial aid packages are put together is not necessarily carved into stone. Sometimes there is room to negotiate. The point is that you need to work with the college financial aid officer. She or he is your ally, not your antagonist.

Eligibility

Students must meet several eligibility requirements to qualify for federal financial aid, one of the main ones being that a student must be enrolled at least half-time in a college — including universities, four-year colleges, two-year colleges, community colleges, vocational schools, technical schools, and hospital schools of nursing — recognized by the U.S. Department of Education. Other requirements include registration with the Selective Service, not being in default on previous education loans, making satisfactory progress toward a degree, and the like.

There are several basic federal programs — grants, loans, and work study — for financing higher education. Some are student-based. They award or loan money directly to students or parents. Others are campus-based. The government funds the colleges, which in turn allocate money on the basis of federal guidelines. The six major federal financial aid programs are as follow:

Grants

- *Federal Pell Grants.* The Pell Grant Program accounts for about 25 percent of all federal money spent on financial aid and is the second largest federal program. It awards money to qualified undergraduates with moderate to extreme need, including students who attend less than half-time. The awards are administered by colleges.
- *Federal Supplementary Educational Opportunity Grants.* These are awards to undergraduates with extreme need. Priority is given to recipients of Pell Grants. The program is open to both full-time and part-time students. The funds are administered by colleges.

Loans

- *Federal Perkins Loans.* These loans are made by colleges at favorable interest rates to undergraduates and graduates. Preference is given to students with extreme need, including students who attend less than full-time. There is a $3,000 annual limit to the loans and students pay no interest while in college but must repay the loans with interest when they leave college. The loans are administered by colleges.
- *Federal Stafford Loans.* This is the largest federal loan program and accounts for about 45 percent of all federal dollars spent on aid. Loans are made by a bank, credit union, or savings and loan association and are insured by state and federal agencies. Undergraduates, graduates, and professional students who are enrolled at least half-time are eligible. The federal government pays the interest on the loans for needy students while they are enrolled in college. Upon completion of schooling, students must repay the principal and interest.
- *Unsubsidized Federal Stafford Loans* are available for students who cannot demonstrate need. Interest may be capitalized or paid as it accrues.
- *Federal Parent Loan for Undergraduate Students.* These loans, sometimes called FPLUS or PLUS loans, are available to all parents of undergraduates and are not based on financial need. The loans are available to parents up to the full cost of education less any financial aid received by the student. The interest rate is tied to treasury bills and capped.
- *Federal Direct Student Loans.* This is a new program that went into effect on July 1, 1994. It consists of Federal Direct Stafford Loans, both subsidized and unsubsidized, and Federal Direct PLUS Loans. The difference is that the lender is the U.S. Department of Education rather than a bank or credit union, and the loan is processed through colleges rather than through private lenders.

Work Study

■ *Federal Work-Study Program.* This program provides subsidies to colleges for jobs for undergraduate and graduate students who need financial aid. The major part of the salary is paid by the federal government. The amount of pay the student receives depends on need and the kind of work he or she does. Federal Work Study is administered by the colleges.

In addition, in 1993 the federal government created AmeriCorps, the first program in the national service concept. In return for community-service work, AmeriCorps pays up to $4,725 a year for up to two years for college tuition or to repay college loans. By the end of 1994, the program will involve 20,000 paid volunteers.

The names, number, and details of federal financial aid programs change from year to year. The best way to stay informed is to ask for *The Student Guide* published by the U.S. Department of Education, which is available without charge from high school career counselors, career centers, and college financial aid officers. Alternatively, call 1-800-433-3243. For information on AmeriCorps, call its hotline at 1-800-942-2677.

Other Forms of Financial Aid

Most financial aid originates with the federal government — over 70 percent; but another 30 percent originates with state financial aid programs and other forms of aid located in the private sector.

Each state has its own program of financial aid for higher education. No two state programs are the same. A few states have brochures that contain information on all financial aid programs within their particular state. Generally, however, several different agencies administer state programs, and students and their parents may have to piece together the information from different sources. The amounts of available state financial aid are not large and, in total, represent only about 5 or 6 percent of all available financial aid.

In his book, *Don't Miss Out*, Robert Leider classifies the different categories of state financial aid programs as these:

Need-based grant programs

■ Grants restricted to in-state study
■ Grants to study in other states with reciprocity agreements
■ Grants for study in accredited schools in any state

Miscellaneous grant programs

- Merit programs are grants based on academic accomplishment
- Loans are programs in which the state operates as guaranteeing agency under the federal Guaranteed Student Loan program
- Special fields refers to programs that train people in areas in which the state experiences labor shortages
- Minority group programs are generally limited to native Americans
- State work-study programs are job programs similar to federal work-study programs
- Veterans' programs are earmarked for state residents who served in the military, usually in time of war
- National guard programs refer to special benefits for people who serve in the state's national guard

Dependent programs — special state financial aid programs for dependents of:

- Deceased or disabled veterans
- Prisoners of war or personnel missing in action
- Police officers or firefighters killed on duty

Parents and young people who need information about state aid programs should contact the state education office listed for each state and college admissions offices listed in college reference books. High school guidance counselors may also be knowledgeable about state financial aid programs.

Other Assistance

Other sources of financial aid are available. Cities and towns provide assistance to young people through civic groups and business associations. Private foundations award loans and scholarships based on competition. The community affairs column in local newspapers occasionally carries notices of awards for which residents may qualify. Young people may qualify for loans, grants, or scholarships on the basis of parental military service, union membership, membership in fraternal or religious organizations, or employer programs. Similarly, young people's characteristics and activities — including jobs held, religious affiliation, minority membership, nationality, being female, being disabled, having particular career interests or talents — may also qualify them for financial aid. Another possibility is to take advantage of military educational benefits, which I discuss in Chapter 12.

If your son or daughter is enrolled in high school, check with the school guidance center about local sources of financial aid.

Employer Tuition Programs

Since 1978, federal legislation enables employers to deduct educational assistance costs as business expense, and many companies have been paying part of their employees' educational expenses. Tuition aid from employers is probably the most overlooked source of funds for students. Ivan Charner, research director for the National Institute for Work and Learning, reports that more than 80 percent of companies with 500 to 1,000 employees have tuition benefit programs; 92 percent of companies that employ between 1,000 and 10,000 people offer tuition plans; and 95 percent of companies with more than 10,000 workers offer tuition plans. Yet most workers do not know they are eligible, the plans are not well-understood, and company tuition plans are never thought of by most employees.

Employer tuition benefit programs may benefit you in two ways. First, your son or daughter may work for an employer that has an employee tuition program. Check it out, especially if your son or daughter works for a large firm. Second, you or your spouse may work for a firm that has hidden employee family benefits. Again, check it out if that seems reasonable. Only small percentages of employees take advantage of employer tuition programs.

Financial Aid Guides

Many publications are available on various financial aid programs — far too many to list. Following are examples that may be useful to parents and young people who need to explore financial aid information.

In this section, I list the publications by topic, beginning with an example that explains how student financial aid works and how to apply for it, and then listing examples of publications on general sources of financial aid. I end with references for special programs for which your daughter or son may qualify. For each example, I list the title of the book, and then give a summary of the contents, which is usually one sentence long. I favor examples that are revised annually, which assures that the information is current. I list mailing addresses where the publisher may be contacted, and I include current costs, which may affect a parent's decision to purchase. These references may be available in some career centers and libraries; otherwise, find the publication through bookstores.

Financial Aid Process

College Costs & Financial Aid Handbook

This *Handbook* outlines the financial aid process from start to finish, reviews major aid programs, and lists current costs and scholarship opportunities at 3,200 two- and four-year public, private, and proprietary schools. The *Handbook* includes indexes to colleges that award scholarships in specific areas. It is published by the College Board and is widely available in career centers, libraries, and bookstores ($16, plus $3.95 handling). Order from College Board Publications, Box 886, New York, NY 10101-0886.

General Financial Aid Information

The Student Guide

Official source of government information on federal student aid programs, eligibility rules, application procedures (free). Available from career centers or order from Federal Student Aid Programs, P.O. Box 84, Washington, DC 20044, or phone 1-800-433-3243.

Need a Lift?

Guide to loans and scholarships for all students, with emphasis on scholarships for veterans, their dependents, and children of deceased or disabled veterans. It is an inexpensive public service booklet ($2 prepaid). Order from National Emblem Sales, P.O. Box 1050, Indianapolis, IN 46206.

Annual Register of Grant Support

Lists more than 3,000 grant programs in the humanities, education, social sciences, physical sciences, life sciences, race and minority concerns, environment and urban affairs, international affairs, technology and other areas ($175). Order from R.R. Bowker, 121 Chanlon Rd., New Providence, NJ 07974.

Chronicle Financial Aid Guide

Provides information on more than 1,600 financial aid programs including grants offered by noncollege organizations, labor unions, and federal and state governments ($22.47, plus postage and handling). Order from Chronicle Guidance Publications, Inc., 66 Aurora St., P.O. Box 1190, Moravia, NY 13118-1190.

The Scholarship Book: The Complete Guide to Private Sector Scholarships, Grants, and Loans for Undergraduates

Lists over 50,000 private-sector scholarships, grants, loans, fellowships, internships, and contest prizes covering major fields of study. Includes samples of letters requesting financial aid information ($19.95, plus postage). Order from Order Processing Center, P.O. Box 11071, Des Moines, IA 50336-1071, or phone 1-800-947-7700.

Special Groups

Bureau of Indian Affairs Higher Education Grants and Scholarships

Gives sources of financial aid for native Americans, Alaskan natives, and other tribes recognized by the Bureau of Indian Affairs (free). Order from Office of Indian Education Programs, Code 522 Room 3516, 18th and C Streets NW, Washington, DC 20240.

Directory of Financial Aids for Women

Lists more than 1,750 sources of financial aid for women ($45, plus postage and handling). Order from Reference Service Press, 1100 Industrial Rd., Suite 9, San Carlos, CA 94070.

Higher Education Opportunities for Minorities and Women

Suggests financial aid sources for minorities and women ($8). Order from Superintendent of Documents, U.S. Government Printing Office, Washington, DC 20402-9325.

Educational Assistance and Opportunities Information for Army Family Members

Lists financial aid programs for dependents of Army personnel (free). Order from Commander, U.S. Army Personnel, Attn: TATC-POE, 2461 Eisenhower Ave., Alexandria, VA 22331.

Financial Aid for Veterans, Military Personnel and Their Dependents

Gives financial aid sources and internships for military personnel ($37.50, plus postage and handling). Order from Reference Service Press, 1100 Industrial Rd., Suite 9, San Carlos, CA 94070.

Federal Benefits for Veterans and Dependents

Lists financial aid benefits for dependents ($3.25). Order Fact Sheet IS-I from Superintendent of Documents, U.S. Government Printing Office, Washington, DC 20402.

Financial Aid for the Disabled and Their Families

Lists financial aid programs for the disabled, including their children and parents ($38.50, plus shipping). Order from Reference Service Press, 1100 Industrial Rd., Suite 9, San Carlos, CA 94070.

Cutting Costs

A second way to manage educational expenses is to cut costs.

One way to cut costs is to "shop for credits" — that is, compare the cost per credit hour at various institutions. Costs per credit hour at state universities, state colleges, or local community colleges will usually be less than at private schools.

Another way to cut costs is to start out at an inexpensive two-year or four-year college, take the basic courses required in most colleges, then transfer to a more expensive four-year college. The student earns a more prestigious degree without paying the higher costs for four years. The *Wall Street Journal* reported an example of a student who transferred out of Georgetown University to a less prestigious college because he could transfer the credits back to Georgetown and it would cost him $7,300 less.

Some high schools offer advanced placement courses that carry college credit that may reduce later college costs. Your son or daughter may be able to save time and expense through College-Level Examination Programs (CLEP), which enable students to satisfy course requirements by examination rather than by course enrollment. Parents and young people contemplating this possibility may wish to consult *The Official Handbook for the CLEP Examinations.* The *Handbook* gives information about earning college credit for courses taken elsewhere and includes descriptions of examination, test preparation advice, sample questions from CLEP exams, and a list of 1,200 CLEP test centers by city and state ($15, plus $3.95 shipping and handling). Order from College Board Publications, Box 886, New York, NY 10101-0886.

Other economies may be achieved. Some colleges offer a book rental program. Students can make-do with used textbooks, live in a low-cost apartment, use public transportation instead of personal car, or take four years of credits in three years' time. The College Board estimates that in 1994–1995, undergraduates enrolled in public four-year colleges who live at home will save $1,836.

Though it is unlikely that students can earn more from summer employment than their annual college costs will be, many can save more from summer earnings than colleges expect of them, which is a net advantage to students in terms of financial aid. Finally, many students are responding to increased education costs by enrolling part-time and working. Part-time enrollments have been increasing more than full-time enrollments as many students take lighter academic loads in order to keep up with both work and study.

SENSE AND CENTS

I am not an attorney. Nor am I an accountant, a financial aid consultant, or a college financial aid officer. Rather, I am the father of three sons who has gone through the financial aid scenario more than once. I am a research sociologist who follows everything that has to do with youth career development. And I am a private citizen who hears about and reads about financial aid. Putting it all together, I can appreciate the anxiety that parents feel when they stare at college costs, and I understand the confusion they feel when they try to understand financial aid programs. I've been there.

Financial aid is big business — $35 billion per year! Because it involves big bucks it is the subject of newspaper headlines, magazine articles, government brochures, and over-the-fence and across-the-grocery-cart neighborly conversations. But not all of the information is helpful. And some of the information may be ill-advised if not erroneous. Both the popular press and folk-talk can be unreliable guides for planning college finances and maximizing the benefits of the financial-aid system. By "folk-talk" I mean beliefs and ideas, even schemes, for "getting around" financial aid requirements.

In this section, I suggest some cautions and questions to answer before adopting a beat-the-system strategy that may cost you. My advice is simple: Measure twice, then saw. Check it out, then act. Financing a college education involves large sums of money, and parents should get the same legal and financial advice they would get for such expenditures as purchasing homes, setting up trusts, or establishing retirement programs.

Following are "folk tales" that you may want to check out before organizing your financing-a-college-education plans around them.

Folk Tale # 1: Put money away for your child's education by setting up a trust fund in your child's name under the Uniform Gifts to Minors Act.

Folk Tale # 1 goes something like this: You can give substantial amounts of money to your child without your child having to pay either gift or income taxes on the gift. The gift legally transfers the money away from parents who, presumably, are in a higher income bracket to the child who, presumably, is in a lower tax bracket. Therefore, the argument goes, any income earned on the money will be taxed at a lower rate because it belongs to the child rather than the parent.

The basic reasoning may be sound, but whether sense makes cents is another question. Parents need to check it out. Tax implications regarding financial aid are comparable to tax implications for any kind of financial planning. It's a bit of a cat-and-mouse game, and tax laws change. Parents need to answer two questions:

> ■ How much in tax savings will actually accrue?
> ■ How much in financial aid will the student lose by benefiting from parental gifts?

The formulas that establish whether students qualify for financial aid take into account both the resources parents have and those that students have, and in recent years students have been required to contribute substantially larger percentages of their assets than parents. For example, students may be required to contribute 30 to 35 percent of their resources whereas parents may be required to contribute only 5 or 6 percent. Therefore, the advantage of transferring assets to children is eroded.

The tax savings in income earned on the money is only one consideration. The second consideration is the rate at which parents' and their daughter's or son's assets will be assessed for purposes of determining eligibility for financial aid. Both assessments should be made to determine whether savings should be accumulated in the parents' or child's name.

Folk Tale # 2: *You can get around some of the financial aid requirements by locking up a trust in your son's or daughter's name that is not payable until she or he leaves college.*

Whether parents can set up such a trust is a different issue than whether the trust will be assessed for financial aid purposes. Parents need to check it out.

Assuming parents can set up such a trust — which is likely — parents need to answer three questions:

> ■ Is a trust, set up in the child's name and payable only after the child leaves college, exempt from determining the parent's and child's assets for financial aid purposes?
> ■ If the trust is assessable, what is the rate at which such a trust is assessed for purposes of determining eligibility for financial aid?
> ■ Is there an advantage to establishing such a trust?

Folk Tale # 3: *There is a family income ceiling of, say, $30,000 to qualify for financial aid.*

There is no fixed family income ceiling for establishing eligibility for financial aid. Indeed, students from families with even larger incomes may qualify. The formula that establishes the level of family assets is complex and, in some cases, allows even families with sizeable incomes to qualify. Eligibility for financial aid is determined not only by family income and assets, but also by the relative costs of college, which vary from college to college.

Eligibility for financial aid is established on the basis of the difference between college costs and family assets; and because both may vary, some families with relatively large incomes may qualify.

Folk Tale # 4: Don't apply for financial aid until a son or daughter is accepted for admission — because you don't want a financial aid application to jeopardize the chances for admission.

This is simply bad advice and, I would guess, it is probably always wrong for these reasons:

- It is usually the case that parents and students must process financial aid applications before a student is admitted for enrollment. Waiting may result in missing deadlines and jeopardizing the student's chances for any financial aid whatsoever.
- Students are often admitted for enrollment before a college makes decisions regarding financial aid.
- Except in marginal cases, such as when a college may be selecting students for the last available enrollment openings, enrollment admission decisions and financial aid decisions are made independently by colleges.

Folk Tale # 5: The "real money" in financial aid comes from scholarships and grants that aren't widely publicized, and finding these is where parents should spend their time and effort.

This isn't true, and it is seldom good advice. Occasionally, parents and students will stumble across a windfall in the form of little-known grant or scholarship money for which they qualify, but these lucky pots of gold help only a few. Almost all financial aid money comes from publicly known sources: most of it from the federal government, substantial monies from state governments, some from private organizations, and additional monies from college grants and loan programs. "Secret money" is usually wishful thinking, a notion based more in fantasy than in reality.

Nonetheless, check out all possibilities. That's why I listed references for financial aid programs earlier. Follow through on sources you hear about, and make a special effort to determine whether your employer, professional associations, or organizations to which you belong have financial aid programs that may benefit your son or daughter. It doesn't hurt to check it out.

Folk Tale # 6: The best deal is a state-guaranteed tuition plan.

Increasingly, states have gotten into the business of setting up programs whereby parents pay in advance to finance a college education at a state school. This may or may not be a good deal. Parents need to check it out, and then decide. Be sure to answer these three questions when making that decision:

> ■ What if, when it comes time to apply, you and your child decide that an out-of-state college is the best choice? What are the provisions in the plan for this contingency?
>
> ■ What if parents' employment or other considerations necessitate their relocating to another state before the son or daughter enrolls in college? What provisions apply to this contingency?
>
> ■ What if your son's or daughter's academic performance is not what you had hoped, and he or she is not eligible for admission to one of the better schools in the state? What are your options?

Before entering a guaranteed tuition plan, parents should satisfy themselves that their hands are not tied.

Folk Tale # 7: College certificates of deposit are the best protection against inflation in college costs.

Certificates of deposit are offered by certain banks that tie interest rates on the deposit to tuition increases and thereby suggest that the principal will accumulate at a rate comparable to the inflation of college costs. Parents need to check it out. Questions to be answered include:

> ■ What is the annual rate of return on the certificate?
> ■ What is the service charge or commission?
> ■ Is the income produced by the rate of return taxable and, if so, how much does that affect the realized rate of accumulation?

Parental Involvement

Most of the loopholes in the financial aid system have been closed. Nonetheless, there are things parents can do to assist their daughter's or son's career development. First of all, if financial aid is a confusing prospect for parents, consider what it must be for inexperienced students. Throughout the financial aid process, it is best for parents to represent their sons and daughters. Parents are much more experienced in financial matters. They are less intimidated. They aren't as likely to be swept away by big numbers. And only parents can speak for what the family is in a position to do. Most parents are likely to foot some of the cost for a college education — perhaps even most of the cost. Parental input is absolutely necessary when it comes to securing financial aid.

Second, parents can start the process early — earlier than most students would think about starting it or be concerned about it. Students begin thinking about financial aid at about the time they take the PSAT in their junior year, or not until the Fall term of their senior year. But parents are in a position to anticipate and should get involved in the financial-aid process even earlier — as early as the student's freshman or sophomore year in high school. That is not the time to start saving for a college education, and it is not the time to apply for financial aid; but it is the time for parents to begin to study the financial aid process and to review financial aid application forms and procedures.

Third, there may be possibilities for parents to "move money around" to advantage, if they do so in advance. Family finances during the student's junior year in high school will figure prominently in determining eligibility for financial aid. That is because the family financial aid application, which will be processed in January of the student's senior year, must be supported by income tax information from the previous year. To the extent that parents can control their income, it is to their advantage to reduce their income after January 1 of their son's or daughter's junior year. They may wish to take as much income as they can prior to that date and to delay expenses as possible until January of the junior year. Planning for financial aid involves some of the same considerations as planning income and expenses for income tax purposes.

Finally, processing family financial aid forms occurs largely behind the scenes, though it involves hundreds of thousands of families every year. Meeting deadlines is critically important, as is giving careful attention to detail and answering queries promptly. These are additional reasons for parents to get involved in the financial aid process from start to finish.

Next Steps: What Parents Can Do

Confusion and frustration often go together. Confusion comes from not knowing what to do, or when to do it — which is frustrating. Add to that the prospect of spending large sums of money and the frustration intensifies. One way to lessen the confusion and frustration that comes with choosing a college and applying for financial aid is to know what parents and young people need to do, as well as when, where, and how to do it.

I've tried to answer those questions for you with a checklist that summarizes key steps in preparing for a career with additional schooling, and puts the steps on a timetable. If your daughter or son is college material, start following the checklist during the sophomore year and stay on schedule through the senior year. Your local circumstances may require that you make some adjustments along the way, but the checklist keeps track of the main "to-dos."

Check each box as you complete the task. Also, draw a line through boxes that do not apply to you. That way, only the unmarked boxes indicate what you need to do and when.

SOPHOMORE YEAR: FALL SEMESTER

This is the year to familiarize yourself with available services, information, and procedures, and to do some advanced planning. It's time to make sure you understand two processes:

- Applying for college admissions
- Applying for financial aid

Here are the "to-dos" for the sophomore year.

❑ Visit your local bookstore.

Browse for occupational careers information — probably in the business section.

Look over the information on college planning — probably in the self-help section.

Consider purchasing a copy of the *Occupational Outlook Handbook* for the coffee table in your family room, if you haven't already done so.

❑ Visit your local library.

Explain to the reference librarian that you are interested in materials on occupational careers and college planning. Ask what materials are available and whether there are special sections of material on career planning.

249

SOPHOMORE YEAR: SPRING SEMESTER

This is the semester to finish your preliminary planning.

❑ Locate the telephone number for your State Occupational Information Coordinating Committee (see Chapter 7).

> Call your SOICC office, explain that you have a son or daughter contemplating college, and request free information on occupational careers and career preparation programs in your state.

❑ Visit your high school career center with your daughter or son.

> Introduce yourself to your son's or daughter's career counselor. Explain that you are trying to understand the planning for college process.

> Ask what services the career center offers parents and students. Make notes of important activities such as career fairs and other scheduled events, and services such as interest inventories and aptitude tests. Some high schools give interest inventories and aptitude tests only on request. Some charge; others don't.

> Ask for free handouts and literature on

> ☞ The PSAT
> ☞ Financial aid programs for college — for example, *The Student Guide*
> ☞ Other materials on planning for college

> Familiarize yourself with basic reference materials available in the career center — such as the *Occupational Outlook Handbook* and *College Costs & Financial Aid Handbook*.

> Check what other reference materials are available, including computerized career information systems.

> Have your daughter or son demonstrate how a computer career explorations program works.

❑ Explore whether you should rearrange any family finances in anticipation of submitting financial aid application forms.

❑ Set aside a place in your home where you can file or store college planning materials.

JUNIOR YEAR: FALL SEMESTER

Fall semester, junior year, is the time to begin pulling things together.

❑ Help your daughter or son clarify what she or he wants from the college experience. Thinking through college possibilities is one way to do that. See Chapter 9, "Choosing a College," for ideas. See, also, the introductory material in *The College Handbook* or similar guides. Begin to sort out kinds of colleges that interest you and your daughter or son.

❑ Consider purchasing a copy of *The College Handbook* or other guide to colleges for the coffee table in your family room.

❑ Take final stock of family finances for the following year, January 1 through December 31, to determine whether family finances might be adjusted in anticipation of submitting a financial aid application the following year.

❏ Sign-up with the guidance counselor for taking the PSAT in October. Note the date on your family calendar.

❏ Review PSAT/SAT descriptive information with your daughter or son.

❏ After your son or daughter has taken the PSAT, help him or her decide whether to purchase SAT review course and study materials from a bookstore.

❏ Encourage your daughter or son to be involved in a community service activity and/ or school extracurricular activity that can be listed favorably on a college application form. Encourage your son or daughter to seek a leadership role.

❏ Get a realistic picture in your mind about the cost of a year of college at the institutions your son or daughter may be considering, what family resources are available, and whether your son or daughter is likely to qualify for scholarships or grants. Discuss "what's in the ball park" with your son or daughter so that, later, you can arrive at a mutually acceptable decision.

JUNIOR YEAR: SPRING SEMESTER

This is the semester to get serious about identifying colleges that match your child's interests. Come up with several college possibilities and don't eliminate any solely on the basis of costs. Remember, financial aid is based on estimated need — the difference between costs and resources. Use *The College Handbook* or a similar college reference to get preliminary information.

❏ With your daughter or son, call or write to several colleges that interest you. Ask for an undergraduate catalog, admissions forms, financial aid information, and other available information.

❏ Attend college fairs in your community with your son or daughter and speak with college representatives.

❏ Talk with young people who are attending colleges that may interest your son or daughter. Speak with their parents, too. Get as much advance information as you can so that you have specifics to talk about when it comes to trying to match your daughter's or son's interests with school characteristics.

❏ Visit nearby colleges. Schedule meetings in advance with the admissions officer and financial aid officer.

❏ Determine what admissions tests are required by the colleges that interest your son or daughter. This information is available from college catalogs, college reference books, and career counselors. Verify with the college admissions office.

❏ Meet with the high school counselor to discuss college plans and financial aid possibilities.

❏ Encourage your daughter or son to take the SAT or ACT, whichever is required, and register to take the test during Spring semester of the junior year (currently, ACT in April and SAT in May). This allows an opportunity to retake the test, if your son or daughter wishes, during the Fall semester of the senior year.

❏ Encourage your son or daughter to read the booklets in the registration packets and to take the practice tests. This will help him or her avoid confusion and reduce anxiety.

❏ When you receive the SAT or ACT test report, work through the results with your son or daughter so that both of you understand what the scores mean. Decide with your daughter or son and career counselor whether to retake the test in the Fall.

SUMMER

Summer is a good time to talk with students home from colleges that your son or daughter may be thinking of attending.

SENIOR YEAR: FALL SEMESTER

Fall semester in the senior year is the time to pay special attention to financial aid announcements: deadlines for application, application procedures, and special programs.

❏ Suggest that your son or daughter check high school information sources for program announcements and deadlines on a weekly basis.

❏ Note important application dates on your calendar.

❏ Your daughter or son should apply to take the ACT or SAT or ACH (College Board Achievement Tests) if she or he did not take it earlier or if there are good reasons to retake it. Watch for December scheduling dates.

❏ Be alert for announcements of career days and college fairs.

❏ Visit colleges, if possible, with your son or daughter. Try to visit on weekdays when students are on campus and administrative offices are open. Make an appointment to discuss policies, forms, and procedures at the college financial aid and admissions offices.

❏ Try to narrow college prospects to a manageable number — say, three or four.

❏ Pay close attention to the admissions process and admissions and financial aid deadlines for colleges that interest your son or daughter. Note deadlines.

❏ Meet with the high school counselor to discuss college choices and financial aid.

❏ Arrange for teachers to write letters of recommendation as required by college application materials.

❏ Take ACH (College Board Achievement Tests): English with an Essay (ES), Math Level 1, and any other requirements.

❏ Complete, check, and mail all college admissions forms by deadlines.

❏ Get financial aid application forms from high school counselors and college financial aid offices. Begin to prepare applications.

SENIOR YEAR: SPRING SEMESTER

This is the semester for decisions and deadlines.

❑ Encourage your daughter or son to continue checking high school information sources for program announcements and deadlines on a weekly basis.

❑ Financial aid application forms are due shortly after the beginning of the year. Complete all forms carefully and mail to the appropriate need analysis service at least six weeks before the financial aid deadlines.

❑ Keep a copy of all application materials submitted.

❑ You will receive a report from the financial need analysis service that gives your "estimated family contribution." Use that figure as a rough guideline to determine your son's or daughter's "estimated need" by subtracting the estimated family contribution from the estimated college costs. Estimated need is the figure that college financial aid officers will try to meet.

❑ Colleges may notify students of admission acceptance as early as February. Students admitted to more than one college will have only a few weeks to choose. Prepare to make the choice.

❑ Forward the required monetary deposit to the college of your son's or daughter's choice.

❑ Complete and return additional registration materials as required — for example, room and board application. Normally, it is to your daughter's or son's advantage to respond early.

❑ Notify colleges to which your daughter or son has applied but has chosen not to attend.

PART IV
CAREER PREPARATION:
EARNING WHILE LEARNING

Vocational Preparation Strategies

Basically, anyone who wants to go to college can do so. The majority of colleges have open admissions policies — they admit everyone or nearly anyone who applies. Four-year colleges and universities tend to be more restrictive. State universities, for example, typically admit two-thirds to three-fourths of applicants. Some colleges admit only about half their applicants. Only a very few select colleges and universities admit a fourth or less of their applicants. Everyone who wants to go to college can find a college somewhere that will admit her or him.

But that doesn't mean that everyone wants to go to college, or that everyone should go to college, or that it necessarily makes sense to go to college — certainly not for four years. And most people don't. Of high school graduates, 62 percent enroll in two- or four-year colleges, and 40 percent of them end up with a four-year degree. Only 22 percent of persons 25 years and older hold four-year degrees.

Every year, thousands of students go to college for the wrong reasons, and they do not belong there. Other people — parents, guardians, well-intentioned relatives, employers, spouses, and college talent scouts — have all kinds of reasons for sending other people to college, but from the individual's point of view there are only two good reasons to enroll. One is because a person has "fire in the belly," to borrow a Lee Iacocca expression, to study traditional academic subjects like the classics, literature, history, philosophy, physics, or biology. A second good reason to go to college is because a person needs a college degree to achieve a career goal. She wants to be a doctor or he wants to be a lawyer. The first reason to go to college is because you want to go. The second is because you have to go.

A plumber's wife who works as a practical nurse in a doctor's office put it this way:

> *" I will not push my children — I have three — to go to college. I want them to do the best they can and will do all I can to help them pursue what interests them. If a certain field interests them, I will help them see the pros and cons of that field so they know what to expect so as not to be shocked later if they enter that field."*

Similarly, a sales manager in Colorado told us:

> *" Too many dream of glamorous jobs such as doctor, lawyer, or airline stewardess where competition runs high as does the expense and years of training. It's not important what job you do, but how well you do it that gives you satisfaction."*

And a postal clerk with a B.A. in history said the same thing: "Some people, including myself, would rather do physical labor than sit behind a desk and get fat."

A college education is no longer the only way to get a job, and it may not be the best way for people who don't want a college education or for jobs that don't require additional schooling. A society in which a fourth of all workers are already overqualified doesn't need an even larger glut of college graduates — 30 percent of workers may be overqualified by the year 2005. It is true that the nation needs scientists and professionals and others with higher education credentials, but it is also true that three-fourths of the job openings in the U.S. do not require a college education. Finally, there is nothing automatic about a college education preparing a young person for a career. The son of a grocery store manager, who has a master's degree in personnel and labor relations, commented:

> *" I was led to believe that if I went to college, the American dream would be mine and my life would be set. Most importantly, I thought I'd know what I wanted to do with my life. Well, here I am [age 30] and I still don't know — and perhaps I never will."*

Yet all jobs require an education, most prefer more than a high school education, and virtually all require at least a high school diploma. Early in our country's history, few finished high school. Instead, most took jobs. That made sense. There were roads to build and streets to sweep — by hand. There were crops to plant and cultivate and harvest — by hand. There were cash registers to punch and books to keep — by hand. There were a lot of factory and common labor and unskilled jobs.

But that isn't the way it is today, and that certainly is not the way it will be tomorrow. People who do not want to go to college need to understand that there are nearly no more jobs for people without education and skills. The preferred preparation for a typical job in the U.S. labor force today is about 13.5 years of education/training. That is a high school diploma plus a year or two of vocational preparation beyond high school. And that means that the critical decision for an intelligent and responsible young person to make is what kind of additional schooling and training to get. It doesn't have to be four years of college. It doesn't have to be two years of college. It doesn't have to be formal education at all. It can be practical training that converts personal interests and abilities into basic skills that secure a good job and a stable career. It's "hire education." I call these programs "earning while learning."

There are many careers out there — in fact, most careers! — that do not require a college education but do require more than a high school diploma. It takes some courage to explore earning-while-learning options, because the popular notion is stronger than ever that college is the best or the only way to prepare for a career. According to the U.S. Department of Education High School and Beyond Study, more sophomores reported that they were encouraged to attend college after high school by parents, teachers, and counselors in 1990 than in 1980. Parents were still more likely to advise college attendance, but guidance counselors and teachers were twice as likely to recommend college attendance in 1990 as in 1980. This advisement tilt toward college occurred at the same time that the college graduate glut increased, education requirements for most entry-level positions decreased, and the number of ways to prepare for careers other than traditional four-year college enrollment expanded considerably. A veterinarian in our Career Development Study told us: "I do not feel that college is for everyone . . . technical schools and on-the-job training should be encouraged with the same social acceptance as college." And a dental hygienist echoed the same theme:

> *"I felt pressured to attend college after graduation from high school as my peers were doing. . . . I feel college should not be made to seem so attractive, as the only means of becoming a success."*

In this chapter, I examine 12 ways to add vocational training to a high school education. And in the following chapter, I explore three more options.

VOCATIONAL EDUCATION

There is much confusion about vocational education. People say that vocational education is "trade courses in high school," "what community colleges offer," "what technical schools do," or "a special program in four-year colleges." What vocational education is gets even more confusing if we consider definitions used by the National Institute of Education, the National Center for Education Statistics, or the Bureau of the Census. Perhaps that is why the Carnegie Council on Policy Studies in Higher Education published a chapter with this title: "Vocational Education: Change Everything, Including the Name."

When I use the phrase *vocational education*, I mean two things: programs in which the primary goal is to provide skills at the technical, paraprofessional, and skilled occupation levels; and programs that are usually of shorter duration

> *"Today, there are 6,961 institutions that provide vocational education — nearly twice as many as the total number of all four- and two-year colleges."*

than four-year baccalaureate programs. Often vocational education programs are shorter than two-year associate degree programs. My definition includes degree and certificate programs offered by four-year colleges, two-year colleges, and noncollegiate schools. It also includes programs that begin in high schools. I do not include correspondence schools where the primary mode of instruction is based in neither the job nor the classroom.

Background

In 1963, Congress passed the Vocational Education Act. Passage gave formal recognition, increased visibility, new status, and multibillion-dollar financial impetus to vocational education programs. Today, there are 6,961 institutions that provide vocational education — nearly twice as many as the total number of all four- and two-year colleges. A third of all high school students enroll in vocational education programs; about one in seven enroll within a year and a half after high school graduation; and four of five high school students go on to some type of postsecondary schooling within 12 years after high school graduation. If those proportions hold, as I expect they will, nearly 400,000 students from this year's high school graduating class will enroll in some kind of vocational education program within 18 months after high school; and two million of them will enroll within 12 years. With the current federal initiatives of work force preparedness, school-to-work transition, and education reforms, the numbers of participants in vocational education will surely increase.

Apparently, more and more young people agree with what a firefighter with 10 years' experience told us: "College should not be deemphasized; but vocational education should be emphasized more."

Major Program

There is no single system in general use for classifying vocational education programs. However, the National Center for Education Statistics classifies 66 sub-baccalaureate awards, and 85 percent of the less-than-one-year awards are given in five general areas.

Health services is the largest single area, followed by business and management, engineering technologies, protective services, and visual and performing arts.

Program Area	Percentage
Health Sciences	33
Business and Management	27
Engineering Technologies	15
Protective Services	6
Visual and Performing Arts	6
All Others	15

The number and types of programs available varies by institution and region of the country. Some schools specialize in a single occupational area. For example, for years nearly half of technical education students in Michigan were enrolled in electronics technology. Other schools and regions offer a more diversified menu, and chances are that a varied selection of programs is available in your area.

Occupations

Many areas exist for which specialized training is required, and vocational education programs provide the necessary training for many of them. Vocational education is not an entry ticket to all occupations, and it is not the best form of career preparation for some occupations; but it is a good way to prepare for many occupations.

There are many things to consider in determining whether a vocational education program is the best way for your daughter or son to prepare for a particular career:

> ■ What occupation is your son or daughter thinking about?
> ■ What does the *Occupational Outlook Handbook* indicate are the minimum and the preferred entry qualifications for that occupation?
> ■ What colleges offer vocational education for that occupation?
> ■ What is your son's or daughter's potential?

Each of these must be considered, and there is no set answer that suits everyone.

Also, remember how vocational preparation programs fit into the grand scheme of things. This will give you further guidance for figuring out your particular situation. Think again about the occupational projections reported in Chapter 6. I differentiated there, as I have throughout this book, between projections based on number of employment openings in an occupation and projections based on growth rate — a critical distinction. To illustrate how vocational preparation programs relate to employment possibilities, consider what form of minimal career preparation is advised for the 15 occupations that will have the most employment openings over the next decade. Before commenting, allow me also to list the occupations projected to have the fastest growth rates together with the form of career preparation advised for these (see the following tables).

Note four things about the preferred minimal education and training for these 30 high-opportunity areas:

> ■ High school and vocational preparation is the most preferred minimal preparation for most employment openings.
> ■ High school is adequate for many of the occupations that have the most employment openings.
> ■ A college education is preferred more often for occupations with fast growth rates.
> ■ Advancement within occupations almost always requires additional schooling or training.

PREFERRED ENTRY-LEVEL CAREER PREPARATION FOR 15 OCCUPATIONS WITH THE MOST EMPLOYMENT OPENINGS, 1992–2005

Occupations	High School	Vocational	College
Salespersons, retail	x		
Registered nurses		x	
Cashiers	x		
General office clerks	x		
Truck drivers, light and heavy	x		
Waiters and waitresses	x		
Nursing aides, orderlies, and attendants	x		
Janitors and cleaners, including maids and housekeeping cleaners	x		
Food preparation workers	x		
Systems analysts			x
Home health aides	x		
Teachers, secondary school			x
Childcare workers	x		
Guards	x		
Marketing and sales worker supervisors			x

PREFERRED ENTRY-LEVEL CAREER PREPARATION FOR 15 FASTEST-GROWING OCCUPATIONS, 1992–2005

Occupations	High School	Vocational	College
Home health aides	x		
Human services workers		x	
Personal and home care aides	x		
Computer engineers and scientists			x
Systems analysts			x
Physical and corrective therapy assistants and aides	x		
Physical therapists			x
Paralegals		x	
Teachers, special education			x
Medical assistants		x	
Detectives, except public	x		
Correction officers	x		
Childcare workers	x		
Travel agents		x	
Radiologic technologists and technicians	x		

Vocational Education Resources

Young people do not always know the connection between degrees or certificates and jobs. Often, someone needs to point out the connections. Take the case of this young woman, who graduated with a bachelor's degree in psychology from a college in New Mexico. The biggest problem she said she faced was "deciding early in high school the degree I wanted to pursue, but having no real knowledge of the job(s) this degree would qualify me for." The best way to determine what form of education and training is preferred for a particular occupation is to read about the occupation in the *Occupational Outlook Handbook* (see Chapter 7).

Several sources of information about particular vocational preparation programs are available, but two stand out as excellent places to start. If you are interested in programs in four- or two-year colleges, check the indexes in *The College Handbook* or other college reference books. If you are interested in programs only in your state, region, or community, check the information from your State Occupational Information Coordinating Committee (also covered in Chapter 7).

Costs. Costs for attending vocational education programs vary by programs. Tuition charges at most public two-year colleges are modest — an average of $1,298 for the 1994–'95 school year. Often students in two-year colleges live at home and commute, with the result that transportation costs increase but room and board costs remain about the same as when the student was in high school.

Tuition charges in proprietary noncollegiate schools — that is, for-profit business, trade, and technical schools — are usually based on a flat fee for a particular program. Sometimes the fee includes costs of books and supplies. Sometimes it doesn't. You need to check.

There is no direct comparison of tuition costs between public, private, and proprietary schools; or between four- and two-year colleges; or between colleges and noncollegiate institutes and trade schools. Community colleges list programs in terms of credit hours, but noncollegiate schools list programs in terms of duration — that is, in weeks. In community colleges, students spend between 15 and 20 hours in the classroom or laboratory per week, but in noncollegiate proprietary schools, students generally attend between 25 and 30 hours. That gives them about one-third more instruction time per week.

Other differences that make cost comparisons difficult include whether a person views the general courses offered in community colleges as a bane or a bonus; whether the flat rate of noncollegiate proprietary schools includes books, supplies, and fees that are extra assessments in two-year colleges; and whether income deferred in programs of longer duration in four- and two-year colleges is viewed as a cost. Parents and their sons and daughters will want to consider the relative costs from a number of different perspectives.

Uneven Information. Vocational programs are comparatively recent additions to the U.S. education/training scene — they're only 30 to 35 years old; the programs have experienced rapid growth and change; the areas are not tightly conceptualized into standard categories; the nearly 7,000 vocational preparation institutions are not governed or regulated by a single agency; and few rigorous studies of the effects of vocational education on later careers have been done. As a result, the information about vocational education programs is less plentiful and reliable than that available for college degree programs. The information is uneven. There is much about some programs but little about others. A 1994 National Assessment of Vocational Education Report describes research on vocational education as a maze of "complicated and often contradictory findings."

Vocational education programs are offered in four-year colleges, two-year colleges, and noncollegiate schools. Two-year colleges, junior, and community colleges are the most popular settings and enroll two-thirds of all students in vocational preparation programs. Another fourth are enrolled in noncollegiate schools, and the remainder are enrolled in vocational education programs in four-year colleges.

The following sections review vocational education options. I begin with options available during the high school years, then the college years, and close with noncollegiate possibilities. I briefly describe the unique features of each program, point out the main advantages and disadvantages, and, where available, I incorporate findings from evaluations of the programs. I also suggest where and how to get information on the programs.

HIGH SCHOOL VOCATIONAL EDUCATION OPTIONS

Vocational education programs are available at every level, beginning in high school. In this section, I review four vocational education programs commonly available in high schools.

Alternative High Schools

Going to college is not the only way to prepare for a career, but graduating from high school is a must. Young people must understand the relationship between credentials and careers. Heading out to find work without a high school diploma is like going fishing without bait. A young person's only hope would be to accidentally snag something — while friends and classmates are baiting hooks and flipping out lures. Young people must be taught how the social system works. When it comes to jobs, society stands at the door and takes tickets. Diplomas get you through the door.

For nearly a decade, I was director of research at the Boys' Town Center for the Study of Youth Development, Father Flanagan's Boys' Town. In that position, I came to realize how many young people have a poor understanding of the way the social system works, of the relationship between school and work and between career preparation and later career stability. It was not unusual for boys at Boys' Town to want to drop out of high school and become lawyers. They didn't understand the connection between occupational choices and career preparation decisions. They didn't understand their career preparation options, either.

The first rule in career preparation for young people is to finish high school. That's the bottom line. And the second rule is to do as well in high school as they can. That includes taking the most demanding programs and the toughest courses. It means not just getting by but mastering the basics. What is at stake is a stable career. That's more than just getting a first job — which may be a dead end as far as a career is concerned. Stable employment also means keeping a job and staying employed over the long pull.

But some young people are lost to traditional high schools already at an early stage. For whatever reason, they need an environment different from the conventional setting — which is the mission of alternative high schools. One mother, a manpower analyst for the U.S. Marine Corps whose husband is a military barber, explained that her son would like to be a farmer:

> *" I don't think our schools are adequately preparing those students that have no interest in going to a four-year college or university. I think more emphasis should be placed on 'basic living' skills to prepare our children for life as well as a career or profession. Some students do not perform well in the traditional classroom but thrive on hands-on activities."*

Alternative high schools are usually small and focus on 16- to 19-year-olds who are at risk in traditional high schools. Flexibility to accommodate individual students' needs is their defining characteristic. The flexibilies include nontraditional school hours, lower student/teacher ratios, and individualized instruction. In addition to offering minimum competency and general academic programs that reinforce basic employment skills, alternative high schools stress vocational education. Home economics programs may include parenting, child development, childcare services, and foods and nutrition. Business programs may include courses in typewriting or keyboarding, introduction to computers, computer applications, accounting, employability skills, and administrative support occupations. Alternative high schools pay attention to individual students' problems and offer strong guidance programs, including personal/social, educational, and vocational counseling. This may extend to case management programs, personal management programs, and special services including infant-care centers. In addition to offering minimum competency academic courses, alternative high schools stress vocational education.

Many young people need basic survival skills. A high school junior in our Youth and Careers Study told us her career aspirations: "That I can make it . . . to where I can support my son and so that I don't have to depend on my mom and dad forever." Another, one of nine children, told us:

> *" As I think ahead I worry about my child and how she will grow up without me. I think how good a mom I am to her. Am I going to be there when she really needs me? A lot of questions about that subject come to mind."*

And a mother, never married, who works in a chicken processing plant, expressed a similar concern about her daughter:

> **" I worry about her safety out in the world, her health because there's so many diseases going around. And most of all, I worry about her being a good parent to her daughter."**

Alternative high schools offer no pretense of preparing young people for Harvard or for winning National Merit Scholarships, but they do offer an alternative to traditional high schools, which don't work for everyone. They offer education in the basics, training in pre-employment, and a high school diploma.

For more information on alternative high schools in your area, phone your county school system.

Vocational Education Programs in Comprehensive High Schools

A high school diploma is better than no diploma, but a young person's long-term career interests also depend on the academic program she or he takes while in high school. Vocational education programs are popular in high schools. A third of all high school students enroll, as do a fourth of students in comprehensive high schools. The programs have the advantage of offering disaffected students an alternative to traditional academic courses. Vocational education (vo-ed) programs give students a chance to try out a trade or occupation before they hit the real world of work. And following the vo-ed path is convenient. Students can slip into them without changing schools, bus routes, extracurricular activities, peer groups, friendships, and the like.

But high school vocational education programs have been roundly criticized. The basic criticisms are that vo-ed programs are dated, teachers are out of touch and past their prime, equipment is old, course offerings are superficial, school administrations are not supportive, and programs are offered in areas where employment is declining (for example, agriculture, home economics, and industrial arts) rather than expanding (such as training as technicians). The result, critics argue, is that students receive obsolete job skill training, and that many employers will not recognize high school diplomas awarded for vocational education.

Apparently, the criticisms are not without foundation. The National Assessment of Vocation Education conducted by the U.S. Department of Education concluded that the typical high school vocational education program "neglects academic skill development, trains for occupations not in demand, teaches with outmoded equipment, and offers limited placement assistance." The same report concludes that, generally, fewer than half of high school students were able to use the vocational course skills they learned in the jobs they took after graduating. Examples of selected course utilization rates are shown in the following table.

In addition, unemployment rates for graduates of vocational education programs in comprehensive high schools were high, and wages were low. The summary evaluation for high school vocational education programs nationwide is that they are seriously inadequate. The 1994 National Assessment of Vocational Education final report to Congress depicts a haggard vo-ed program in need of change. Indeed, the report recommends

Vocational Education Course	Men	Women
Agriculture	44%	27%
Business	32%	65%
Health	8%	79%
Occupational Home Economics	14%	32%
Mechanics and Repairers	46%	35%
Transportation	6%	0%
Average for all courses studied	38%	53%

Source: National Assessment of Vocational Education, U.S. Department of Education

eliminating general track studies in high schools in favor of more rigorous course work for all students. The same report recommends replacing occupation-intensive courses with the basics of mathematics and science.

Unfortunately, the evaluation masks excellent vocational education programs found in some comprehensive high schools. There are, without question, sterling programs in selected high schools. One thing I learned from my own experience as a parent, however, is that parents must never assume that their child's best interests are automatically served by the school. The only way you can have that peace of mind is by getting in there and checking it out. Talk with other parents. Get to know a teacher. Talk to employers — the personnel director, a supervisor, an executive from a company in your area, people you know in business. Ask them pointed questions: "Do you know anything about the vocational education program at X high school?" "Have you worked with its graduates?" "What has been your experience?" "What can you tell me about it?"

Vocational education courses in comprehensive high schools will remain a possibility, at least for the short-term future. Nonetheless, tough academic programs take no more time than slide-by programs. Aim high.

Vocational-Technical High Schools

All students in vocational-technical (vo-tech) high schools major in some program of vocational education. In addition, all take traditional high school academic courses. Vocational-technical training is the reason vocational-technical high schools exist, and they generally exhibit a much stronger commitment to vocational education than do comprehensive high schools and alternative high schools with vocational education courses and programs.

Many vocational-technical high schools offer quality vocational education programs. People skilled in crafts teach the courses, equipment is modern and up-to-date, the schools have strong placement services and maintain close ties with local industries, and employers generally value diplomas from vocational-technical high schools. Strong vo-tech high schools integrate traditional academic instruction with in-depth technical training and graduates are well-trained. The relevance between education and work is demonstrated.

And the quality of vocational-technical high schools is generally respected. Vocational-technical high schools are the answer for mothers like this secretary for a construction company in our Youth and Careers Study: "I think high schools need to expand on their career teaching and take more of a 'hands on' class. Be more realistic."

Unfortunately, there are fewer than 500 vocational-technical high schools in the nation and most communities are without one. This has left vocational-technical high schools, whatever their merits, as minor players in preparing today's youth for the contemporary world of work. But if you have a daughter or son with vocational leanings and there is a vo-tech high school in your community, check it out. Ask the same hard questions I posed of vocational preparation programs in comprehensive high schools above.

High School Cooperative Education Programs

Cooperative education programs occur at both the high school and college level, and cooperative education may offer one of the best values in vocational education available today. At both the high school and college levels, the concept is the same: Integrate traditional academics with a part-time paying job at a local company. Current national initiatives, including work force preparedness and school-to-work transition programs — while modeled after the apprenticeship programs of Japan and Germany — have much in common with cooperative education programs that are already in place in U.S. high schools. A typical high school cooperative education program offers vocational courses at a comprehensive high school in the morning and a job for pay with a cooperating company that provides instruction and close supervision in the afternoon. Co-op programs at the high school level would seem to be exactly what a lawyer's daughter who works as a secretary in business told us: "High school education should give students more insight into the working world and some experience with working skills so that they won't waste so many years trying to figure out what type of employment might be satisfying."

A major plus for high school cooperative education programs for students is that they allow them to test their choice of college/occupational major or, if they are undecided, to explore career fields. They give them access to professionals in their chosen field, to state-of-the-art equipment, and to business, industry, and government cultures. In addition, the programs put work experience on their resumes, making them more marketable when they graduate.

Another plus is the close working relationship between vocational education teachers and employers. Teachers bring an academic structure, rigor, and a passion for youth development to the equation. Employers and companies add contexts for real-life experiences, modern equipment, and hands-on opportunities. The close ties between industry and education can be a major asset in placing students in jobs following graduation.

Unfortunately, the quality of traditional academics offered in cooperative education programs may vary widely across high schools. High schools committed to the concept can provide excellent vocational education, but high schools that view academic education as their primary goal and vocational education as a weak secondary goal may offer inadequate vocational education, even though cooperative education students need the same basic skills as do students on academic tracks. This is not a small problem. The numbers tell the tale. The lack of secondary school commitment to cooperative education is evident in that only about 3 percent of comprehensive high school students are formally enrolled in co-op programs.

There is a second disadvantage to the high school cooperative education concept. In order to take full advantage of a strong cooperative education program, a high school student must commit to the program early, which means having some idea of an occupation and trade in which she or he chooses to specialize by the sophomore year. These are 15- and 16-year-old students. One question is whether this forces students to firm up their career plans too early.

Some years ago, I worked on a study of more than 50,000 high school students with Archibald Haller of the University of Wisconsin. That research showed that it was not until young people were juniors, or about 17 years old, that their career aspirations firmed up and focused. This was a study of typical young people. But we know that people from culturally and economically deprived backgrounds, many of them prime candidates for vocational preparation programs, firm up their career goals even later in life — not earlier. They also have a poorer understanding of the relationship between school and work, of their career preparation options, and of the relationship between career preparation and career stability. My concern with high school cooperative education and vocational education programs generally at the high school level — and I have the same reservations about some of the career preparation initiatives coming out of the federal administration — is whether the programs are in sync with what we know about youth development in the U.S.

A counter argument, of course, is that German schools routinely assess students at age 10 to determine their suitability for vocational or college-prep high schools, and that Japanese students take a similar test at the end of the ninth-grade equivalent year. But the argument against severe tracking in American schools is that the U.S. policy has been to share access and to always guarantee a second chance, whereas Germany and Japan have controlled access to postsecondary programs at an early age.

I note in passing that, increasingly, our society has been pushing youngsters into adulthood — high heels by grade eight and football helmets by grade four. Some years ago, I received a telephone call from a state legislator in another state asking for an opinion. After reviewing legislation he was proposing that would require youngsters in public schools to commit to a career track at an early age, he asked whether, in my opinion, young people couldn't make a career decision by sixth grade, and whether he could quote me. I agreed that he could quote me. But my opinion was not what he wanted to quote.

COLLEGE VOCATIONAL EDUCATION OPTIONS

Colleges are the main settings for vocational education programs in the U.S. Following are the principal options.

College Cooperative Education Programs

Some of the finest vocational education programs available today are housed in college and university cooperative education programs. The concept is the same as cooperative education at the high school level: Integrate traditional academic studies with a part-time paying job in a five-year program. Colleges assure the viability of the program as a bona fide academic experience, and local companies offer hands-on and real-life work experience.

Some programs have improvised on the traditional program that involves alternating full-time academic semesters or quarters with full-time work semesters or quarters — alternating work plans. Some colleges, primarily community colleges, allow students to work part-time while carrying reduced course loads — parallel work plans. Vocational education programs typically include agriculture, natural resources, business, computer science, food service, construction, applied arts and crafts, repair and maintenance occupations, and trade and industrial occupations.

College cooperative education programs have picked up much momentum in recent years, and for good reasons. Students who do well increase their probabilities of a job after graduation. Forty percent take jobs with the same employer after graduation; another 40 percent take jobs in the same field as their cooperative education experience; 15 percent go on to additional schooling, a bachelor's degree, or even graduate school; which leaves only 5 percent without a clear career trajectory following graduation. The programs are offered in 48 states and the District of Columbia. Cooperative education programs are available at about 1,000 public and private two- and four-year colleges and universities and involve more than 250,000 participants each year. Corporate collaborators include such blue chip companies as Duke Power, American Telephone and Telegraph, and Walt Disney World.

If there are disadvantages to college cooperative education programs, they are unevenness and lack of standardization across programs — which is typical of new and diverse programs. I expect that college cooperative education programs will be beneficiaries of some of the new federal initiatives that stress apprenticeship-like experiences associated with formal education. I expect that some of the initiatives will merge rather than compete with cooperative education.

Cooperative education at both the high school and college levels appears to be an idea whose time has come. Federal initiatives stress highly skilled and highly productive workers, qualities that colleges and universities can produce; and employers and firms offer the applied settings and real-world experiences that young people also need. I think it will be a happy marriage.

For information on cooperative education programs, phone (617) 437-3778, or write for the *Cooperative Education Undergraduate Program Directory,* the National Commission for Cooperative Education, 360 Huntington Avenue, Boston, MA 02115. The *Directory* lists all colleges that offer cooperative education programs, the courses they offer, and the companies that participate in the programs.

Tech-Prep Programs

Tech-prep is a relatively new concept on the vocational education scene, still in the federal demonstration site stage in selected locations. Federal demonstration programs are a common method for exploring the potential of new concepts. Typically, a federal agency will provide incentive money for three to five years to five or six sites that have bid successfully on developing a concept. Each site then develops a model along general guidelines but in ways that suit local circumstances. One of the requirements is that the model be transportable — that is, suitable for use in comparable situations elsewhere. Over the duration of the demonstration funding period the concept is developed, implemented, and fine-tuned, and the model is evaluated. Depending on the results, together with the political and policy climate at the close of the project, the program may become the prototype for a more expansive program or the experiment may be shut down. Tech-prep is a survivor: 5,400 of the country's 11,500 public school districts have instituted tech-prep in some fashion, although only 475 have used the federal vocational education law as a model.

Tech-prep spans the last two years of high school and extends another two years at a two-year college, typically a community college. For that reason, it is sometimes referred to as "Two-plus-two" (or "2 + 2") tech-prep. The concept responds to the same theme that drives all vocational education programs: namely, it prepares students for the job market by combining traditional academics with technically oriented vocational courses. The target group for tech-prep study is high school students whose interests are in neither the professions nor four-year colleges and universities, but who would benefit from vocational education courses in comprehensive high schools that emphasize concepts, theories, and applications coupled with technically oriented courses at the community college level.

The distinguishing feature of tech-prep is that it is a coordinated course of study that spans the last two years of high school and two years of community college. It is a four-year program. It differs from cooperative education programs in that tech-prep offers an organized transition from high school to community college, whereas cooperative education, at both the high school and college levels, integrates the academic with real-world work experiences.

Tech-prep is new, still in the experimental stage, and it is not widely available. But this could change rapidly, because the primary requirement for establishing tech-prep programs is to align and refine vocational preparation curricula in comprehensive high schools with those in community colleges. These are not issues of brick and mortar but issues of curriculum reform and program policy — which is not to suggest that it is easier to change curriculums and educational policies than brick and mortar, only that it should be less expensive. Because tech-prep is based within high school and community college systems, and each looks over the shoulder of the other, one should be able to relax in the knowledge that the program receives careful oversight.

There are other pluses. Because the programs are new and have to prove themselves, program administrators are keeping careful records, and information on program outcomes is readily available. For example, I have before me two reports on the Richmond County, North Carolina, tech-prep program. One report, "Tech-Prep Results," is six pages of numbers. The other, the "Report Card," is 12 pages of charts and graphs. Both cover the years 1986 to 1993 and tell me everything I want to know — and more! — about tech-prep enrollments, dropout rates, specific course enrollments, standardized test scores, graduate follow-up information, and the like. Also, tech-prep has the advantage of keeping the college option open. Assuming a student performs well in traditional academics, she or he may go on to a four-year college and bachelor's degree and even a graduate school. A student is not locked into a two-year vocational education program.

I have other information before me that reports that more than 90 percent of graduates find work in the fields in which they were trained, and that the average starting wage is about $9 per hour. One reason for these enviable outcomes may be that tech-prep programs found early support and took root in communities where there was an established need for workers with technically oriented educational backgrounds. The same industries may pay well. But this is not to demean the quality of tech-prep programs. Tech-prep is an enterprising effort to integrate community resources — namely, comprehensive high schools, community colleges, and industry — into a coordinated career preparation program. And it has the potential for bringing the strengths of each partner to the program.

Unfortunately, tech-prep is a new kid on the block, and people are standing around watching it, wondering how it will fit in with the rest of the community, whether it is safe for the neighborhood, and whether it will ever amount to anything. Tech-prep is not available everywhere. But check it out in your community. Ask about tech-prep. If the answer is "huh?" you are ahead of your time. Then ask, "What vocational preparation programs are available in our area?" The information is only a phone call away. Call the information desk at your county school system.

Community Colleges

The Vocational Educational Act of 1963 gave impetus to community colleges nationwide. The concept embodied in the federal legislation was that two-year public academic institutions based in communities would be a transition between high schools and established four-year colleges and universities, and that they would serve the local needs of employers. The tremendous success of community college systems over the past 30 years is evident in the fact that most people who enroll in colleges today enroll in two-year colleges, not in four-year colleges. Today, the third largest campus in the country is a community college with 51,768 students — Miami-Dade Community College.

A mother in our Youth and Careers Study who works as a retail clerk in a drug store told us her hopes for her son:

> *" . . . that he will hopefully go to community college for a year or two for more education on body work, mechanics, and welding. This way he may someday open his own business and have plenty of respect for himself and earn a good income so that he doesn't have to struggle for the rest of his life."*

But not everybody wants to complete a program. A young woman in our study, whose father is a factory worker and whose mother drives a bus, wants ". . .to be able to complete some business course to help me open my own business someday."

Variability. There is much variability in community colleges across the country. That happens for two reasons. First, community colleges have been true to their charters, which emphasize local needs. They have offered both traditional academics and vocational education. They have prepared students both for four-year colleges and for local industries. The latter may mean training fire fighters in one community, health care workers in another, or hotel and restaurant managers in another. Moreover, community colleges have opened their doors widely. Most have open admissions policies. Many do not require a high school diploma for admission. They have full-time and part-time students, young and old, students pursuing certificates and degrees and persons interested only in selected courses. They are truly community resources and as diverse as the communities they serve.

The second reason for the variability across community colleges is that the concept is still in its infancy. Thirty years in American education is not very long compared with, say, the nation's first colonial college, now Harvard University, founded in 1636. The recency of the concept, together with the local character of community colleges, makes them a very diverse group. And the diversity makes them a difficult subject of study and a difficult basis for generalizations and conclusions. There are fewer studies of community colleges, the studies are of short duration, and the rigor of the studies is more open to dispute than studies of four-year colleges. We simply know much less about the effectiveness of community colleges than we know about four-years colleges and universities, which have been studied in depth for 150 years.

Community colleges have been on the forefront in developing and offering vocational education programs. What this means academically for a particular college may vary from a strong emphasis on traditional academics as preparation for admission to four-year colleges and universities to strong emphasis on hands-on, experiential learning leading to a certificate and a job. What it means by way of vocational preparation is innovative programming including tech-prep programs with comprehensive high schools and cooperative education programs with industry.

The point I emphasize here, however, is that community colleges have long been the leader in stand-alone independent vocational training programs. Most do not offer comprehensive vocational training but specialize in one or two areas — for example, allied health, business, or engineering. Most also nurture close ties with local industries and have active placement services. Their mission is job preparation and job placement. But what job training is available varies from community college to community college.

Quality. The quality of community colleges is probably as broad as their diversity. Many are exceptionally good, although occasionally there is media coverage of one that is very bad. The quality of most is, undoubtedly, between the extremes, but always a subject worth investigating. The jury of public opinion is not yet in. That is evident in the numbers. Only about 60 percent of community college students are able to use the vocational training they get, and the unemployment rates of community college graduates continue to be high. However, the high rates of unemployment for community college graduates may be due to students not taking enough courses in their vocational areas. Thus, the National Assessment of Vocational Education reports a direct relationship between the number of credits students take in their major vocational subjects and their unemployment rates.

Course Credits Taken After One Year	Unemployment Rate	Average Hourly Starting Wage
12 credits	16%	$6.58
30	11%	$7.05
50	7%	$7.39

Source: National Assessment of Vocational Education, U.S. Department of Education

The same relationship holds for starting wages.

The guiding principal, then, for parents and young people enrolled in vocational education programs in community colleges is the same as for other forms of education and training: namely, education and training pays. The more education and training you get, the more you will benefit.

For information resources on community colleges, see *The College Handbook* and Chapter 7 regarding State Occupational Information Coordinating Committees and Career Information Delivery Systems.

Private Junior Colleges

Private junior colleges are much the same as community colleges but differ in that they are privately operated. Many have religious affiliations and began as liberal arts institutions. But with the rise of the vocational education movement during the '70s, junior colleges modified their course offerings and, today, are virtually indistinguishable from community colleges. Like community colleges, they serve a broad clientele. And many offer special programs including cooperative education.

Because of their historic roots in liberal arts and residence campuses, private junior colleges tend to maintain stronger ties with traditional academics and offer broader programs and more by way of athletic programs and extracurricular activities — holdovers from the times when they were boarding schools for full-time resident students.

Some private junior colleges offer superior programs and maintain excellent academic reputations. One reason, therefore, to consider a private junior college for vocational education purposes is that the program excellence may extend to vocational courses and job placement services. But this is not necessarily the case, and parents and young people must exercise the same good judgment about private junior colleges as they would of any other form of vocational preparation. Institutions, like programs and courses, must be evaluated on their merits.

Although it is often the case that private junior colleges are better academic institutions than community colleges, there is also a possible disadvantage. Private junior colleges usually cost more than community colleges.

For information resources on private junior colleges, see *The College Handbook* and Chapter 7 regarding State Occupational Information Coordinating Committees and Career Information Delivery Systems.

Four-Year Colleges and Universities

Reverse transfers, people who return to two-year colleges and noncollegiate schools for skill training after taking a four-year degree, have become increasingly common, and the strategy has become increasingly rewarding. In our Career Development Study of the early careers of 7,000 young men and women, nearly equal percentages of students took some college, then entered a vocational preparation program; took vocational preparation first, then some college; or ended up with both a college degree and some form of vocational preparation. The point is that there are vocational preparation programs that either prepare a young person directly for an occupation or complement high school diplomas and college degrees in ways that give a person an employment advantage. For some, including this university research assistant in the Career Development Study, it may be a way to prepare for a career after the college years are over:

> *" My major problem was not having any definite plans about what I wanted to do, which isn't all that bad, but I still hadn't made up my mind by almost thirty. Had gone to college for four years and got a B.A. only because college was just the thing to do."*

Four-year colleges and universities are usually considered only as degree programs, but many colleges have followed the lead of the vocational education movement and now offer extensive vocational training programs. College cooperative education programs are one example.

There are other forms of vocational education on college and university campuses. Some are institutes. On my campus, there is an Agricultural Institute that provides two-year training and certification. As an example, it offers a turf management program that prepares young people for employment at golf courses. Other examples are swine and poultry production programs that teach people the essentials of business, nutrition, and disease control in these industries. As is the case with community college programs, these programs vary widely from campus to campus.

Other vocational education options exist on four-year college and university campuses. As with two-year college programs, one does not have to enroll in degree-granting programs on college and university campuses. Rather, one can be selective. Pick from the smorgasbord of courses and programs. Make inquiry, talk to the professors and students, and choose the courses needed to learn a trade or to upgrade skills.

Colleges and universities also offer continuing-education and life-long learning programs. These are not programs in the sense of course sequences, and they do not add up to a degree or certificate. They are stand-alone programs, but with a little imagination, programs can be packaged to suit individual interests and needs. They may be just what your daughter or son is looking for, and the courses may be taught by the same faculty members who teach the more expensive and demanding degree programs. Many of these offerings occur in conference centers associated with colleges and universities — which, incidentally, is a good place to stop and pick up information on program offerings. Another good place to start, of course, is by calling the registrar's office on campus.

The advantage of vocational education experiences on a college campus is that the learner can have the benefit of more intensive and in-depth learning. A person can choose from the wide variety of college and university course offerings — many not offered by two-year colleges — to supplement vocational training and other academic programs. Courses may be taken by audit or on a pass-fail basis. Finally, large colleges and universities typically offer the most extensive resources, including libraries and laboratories, field settings, and services including career counseling and job placement services.

One disadvantage is that costs at four-year colleges and universities may be higher than at community colleges. Another is that locations are not as convenient. And a third is that large institutions can be intimidating, hard to find your way around and through the red tape. But, depending on interests and needs, the necessary persistence may be well worth the effort.

NONCOLLEGIATE OPTIONS

There are also noncollegiate vocational education possibilities — that is, programs that normally do not offer degrees. This section explores the main possibilities.

Technical Institutes

Technical institutes are like community colleges in that they usually are two-year schools. Technical institutes are unlike community colleges in that they are more highly specialized, focus more narrowly on technical training, and seldom offer traditional academic programs. Young people considering enrollment in a technical institute must keep in mind the difference between an institute and a college. Technical institutes make no pretense of competing with colleges. They assume that students know the basics — written and oral communications, math, relevant sciences, and other program requirements. They assume, further, that if students do not have the basics, they will go elsewhere for remedial work. Technical institutes do not offer degrees. They are "noncollegiate."

Technical institutes often have a reputation for high-quality programs. The teachers may be industry professionals, up-to-date and in touch with industry. Technical institutes have close working relationships with industries, may be sponsored by industries, and usually have a vested interested in preparing workers for industries. One of the advantages of vocational education in technical institutes is that they usually have extensive job-placement services.

Technical institutes provide in-depth training and require intensive study. For that reason, most recommend full-time enrollment and discourage part-time employment. Moreover, technical institutes can be expensive, particularly compared to community colleges. Further, because technical institutes are narrowly specialized, the employment rates of their students can be subject to the vicissitudes of the national economy. When the industry thrives, employment opportunities are plentiful. If the industry is depressed, there is no assurance of employment.

The National Assessment of Vocational Education notes that, despite in-depth training, only 84 percent of graduates find work. That is only 2 percentage points higher than the same evaluation reports for students trained at community colleges. The report indicates that 60 percent of students report that they are able to use their technical training on the job. That is the same course-utilization rate as the evaluation reported for community college students.

Yet another parallel exists in the findings for technical institutes and community colleges reported by the National Assessment of Vocational Education. As is the case with community college graduates, rates of unemployment and starting wages for graduates of technical institutes are directly related to the number of credits students earn in their vocational major.

Credits Taken After One Year	Unemployment Rate	Average Hourly Starting Wage
12	19%	$5.84
30	12%	$6.61
50	6%	$7.19

Source: National Assessment of Vocational Education, U.S. Department of Education

Three additional considerations bear on technical schools as a vocational preparation option. The first is that there are not many technical institutes around — certainly far fewer than community colleges. Thus, enrolling probably means also making arrangements for room and board. Second, technical institutes are almost always more expensive than community colleges, sometimes much more expensive. Third, they require more intensive study.

For more information on technical institutes, see the index of specialized colleges in *The College Handbook* or comparable references, and see Chapter 7 regarding State Occupational Information Coordinating Committees and Career Information Delivery Systems.

Proprietary Trade Schools

Proprietary trade schools are the only places a person can learn some skills. There simply is no other place to learn to be a barber or a bartender. Like technical institutes, proprietary trade schools are noncollegiate. They do not offer degrees. Trade schools offer no courses in traditional academics and all training is narrowly focused on one field. For example, a trade school might be a barber school, a flight school, or a school of cosmetology — nothing more.

Trade schools have little regulation and, therefore, there may be little comparability from one trade school to the next. Teachers' levels of training and experience may vary considerably. Some may be teaching as a hobby or pastime after successful careers. Others may be just out of trade school themselves. Teachers in trade schools are paid considerably less than teachers in community colleges and technical institutes, which might reflect on their skills.

According to the National Assessment of Vocational Education, unemployment rates for graduates of proprietary trade schools are extremely high, more than 50 percent higher than for graduates of community colleges and technical institutes. This is a serious criticism. If the purpose of vocational education is to prepare for and find a job, what is its value if it doesn't accomplish that result?

Course utilization rates for graduates of proprietary trade schools are also low, about 15 percent lower than rates for community colleges and technical institutes. However, the average starting wage for trade school graduates is better than starting wages for graduates of community colleges and technical institutes — 15 to 25 percent higher.

Institution	Unemployment Rate	Course Utilization Rate	Average Hourly Starting Wage
Community College	19%	61%	$6.63
Technical Institute	17%	60%	$5.92
Proprietary Trade School	28%	51%	$7.40

Source: National Assessment of Vocational Education, U.S. Department of Education

Although the average starting hourly wage for graduates of proprietary trade schools is higher than that for graduates of community colleges and technical institutes, hourly wages for proprietary trade school graduates do not increase over work careers as readily as do wages for graduates of community colleges and technical institutes. That is because most trades are single-level occupations. There is no career ladder or advances in rank in bartending, barbering, hairstyling, or truck driving to which wage increases are attached. Unless graduates of the proprietary trade schools establish their own businesses — taverns, barbershops, and the like — their wages will remain relatively constant across their careers except as they themselves adjust their wages for inflation.

The biggest disadvantage to seeking vocational education through proprietary trade schools, however, is the possibility of running into a scam. Proprietary trade schools operate under a cloud of suspicion and questionable conduct. They are subject to few regulations and, unlike the professions, they do not police themselves through professional associations and ethics committees. It is not unusual to see media coverage of a proprietary trade school that has closed shop and left town with enrollment deposits, or that doesn't deliver programs or financial aid or job placements as advertised, or that is under investigation for abuses. A recent U.S. government study of proprietary trade schools concluded as follows:

> *" Our study found patterns of misrepresentation to prospective students, lack of attention to . . . standards, low [student] completion rates, and faulty use of federal financial aid programs. Three-quarters of the students admitted without a high school degree and half the students with a high school degree dropped out . . . certificates for many proprietary schools have little reliability."*

Since the middle and late 1980s and early 1990s, several trade schools have been investigated by the Department of Education's Office of Inspector General for defaults on refunds to the Department when students on financial aid drop out, for inflated default costs, and for over-subsidies to loan holders. The scams leave student borrowers who drop out liable for the trade school's failure to pay refunds to the Department of Education. Recently, several trade schools have been shut down in related court actions.

Unfortunately, good proprietary trade schools are tarred with the brush of public suspicion and malpractice. That means that prospective students must be wary and careful about programs offered by proprietary trade schools.

There are, however, good reasons to enroll. One is that the trade a young person wants to learn is taught only in proprietary trade schools. A second is that there may be a good and reputable proprietary trade school in one's community. If both are true, enrollees may proceed cautiously but, at a minimum, they need to protect themselves in three ways:

- Be certain that the school is accredited by the National Association of Trade and Technical Schools. That accreditation should be listed in the school's descriptive literature. If it isn't, beware.
- Inquire about the proprietary trade school from your state Department of Education and your local Chamber of Commerce.
- Ask questions. Speak with high school principals and people in business. Find out who owns the trade school, how long they have been in business, and about the reputations of the school and the owner.

A diesel tractor-trailer owner-driver spoke glowingly of his occupation and career, which all started in trade school:

" I own my own rig. Paid 87 thousand for the tractor and 22 for the trailer. That was back in '88. We been together ever since. Got 600,000 miles on 'er. Never touched the engine. Live in my truck. Try to keep 'er lookin' good. When it gets hot I go north and when it gets cold I go south. I go where I wanna go. Nobody tells me. This ole girl 'll go 139 miles per hour if you open 'er up. Did it one time on a stretch in Kansas. Got a Cummins 450 under the hood. I pay my bills and at the end of the year I got $60,000 in the bank. I ain't complaining."

Employer Training and Education Programs

Participation in work-related education and training has been increasing steadily. There are several contributing factors, including technological innovations that require new knowledge and skill, workers seeking employment security by upgrading their skills, industry efforts to be more competitive and profitable, and federal emphases on work force preparedness and highly skilled, highly productive workers. Industry training and education programs also appeal to people who are skeptical of the value of a college education and to people who can't afford it. Finally, the population is increasingly hearing the message that most employment openings require high school plus additional training, but not necessarily a college degree. "Train them for the real world," a welder told us, "not some fantasy where everybody goes to college and lives happily ever after."

Two different types of employer-sponsored vocational education programs exist. One is on-the-job training (OJT). The other is employer-sponsored educational programs. On-the-job training programs are designed to improve workers' skills to perform a specific job. OJT is almost always conducted in-house by company employees and on company time. The beneficiaries of OJT are two groups: new workers and current workers in need of retooling. Educational programs, by comparison, are as likely to occur after work hours and in off-work sites. Educational programs are more likely to incorporate external resources including local college or technical school instructors and facilities. Sometimes employer education programs are very much "hands off," as is the case with company tuition-aid plans that provide employees with partial or complete reimbursement for college courses taken during or after working hours.

Studies and published information on the extent and effectiveness of employer training and education programs are sparse. In part that is because there is much variation in employer-sponsored programs due to the differing requirements of occupations and the differing characteristics of companies in which workers are employed. In other cases, companies regard such information as proprietary — that is, private and nonpublic.

On-the-Job Training. Firms normally give new workers an initial orientation to the work and performance standards of the jobs for which they were hired. In many cases, the orientation is informal and unstructured, simply showing new employees what to do and then turning them loose except for ongoing supervision.

On-the-job training programs are more structured and last longer than orientation sessions. Acceptance into on-the-job training programs may require a high school diploma or, in the case of advanced programs, may require completion of related training in a two-year college or technical school. Or the firm may require a certain level of experience or competency. OJT programs typically enroll only company trainees, which means it is necessary to work for the company to qualify. Length of training may vary from a few days to several weeks; and most training is "hands-on," with company instructors or experienced workers providing the instruction, though some programs may require additional classroom instruction. Some companies train workers for a specific job with little possibility for advancement. Others provide training programs and encouragement for workers to advance according to their interests and abilities.

On-the-job training programs are offered most often in the fields of health occupations and secretarial work, insurance, telephone communications, computer programming, and banking. They serve an important function in industry, as an artist for an advertising agency observed: "There is too much pressure and importance put on college. The trade schools and actual on-the-job working with people is equally if not more important."

Education Programs. A Rand Corporation Study indicates the heavy reliance many workers have on their employers for education and training, as shown in the following table.

Like other career preparation options, employer training and education programs offer young people both advantages and disadvantages. The primary advantage is that

Job Category	Men %	Women %
Professional and technical workers	62	64
Sales supervisors representatives and clerks	41	29
Trade and crafts workers	39	31
Office and clerical workers	38	34
Machine operators and assemblers	27	20
Transportation workers	17	45

Source: Rand Corporation Study

employer programs provide job experience and earnings while a young person learns a specific skill. The programs are truly "applied." They relate directly to the job. And they are widely available. Also, some companies have internal career ladders for people who take advantage of the programs to improve their skills and abilities.

There are also disadvantages, and these, too, should be noted. The main disadvantage is that training specific to one company may not be accepted as qualification for a similar job in another company. On-the-job training does not offer the same portability as a college degree, certificate, or apprenticeship credential. What is good for one's job, therefore, is not necessarily good for one's career.

Like other more involved forms of career preparation, employer training and education programs offer young people a way to invest in themselves, to earn while they learn. At the same time, investing in employer training and education may be like investing the minimum during a period of exceptionally good investment opportunities — namely, during one's early career. Investing something is better than nothing, but the career preparation years occur once in a lifetime, and that's the time to make major commitments to acquiring knowledge and skills.

The primary sources of information about employer training and education programs are the companies that offer the programs. There are three ways to identify those companies:

- The local office of the state Job Service Office can provide names of companies with programs in particular areas. It is best to go to the Job Service Office and talk face-to-face with a counselor to get the necessary information.
- School personnel — high school counselors, counselors in local two-year colleges or technical schools, high school or college instructors who teach classes in areas of interest — also are in a good position to suggest local companies that offer employer training and education programs.
- Large companies in the region are the most likely to have training and education programs. (Companies with fewer than 50 employees are not likely to offer programs.) Company personnel can provide that information.

All of the above are anxious to provide such information. It's in their best interest as well as yours.

There is no way to know in advance whether a particular training or education program will offer a career advantage, but there is a principle young people should follow: They should invest in themselves, take advantage of every opportunity to learn while they earn. But also, young people should realize that there are many ways to find meaning and satisfaction in work. A civil engineer in Hawaii shared his experience:

> *" I was encouraged to believe a college education was essential to be a 'successful' person. I don't believe this is true for everyone. Being a success just to be looked up to is bunk. If one is satisfied and happy, I think he is a success to himself and that's really all that matters."*

Apprenticeships, Federal Civil Service, and Military Service

Three additional career preparation options must be included in the 15 earning-while-learning strategies: apprenticeships, federal civil service, and military service. These programs have several things in common. Each is highly organized and highly structured. Each is a nationwide program. And each tends to be available a little later in early career — certainly not during the high school years. Each program may offer extraordinary career preparation and employment possibilities, yet the prospects in each are not widely understood and information can be difficult to find. Nonetheless, each offers the incentive of clearly defined education and occupational training benefits, and these options, too, should be considered.

APPRENTICESHIP PROGRAMS

For thousands of years, skilled artisans taught their crafts to young workers in a master-apprentice system. The apprentice lived with the master craftsman and received food, clothing, and shelter in return for working at and learning the craft. When the apprenticeship period was over, the apprentice was recognized as a journey worker. Apprentices submitted a masterpiece for inspection and approval by the master craftsman as a final test of competency.

Apprenticeships have existed in the United States since the 17th Century, but structured programs began with the National Apprenticeship Act of 1937. Today's apprentices are regular members of the labor force, earn wages, work a normal work week, and live in their own homes. They are certified as journey workers upon completion of the apprenticeship contract.

Apprenticeship Programs

Apprenticeships are formal training programs, usually for manual occupations, that require workers to have a broad understanding of their work and knowledge of how their work relates to other tasks and workers on large projects. For example, workers who build the internal walls in high-rise office complexes must have a general understanding of the requirements for heating/air conditioning ducts that other trades people will install later. Apprenticeships combine supervised on-the-job training with related technical studies.

An apprentice is an inexperienced worker who signs a contract to participate in a trade-training program. Journey workers, the next highest level of certification, teach the entire range of skills within an occupation. Programs require about 2,000 hours of carefully supervised, on-the-job training plus related classroom instruction. The apprentice must perfect skills at established levels of performance, speed, and accuracy to master the occupation. It's a challenging training program, as a cabinetmaker in a furniture manufacturing company pointed out: "A 4-year apprenticeship is just as difficult, stimulating, and rewarding as a 4-year college degree, I would say, having experienced both."

About 95 percent of apprentices work in about 50 occupations in three industrial sectors: construction, manufacturing, and service. Nearly two-thirds are in the building trades, and carpenters, electricians, and the pipe trades account for a third of apprentices. Manufacturing claims the second largest number of apprentices, about a fourth of the total, in such occupations as machinists, tool and die makers, and welders. The remaining apprenticeships are in service occupations, including meat cutters, auto body repair mechanics, and dental laboratory technicians. Some people like to work with their hands and, for that reason, they find apprenticeships appealing. A clerical worker for an electrical equipment manufacturer told us: "I have an excellent job, but I'd like to get out of the 'professional' field and do a trade to work with my hands."

Qualifications

Apprenticeship sponsors look for people who have the mechanical and mental abilities to master the techniques and technology of the trade. Requirements emphasize four qualifications: age, education, physical condition, and aptitude.

Most programs set minimum age for entry at 18. The minimum level of education varies by program, but most require a high school diploma. Regardless of formal requirements, apprentices need a solid background in traditional academics. Some programs have special math requirements. Most programs require a physical examination, and many require that applicants demonstrate certain aptitudes. Some test applicants' familiarity with the tools and terms of the trade. Service occupations may require that applicants have interpersonal skills. Applicants are in competition with each other, and it is to their advantage to demonstrate a willingness to learn the trade and give evidence of interest and motivation.

In practice, the average age of an entering apprentice is 23. Most have 12 years of schooling, and many have additional formal education. More than a third are veterans. Most had other jobs before entering their apprenticeship, and about a third of entering apprentices have a relative in the same trade. Traditionally, an applicant with a close relative in the trade had an advantage in competing for an apprenticeship. "Not anymore," say the sponsors. By law, the selection process must treat all applicants equally. Nonetheless, people who have close contact with craft workers are likely to be more familiar with that trade, and that is an advantage.

I stated in Part I that I cannot tell my son very much about shrimp boats, and I really don't know very much about lobster fishing off the Maine coast; but I can show him what's in my briefcase and in my office. Families in the trades pass along important career information in the same way.

Employment

Apprenticeship programs involve written contracts. The employer agrees to provide instruction and practice that lead to the acquisition of specific skills, to make every effort to keep the apprentice employed, and to comply with program standards. The apprentice agrees to follow the guidelines and to work for the employer at a fixed rate of pay. Apprentices' pay starts at about 50 percent of the journey workers' wage and, by the end of the program, is about 95 percent of the journey worker's rate.

Traditionally, apprenticeships last up to six years, though the duration depends on how long it takes the apprentice to complete the hours of work and class time. If the apprentice is laid off, it takes longer to complete the program. Apprentices must attend classes whether or not they are working. When the apprentice has successfully met all program requirements — including work experience, performance standards, and required classroom instruction — the apprentice is awarded a journeyman card. The journeyman card is a form of certification that entitles the worker to higher pay, increased job security, and often supervisory responsibilities at work sites. The highest level of skill is master craftsman status.

Apprenticeships include a probationary period during which sponsors may ask apprentices to leave the program without cause. Lack of interest, bad attitude, poor attendance, tardiness, poor work habits or course grades, lack of interpersonal skills, and bad reports from supervisors are often the reason apprentices are asked to leave. Probationary periods may be hard times for apprentices. Not only are they trying to prove their performance levels on the job, but hazing often is part of the expected initiation ritual. There is a fraternal character about apprenticeships, and the initiated expect the new apprentice to accept it. Assignment of menial tasks, tricks, name calling, and ridicule are often part of the process. In his book, *Ten Thousand Working Days*, Robert Schrank reports such a distasteful hazing experience and the intensity of his own emotions:

> *"Covered from head to foot with pieces of toilet paper . . . , I finally found a way out of that flooded room, and there were the guys holding their noses and rolling with laughter. I was filled with rage, tears, and fury."*

Of course, work-related problems don't necessarily end after the probationary period. An apprentice carpenter described "what the world is really like" this way:

> *" When you get the job you have to put up with power hungry bosses and back-stabbing, brown-nosing co-workers. It doesn't always happen but it's best to be prepared. Tell them that sometimes you have to close your eyes, grit your teeth, and plunge right in!"*

Apprenticeships may be the ultimate real-world work experiences.

Advantages and Disadvantages

Apprenticeships offer a number of advantages. There are nearly a thousand apprenticeship programs in the U.S. They are a planned, organized, and efficient way to acquire skills, a combination of on-the-job and classroom training. Apprenticeships start workers in entry-level positions on a career ladder. Compensation is usually above minimum wage. Unions monitor labor force supply and demand within the trades, which assures workers of employment stability and a good standard of living. The journeyman card is transportable and enables the card carrier to relocate with established qualifications. Apprenticeships are what some some young adults, including this flight attendant in the Career Development Study, complained they missed in high school: "I certainly wasn't taught survival skills, such as an apprenticeship for a trade, or anything preparing me, specifically, for any occupation."

Apprenticeships also have disadvantages. In recent years, acceptance into apprenticeship programs has been slow. That is because most programs are oriented toward the trades where the economy is slow. Beginning apprentices may feel that their work is menial, boring, technically difficult, or physically demanding. Advanced apprentices may feel they are underpaid. In addition to a full work schedule, the apprenticeship requires three hours or more of class work per week. Apprenticeships teach all aspects of a trade, which makes workers more adaptable; nonetheless, skilled workers are not totally shielded from technological advances, and there are shifts in employment demands. For example, artificial brick and bricklaying machines have increasingly reduced the demand for bricklayers, and drywall has reduced the need for plasterers. At the same time, new types of apprenticeship trades continually emerge, and displaced journey workers may retrain in areas that take advantage of their technical knowledge and skills.

Little systematic study has been done of the effects of apprenticeships on workers, but the studies that do exist suggest that apprenticeship training gives craftsmen considerable advantage over those trained by informal means. Apprentices are better educated, learn their trades faster, work more steadily, and are more likely to be supervisors than nonapprenticed craft workers. The studies report that apprenticeship systems produce better skilled, more productive, and safer craft workers. Apprentices and journey workers are better paid. They experience fewer and briefer periods of unemployment. Employers often specifically request workers with apprentice training.

Information

When seeking information about apprenticeships, the best place to begin is with the *Occupational Outlook Handbook*. The *OOH* gives general information about apprenticeship possibilities, if applicable, in the section for each occupation titled "Training, Other Qualifications, and Advancement." Your local office of the Bureau of Apprenticeship and Training or the Apprenticeship Information Center is a good source of information for programs in your community. The Bureau is listed in the telephone directory under United States Government — Department of Labor.

If your daughter or son has a particular occupation in mind, contact the local union office or a large company that employs workers in that occupation. These sources can help you contact the apprenticeship committee that has specific information on qualifications and application procedures.

Federal Civil Service

Government service offers career preparation opportunities that young people may overlook. Consider the following:

- The federal government is charged by public law and executive order to provide training for government employees to enhance their careers.
- The government offers training programs for new employees designed to bring them to their full productive and earning capacity as rapidly as possible.
- All of the large federal departments and agencies operate their own continuing training and development programs.
- The government has executive training programs designed to recruit college students and develop them as top executives.
- The government sponsors national student employment and work training programs for high school students.

The training opportunities, coupled with the fact that the federal government is the nation's single largest employer, make government service a unique opportunity from a career preparation point of view. Government service is one of the nation's largest industries — employing one of every seven workers in the labor force.

The federal government employs about 5 million people, total, of whom 3 million plus are associated with governance. One of four federal employees works in an administrative or clerical position. Every year more than 300,000 new workers fill new positions or replace employees who retire, die, or leave government service. One-fifth of the newly hired are young, recent college graduates hired for entry-level positions. Thousands of other young people, mostly under age 30, move into government after experience in private business and industry.

Opportunities in Government Branches

The federal government is organized in three major branches. The legislative branch includes Congress, the Library of Congress, the Government Printing Office, and the Congressional Budget Office. The judicial branch includes the Supreme Court and the Federal Judicial Center. Only 38,000 work for the legislative branch, and 25,000 for the judicial branch. There is keen competition for positions in these branches, and employment opportunities are limited.

The executive branch is the largest of the three branches, and it employs nearly 3,000,000 people. The executive branch includes the president, executive office of the president, office of the vice president, 14 cabinet departments, 45 agencies, and more than 100 committees, commissions, and international organizations. Two-thirds of all federal employees work for the 14 cabinet departments, and another third work for the 6 largest agencies.

The Department of Defense is by far the largest federal employer, employing more than a million civilians, a third of all federal workers. Other major employers are the U.S. Postal Service, the Veterans' Administration, the Department of Health and Human Services, and the Departments of the Treasury and Agriculture.

Fourteen percent of federal government jobs are located in the greater Washington, D.C., area, with the rest scattered throughout the U.S. and its territories. Five percent are situated outside U.S. boundaries.

Categories of Federal Jobs

There are five categories of federal jobs:

- Administrative Careers
- Public Safety Occupations
- Specialized Occupations
- Technical Occupations
- Clerical and Administrative Support Positions

Administrative Careers. Administrative Careers is a large, catch-all group of entry-level administrative and professional occupations. Most require a college degree or equivalent work experience, although many do not have specific background course requirements.

Administrative Careers are filled by written application, including a written examination or acceptance of scholastic achievement as indicated by grade point average. Candidates may apply for Administrative Career jobs within nine months of graduation from college, upon successful completion of the qualifying academic courses required of specific areas, or with three years of work experience in the area. Positions in this category usually start at GS-5 (about $17,000 per year) or 7 (about $21,000 per year), depending on the applicant's credentials.

Applicants can choose to take one or more tests in six occupational groups. One example is health, safety, and environmental occupations. Another is law enforcement and investigation. Each exam consists of a written test and a multiple-choice Individual Achievement Record (IAR). The written test assesses the candidate's reasoning and job-relevant abilities. The IAR questionnaire solicits biographical information. Examinations are conducted as employment opportunities occur in the six occupational groups.

Administrative Careers also take applications as vacancies occur for 16 non-test positions. Although these positions do not require completion of a written test, they do require completion of specific college courses, such as archeology, economics, history, or sociology. Hiring for these positions is limited to the number and timing of vacancies that occur. When vacancies occur, a federal agency may hire candidates directly based on the candidate's education and work experience or by GPA/scholastic standing.

Specialized Occupations. The Specialized Occupations require completion of specified college-level courses. A degree in the field normally qualifies candidates and no written test is required. These positions start at the GS-5 and 7 levels. Examples of occupations include accountant/auditors, biologists, engineers, foresters, mathematical scientists, and physical scientists.

Public Safety Occupations. Public Safety Occupations are technical and have more general educational requirements than do the Specialized Occupations. A bachelor's degree or equivalent experience is required, but the degree need not be in a particular field. However, a written test must be taken for each specialty area. The Public Safety positions are GS-5 and 7. Examples include air traffic controller, Deputy U.S. Marshall, Treasury Enforcement Agents, and U.S. Park Police Officers.

Technical Occupations. These positions are often called *paraprofessional*. They are support and technical assistance positions for professionals in particular areas. Technical Occupations require practical knowledge of specialized subjects based on a two-year degree, two years of technical experience, or a combination of two years experience plus education beyond high school. A written test may be required. Technical occupations usually open at the GS-4 level.

Clerical and Administrative Support Positions. Clerical and Administrative Support Positions is the largest group of government employees. The positions start at the GS-2 level, which usually requires a high school diploma. Positions are generally available, and for many it is a way into the federal system. Many people in top government jobs began their careers in Clerical and Administrative Support Positions.

Application Procedures

The notion that a person "works for the federal government" is somewhat misleading because government is so large and so diverse that it cannot be considered a single entity. Rather, government is a many-layered and sprawling bureaucracy with organizational units of all kinds, complexities, and sizes. With the diversity of agencies and departments, it would be impractical if not impossible to fill government position openings out of a single employment office. Rather than one way, there are three ways to apply for a federal job:

> ■ Apply directly to a federal department or agency
> ■ Apply with the Office of Personnel Management (OPM)
> ■ Apply through a special employment program

How an applicant proceeds depends on what she or he has to offer and her or his interests.

Information on Federal Jobs

The Office of Personnel Management acknowledges the problem of getting information about and applying for federal job opportunities, and it has put in place a program called "Career America" to encourage people to consider federal careers and to make the hiring process more understandable and user friendly.

Federal Career Directory. As part of Career America, OPM has published a *Federal Career Directory*. The *Directory* is an excellent resource for locating department and agency occupational information. It is an inexpensive paperback. My copy, a reprint, is 261 pages long, costs $14.95, and is published under the title *America's Federal Jobs* by JIST Works, Inc., Indianapolis. Check for a copy with your bookstore, library, or career center.

The *Directory* is easy to use. The book begins with material on "The Federal Government — The Nation's Largest Employer" and "Civil Service, At Your Service." Then follows a 200-page section titled "Introducing the Federal Agencies and Departments," which gives a profile of each department's or agency's mission, function, and entry-level types of openings. The book ends with a series of short articles that give additional insight into working for the federal government. Examples include: "Employee Benefits," "Training and Development Opportunities," "Federal Pay Systems," and the "Personnel Classification System."

One article, "Index of College Majors/Areas of Study," is a reverse index of college majors and areas of study, identifying agencies that hire college graduates with degrees in these areas. For example, a college graduate with a degree in archeology will find that the Bureau of Land Management (Department of the Interior), the Forest Service (Department of Agriculture), the National Endowment for the Humanities, and the National Park Service (Department of the Interior) hire candidates with degrees in archeology. A potential applicant then can turn to information on the agency's mission and function, the address and telephone number of the personnel office of each agency, and such other relevant information as availability of student work-study programs.

"National Student Employment and Work Training Programs" outlines several federal employment programs for high school students. The federal government is, for example, the largest employer of co-op students in the country. "How to Apply for Federal Employment" is a summary statement on job application procedures.

No single volume can answer all questions about employment in the federal government, but the *Directory* gives excellent coverage, both in breadth and depth.

Vacancy Information. A second kind of useful information is helpful for prospective applicants: namely, finding out where vacancies exist. Again, there is no central listing of government openings, and it is up to the individual to locate the information. Here are some ways to do that:

- Contact the federal departments and agencies directly. Many have job information hotlines and toll-free numbers available 24 hours a day. Check Section IV of the *Directory*, "Introducing Federal Agencies and Departments," pages 11ff, for how to make contact.
- Contact an Office of Personnel Management's Area Office or a Federal Job Information Center. Phone numbers are listed on page 252ff of the *Directory*.
- Visit one of the more than 2,000 State Employment Service Offices of the Department of Labor. Ask for federal job vacancies listed on the computerized Federal Job Opportunity Listing.
- Check with local libraries and high school and college career centers, which may also have copies of the Federal Job Opportunity Listing.
- Check local libraries for federal job vacancy listings in nongovernment newsletters.

Also, people interested in federal careers may call the Career America Hotline at 1-900-990-9200 (912/471-3755 in Alaska) for career and application information for college students and recent graduates. Hotline users hear a list of topics that lead to recordings of information about current entry-level opportunities for specific job categories together with general information on pay and benefits and how to apply. Callers also have the option of leaving voice-mail messages to request more information including application forms. The Career America Hotline is available 24 hours a day, and requested materials are processed within 24 hours. Callers are billed for the service by their telephone companies at a rate of about $.40 per minute of calling time.

Office of Personnel Management. The Office of Personnel Management (OPM) functions in two different capacities. For occupations that are common to many departments and agencies — for example, computer-related occupations and accounting — OPM functions as a search firm. It accepts applications, evaluates them, rates them, and refers qualified candidates to agencies. But in the case of agencies that have positions somewhat unique to the agency — for example, air traffic controllers in the Federal Aviation Administration — the agency may be authorized to recruit on its own. The same is true in the case of agencies facing critical shortages. The point is that the only way to know whether application should be made directly with the agency or through OPM is to find out from the agency or OPM.

Vacancies in the federal civil service are filled by open competition, promotion from within, reassignment, transfer, or reinstatement of a former employee. About 80 percent of all federal civilian jobs are competitive — that is, job opportunities are announced publicly and applicants are evaluated, ranked, and employed on the basis of merit. Applications are accepted based on the number of openings agencies estimate they will have in various locations over a period of time.

Evaluation Procedures

Office of Personnel Management examiners evaluate applications to identify people who qualify for particular positions. Applicants' qualification ratings are based on a written test score or work experience, education, and training. The criterion for rating depends on the position. If qualified, the name of the applicant is entered on a list with the names of other qualified candidates.

When a vacancy in a government agency appears, the agency requests the names of qualified candidates, and OPM refers the top qualified candidates to the hiring agency. Applicants who are not selected continue on the referral list until they are either hired, their eligibility expires, or the list is terminated.

Most federal jobs do not require that candidates take a written test, although some — for example, general and social administration positions — do. The Professional and Administrative Career Examination (PACE) is the written test used most widely for federal civil service. PACE covers applicants' verbal and quantitative abilities and is the principal screening mechanism for filling entry-level positions for college graduates. Persons planning to take PACE may wish to consult some of the commercially available review workbooks that are available in bookstores and in some career centers.

A high score on the examination opens a long list of entry-level positions to young people, regardless of their undergraduate major. Students may qualify for federal jobs that require specific college course work even though they do not have a degree in that field. For example, a student does not need a degree in economics to work as an economist. Anyone who meets the minimal requirements may qualify.

People who do not hold a college degree may qualify for some professional jobs on the basis of work experience, though it is difficult to obtain a position on this basis. Qualification for entry-level positions typically require:

- Six months of work experience
- A high school diploma
- Up to two years of college, vocational training, or specialized work experience
- Combinations of education and experience

Qualifications for manual jobs are based on skill levels rather than on education or experience. Skill level is assessed in a variety of ways including written or performance tests, school records, and work histories.

Civil Service Advantages

Federal civil service offers extraordinary career development opportunities. Workers can advance in the civil service based on initiative, ability, and willingness to accept responsibility. Like employment, advancement is competitive and based on performance and merit. Opportunities include advancement within agencies, transfer to other agencies, and advancement across organization lines. Career development is a way of life for federal workers, and there are ample opportunities for training. Almost without exception federal agencies provide lifetime employment and associated privileges that young people can rarely match in the private sector.

In 1962, Congress passed the Federal Salary Reform Act that provided substantial pay increases and established the policy that annual compensation for government employees should be comparable to that of private employees for work at the same level of difficulty and responsibility. Pay increases have been regular and predictable over the last 30 years. Raises occur in October, and they are based on the Department of Labor's cost of living index.

The federal government's benefits package is an excellent feature of federal employment. It provides a measure of income protection for disability, death, and retirement. Other benefits are sick leave, vacation, health insurance, cost of living allowance for certain geographical areas, mobility, paid holidays, severance pay, group life insurance, and unemployment compensation. The federal government provides flexible work schedules including, in some cases, flexible workplace employment — that is, work at home.

Government employment also offers unparalleled job security. The federal government is as permanent an organization as exists anywhere. That is not to deny RIF (reduction in force) notices that have occurred in recent years. Nonetheless, the federal government is not going out of business, is not about to merge with another corporation, and is not about to be taken over by a corporate raider.

Civil Service Disadvantages

Federal employment also has its drawbacks, and these, too, should be considered. Though federal salaries are competitive, the government cannot match private-sector salaries for occupations in high demand, such as high-level executives. The federal government is not the place to "strike it rich," and federal employment is not the place for the young person who wants to be self-employed or to own a business.

Federal employment may not be the place to be if a person has strong political or partisan ideals. Federal employees are forbidden to strike and must sign an oath stating that they will not strike, as evidenced in the aftermath of the 1981 air traffic controllers' strike. According to the Hatch Act of 1939, most federal employees cannot take an active part in partisan political campaigns. Some federal jobs also involve health hazards. Radioactive exposure, terrorism, and assassination are examples. Civilian employees may lose their lives, as occurred in Vietnam, Iran, Lebanon, Kuwait, and Oklahoma City. FBI and CIA agents face possible injury and death in carrying out special assignments.

The federal government is an extremely large and complex organization. Regulations and red tape are ways of doing business, and delays in work schedules and personal frustrations are commonplace. The snail's pace may be particularly annoying to activists and the young. Another annoyance may be the rationale for government action — or inaction. Some time ago, I made a comment to a friend in a federal agency, something about Washington acting politically rather than logically. "In Washington politics *is* the logic," he reminded me. Idealists may be disillusioned.

Government employment will probably grow more slowly than the average rate of growth for all industries through the year 2005. Public concern about rising taxes is restraining government spending and slowing growth in employment. Federal agencies are reducing staffs as government is "reinvented," some regulating functions are abolished, and other administrative responsibilities are transferred to state and local governments. The Gramm-Rudman Bill is forcing other limits and reductions.

Nonetheless, there will be new jobs and there will be openings to replace federal employees who leave government service, retire, or die. Opportunities will occur in occupations in which employment is relatively stable as well as in those in which employment is rising. There will always be room for competent young people, though competition will continue to be intense. A major reason for the competition is the extraordinary career preparation opportunities offered by federal civil service employment.

EDUCATION AND OCCUPATIONAL TRAINING IN MILITARY SERVICE

About 200,000 young men and women will join the military services this year. But whether military service is a bummer or the chance of a lifetime is a controversial issue. A Navy veteran who now works as a telephone lineman in the state of Washington told us, "In my opinion the military (I was in the Navy for six years) did twice as much in preparing me for the future as high school did." But an Air Force veteran, now an air traffic controller in Oregon, had a much different opinion. He said, "The demands of military service, especially family separations, precipitated divorce and disrupted my life for about eight years after high school."

You will find good reasons to consider the implications of military service for young peoples' careers:

> ■ Large numbers of young men continue to serve in the armed forces; and opportunities for military service are increasingly open for women.
>
> ■ The possibility of military service occurs at the same time that young people make other career decisions.
>
> ■ The All Volunteer Force competes with industry, college, business, trade, and technical schools for recruits. Reserve Officers Training Corps (ROTC) and the Marine Corps Platoon Leaders Class (PLC) programs are closely integrated with college education and training programs.

> ■ The All Volunteer Force presents itself as a way to pay for education and training before, during, and after military service is completed.
>
> ■ The All Volunteer Force also presents itself to young people as an opportunity for occupational training.

Given the differences in opinion about military service and the nature of the commitment — a signature on the dotted line may mean an eight-year hitch and the risk of combat — it is wise to set aside the "M.A.S.H." and "Hogan's Heroes" view of the military and consider a more factually based orientation to the opportunities and obligations offered by the modern military.

Unfortunately, neither of the two most popular sources of information, military recruiters and protest/anti-war/CO groups, has established itself as an even-handed evaluator. I try to balance the pros and cons in the pages that follow. As a parent of three, I resent anyone trying to sell my sons a bill of goods, whether that be a political or religious ideology, a bad used car, street-corner drugs, or anything they have not thought through or, upon reflection, would not choose to do. At the same time, I want my children to sort out their options and take advantage of whatever opportunities there are that appeal to them. My guess is that most parents feel the same.

I emphasize two themes in this section, the same themes that apply to all career decisions. First, just as choosing additional schooling is a choice for a different lifestyle than is choosing full-time work after high school, so military service involves choosing a much different lifestyle. The single most important characteristic of military service is that once you sign on the dotted line, you have signed away a substantial amount of control over your life. Second, as with any other career decision, information is available, and you need to check it out. In the sections that follow, I try to describe what military service offers young people by way of recruitment incentives, and I raise a number of questions that young people who are considering military service should ask, talk through with their parents, and answer.

Parents should not assume that young people know all there is to know about military possibilities. Young people have the same Hollywood version of the military as they have of other occupational careers. A former postal clerk in the Navy told us that his major problem with military service was deciding "what branch to go into and what field of training might help in getting a job once you get out." I offer the following considerations for parents and young people who want to examine the career implications of military service in more detail.

The Modern Military

Since 1973, the military has been an all volunteer force, and the modern military has had to adjust to the numbers, quality, and composition of personnel that it is able to attract. It was a lot simpler for the military when Uncle Sam did the choosing.

A second major change occurred in 1976, when women were admitted to the service academies. Since then, their numbers have increased in the officer corps and among enlisted personnel. Women are now eligible to enter most military specialties, all but those that involve combat duty. The combat exclusion policy is under review.

Women in the Military

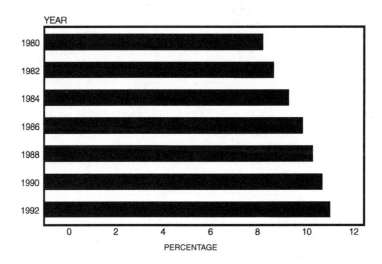

Figure 12-1 *Source: Military Careers, U.S. Department of Defense, 1992*

A third major change is that the modern military relies on advanced weapons systems whose effectiveness hinges on a small number of highly trained and widely dispersed personnel and a large support service. Sophisticated and complex equipment requires more intelligent and better-trained men and women to operate it. Instant communication and information processing is the glue that holds it all together. Computers will never replace soldiers in the trenches, but the military services are at the leading edge of the technological revolution.

That doesn't mean that everybody in the military plays computer wargames, flies helicopters, or wears white lab coats while making technical adjustments on missile guidance systems. The hot, noisy engine rooms in the bottoms of ships are still there, as are the jungle swamps to slosh through and the desert stockades to guard. But today's armed services are different organizations than good ol' Dad or Uncle remembers from years gone by. Skilled personnel, sophisticated equipment, and instant communications characterize the modern military.

The military must compete successfully for recruits with higher education and the labor force, and the military has had to upgrade the quality of life it offers. Today's military pay schedules are much more in line with pay scales in the civilian labor force. Also, the military has taken strides to integrate its occupations into the structure of the civilian labor force. Several forms of occupational training in the military now count toward apprentice training in the civilian labor force. The military has added other inducements and a variety of training options that, under the draft system, had been assignments.

Recruitment Themes

The military has responded to its change in status to an all volunteer force and its need to recruit successfully with a high-powered advertising recruitment campaign. The military spends millions each year in advertising that is geared to get young people thinking about military service as a career option. It employs the same advertising imagination that sells dog food, Toyotas, and lawn mowers on TV. Advertisements dramatize the breadth of job possibilities available to young people, and they feature young men and women having the time of their lives including playing coed volleyball on the beach and enjoying holiday weekends abroad. The ads skillfully respond to the kinds of questions young people ask:

- How can I get out of this dead-end job?
- How can I meet guys or girls and have some fun?
- How can I learn skills that I need to get the kind of job I want?
- How can I get out of here — home, school, community?
- How can I get away from dad, mom, brother, sister, or a romance gone sour?

Military service offers an out for a lot of problems young people face, one being that no one wants to hire them. The daughter of a foreman for an aluminum manufacturer started out as an assembler in a plastic products company and held 12 different full-time jobs in as many years after leaving high school. Her comment was that "between the ages of 18 and 25 it is difficult getting a job, as employers feel that this is a young and unstable age."

Military service solves some of these problems. It gives young people options. It gives them a group, an identity, even a slogan they can relate to:

" Be all you can be" — Army

" It's not just a job, it's an adventure" — Navy

" Aim high"— Air Force

*" We're looking for a few good men and women"
 — Marine Corps*

Each branch of the service, plus the Coast Guard and National Guard, has its own mission and character. They also have their own incentives, bonuses, and recruitment strategies.

Active Duty or the Reserves

All branches of the services are structured into active and reserve duty components. Both receive the same training, work with the same machinery and equipment, and are paid at the same rate. The big difference is how much time is spent on the job. Active duty means full-time work and full-time wages. Reserve duty means part-time work and part-time wages, or none at all, depending on the branch of the service.

The military hitch is eight years, whether a person signs up as an enlistee or an officer. The time spent on active duty may range from two to eight years, depending on the military branch. Eight years minus the time on active duty is the amount of time a person will spend in the reserves.

Reserve time may be divided into Ready Reserve and Standby Reserve. Ready Reserve members are ready to be called to active duty. They train and are paid one weekend a month and 15 days during the year. Standby Reserve members have time left on their eight-year military obligation, but they are not in active training and they do not get paid. They can be called up if Congress declares war or if there is a national emergency.

There are two other reserve units. The National Guard is a special reserve force, available for domestic disasters or civil disorders. The National Guard reports to both the federal and state governments. Members of the Retired Reserve have put in enough time to qualify for retirement benefits. They are no longer paid.

The biggest advantage of reserve duty is the money it pays together with the associated benefits. It's like having a second job. It pays a couple hundred dollars a month and includes benefits: low-cost life insurance, eligibility to buy things at low-cost military stores, recreational privileges at military installations, and such veterans' benefits as low-cost mortgages and retirement programs. The reserves also offer occupational training, in which a young person can learn in conjunction with running a civilian business. Financial benefits for a college education are available to members of the reserves.

Being a member of the reserves has some disadvantages. One is that if you are in the active reserves, you have no guarantee that you can stay at home. There is no assurance that the amount of time will be limited to a weekend a month plus 15 days a year. If your reserve unit is activated, then you are activated, too — no ifs, ands, or buts about it. You have to go.

Another disadvantage may be time away from work. Military obligations can interrupt company time at critical periods. A civilian employer may have to rely on somebody else to be absolutely certain that a big project gets done; and, of course, the outside obligation can show up in the paycheck and at times for promotions. Likewise, monthly weekends and 15-day stints away from home will conflict with birthdays, anniversaries, family reunions, neighborhood get-togethers, school events, church events, and a whole host of other things. It can be inconvenient.

Officer or Enlisted Person

Another choice a young person thinking about a military career might make is whether to enter as an enlisted person or an officer. Going in as an officer means more money and more rank, but the choice isn't simple. The basic question is whether the young person sees military service as a short- or long-term commitment.

A short-term commitment means that a young person goes in to get occupational training or to get money for college. A long-term commitment means that a young person is thinking about making the military a career.

Each branch of the service has its own package to offer, and young people thinking about military service should get the latest information from recruitment offices. There are, however, similarities across the services in the officers and enlisted members of the services. An officer in a military service functions like the manager of a corporation in the private sector. Officers in the military are well-educated, highly trained, and enjoy special benefits. More than 90 percent of them are college graduates and, therefore, they are the most likely to have access to such special education/training programs as graduate school or management training.

Advantages of Military Service

Joining a military service can be the first step to a very satisfying and rewarding career. Whether a young person enters with the intent of making a career of it or as a stepping stone to something else, the military has a number of things to offer.

The military takes care of you and provides the basics: a roof over your head, a bed or cot to sleep on, shirt and shoes, food to eat, and a place to hang out. There's a doctor to go to if you get sick, a dentist if you chip a tooth, a chaplain if you are so inclined, and fun things to do: pool, poker, bowling, and places to go. It isn't the Ramada Inn, but it is a home-of-sorts away from home. And you're on your own.

Education and occupational training alternate as the number one military recruitment themes. Currently, the emphasis is on education. Military service can be the way to finance a college education either totally or in part. Service personnel can take courses as part of their regime and they may get veterans' education benefits after they are discharged. Those who have been to college and want to go to graduate school, especially to medical school, may have all costs paid while they earn a salary.

Occupational training runs a close second in recruitment themes. The military is one of the nation's largest employers and it offers virtually every job that is available in the civilian labor force plus a number that aren't available, such as adjusting atomic warheads, testing submarines, and repairing tank gun-turrets. The trucks, tanks, helicopters, and ships all need someone to run and maintain them. The same is true of computers, radar screens, and potato peelers. Many military occupations require no previous experience or training. The military will teach you how, and then pay you to do it.

A hitch in the military also involves an opportunity for young people to "sort things out" and to "get their act together." It is an opportunity to get away, to get some skills training, to meet new people, to travel, and to get a fresh start.

Finally, military service also provides an opportunity to participate in a very honorable tradition, that of protecting the American people and defending the United States. This is a necessary and worthy vocation and those who follow it have the rest of us in their debt.

Disadvantages of Military Service

Military service can also be the source of a lot of frustration and anxiety, as is true of all occupations. Military regimes can be confining. Joining the military means giving up a lot of control over your life.

Young people thinking about military service are well-advised to remember that the number one purpose of the military is not to provide occupational training, is not to provide educational experiences and benefits, and is not to provide flight training in Cobra helicopters. Military service was not designed to be and it does not operate as a young person's welfare program, travel bureau, or holiday weekend service. The military offers a lot because it expects a lot in return: control over young people's lives. When push comes to shove, both in peacetime and in wartime, the decisions that are made are in the best interests of the military. What happens to a particular young person is a secondary consideration. Perhaps it needs to be said that you can get hurt in the military. The military ads and brochures don't picture the wheelchairs, amputees, veterans' hospitals, burials at sea, broken families, and broken lives that are also part of the military scene. They don't picture military cemeteries.

Military combat is a dirty business, and nobody asks for a recruit's opinion about a particular military order. *Robert's Rules of Order* is not the way of doing business. The recruit's assignment is to follow orders and that's what he or she agreed to do. And if they don't like it, they can't just process a drop/add card as they do in college. They can't just quit. As with any career decision, there are costs as well as benefits to enlisting.

Enlistment Packages and Procedures

Since the end of the military draft, the armed services have had to recruit to maintain their personnel quotas. In order to compete successfully, the services have come up with a number of benefit packages to attract young people. Because the services are in competition with each other, they are constantly modifying the incentives: phasing in new programs, phasing out old programs, increasing benefits, offering more alternatives, and the like. I don't try to review all the recruitment options here — only the ones that relate most immediately to careers and career preparation.

Three steps are involved in enlisting in the military: taking an aptitude test, talking through your options with a recruiter, and going through a military processing station.

The Armed Services Vocational Aptitude Battery. The military services use a special aptitude test called the Armed Services Vocational Aptitude Battery (ASVAB). The ASVAB is a multiple-choice test that covers 10 different subject areas with a total of 334 multiple-choice questions. It takes about two and one-half hours to complete. The ASVAB is somewhat similar to college entrance exams such as the ACT and the SAT, but the ASVAB focuses more on vocational aptitudes and less on intellectual abilities. The military uses the ASVAB to identify which jobs and how many jobs in the military will match a person's interests and abilities.

If your son or daughter is thinking of taking the ASVAB, suggest he or she take it at least a day or two before meeting with a military recruiter. This will give your child time to think about the results and to decide what to talk to the recruiter about.

Two additional pieces of information may be useful. One is the ASVAB Information Pamphlet, which describes the test and includes sample test questions. These are available at most career centers; otherwise, check your local recruitment office. Another useful pamphlet is an ASVAB practice book. The book provides sample questions and practice at taking the test. Practice books are available in bookstores and sometimes in libraries.

After taking the ASVAB, a young person should examine the scores before going to the processing station. Ask a high school career counselor for a copy of *Military Careers,* which should be available in high school career centers. This book describes 197 enlisted and officer occupations in 12 broad military occupational groups and explains what ASVAB scores are needed in order to qualify for the jobs. Young people should speak with their career counselors and parents about the match between their aptitudes and their scores and think about the questions they want to ask a military recruiter.

Visit a Service Recruiter. Many young people are understandably cautious about setting foot inside a recruitment office. It occurs to them that the door might blow shut and lock behind them, they might accidentally sign something, their hair might get chopped off, and they could get stuck on a bus headed for boot camp — and nobody will ever know what happened to them.

That is not likely to happen. It isn't likely because the military cannot afford to drag young people kicking and screaming into service against their will. It is in everyone's best interest — the military's, the recruiter's, the young person's, and parents' — that young people enter the military only if they and the military seem to be a good match. The military is not a dumping ground. As military equipment has become more sophisticated, it takes more intelligent and better qualified young people to make the grade. A fair amount of a recruiter's time is spent discouraging young people who won't make the grade. Today's military services are highly specialized. Recruiters are not looking for just "any ol' signature."

Recruiters are skilled at what they do. They make a good impression. They are attractive and well-groomed. Their military uniforms fit well and their shoes shine. Their ribbons and medals are colorful and impressive. Recruiters have self-confidence, a friendly smile, and a cabinet full of videotapes that leave just the right impression. Most recruiters are in the military because they like it. They have already reenlisted. Like all good sales-people, they will emphasize the positive features of the military and will probably ignore the negative aspects.

A recruiter can be a valuable resource for a young person who has specific questions in mind. The recruiter will have his or her own objectives to cover. Basically, these are to make an assessment of whether the young person is really a prospective recruit. The recruiter will tactfully steer the conversation into a number of areas. What were the young person's interests in school and how well did she or he perform academically? Illnesses? Brushes with the law? Drug use? Jobs of interest? The recruiter may suggest the young person take a short screening test or a practice version of the ASVAB. And you can be sure that the recruiter will establish whether or not the young person is 18 years old. If not, the whole process will come to a screeching halt until parental permission is furnished.

If the young person continues to be interested and the recruiter judges that the young person is a potential recruit, the next step is to schedule an appointment at a military entrance processing station, which the recruiter will arrange. The recruit should be sure that all questions have been answered. One way to make sure that the right questions have been asked and satisfactorily answered is to take someone along to the sessions with the recruiter, a parent or friend. Another way to make sure that necessary information is given is to make several trips to the recruiter. Get information, think about it, talk to other people about it, and then head back to speak with the recruiter again. Have the recruiter schedule the appointment at the military processing station when, and only when, the young person is ready.

Take your time in all of this. There is no hurry — other than youthful impatience.

The Military Entrance Processing Station. The military processing station is where the real details are worked out, final agreements are made, and signatures go on the dotted line.

To begin with, the people in uniform will give careful attention to whether the requirements for getting into service are met. A liaison officer will check through the recruit's paperwork. The recruiter will specify in advance what the recruit needs to bring along — for example, a Social Security card, identification, contact lens prescription if contacts are worn, medical documents, ASVAB test scores if the test has been taken, and the like. Assuming these materials are in good order, the next step is the physical examination.

Although the general requirements are much the same across the services, each branch of the military and units within the branches have special requirements or restrictions. Thus, although the maximum height accepted is 6 feet and 8 inches, it is unlikely that recruits that tall will end up in Army tanks, Air Force fighter jets, or Navy submarines. Conditions that can keep a young person out of the military go beyond low ASVAB scores and height and weight requirements to include such "innocent" conditions as braces on the teeth, wool allergies, and bee sting reactions. Before the process continues, the young recruit must pass the physical.

If the recruit passes the physical exam, military interest in the recruit intensifies. If the paperwork is in good order and the physical exam has been passed, most of the concerns that the military has about the recruit have been satisfied. But that does not mean that the recruit's interests have been satisfied, and there can be a lot of momentum at this point to just get the enlistment business over with. At this point, recruits need to remember two things. First, from the recruit's point of view the most important things— like job assignment and enlistment benefits package— are yet to be decided. Second, the recruit hasn't yet signed or enlisted and it is perfectly appropriate to head back home. Recruits should take their jolly-good time making sure they get what they want. They are making an eight-year commitment.

A job classifier works with recruits to help them decide which field they will enter. Of the hundreds of jobs in the military, those open to a particular recruit will be determined by ASVAB scores. The recruit will have to choose a military specialty, and the classifier will use a computer to determine when the next job opening in that specialty will be posted and whether the recruit's training will be completed in time to fill the open position.

It is not unusual for recruits to have to wait, perhaps for a year, for a job in their chosen specialty to open. When delays happen, recruits may feel self-imposed pressure to choose another specialty — something else, anything — that will enable them to enlist immediately and get on with it. The job classifier, who wants to keep the line moving, may encourage an "it really doesn't matter that much" attitude. But this is a critical point in the enlistment process. Recruits need to remember that they will live with the specialty they choose for four to six years, and they shouldn't allow themselves to be stampeded into anything. Keeping the line moving is not their problem. They are not in the military and nobody can order them around — at this point. They have options other than to sign on the dotted line for a specialty that is not their choice.

Recruits have three options if the job they want isn't immediately available or if their ASVAB scores are too low in their preferred specialty:

- The recruit can ask for a waiver, a request for special permission to take the job even though the formal requirement isn't met. The commander of the processing station is authorized to grant waivers and the recruit should not be reluctant to go to the commander and ask for a waiver.
- The recruit can return home and wait. The military job situation changes day by day. So do the entry-level qualifying scores that recruits must meet. It all depends on supply and demand in the military labor market. The recruit can ask the job classifier to make contact if the job situation changes.
- The recruit can return home and talk to the local recruiter. The recruiter's job is to match the recruit with the military. The recruiter can monitor the job situation and inform the recruit when things change.

I encourage recruits to go back home if they don't get what they want. That is their right, and it is the wisest thing to do if they are not completely satisfied with the package the military offers them. There is little if anything to be lost by doing so. Their physical exam is good for 30 days — and what if they had to take it again sometime later? They passed it the first time. There is little reason to believe they wouldn't pass it the second time. The point I make is that the recruit should hold out for the job that interests him or her. That's how to make an intelligent and responsible military career decision.

Suppose, however, that the job that interests the recruit is available. Then, especially, the job classifier may want to get the file closed and keep the line moving. I strongly urge, however, that the recruit make sure that he or she has answers to these questions before signing:

- If I choose this option, how long must I stay in the military?
- Are there any other tests I must pass or requirements I must meet in order to get this job? If there are, and I don't pass them, then what happens?
- Is special training required for this job? What happens if I don't complete the training satisfactorily?
- If I take this job, do I have a choice of where I will be stationed? What are the probable places I will be stationed? How long am I likely to stay there?
- If I take the job under the buddy plan — that is, I sign up with a friend — how long can the two of us stay together?
- If for some reason this job turns out not to be available, then what happens?

Advanced planning, knowing what questions to ask, will help move the process along.

Assuming that the military and the recruit can agree on a job and date to enter military service, the nuts and bolts of the enlistment process have been completed. There are other details to take care of, but the oath of enlistment has not been administered. That means there is still time to call time-out and to think about it for a few days, weeks, even months. "It isn't over till it's over," Don Meredith was fond of saying as an announcer on "Monday Night Football." That is true of the enlistment process, too. It isn't over until the recruit signs the dotted line and takes the oath of enlistment. It's over when the recruit raises his or her right hand and repeats the following:

> *"I do solemnly swear that I will support and defend the Constitution of the United States against all enemies, foreign and domestic; that I will bear true faith and allegiance to the same; and that I will obey the orders of the President of the United States and the orders of the officers appointed over me, according to regulations and the Uniform Code of Military Justice. So help me God."*

The Military and Careers

Employment in the military offers some people many of the same advantages as nonmilitary government employment. A stock clerk in the Navy told us his experience:

> *"When I got out of the Army in 1971 there were no jobs available . . . so I went to college. In sheer desperation I joined the Navy in 1973, where I have been ever since. Although I don't like being in the service (because I feel there is a stigma attached), I like the job security."*

Career officers, if competent, enjoy a high degree of job security and possibly rank and status well into middle age.

Also, the military may provide an extraordinary opportunity for administrative and general management experience. The military is a large and tightly structured bureaucracy, and people who work their way up through the ranks gain first-hand complex organization experience from many different angles. They receive on-the-job training and hands-on experience in management and administration that has broad nonmilitary applications. First careers in the military have been important stepping-stones for high-level civilian administrative positions in industry, government, and education.

But what about the noncareer recruit? The military services are working hard to equip young people with skills and to ease their transition back into the civilian labor force. For example, the services have structured apprenticeship programs into Army, Navy, and Marine training programs by agreement with the Department of Labor. These programs assure that service people receive apprenticeship accreditation that can be logged toward civilian journeyman status.

There are also examples of non-apprenticeable technical training learned in the military that is transferable to civilian occupations. Certainly that is true of such specialties as commercial air pilots who are able to accumulate experience and log flying time in the military. It may also be true of training in communications systems, computing technology, and clerical work.

In their monograph *Employment and Training Programs for Youth,* Mangum and Walsh state, "Ninety percent of the training is related to civilian occupations, whether or not the individual chooses to or has an opportunity to pursue a related occupation." That state- ment is at the center of a major controversy regarding military service as a career prepara- tion option, however. I cannot resolve the conflict here, but I can summarize four basic criticisms of occupational training in the military, and then let parents and young people decide for themselves.

Criticisms of Occupational Training in the Military

Some are disillusioned over military service, and military education and training appears to be a major sore point. In hearings before the Senate Subcommittee of Manpower and Personnel of the Committee on Armed Services, Jerry Reed, acting on the commission of Congressman Frank Beard, suggested that accessibility to military education programs is a major problem. Reed testified that 80 percent of the first-term enlisted personnel stationed overseas that he interviewed sought a college education in the military, but only 5 percent had been able to take college courses. Reed states that 90 percent of military personnel who applied for college course work were repeatedly turned down by their unit commanders. Similar comments were made by soldiers who wanted to finish their high school require- ments for a diploma.

A second criticism is that where education or training is offered, enlistees are not able to take the courses they want. This criticism can be stated simply. Even if Mangum and Walsh are correct that the military offers 900 specialized skill courses, the reality is that no ship at sea or remote outpost on land can offer more than a small fraction of the total number of specialized skill courses; and the courses offered are the result of military need, not individual preference. Job duties are changed on the basis of service requirements, not personal preference.

A third criticism is the military's option to assign personnel to jobs other than those for which it trained them. The military guarantees education and training, but it does not guarantee a job and experience in the same area that the recruit was trained.

A fourth criticism is that skill training may not transfer to civilian occupations. A Navy veteran who now works as a pipefitter for a gas and steam supply system but wants to be an elementary school teacher told us his experience:

> *"After graduation I went into the service and was trained in a field with no civilian counterpart. After leaving the service I had no training and, even though a veteran, was given no opportunity in the field I wanted to follow."*

A radio/TV repairman told a similar story:

> *" I completed four and one-half years in the Navy as an aviation electronics technician. I was discharged with the knowledge and confidence that I was well-trained and with work experience in the electronics field. I had difficulty getting a job. I was told by more than one potential employer that the credentials that I produced showing my training experience just wasn't important."*

Another Navy veteran who now works as a surveyor for state government told us his experience:

> *" I had four years as an equipment operator but only military. Everywhere that I sought employment I was told I did not have enough experience. It didn't make any difference that I had the training in the construction field; the employers always seemed to tell me that they wanted someone that had gained their experience in the civilian world. Therefore, the first four years I had to be satisfied with part-time jobs or jobs completely foreign to what I'd been trained to do."*

Every year thousands of recruits receive extensive training in a variety of fields. When they leave the military, they may or may not possess skills that are useful in the civilian labor market. Even if the skills are comparable to those needed in civilian jobs, many need additional training after they leave the service to qualify for civilian jobs in which they can apply their military skills.

Strong differences of opinion exist about the career preparation outcomes of military service. Unfortunately, no definitive studies are available to settle the controversy. Until such studies are done, parents and young people will have to rely on the best information they can get and their own best judgment.

Informed Decisions

It is not my purpose to try to convince young people either to join the armed services or to stay out. I have tried to point out both the opportunities and the obligations. Some people find a home in the military. Others hate every minute. Each young person must decide, hopefully in advance, whether military service offers a viable career preparation option.

The favorable and unfavorable examples cited are probably extremes in terms of what the military has to offer and what it delivers. I doubt that either extreme presents an accurate picture. The possibilities of military service as career preparation undoubtedly fall somewhere in between. As with any other career decision, parents and their young people will want to get as much information as possible, think it through, and make their own decisions.

Young people contemplating military service to gain skills for a civilian career should do their homework before choosing a military specialty. Above all, they should remember that, whatever else the military offers by way of opportunity or obligation, it is first and foremost an appeal for "service." Young people should find out whether there are civilian employment opportunities that relate to the military specialties that interest them. They should also inquire about the entrance requirements for the related civilian job, whether military training is sufficient to enter the area, and, if not, what additional certification, licensing, educational levels, or training are required.

With respect to military service, I urge parents and young people to remember two things:

> ■ The number one purpose of the military is to defend the United States, not to provide education and training for young people.
>
> ■ The All Volunteer Force concept puts the service in competition with civilian educational and occupational opportunities; and parents and young people must not expect more from the military than it can provide.

College and Career Prep: Do They Pay?

I t costs well over $100,000 to raise a child to age 18 — at least $100,000 in the rural Midwest and at least $125,000 in the rural West. Of course, if you want to include a college education, the costs could double.

With increasing college costs, cuts in appropriations for federal financial aid, an oversupply of college graduates, and primary demand for workers in service industries, is a college education worth the cost? A college professor in our Career Development Study didn't seem to think so. He told us:

> *" I do find it frustrating that I hold the rank of assistant professor at a state university and still can't buy a house. So much for the American dream. The days when hard-working, well-educated people could be assured of a higher standard of living than their parents are long gone."*

Is the cost of a diploma worth its price in tuition, room, board, and four years without income? How does the earning power of a $2,500 vocational certificate compare with the earning power of a $50,000 sheepskin? Those are fair questions to ask if you are a parent and face the prospect of picking up much of the tab. They are also reasonable questions for young people to ask.

None of us has a crystal ball with which to view the future, but we do have information about the past, knowledge of trends, studies that provide some sense for how things are changing, and a good idea of whether education and training will pay in the future.

I limit this discussion to two kinds of programs: four-year college degree programs and less-than-four-year vocational preparation programs. I ask the same question of both: Will they pay? Are they worth the cost?

FOUR-YEAR COLLEGE DEGREES: ARE THEY WORTH IT?

There are different ways to consider whether a four-year college education is likely to "pay" in the years ahead. One way is to look at college as an economic investment. A college education will cost a certain amount of money, and that investment should pay off in dollars and cents. That's the cost-benefit approach to answering the question.

College as an Economic Investment

The annual cost of a college education has been increasing, and the job market for college graduates has been getting tighter. In addition, it takes most students more than four years to get through college. Only 43 percent complete a bachelor's degree within four calendar years of their graduation from high school. On the average, 6.2 years pass from the time they receive their high school diplomas until they receive their bachelor's degrees. Some argue that "the juice has to justify the squeeze," that the principles of investment-returns analysis should be applied to education just like anything else.

These analysts view education as an investment in people in much the same way they would look at buying stock as an investment in a business. It's a "human capital" approach. People can invest in many different things. The question is whether investing in a college education is likely to yield a better return to the individual than investing in noncollege opportunities like stocks, bonds, and real estate.

From an economic point of view, where would you put your money? In a college education? Or in some other investment — stocks, bonds, real estate, or savings?

Past Investment Returns. A college education has definitely been worth it in the past. College degrees have produced higher lifetime earnings. The demand for college graduates has been especially high in professional and technical occupations. During the 1960s, the average lifetime income of a white male with a four-year college degree was almost $200,000 more than the earnings of a high school graduate. The 1960s were good years to enter a career because the number of jobs was greater than the supply of college graduates. From 1962 to 1969, roughly 575,000 college graduates entered the labor force each year, and 73 percent went into professional and technical jobs. Those jobs paid well.

But things changed dramatically during the 1970s. Twice as many college graduates entered the labor market annually as during the decade earlier, and college graduates faced stiffer job competition. Then the economy went sour. Many people began to believe what a city fireman told us in the Career Development Study:

> *" This is probably an old argument, but I believe that more vocational type courses are needed. . . . Most classes were geared toward a college education, but in reality only a minority attended college and many of those got jobs not requiring a college education."*

During the 1980s and early 1990s, businesses trimmed administrative positions and "lean-at-the-top" management styles took over. Graduates experienced difficulty finding high-paying positions and movement up the job ladder slowed. Less than 50 percent entered professional and technical jobs, down more than a third from a decade earlier. In greater numbers, graduates went into managerial and administrative positions, sales, clerical, craft, operative, laborer, service, and farm worker jobs, or they were unemployed. A fourth took jobs that traditionally were not held by four-year college graduates. College graduates' lifetime economic advantage over high school graduates declined.

The annual rate of economic return on the cost of a college education averaged 10 percent or more over the 30-year period from 1939 to 1969. That was as good a rate of return or better than most other investments posted over the same period. By 1969, the rate of return for college education climbed to about 15 percent for men and 17 percent for women, and then dropped to about 12 percent by 1980. Today, the rate of return on the cost of a college education probably stands at about 10 or 11 percent for men and 13 or 14 percent for women.

These calculations take into account the cost of a college education, which may be substantial and rose dramatically over the past five years. They estimate the differences in increased earnings for individuals over their lifetime. And they take into account income foregone over the college years. People with four years of college can expect lifetime earnings nearly twice as high as people with a high school diploma, and adding a graduate degree adds about another two-thirds more to the corresponding earnings advantage of a bachelor's degree over a high school diploma. Given recent earnings trends, the advantage of a college education for women is likely to be even greater, though it will not equal the totals earned by men.

Annual Salary Differences. Comparisons of annual salaries is a second way to examine the economic returns to a four-year college education. When these comparisons are made, the dollar return to investments in education and training are apparent. Workers with more education earn more.

DIFFERENCES IN ANNUAL EARNINGS OF MEN AND WOMEN 25 YEARS AND OLDER BY LEVEL OF EDUCATION, 1991

Education	Annual Earnings	
	Men	**Women**
More than bachelor's degree	$51,573	$34,056
4 or more years of college	36,009	22,482
Associate degree	29,220	19,202
Some college, no degree	26,818	16,078
High school graduate	22,482	12,690
Less than 4 years of high school	16,021	8,958
Less than 9th grade	11,733	7,409

Source: U.S. Commerce Department, 1993

The differences in earning power — the advantage to those with more education and the disadvantage to those with less — are dramatic. Men with more than a bachelor's degree earn 4.4 times as much annually as do men with less than a 9th-grade education. Comparably educated women earn even more, 4.6 times as much. Both men and women who graduate from high school annually earn 1.4 times as much as those who drop out of high school. Men with some college annually earn 1.2 times as much as men who graduate from high school. Women earn 1.3 times as much. Men with an associate degree annually earn 1.3 times as much as high school graduates, and women earn 1.5 times as much. Men with a college degree annually earn 1.6 times as much as do men with a high school diploma; and women earn 1.8 times as much.

Over the past 20 years, the earnings advantage of completing a college education has been increasing. For example, between 1980 and 1990 the income for men with five or more years of college who were year-round, full-time workers rose 78 percent; for those with high school diplomas, income rose 37 percent; and for high school dropouts, income rose 30 percent. People with higher levels of education not only earned more, but the amount of their income advantage has been increasingly substantially. Over the same period women's incomes increased faster than men's — 76 percent compared with 51 percent overall. The average incomes for full-time, year-round workers rose from $20,297 to $30,733 for men and from $12,156 to $21,372 for women. In 1990, men with four years of college earned an average of $39,238, and women earned $28,017.

Workers with more education are also less likely to be unemployed. Again, employment rates are directly related to level of education, and the pattern for men and women is much the same. The unemployment rate for men who are high school dropouts is 3.2 times higher than the rate for college graduates. Among women the rate is 3.1 times higher. The unemployment rate for men who are high school graduates is 1.9 times higher than that for college graduates. Among women it is 1.8 times higher. And the unemployment rate for young men with some college but no degree is 1.2 times as high as it is for college graduates. Among women it is 1.8 times higher.

In summary, workers with more education earn more and are less likely to be unemployed. A college education definitely has been "worth it" in the past in terms of a return on the investment, and it is clearly worth it today in terms of annual earnings and employment stability.

Investment Prospectus. Over the past decade, roughly 10 million college graduates entered the labor force, but one-fourth had to take jobs that did not require a four-year degree. College graduates will continue to have an advantage over high school graduates when it comes to employment, but college graduates will face increasing competition in many fields from community college graduates with job-related skills.

The employment outlook is not as rosy as it once was for four-year college graduates, but that does not mean that the future looks bleak. Consider employment/population ratios — the number of persons employed as a percentage of the population. College graduates invariably fare better than any other category when it comes to claiming available jobs. Thus, whereas two-thirds of the total population is employed, 8 or 9 of 10 college graduates are employed. All indications are that college graduates will continue to have an employment advantage in the future, just as they do today.

Lower unemployment rates mean that college graduates have more stable incomes. In addition, college graduates have better benefits packages: sick pay, health insurance,

UNEMPLOYMENT RATES BY SEX, AGE GROUPS, AND LEVEL OF EDUCATION, 1992

Education	Men			
	Total	16–19 yrs	20–24 yrs	25+ yrs
All education levels	15.1%	22.0%	13.0%	6.4%
Bachelor's degree or higher	7.7	—	7.7	3.3
Some college, no degree	9.4	10.6	9.2	6.1
High school graduate	14.7	19.5	13.5	7.3
Less than high school graduate	23.6	26.8	21.1	11.4

Education	Women			
	Total	16–19 yrs	20–24 yrs	25+ yrs
All education levels	13.3%	21.4%	10.9%	5.7%
Bachelor's degree or higher	5.5	—	5.5	3.0
Some college, no degree	9.8	12.2	9.4	5.8
High school graduate	10.0	18.0	11.4	6.2
Less than high school graduate	27.1	29.3	24.8	11.4

Source: U.S. Department of Labor, 1993

retirement programs, and employee assistance programs. Lower unemployment rates together with employment in better paying positions with better benefit packages boosts college graduates' economic advantages further; and there is nothing on the horizon to suggest that these trends will change.

Of course, what happened in the past is no guarantee for the future. Nonetheless, one way to project the future is to look at the past and extend the trends. I offer three observations:

LABOR FORCE PARTICIPATION RATES BY AGE AND LEVEL OF EDUCATION, 1992

Education	16–24 yrs	25 yrs+
All education levels	68.1%	62.3%
Bachelor's degree or higher	88.9	78.7
Associate degree	86.8	75.8
Some college, no degree	79.2	69.1
High school graduate	71.4	61.7
Less than high school graduate	46.5	36.1

Source: U.S. Department of Labor, 1993

- ■ In terms of return on investment and annual earnings differences, there have been substantial economic benefits to a four-year college education in the past.
- ■ The annual earnings advantage to education has been increasing over the past two decades.
- ■ The earnings advantages of education are likely to continue in the years ahead.

The calculation of returns-on-investment approach takes into account that, while higher education costs have increased, the costs to individuals have not outpaced inflation until recent years. Except for the last few years, the investment costs have remained fairly constant. Only the returns have changed. They have decreased as a percentage of investment costs, though the earnings advantage to education has increased. The same outcomes do not necessarily apply to every college program and degree, and the outcomes do not tell us how our daughters and sons will fare in the future. However, they do suggest a cost-benefit return to a four-year college education for the total work force if the long-term trends continue.

Return on investment percentages are based on average lifetime incomes, and salary difference percentages are based on average or median annual incomes. My best guess is that four-year degrees will continue to pay economic dividends of at least 10 percent annually, and salary advantages of perhaps 50 to 60 percent per year for those who graduate from college compared with those who graduate from high school. College graduates will continue to earn considerably more over their lifetimes than do high school graduates, though the differences may not return to the large advantages enjoyed by college graduates in the 1960s. People who believe what a hospital administrator told us, that today "blue-collar labor earns the same or more than most college graduates," should remember that the increased wage levels of blue-collar workers is largely due to their increased education levels.

Figuring out the economic returns on a college education is an important and interesting question, but it isn't the only question to ask; and, from my point of view, it isn't the most important question. Some years ago, Stanford University provost Al Hastorf suggested a very practical consideration: "Don't study what you think is going to have a big economic payoff, because that may not be true 10 years from now." There are also noneconomic ways to assess whether a college education is likely to pay in the future.

Noneconomic Returns

The phrase "noneconomic consequences" refers to the other-than-financial effects of a college education. How does college affect a young person's development, attitudes, behavior, way of thinking, and lifestyle? Each young adult is a unique person, and no one can say how college will affect a particular individual. But studies indicate how college life and education affect young people in general. They offer a rough guide for what parents can expect.

Knowledge and Thought. The evidence is persuasive that four years of college raises people's knowledge level and the quality of their thought processes. Studies also show that a college education leads to moderate increases in ability to communicate, intellectual toler-ance, and aesthetic sensitivity, and to small increases in mathematical skills, rational thinking, and creativity.

Students gain in their ability to think critically. They are more reflective and show greater intellectual flexibility and independence of thought. The ability to think indepen-dently is associated with individual enjoyment, on the one hand, and with career advance-ment, on the other. A librarian in Seattle made the same point:

> *" I was told that this [going to college] would be necessary in order to get a good job. . . . Of course, I know that is not true. No one ever told me that ideas are exciting. Certainly no one ever encouraged me to question what my textbooks said or what it means to research an issue, to analyze information, to reach an informed conclusion. . . . I believe it is important to help students learn how to think independently, also to teach them the ability to learn on their own."*

College-educated people are more future-oriented than are noncollege graduates. They are more likely to defer immediate gratification for the sake of long-term benefits. College-educated people do more planning. They take more reasonable risks. Level of education is associated with being resourceful, being adaptable to change, and being willing to compromise and keep options open.

Education provides building blocks for the kind of learning and development that continues throughout life. The details of Outer Mongolian history, cell physiology, and baroque music may fade from memory, but what remains is the know-how for getting and organizing information, analyzing, and thinking, tools that are useful and help people understand and work in our complex culture.

The ability to think independently has been cited often as a prized quality of citizen-ship in a democracy for these reasons:

- College-educated people vote more frequently.
- College graduates participate more often in political and community affairs than do people who did not attend college.
- College graduates are more committed to the basic freedoms outlined in the Bill of Rights than are people who did not attend college.

Americans have long believed that education is crucial to the democratic process, and a college education favors a number of political attitudes and behaviors that are consistent with democratic ideology. For example, as level of education increases, so does voting participation. Using high school graduates as a point of reference for voting behavior in the 1992 presidential election, college graduate ages 25 to 44 were 58 percent more likely to vote, and high school dropouts were 46 percent less likely to vote. The difference in voting behavior by education levels have generally been widening over time.

Beliefs and Values. Colleges provide young people with new experiences, influences, and challenges in contact with people from different backgrounds and ideas. The mark of today's university is its diversity. Life on campus, both in and out of the classroom, challenges young people to think things through for themselves.

That doesn't mean that a student is likely to go through a drastic personality change over the college years. On the contrary, value change studies show that colleges generally accentuate or anchor personality tendencies that were already present when the young person entered college. There are always exceptions, but major personality changes are not the general rule.

When it comes to values and morals, higher education encourages tolerance, permissiveness, and flexibility. College campuses often lead the way in social and political movements. For example, campuses have been at the forefront of movements toward greater sexual permissiveness and the unisex emphasis on men's and women's overlapping attitudes and interests. And campuses have been public forums for debate and social action regarding civil rights, Viet Nam, the environment, alternative lifestyles, gender issues, and the like.

Some observers fear a decline in conventional morality that leaves college students without adequate values with which to structure their lives. Others argue that the movement away from authority and dogmatic standards toward greater openness, tolerance, and honesty is a new, perhaps higher, kind of morality. Each individual, like each generation, must decide.

A similar debate goes on concerning patterns of religious interests and beliefs on college campuses. Since the late 1950s, there has been a decline in the strength of religious values; but, at the same time, class enrollments in the formal study of religion and philosophy have increased. While adherence to traditional forms of religion has decreased, interest in the study of religion has increased.

Behavior. College student behavior — whether swallowing goldfish, rushing to the Florida coast over spring break, or keg and block parties — makes good news copy; and studies show that changes in behavior among college students include an increase in such negative behaviors as drinking, smoking, partying, and gambling. These behavioral patterns vary considerably between institutions, however.

Size of colleges makes a difference. Large institutions reduce a student's chance of involvement in campus activities, while small campuses increase the likelihood of interaction with faculty and participation in campus governance and athletic programs. Similarly, the few remaining single-sex colleges, whether all male or all female, also tend to be small and, therefore, increase the chances of involvement in academic pursuits, interaction with faculty, and classroom participation. Boarding schools historically have emphasized extracurricular activities.

What happens to students also varies by gender. Women generally earn higher grades than men yet, until recently, women were less likely to stay in college and go on to graduate or professional schools. Aspirations for higher degrees increase among men more than among women. Women generally achieve in the areas of cultural knowledge, foreign languages, music, and homemaking. Men show higher levels of achievement in athletics, original writing, and acquiring technical and scientific skills.

Higher education affects later consumer behavior, leisure, and health. Compared with noncollege-educated people at similar income levels, college-educated people spend less money on food, tobacco, alcohol, and automobiles, but more on housing, reading material, and recreation. College-educated people save a higher proportion of their incomes.

College graduates work longer hours and retire later in their careers than do noncollege-educated workers. College graduates have less leisure time, and they use it differently. They watch television less frequently but more selectively. College graduates spend more time reading, going to cultural events, taking part in community affairs, pursuing hobbies, and taking vacations. Generally speaking, college graduates are more discriminating in their behavior.

Family Life, Satisfactions, and Health. College education has lasting effects on people's personal lives, particularly in family life. College-educated people marry at an older age and have fewer children. They devote more time to childcare and are generally more involved with their children. College-educated parents spend proportionately more of their income on education and activities that foster the personal growth of their children.

There is a strong relationship between parents' levels of education and the intelligence and achievement levels of their children. By improving parents' levels of ability and motivation, a four-year college education has the spin-off effect of improving children's life chances. Education has a multiplier effect. People with college degrees generally report that their work is more challenging and rewarding than do those who have completed only high school. That is probably because college degrees qualify people for more desirable jobs; more desirable jobs offer greater personal satisfaction; and greater personal satisfaction on the job is associated with greater quantity and higher quality of productivity.

College graduates have substantially lower rates of disability than do people who do not attend college. Although the reason is not clear, college graduates are healthier than noncollege graduates. They also have the financial resources with which to take better care of themselves. They watch their health more closely, as evident from these samples given in the table below.

In summary, in the past a college education has improved people's resources, opened career doors, and prepared them to take better advantage of opportunities. This is value

PERCENTAGE OF PERSONS 18 YEARS AND OLDER WHO RESPONDED POSITIVELY TO HEALTH-RELATED QUESTIONS BY LEVEL OF EDUCATION, 1990

Question	All Levels	High School		College	
		1–3 yrs	4 yrs	1–3 yrs	4+ yrs
Exercise or play sports regularly	40.7	29.7	37.0	48.5	55.8
Told more than once they had high blood pressure	16.3	21.5	15.7	12.8	12.4
Smoke cigarettes daily	25.5	37.4	29.6	23.0	13.5

Source: National Center for Health Statistics, 1990

received, whether measured as an economic or noneconomic consequence of education. Many people agree with a business woman, a bank officer in Reno, Nevada, who told us:

> *" I believe that the biggest disfavor that can be done to young people today is to play down the importance of a college education and degree. I am faced every day in the business world with individuals who are continually denied opportunities for the lack of a degree. They are frustrated and resentful of those who have the degree and regret their own inadequacy."*

When economists calculate the advantages of increased schooling, they usually take earnings into account but fail to consider such intangibles as working conditions and quality of life. When these are factored into an individual's "true economic well-being," the value of education goes much beyond the increases in earnings that it generates. A study at the Institute for Research on Poverty at the University of Wisconsin-Madison concludes that economists' estimates may measure only about three-fifths of the full dollar value of an education.

VOCATIONAL PREPARATION PROGRAMS: DO THEY PAY?

Vocational education and career education are two congressionally mandated programs that are funded, in part, by the federal government. At the state and local levels there are corresponding entities in the form of vocational schools and vocational programs.

Vocational programs have been controversial for a number of reasons, but at the center of the controversy has been the question of how general or specific career preparation should be. Advocates of vocational programs reason that occupation-specific career preparation gives an employee an advantage in the labor market, whether or not there is job turnover. Opponents argue that occupation-specific training is inefficient because workers typically do considerable job hopping, particularly during their early years. This outcome of vocational preparation programs is likely to remain in question until long-term definitive studies shed more light on the issue.

Knowledge about the outcomes of vocational preparation programs is limited for several reasons:

- Vocational preparation programs take many different forms and vary from school to school.
- Vocational preparation programs are still relatively new, and there haven't been many long-term studies of the results.
- Vocational preparation programs have been controversial, emotionally charged, and political; it is difficult to evaluate them objectively.

With these realities in mind and the forthright acknowledgment that there is little solid information about the consequences of specific vocational preparation programs — "complicated and often contradictory findings" is the way the 1994 National Assessment characterized evaluations — I offer these observations and impressions of the outcomes of vocational programs. I consider the outcomes in terms of placement rates, economic benefits, and noneconomic outcomes.

Placement Rates

Private schools that participate in government-sponsored financial aid programs are required to keep records of placement rates — that is, their ability to locate suitable jobs for their graduates. Placement rates are frequently available for public schools, also. Because vocational training emphasizes occupational preparation, placement in an occupational specialty is the most common measure of program success. Placement rates are also used extensively for marketing and public relations purposes. For that reason, the most attractive numbers are often the most quoted numbers.

True placement rates are not easily determined, however. The basis for calculating the rates — whether they should be based on all students who enroll in programs including those who spend minimal time in training, just those who completed the program and are available for employment, only those placed in occupations related to their specialized training, or graduates placed in any occupation — varies from school to school. Also, what the "base" is and what "successful placement" means differ from study to study. There is no generally accepted way for calculating placement rates, and that's a problem.

An American College Testing study, for example, reports placement rates based on students who completed program requirements or were enrolled for at least four months. Placement rates for all but two programs were over 50 percent, ranging from 5 percent for science programs to 99 percent for registered nursing. Those rates are based on only 57 percent of the total number of students. When the placement rates are calculated on the basis of the total number of students in each program, the rates decline by about a third. Only two programs, auto mechanics and registered nursing, remain above the 50 percent placement level. The average placement rate based on all students probably lies in the 40- to 45-percent range.

There are problems, then, with information reported on placement rates for vocational preparation programs. The problems have to do with the definition of successful placement and the method for calculating the rates. Definitive studies have not been done, and reports are inconsistent, but the general pattern might indicate that about half of program graduates find jobs in their occupational specialties.

Economic Benefits

I review the economic benefits of vocational preparation programs in terms of unemployment rates and earnings. Again, few good studies have been done on these subjects. Nonetheless, increasing numbers of people agree with an airline flight attendant who told us: "College certainly benefits individuals, but it definitely is not necessary to 'make it.'"

Unemployment Rates. One measure of economic benefits to vocational preparation programs is a comparison of unemployment rates for people with various kinds and levels of education and training.

UNEMPLOYMENT RATES BY AGE GROUPS AND LEVEL OF EDUCATION, 1992

Education	Total %	16–19 %	20–24 %	25 yrs+ %
All education levels	14.3	21.7	12.0	6.1
Bachelor's degree or higher	6.5	—	6.5	3.2
Associate degree	6.0	14.6	5.8	4.7
Some college, no degree	9.6	11.5	9.3	6.0
High school graduate	13.9	18.8	12.5	6.8
Less than high school graduate	24.9	21.7	22.3	11.4

Source: U.S. Department of Labor, 1993

Note that persons with some college, particularly persons with degrees, whether bachelor's or associate degrees, do considerably better than do persons with a high school or less than high school education. Some college or an associate degree is better than just a high school diploma, and the unemployment rates for persons with associate and bachelor's degrees are comparable. Indeed, an associate degree, which is conferred after two years, is usually better than some college without a degree. The point is that certification pays. Certification, not number of years of college, is the way to take credit for additional schooling.

Several state studies suggest that the unemployment rates for vocational graduates of community colleges are not much different from the unemployment rates for the total population. Among 16- to 24-year-olds, graduates of vocational programs are more likely to be employed than are dropouts from four-year college programs, and the unemployment rates for community college graduates are equivalent to rates for four-year college graduates. In a related study of 20- to 24-year-olds, graduates of vocational programs had unemployment rates lower than high school graduates. Recent unemployment rates published by the Department of Labor are consistent with these findings.

Three community colleges in California indicated that graduates of vocational programs "experienced significantly less unemployment than general curriculum graduates two years after graduation." However, 12 years after high school, those participants in the Career Development Study whose highest level of training was vocational certification had the highest percentage of workers who experienced at least one period of unemployment, even more than high school graduates. However, the duration of their unemployment was shorter than it was for people with only a high school education. The same group held the highest number of jobs since high school graduation. People with some form of vocational training were more mobile than high school graduates, but neither group was as mobile as were people with three or four years of college. The percentage of people with vocational certification who were employed full-time was higher than the percentage with only a high school diploma.

In summary, graduates of vocational preparation programs appear to have an employment advantage over high school graduates and college dropouts, but they do not fare as well as graduates of four-year colleges.

Earnings. The primary measure of economic returns to education and training programs in our society is earnings, and the general rule is that the more postsecondary schooling a young person has, the higher that person's average yearly earnings are likely to be.

According to the U.S. Department of Commerce, earnings in 1992 were closely associated with levels of postsecondary education and training. For example, the median annual earnings of whites, both men and women, who had not completed high school were about 75 percent of the earnings of those who completed high school. The earnings advantage of those who completed some college was 32 percent greater than those with only a high school education. Finally, the earnings advantage of a bachelor's degree was more than double the earnings advantage of having attended only some college.

Economically, then, graduates of vocational programs fare better than high school graduates, but they do not fare as well as graduates of four-year colleges. The favorable effect of education on earnings tends to increase over the work history so that, by retirement age, the differences are substantial.

Noneconomic Consequences

Few studies look at the noneconomic consequences of vocational preparation programs. In this section, I cull the literature for what it suggests on the topic.

Educational and Occupational Satisfactions. One way to assess the noneconomic outcomes of vocational preparation programs is to examine the levels of educational and occupational satisfactions people report. In an American College Testing study, 92 percent of students expressed satisfaction with their current jobs. Slightly more than 75 percent of the satisfied reported that they would complete the program again if they were to do it over. More than 75 percent felt they could not have obtained their current jobs without the training they received. Usually two-thirds or more felt that their training was necessary.

A national study indicates that on 8 of 11 measures of satisfactions, the differences in satisfactions reported by individuals with four-year degrees and those with some vocational training was less than 5 percentage points. With respect to satisfaction with pay, security, and permanence, vocational program graduates were more satisfied than college graduates. We examined many different forms of job satisfaction and general sense of well-being in our studies of the early careers of 7,000 young men and women and found no differences based on people's education and training.

In a study of the differences in occupational satisfactions of public and proprietary vocational school graduates, graduates of public schools were more satisfied with their jobs and rated their training as more adequate than did graduates of proprietary programs. Graduates of public schools were more likely to say they would choose the same school if they had it to do over again.

There are few studies of educational and occupational satisfactions of graduates of vocational programs. In the few that have been done, the general finding is that graduates reflect positively on their training experience, see an advantageous relationship between their training and job placement, and are satisfied with their current occupations. A government secretary in Oregon is an example. She told us: "A fulfilling life and good jobs can be found with trade or business school and one need not feel incomplete without college." Similarly, a computer systems analyst told us his experience:

> *" I spent several unhappy years with a bachelor's degree in my pocket, going from unemployment to menial job and back to unemployment. I went back to school, a community college, and received education and training in a technical field which has resulted in my being employed in a job which I find to be very interesting, challenging, and satisfying."*

Upward Mobility. One of the supposed values of education in general and of vocational preparation in particular is that the programs increase workers' opportunities and upward mobility. A few studies have tried to compare the gains made by people from different socioeconomic backgrounds.

A Florida study, however, concluded that vocational preparation increased social and economic inequalities rather than equalizing opportunities. The results indicated that people with higher social status benefited more from vocational preparation programs than did people with lower social status. The study also indicated that more high-status individuals were served by vocational programs and that they received greater rewards than people with lower social status.

This conclusion is supported by a study indicating that students with lower social status were more likely to drop out and that earnings relate more strongly to a student's family social status than to whether the student even completed the program. The observation that young men and women from higher-status families tend to benefit most from vocational preparation programs is generally supported by information in the annual reports of the *Condition of Education* published by the National Center for Education Statistics.

The Career Development Study reveals the average levels of occupational prestige that people with different levels of education and training achieve by age 30. On a scale of 0 to 100, young people with only a high school education average occupational prestige scores of 35; with additional levels of education or training, their occupational prestige scores range from 42 to 45; and with a four-year college degree, their occupational prestige scores are about 60. The more education and training a person receives, the higher that person's occupational prestige is likely to be.

Participants in the Career Development Study tended to score much the same on related work characteristics. People with only a high school education were least likely to be in a position with authority to hire and fire. Vocational preparation generally increased their authority, but not nearly as much as three or four years of college did.

So, also, responsibility to supervise others and to set pay rates was much more closely tied to three or four years of college education. A vocational certificate gave a person no more authority in these areas than did a high school diploma. People with only a high school education had the most repetitious work; but people with a vocational certificate were the least likely to expect to be self-employed five years later. Apart from this exception, it is generally the case that where forms and levels of training and education make a difference, people with three or four years of college have a clear advantage over high school graduates, and people with some kind of vocational preparation usually score somewhere between high school and college graduates.

Missouri Vocational Graduates

One of the better studies of the outcomes to vocational preparation programs in recent years was conducted in the state of Missouri. The study followed samples of vocational and nonvocational graduates from 13 area vocational-technical schools and the high schools from which the students came.

The Missouri study found that vocational graduates, as compared to nonvocational graduates:

- Earn more in annual salaries — a 15 to 20 percent advantage
- Have more job stability — the median number of months vocational graduates had worked at their current or most recent jobs was nearly twice as long as nonvocational graduates
- Have higher employment rates — an advantage ranging from 7 to 38 percent over the five-year period
- Have higher percentages holding full-time jobs — an advantage of 24 to 74 percent over the five-year period
- Are more confident of their ability to compete for employment after high school graduation — 91 percent compared to 82 percent thought they would be able to compete "very well" or "fairly well" for a job after graduation

The study also reported that, over the five-year period, an average of 58 percent of vocational graduates were employed in training-related jobs; unemployment rates of graduates ranged from 20 to 48 percent of the state and national rates; from 75 to 80 percent consistently reported that they were satisfied with their current or most recent jobs; and, over the five-year period, 87 to 92 percent expressed satisfaction with their educational program. The study provides several indications that vocational graduates fare better in the job market than do nonvocational graduates.

On balance, graduates of vocational preparation programs reflect positively on their training and feel it favored them in their job placement. Vocational preparation programs appear to successfully place about 50 percent of their students and, in some cases, perhaps more. Income studies support previous research that shows a relationship between levels of schooling/training and earnings. Similarly, there continues to be a strong connection between levels of schooling/training and how well people fare in the labor market.

Many people with vocational training are very happy with their work and their prospects for the future. For example, this is what a journeyman heavy equipment mechanic in Oregon told us:

> *"When I chose to pursue technical skills instead of college, people thought I was very foolish. Today I am a fully qualified heavy equipment mechanic working for a good company with a good future. Since leaving high school I have never been unemployed. I feel that college is important, but technical skills are the backbone of America."*

COLLEGE AS A DECISION-MAKING PROCESS

There is yet another way to examine the benefits of a college education or vocational preparation program. Not much is written on the subject, but it has to do with the way education and training programs help students sort out their career options. Consider the following lifelike scenarios.

Susan's Story

I have always envied the little girl who, at age five, climbs on her father's lap, and a dialogue like this takes place:

Susan:	"Daddy, I want to be a teacher. How can I be one?"
Father:	"Susan, you have to keep going to kindergarten."
Susan:	"Then what?"
Father:	"Well, after a while you will be one of the big kids in grade school. Then you can go to high school and maybe play soccer or play in the band. If you work hard at your studies, you can go to college, where you will learn to be a teacher."
Susan:	"How long do I have to go to college?"
Father:	"Oh, four years or so. It depends on how well you like it and how hard you work. You can probably go longer if you want to."

The story ends with Susan happily skipping off saying, "Good, Daddy, that's what I want to do." Susan eventually goes to college and becomes a teacher, and everybody lives happily ever after.

As I said, I envy Susan. From childhood, she seems to know what she wants to do. Some people are like that. But that's not the way things worked for me, not the way they worked for my sons, and it may not be the way it works for your children. Many young people aren't sure what they want to do when they finish high school. They have some vague notions, enough to get them started in one program or another. But many college students change their majors by the time they graduate. That means they do a lot of soul-searching about careers over the college years.

I think that's good. Although I envy Susan, who knew what she wanted to do at age five, Dad and Mom plotted out the course, and Susan followed in lockstep fashion, I envy today's young people just as much, the ones who have no idea of what they want to do at age five, go through all the popular fantasies, aren't at all sure by the end of high school, but have the chance to go to college. College can help young people sort out their options and get them started on a career path. I think that's one of the most overlooked benefits of going to college.

Susan knew what she wanted to do with her life from childhood, and college figured prominently in her plans. But what about college for young people who haven't made a career decision?

Buck's Story

Consider the tale of twin brothers, Buck and Bill. Neither has chosen a career. One goes to college because he doesn't know what he wants to do. The other doesn't go to college because he doesn't know what he wants to do. Both find themselves in the same dilemma: They don't know what they want to do. And they follow two different courses of action.

Buck graduates from high school but doesn't know what he wants to do with his life. He wasn't a super student, but he wasn't a dummy, either. He could go to college, but he decides not to go because he doesn't know what he wants to do.

So Buck takes a job flipping burgers. He makes some money and buys aluminum wheels and a high-powered stereo for his Ford Mustang. Buck meets Betty, and within a couple of years there are three mouths to feed instead of two: Buck, Betty, and Bucky. Buck changes jobs to make more money for the family, and shortly takes a second job. Betty works, too. Increasingly, Buck does what he has to. The days of doing what he wants to do are largely past.

That doesn't mean that Buck isn't going anywhere. He can still get on-the-job training, enter an apprenticeship, go to community college part-time, or maybe return full-time, if he's lucky. I simply note that going straight to full-time work after high school probably was not the course of action that opened the most options for Buck.

Bill's Story

Twin brother Bill graduated from high school at the same time, got his diploma one step behind Buck, and, like Buck, he's no dummy; but he isn't exactly scholarship material, either. Like Buck, Bill doesn't know what he wants to do, but Bill goes to college.

From day one, Bill has to make decisions: Where should I go to school? What should I study? Do I want to go to a big school or a small one? Can I afford it? Where can I get the money?

Bill isn't sure that it's going to be worth it. He has his doubts. Not only that, he has to take pre-enrollment tests. The results come back and Bill learns that he's strong in math but weak in English. He'll have to take a remedial course in English. Buck thinks he's nuts.

Bill isn't so sure about it, either — plus, he's scared. Registration week comes and off he goes to more testing, registration for courses he's never heard of, and getting to know his roommates, one from the Bronx and the other from Function Junction. What a zoo!

Nobody forces Bill to make the big decision: What do you want to do with your life? But a lot of little things happen that bear on that decision. Six-week tests come back, and Bill discovers he'd better knuckle down in remedial English. He has to write term papers, and he should figure out what he wants to write about. Some guy down the hall talks him into going on a weekend canoe trip, so he tries that. Bill meets Jill. Jill has some strange ideas about politics and comes from a different religion. She talks with a funny accent.

The first semester ends and Bill gets his grades. He did better than he thought in some areas, worse in others. He has a chance to enroll in a special class, and he does that. He thinks about dropping a course, and he does that — another decision.

The semesters pass and Bill finds himself very much involved in a zigzag, sorting out the subjects he likes and those he doesn't care for. He had to take a speech course — didn't like that at all, so he stays away from communications. Bill was always good in math, but now he finds that there are all kinds of ways to use math. He knows an upperclassman studying to be an engineer, and that looks interesting. More and more he takes the courses that interest him, like drafting, and he sorts out areas that don't appeal to him, like Yugoslavian History 203.

Call it a sorting process, a sifting and winnowing, or a zigzag. The point is that going to college forces Bill to make many little decisions. He has to choose courses, and he finds out that some instructors are better than others. He keeps getting feedback from tests, term papers, and grades that helps him understand his strengths and weaknesses and a number of career possibilities, too. Chances are Bill will end up with a college degree in an area that interests him — not a bad set of tools — and credentials with which to launch a career.

College — whether four-year, two-year, or technical school — isn't just for those who know what they want to do. It can also offer a wealth of experiences that help young people figure out their career interests.

In summary, a four-year college education has paid handsomely in the past. Economically, college has been a good investment. In terms of its other effects, developing knowledge and the capacity for critical thought and generally having a positive effect on attitudes and behaviors, college education has improved people's resources and their life chances. The college experience gives many people a chance to identify their interests, develop their abilities, and prepare for rewarding and satisfying careers. Those benefits will certainly continue for young people who graduate from college in the future.

Career preparation programs are more varied, less well-developed, and harder to assess, but they appear to benefit participants with marketable skills, higher earnings, and lower unemployment rates. Many career preparation programs are being fashioned to equip participants for the demands of the global economy — more education and training than a high school diploma, but not necessarily a four-year college degree.

There is a principle for youth to follow: Invest in yourself. And the more you invest, the more you can expect in return. That's the way the social system works.

Next Steps: What Parents Can Do

Choosing a career preparation strategy can be confusing and frustrating for young people, just like choosing a college. It can also be a little bit frightening. Confusion comes from not knowing what to do, or when to do it — and that leads to frustration. One way to lessen the confusion and frustration for young people is to work with them so that these traps, which can only make matters worse, can be avoided:

- Procrastinating — pushing off a decision, not reaching a conclusion
- Not getting the kind of information that can inform decisions
- Not inquiring into the possibilities of financial aid
- Not setting up appointments, not remembering when they are scheduled, or not keeping them
- Not paying attention to details and accuracy when completing written forms
- Not following through — that is, taking the necessary next steps
- Missing deadlines

When any of the above happen, the important things don't get done.

Another reason young people may be confused and frustrated is that no one has paid much attention to their career development needs over the high school years and then, all of a sudden, parents are all uptight about what they intend to do with their lives. One of the criticisms of high school career counseling is that counselors end up dividing their time between the good and the bad students, but neglect the majority in between. A Vietnam veteran in our Career Development Study works as a printer while going to college. He was bitter:

> **" I am very bitter about the lack of counseling for the 'average' student. It seems that the people in the counseling positions spend all of their time with the extremely 'bad' or 'poor' student, and the extremely 'good' or 'smart' student."**

And a two-year-college graduate, who worked full-time but wanted to be a homemaker, told us: "High schools need to give personalized counseling for more than just star students."

Some students were more sympathetic to the plight of schools, teachers, and counselors. A young woman who described herself as "only a C student" and felt that she was overlooked in high school attributed the problem "to lack of guidance counselors and too many students." Similarly, a working mother offered this observation: "The real problem is they have too many students and what really is needed is more counselors." But, for whatever the reason, you as a parent cannot assume that the job of advising your daughter or son about careers has been done by someone else.

If your daughter or son is a good prospect for vocational preparation, there are several things you can do to help her or him. Following is a "to do" list.

IDENTIFYING VOCATIONAL PREPARATION POSSIBILITIES

One way to help is to narrow down the number of vocational preparation possibilities so that the two of you can focus on the real possibilities. Following are the possibilities outlined in Chapters 11 and 12. Check the boxes indicating those programs that you and your son or daughter feel may be possibilities.

Note: You don't have to settle on only one possibility. In fact, I encourage the two of you to keep more than one option open.

High School Vocational Education Options

- ❏ Alternative High Schools
- ❏ Vocational Education Programs in Comprehensive High Schools
- ❏ Vocational-Technical High Schools
- ❏ High School Cooperative Education Programs

College Vocational Education Options

- ❏ College Cooperative Education Programs
- ❏ Tech-Prep Programs
- ❏ Community Colleges
- ❏ Private Junior Colleges
- ❏ Four-Year Colleges and Universities

Noncollegiate Options

- ❏ Technical Institutes
- ❏ Proprietary Trade Schools
- ❏ Employer Training and Education Programs

Three More Options

- ❏ Apprenticeship Programs
- ❏ Federal Civil Service
- ❏ Education and Occupational Training in Military Service

PROGRAM INTERESTS

Is there a pattern to your daughter's or son's program interests? Which kind of programs appeal to her or him the most?

- ❏ High School Vocational Education Options
- ❏ College Vocational Education Options
- ❏ Noncollegiate Options
- ❏ Apprenticeships, Civil Service, Military Service

NEXT STEPS

Where to go to get specific information depends on the kind of program that interests your son or daughter.

High School Vocational Education Options: If your daughter or son is in high school and, together, you have determined that she or he is a good prospect for high school vocational education, call the information desk at your county school system for information on programs available in your area. Consult with the career counselor in your child's high school. Also, see Chapter 11.

College Vocational Education Options: Several of the earning-while-learning career preparation possibilities involve programs in two- or four-year colleges or universities. If your daughter's or son's career preparation interests include some college, then include the checklist and timetable at the end of Part III in your "to dos."

Apprenticeships, Federal Civil Service, and Education and Occupational Training in Military Service: These are each different and distinct programs, and each has it's own admissions standards and procedures. If one of these possibilities appeals to your son or daughter, check Chapter 12 for the necessary steps to follow.

Noncollegiate Options: Following are general "to dos" if your son's or daughter's preferred career preparation strategy tends toward the noncollegiate options.

Sophomore Year

It is important for young people to develop a plan — to begin thinking about what they will do after completing high school to improve their career prospects.

- ❏ Locate the telephone number for your State Occupational Information Coordinating Committee (see Chapter 7). Call your SOICC office, explain that you have a son or daughter making career decisions, and request free information on occupational careers and career preparation programs in your state.

❑ Visit the high school career center with your daughter or son.

Introduce yourself to your son's or daughter's career counselor.

Explain that you are trying to understand what services the career center offers parents and students. Make notes of important activities (career fairs and other scheduled events) and services (interest inventories and aptitude tests). Some high schools give interest inventories and aptitude tests only on request. Some charge for these services, others don't.

Ask for free handouts and literature on vocational preparation programs.

Familiarize yourself with basic reference materials available in the career center, such as the *Occupational Outlook Handbook.*

Check what other reference materials are available, including computerized career information systems.

Have your daughter or son demonstrate how a computer career explorations program works.

❑ Visit your local bookstore.

Browse for occupational careers information — probably in the business section.

Look over the information on vocational preparation programs — probably in the self-help section.

After you get a sense for where things are in the bookstore, pay a return visit — this time with your son or daughter, if possible. Give him or her a sense for the information and resources available and where they are located.

Consider purchasing a copy of the *Occupational Outlook Handbook* for the coffee table in your family room.

❑ Visit your local library.

Explain to the librarian that you are interested in materials on occupational careers and vocational preparation. Ask what materials are available and whether there is a special section on career planning.

❑ Set aside a place in your home where you can file or store vocational preparation materials.

Junior Year

❑ Help your daughter or son clarify what she or he wants from a vocational preparation program. Thinking through different program possibilities is one way to do that. See Chapters 11 and 12. Begin to help sort out kinds of programs that interest you and your daughter or son.

❑ Get a realistic picture of the cost of a year of vocational preparation that your son or daughter may be thinking about, and what family resources are available. Discuss what's in the ball park with your son or daughter so that, later, you can arrive at a mutually acceptable decision.

❑ Call or write to any programs outside your locality that interest your son or daughter. Ask for program information, admissions forms, and other available information.

❑ Attend career fairs in your community with your son or daughter and speak with vocational preparation program representatives.

❏ Talk with young people, and their parents, who are involved in programs that may interest your daughter or son. Get as much advanced information as you can so that you have specifics to talk about when it comes to trying to match your daughter's or son's interests with program characteristics.

❏ Visit nearby vocational preparation programs.

❏ Determine what admissions information and procedures are required by the programs that interest your son or daughter. This information is available from program administrators and, possibly, from career counselors.

❏ Meet with high school counselor to discuss vocational preparation plans.

Senior Year

Fall semester in the senior year is the time to pay special attention to program announcements, deadlines, application procedures, and special programs.

❏ Encourage your son or daughter to check high school information sources on a weekly basis for program announcements and deadlines.

❏ Be alert for announcements of career days and college fairs.

❏ Note important dates on your calendar.

❏ Visit vocational preparation programs, if possible. Try to visit on weekdays when students are involved and administrative offices are open.

❏ Make an appointment to discuss programs with program administrators.

❏ *Very important:* Establish that the program is accredited with the proper accrediting agencies.

❏ Narrow vocational preparation program possibilities down to two or three.

❏ Meet with high school counselor to discuss vocational preparation choices.

❏ Complete, check, and return all program admissions forms by deadlines.

❏ Forward any required monetary deposits for vocational preparation programs.

❏ Complete and return additional registration materials as required.

Chapter Notes

Introduction

I published some of this material earlier in a more technical format, "A Social Psychological Model of the Career Development Process," *Journal of Applied Sociology* 8:19–35, 1991.

Chapter 1

The material on the global economy is informed by Peter Navarro, *Job Opportunities Under Clinton/Gore* (Portland: Williams Publishing, 1993).

The employment outlook for college graduates draws on Kristina J. Shelley, "More Job Openings — Even More New Entrants: The Outlook for College Graduates, 1992–2005"; Gary Steinberg, "The Class of '90" One Year After Graduation"; and Thomas A. Amirault, "Job Market Profile of College Graduate in 1992: A Focus on Earnings and Jobs," in Bureau of Labor Statistics, U.S. Department of Labor, *Occupational Outlook Quarterly* (Summer 1994).

I am indebted to Dr. Franklin Hart, president of the Microelectronics Center of North Carolina, for providing useful material on the Information Highway, including a copy of the legislative briefing paper, "The North Carolina Information Highway Project," prepared by the Governor's Office, May 1994.

L. Russell Herman's article, "Connectivity Under Construction: The North Carolina Information Highway Draws Distant Resources Together," in North Carolina State University Computing Center, *Connect* (January 1994) was also useful.

The history and growth of the Internet draws on material from Paul A. Gilster, "The Internet," *Spectator* (July 23, 1994).

I drew general information from Montieth M. Illingworth, "Your Road Map to the Information Superhighway," *Hemisphere* (August 1994).

The material on private enterprise efforts to create satellite-based communications systems draws on Amy Feldman, "Space Race," *Forbes* (June 6, 1994).

The material on state information systems was informed by "North Carolina: A Superhighway Microcosm," *U.S. News & World Report* (June 27, 1994).

The communications systems metaphors, 17th-Century information dissemination analogy, and related material on the information highway material draw on Michael Rothschild, "Stagecoach Days on the Infohighway," and George Gilder, "Telecosm," *Forbes ASAP* (June 1994).

Chapter 2

I used information on population and labor changes from several public domain resources.

General resources include U.S. Department of Commerce, *Statistical Abstract of the United States, 1993: The National Data Book,* 113th edition (Washington, DC: U.S. Government Printing Office, 1993); U.S. Department of Commerce, *We, The Americans* (Washington, DC: U.S. Government Printing Office, 1993).

I consulted Frederick W. Hollmann, "National Population Trends," and Jennifer Cheesman Day, "National Population Projections," in U.S. Department of Commerce, *Population Profile of the United States* (Washington, DC: U.S. Government Printing Office, 1993).

I also consulted Sam Roberts' book, *Who We Are* (New York: Times Books, 1993).

I used information on race and ethnic populations drawn from the U.S. Department of Commerce series, "We the . . . ," published by the U.S. Government Printing Office, 1993. Specifically, I drew material from *We, The American Blacks; We, The American Hispanics; We, The American Asians; We, The American Pacific Islanders; We, The First Americans;* and *We, The American Foreign Born.* I also drew material from these more general sources: *We, The American Women; We, The American Elderly;* and *We, The American Children.*

I consulted these chapters in U.S. Department of Commerce, *Population Profile of the United States* (Washington, DC: U.S. Government Printing Office, 1993): Claudette E. Bennett, "The Black Population"; Susan J. Lapham, "The Hispanic Population"; Claudette E. Bennett, "The Asian and Pacific Islander Population"; Susan J. Lapham, "The Foreign Born Population"; and Arnold A. Goldstein, "The Elderly Population."

I drew information on labor force trends from these articles in the *Monthly Labor Review* (November 1963): Ronald E. Kutscher, "Historical Trends, 1950–92, and Current Uncertainties"; Norman C. Saunders, "The U.S. Economy, Framework for BLS Projections"; Howard N. Fullerton, "Another Look at the Labor Force."

I also consulted Bureau of Labor Statistics, U.S. Department of Labor, *Occupational Outlook Quarterly* (Fall 1993); Bureau of Labor Statistics, U.S. Labor Department of Labor, *Occupational Outlook Handbook,* 1994–'95 edition (Washington, DC: U.S. Government Printing Office, 1994); and Jeanne Benetti and Selwyn Jones, "Labor Force and Occupation," in U.S. Department of Commerce, *Population Profile of the United States* (Washington, DC: U.S. Government Printing Office, 1993).

The section on the U.S. response to the new realities was informed by "Science in the National Interest," Office of Science and Technology, Executive Office of the President, August 1994.

Chapter 3

This chapter follows the outline of the author's chapter, "Family Influences on Youths' Occupational Aspirations and Achievements," in Geoffrey K. Leigh and Gary W. Peterson (eds.), *Adolescents in Families* (Cincinnati: South-Western Publishing Company, 1986), pp. 226–255 .

Chapter 4

The material on racial minorities and careers draws on several sources of public domain information. I used U.S. Department of Commerce, *We, The American Blacks*

(Washington, DC: U.S. Government Printing Office, 1993); I also used these article in U.S. Department of Commerce, *Population Profile of the United States* (Washington, DC: U.S. Government Printing Office, 1993): Claudette E. Bennett, "The Black Population"; Robert Kominski and Andrea Adams, "School Enrollment"; Robert Kominski and Andrea Adams, "Educational Attainment"; Donald J. Hernandez, "When Families Break Up"; Arlene Saluter, "Marital Status and Living Arrangements"; Louisa Miller, "Marriage, Divorce and Remarriage"; Robert Cleveland, "Money Income"; Eleanor Buagher, "Poverty"; and Kathleen Short, "Health Insurance."

I used comparative information from U.S. Department of Education, *The Condition of Education, 1994* (Washington, DC: U.S. Government Printing Office, 1994); also, the National Center for Education Statistics, *Digest of Education Statistics, 1993* (Washington, DC: U.S. Government Printing Office, 1993).

Chapter 5

The standard reference for the Standard Occupational Classification system is U.S. Department of Commerce, *Standard Occupational Classification Manual* (Washington, DC: U.S. Government Printing Office, 1980).

I also used the U.S. Department of Labor, *Occupational Outlook Handbook*, 1994–'95 edition (Washington, DC: U.S. Government Printing Office), in preparing this material. Descriptions of the 18 occupational clusters are informed by an article by Martha C. White in the *Occupational Outlook Quarterly* (Spring 1988).

The information on professional athletes is based primarily on correspondence with professional associations. Keith Kimble assisted with gathering that information. I also consulted William R. Heitzmann, *Opportunities In Sports and Athletics Careers* (Lincolnwood, IL: VGM Career Horizons).

Chapter 6

Employment projections came from several public domain resources. I used the following articles in the *Monthly Labor Review* (November 1963): Norman C. Saunders, "The U.S. Economy, Framework for BLS Projections"; Howard N. Fullerton, Jr., "Another Look at the Labor Force"; James C. Franklin, "Industry Output and Employment"; and George T. Silvestri, "Occupational Employment: Wide Variations in Growth."

I used information from the introductory material in U.S. Department of Labor, *Occupational Outlook Handbook*, 1994–'95 edition (Washington, DC: U.S. Government Printing Office, 1994).

I drew information from Geoffrey C. Gradler and Kurt E. Schrammel, "The 1992–2005 Job Outlook In Brief," Bureau of Labor Statistics, U.S. Department of Labor, *Occupational Outlook Quarterly* (Spring 1994).

I also relied upon the special issue on "The American Work Force: 1992–2005," published by Bureau of Labor Statistics, U.S. Department of Labor, *Occupational Outlook Quarterly* (Fall 1994).

Chapter 7

The material on national information sources is drawn primarily from U.S. Department of Labor, *Occupational Outlook Handbook*, 1994–'95 edition (Washington, DC: U.S. Government Printing Office, 1994).

I am indebted to Juliette N. Lester, executive director of the National Occupational Information Coordinating Committee, for supplying annual reports, fact sheets, bulletins, status reports, program guides, brochures, and other publications, including "From Pilot to Practice," from which I developed the sections on the National Occupational Information Coordinating Committee, the State Occupational Information Coordinating Committees, occupational information systems, and the Career Information Delivery Systems. Joyce Kinniston provided additional useful materials.

Chapter 8

I relied on information from four primary sources for this chapter: U.S. Department of Education, *The Condition of Education, 1994* (Washington, DC: U.S. Government Printing Office, 1994); the National Center for Education Statistics, *Digest of Education Statistics, 1993* (Washington, DC: U.S. Government Printing Office, 1993); U.S. Department of Education, *120 Years of American Education: A Statistic Portrait* (Washington, DC: U.S. Government Printing Office, 1993); and *Almanac Issue, The Chronicle of Higher Education* (September 1, 1994).

I also consulted "School Enrollment" and "Educational Attainment" by Robert Kominski and Andrea Adams, in U.S. Department of Commerce, *Population Profile of the United States* (Washington, DC: U.S. Government Printing Office, 1993).

Chapter 9

I illustrate information on colleges with *The College Handbook*. The reference is the College Entrance Examination Board, *The College Handbook 1995* (New York: The College Board, 1994).

Chapter 10

I used material on college costs from the *Almanac Issue, The Chronicle Of Higher Education* (September 1, 1994), in preparing this chapter.

Information on federal financial aid was taken from *The Student Guide*, Federal Student Aid Programs, Washington, D.C.

Chapter 11

This chapter incorporates information on education from these sources: U.S. Department of Commerce, *Statistical Abstract of the United States, 1993: The National Data Book,*

113th edition (Washington, DC: U.S. Government Printing Office, 1993); U.S. Department of Education, *The Condition of Education, 1994* (Washington, DC: U.S. Government Printing Office, 1994); also, the National Center for Education Statistics, *Digest of Education Statistics, 1993* (Washington, DC: U.S. Government Printing Office, 1993); U.S. Department of Education, *120 Years of American Education: A Statistic Portrait* (Washington, DC: U.S. Government Printing Office, 1993); and *Almanac Issue, The Chronicle of Higher Education* (September 1, 1994).

I also consulted the National Association of Trade and Technical Schools, *Handbook of Trade and Technical Careers and Training* (Washington, DC: National Association of Trade and Technical Schools, 1994).

Myrtle Stogner, director of the NC Prep Leadership Development Center, provided information on Tech-Prep.

Chapter 12

Information on apprenticeships was provided by the National Apprenticeship Program, U.S. Department of Labor, Employment and Training Administration.

I drew upon several sources for material on federal civil service, including *America's Federal Jobs: A Complete Directory of Federal Career Opportunities* (Indianapolis: JIST Works, Inc., 1991); Kathleen Green, "Working for the US in the 1990's," *The Occupational Outlook Quarterly* (Summer 1993); and William B. Johnston, *Civil Service 2000* (Washington, DC: U.S. Government Printing Office, 1988).

My sources for information on occupational training in the military include *Military Careers* (Washington, DC: U.S. Department of Defense, 1992); the United States Army Recruiting Command, *Opportunities & Options*, third edition; "What You Can Do For Your Country," Report of the Commission on National and Community Service, January 1993; "Adjusting to the Drawdown," Report of the Defense Conversion Commission, December 1992; and Dyan Machan, "We're Not Authoritarian Goons," *Forbes* (October 1994).

Chapter 13

The primary source for this chapter is Ernest T. Pascarella and Patrick T. Terenzini, *How College Effects Students: Findings and Insights from Twenty Years of Research* (San Francisco: Jossey-Bass Publishers, 1991).

Epilogue

We Are All Self-Employed in Times of Change

A few years ago, in 1962, Thomas Kuhn wrote a paperback that quickly became one of the most widely read and often cited texts on college campuses, a distinction that continues to this day. Kuhn titled his little book *The Structure of Scientific Revolutions*, and in it he developed the thesis that breakthroughs in scientific understanding accompany paradigm shifts, by which he meant entirely new ways of looking at old issues. The best known paradigm shift occurred when the unthinkable notion that the Sun is the center of the universe replaced the folk wisdom that everything obviously revolved around the Earth. Thanks to Copernicus in the 15th Century, we can explore space in the 20th Century.

That was truly a revolution. It wasn't fought with slings and arrows or muskets or cruise missiles. It was a war of words and a battle for people's minds. And it was a world war. There was nothing tame and civil about it. And the timing was terrible. The world had been a cozy place in which to live — not a bad place to raise your kids. Then came the paradigm shift. It challenged established notions about God as much as it challenged principles of astronomy. It was troubling and it was painful. It took generations for the notion to gain acceptance, and the full implications of the paradigm shift have yet to be worked out 400 years later.

Most paradigm shifts are less dramatic. Alternative medicine is a departure from surgical and medicinal practices. Wireless communications are built on different engineering principles than copper-wire technology. Societies grounded in human rights have different priorities than those built on political repression. Wellness is a whole different way of thinking about health than defining well-being as the absence of disease. Many paradigm shifts are welcomed and quickly embraced.

Paradigm shifts don't happen by accident. Rather, circumstances set the stage. The old ideas increasingly fit badly with the world as we know it. At first, it may not be clear what is wrong, but the consensus grows that something is wrong. It's a struggle — figuring out what is wrong, identifying new solutions, choosing better solutions, figuring out how to implement them and how quickly to introduce new programs and policies. One of the characteristics of paradigm shifts is that, once the shift in thinking occurs, the new paradigms generate a momentum of their own. The new ways of thinking extend beyond the original problems and we begin to view all of life and living through new lenses, including our most cherished beliefs and basic assumptions. It can be painful. It can be exciting. It is both.

One of the themes of this book is that we live in a period of global change. We are part of a paradigm shift, and the proportions are worldwide. There is nothing little or trivial about it. It is uncomfortable and the timing is bad. But new approaches to old problems are in motion. There is much uncertainty — including continuing debates about whether there really are any problems, what they are, how to fix them, who should fix them, and how soon. The cork is out of the bottle, and the genie is free to work her mischief as she chooses.

The world of work is not immune to global change. The work world, too, is unstable, and some of the old career strategies are breaking down. In the past people could reasonably assume that, if they were good workers, they would always have a job. Obsolescence, dislocations, downsizing, outplacements, and restructuring were not things to worry about. But today no job is recession-proof, technology-proof, or economy-proof — not at GM, IBM, American Express, Schwinn, or even at Sears. The average stay on a job is less than five years. People change jobs seven, eight, and nine times over their work careers, and they change careers two or three times. The traditional notion of "once a carpenter, always a carpenter" has given way to career lines, successions of jobs and occupations people follow over their work histories. It's a different ball game, and our daughters and sons need to prepare themselves for a different set of rules.

The layoffs we read about have multiple messages. To economists and politicians, the layoffs are measures of how well the economy is doing. To the business community, layoffs are indicators of the financial health and profitability of an industry. But to the individual, layoffs mean that the old social contract between employers and employees is crumbling.

The old contract served us well, though not perfectly. It was an agreement that if workers worked hard, were productive and loyal, the organization would take care of them. People gave up some control over their lives — did what had to be done — in exchange for job security and predictable paychecks, benefits, titles, advancement prospects, identities, and stability. People saw themselves as working for and protected by their places of employment. They came to believe that their companies were responsible for them and that their jobs were entitlements. It was an attitude of dependency.

But that has changed. Today's work environment is more unstable, uncertain, and unpredictable in a more competitive world. The layoffs demonstrate that the company is not responsible for the worker. The layoffs force workers to evaluate not only their jobs and employment, but also themselves. The layoffs mean that workers are on their own. The urgent message of this book is that a dependency mindset among parents and their sons and daughters must be replaced by an attitude of independence and self-sufficiency. We are all self-employed in times of change.

A self-employment mindset requires a new set of attitudes and behaviors. It puts responsibility for employment back in the lap of the individual. It is based not on the premise that people are entitled to work and jobs, but that firms no longer guarantee long-term employment. In place of permanent work, we do piecemeal work in "adhocracies," a term coined by Cliff Hakim. We have work in bureaucracies only as long as they need us, or as long as we can create work within those settings. We are our own career managers. It is up to us to find our next work settings, and it is up to us to prepare ourselves for the changes.

Change puts young people especially at risk for entering and maintaining stable careers. Work and career preparation programs are changing around them, and society does not yet have in place clearly defined and carefully structured school-to-work and work force preparedness programs to ease their career development. That puts today's youth in double jeopardy. And it makes the role of parents in their daughters' and sons' career development all the more strategic and important.

In the introductory chapter, I explained the rationale for this book in some detail, and in this concluding chapter I want to return to those same themes:

- Young people want more help choosing careers.
- Parents, too, are concerned about their daughters' and sons' careers.
- Career decisions involve choosing not only an occupation, but also a career preparation strategy.
- Teachers and counselors have tried to meet students' needs, but schools don't have the resources to give young people the career guidance they need.
- Even if schools had the resources, neither teachers nor counselors could replace the critical influence parents have on their sons' and daughters' career plans.
- If parents are to be effective career advisors for their children, they need to prepare themselves.
- If parents are to prepare themselves, they need programs and materials with which to work.

Fortunately, there are resources parents can use, and I hope this book brings them together for you. Most importantly, I hope this book is useful to you in helping your child choose a career.

Index